W9-CYF-740

USB Complete

The Developer's Guide

Fifth Edition

Jan Axelson

Lakeview Research LLC
Madison, WI 53704

USB Complete: The Developer's Guide, Fifth Edition
by Jan Axelson

Published by Lakeview Research LLC, 5310 Chinook Ln., Madison WI 53704

janaxelson.com

Distributed by Independent Publishers Group (ipgbook.com).

14 13 12 11 10 9 8 7 6 5 4 3 2 1

Printed and bound in the United States of America

ISBN13 978-1-931448-28-4

Contents

Introduction

This book is for developers who are involved with designing or programming devices that use the Universal Serial Bus (USB) interface. If you are a hardware designer, if you write firmware that resides inside USB devices, or if you write applications that communicate with devices, this book is for you.

The USB interface is versatile enough to serve just about any device function. Familiar USB peripherals include mice, keyboards, drives, printers, speakers, and cameras. USB is also suitable for data-acquisition units, control systems, and other devices with specialized functions, including one-of-a-kind designs. The right choices of device hardware, software drivers and development tools and techniques can help you design devices that perform their functions without errors or user aggravation. This book will guide you along the way.

What's Inside

The USB specifications are the ultimate authority on the USB interface, but by design the specification documents omit implementation tips, example code, and information that applies to specific device hardware, software, and other tools and products. This book bridges the gap between the specifications and real-world designs.

These are some of the questions this book answers:

- *How can I decide if my device should use a USB interface?* Find out whether your device should use USB or another interface. If the choice is USB, you'll learn how to decide which of USB's five speeds—including USB 3.1's SuperSpeed and Super-SpeedPlus—and which of USB's four transfer types are appropriate for your application.

- *What controller hardware should my device use?* Every USB device contains an intelligent controller to manage USB communications. A variety of chip companies offer controller hardware with different architectures and abilities. This book will help you select a controller based on your project's needs, your budget, and your preferences for chip architecture, programming languages, and tools.

- *How can applications communicate with my devices?* On PCs, applications access a USB device by communicating with the driver the operating system has assigned to the device. You'll learn if your device can use a class driver provided by the host system's operating system. For devices that don't fit a supported class, you can explore options such as Microsoft's WinUSB driver, other generic drivers, and custom drivers. Example code shows how to detect and communicate with devices from Visual C# applications.

- *What firmware does my device need to support USB communications?* Find out how to write firmware that enables your device to respond to USB requests and events and exchange data for any purpose.

- *Does my device need its own power supply?* The USB interface can provide power to devices, including charging current for battery-powered devices. Learn how to determine if a design can obtain all of its power from the bus, how to meet USB's requirements for conserving power, and how to charge battery-powered devices from the bus.

- *How can I implement wireless communications?* A variety of USB and other industry standards and technologies enable USB devices to communicate wirelessly. Learn which technology is right for your device.

- *How can my device access other USB devices?* Find out how to develop a host for an embedded system or a USB On-The-Go device that can function as both a USB device and a limited-capability host that accesses other USB devices.

- *How can I ensure reliable operation?* All devices must respond to requests and other events on the USB port. The host computer must detect attached devices, locate appropriate drivers, and exchange data with the devices. This book provides tips, example code, and information about debugging software and hardware to help with these tasks.

To understand the material in the book, it's helpful to have some experience with digital logic, application programming for PCs and writing embedded code for peripherals. You don't have to know anything about USB.

What's New

The core of USB has remained much the same since the release of USB 1.0 in 1996. But the interface has expanded to support faster bus speeds, improved power delivery and management, more device classes, wireless communications, support for embedded systems that access USB devices, and more. New and improved chips and development tools have eased the task of developing devices and the software to access them.

This Fifth Edition is revised and updated throughout. New topics include an introduction to USB 3.1 and SuperSpeedPlus, enhanced power delivery and power management, new abilities using USB Type-C connectors, designing devices that use the WinUSB driver without requiring a vendor-provided INF file, new device classes, and how to use free debugging tools.

Much of the information in this book applies to any device hardware and host computer. The example code for applications uses Visual C#.

Updates and More

To find out more about developing USB devices and the software that communicates with them, I invite you to visit my website, *janaxelson.com* You'll find code examples and links to articles, products, tools, and other information related to developing USB devices. The website includes a PORTS forum where you can ask questions and discuss topics related to USB and other interfaces.

Corrections and updates to the book will also be available at *janaxelson.com*. If you find an error, please let me know.

Example Code

The .NET example code in this book is compatible with the .NET Framework Version 4.5 and later.

Example applications are available for free download from *janaxelson.com*.

Acknowledgments

USB is much too big a topic to write about without help. I have many people to thank.

My technical reviewers provided feedback that helped make the book as complete and accurate as possible. With that said, every error in this book is mine and mine alone. For their help with this edition, a big thanks to Paul E. Berg, Lane Hauck, Kosta Koeman, Dhanraj Rajput, and Rajaram Regupathy.

Others I want to thank for their support are Traci Donnell of the USB-IF, John Hyde of *usb-by-example.com*, and Jeff Ravencraft and Brad Saunders of the USB 3.0 Promoter Group.

For their help with the previous editions this edition builds on, thanks to Phyllis Brown, Greg Burk, Joshua Buergel, Gary Crowell, Fred Dart, Wendy Dee, Michael DeVault, Lucio DiJasio, Keith Dingwall, Dave Dowler, Robert Dunstan, Mike Fahrion, David Flowers, John Garney, David Goll, John M. Goodman, Laurent Guinnard, Tim Harvey, Blake Henry, Rahman Ismail, Bill Jacobus, David James, Christer Johansson, Geert Knapen, Matt Leptich, Alan Lowne, Jon Lueker, Brad Markisohn, Dr. Bob Miller, Rich Moran, Bob Nathan, Walter Oney, Amar Rajan, Marc Reinig, Rawin Rojvanit, Glenn M. Roberts, Jeff Schmoyer, Robert Severson, Craig R. Smith, and Dave Wright.

I hope you find the book useful and welcome your comments at *jan@janaxelson.com*.

Abbreviations

This book uses the abbreviations and symbols below to express quantities and units:

Multipliers

Symbol	Description	Multiplier
p	pico	10^{-12}
n	nano	10^{-9}
μ	micro	10^{-6}
m	milli	10^{-3}
k	kilo	10^{3}
K	kilo	2^{10} (1024)
M	mega	10^{6}
G	giga	10^{9}

Electrical

Symbol	Description
A	ampere
F	farad
Ω	ohm
V	volt
W	Watt

Time

Symbol	Description
s	second
Hz	Hertz (cycles per second)

Distance

Symbol	Description
m	meter
mm	millimeter

Data

Symbol	Description
b	bit
B	byte
bps	bits per second

Number Systems

Binary values have a trailing subscript b. Example: 10100011_b

Hexadecimal values have a leading $0x$. Example: 0xA3

All other values are decimal.

USB Basics

USB is the most successful personal-computer interface ever. PCs, tablets, phones, and other devices have USB ports that can connect to everything from keyboards, mice, and game controllers to cameras, printers, drives, audio and video devices, and more. USB is versatile, reliable, fast, power-conserving, inexpensive, and supported by operating systems for computers large and small.

With continued improvements and enhancements such as SuperSpeedPlus and more flexible power delivery, USB is likely to continue to dominate as the interface of choice for an ever-expanding range of devices.

This chapter introduces USB, including its advantages and limits, some history about the interface and recent enhancements to it, and a look at what's involved in designing and programming a device with a USB interface.

Uses and limits

USB is a likely solution any time you want to use a computer to communicate with a device. The computer can be a conventional PC or a device with an embedded processor. Some PCs have internal devices, such as fingerprint readers, that connect via

USB. The USB interface is suitable for mass-produced consumer devices as well as specialized, small-volume products and one-of-a-kind projects.

To be successful, an interface has to please two audiences: the users who will buy the devices and the developers who design the hardware and write the code that communicates with the devices. USB has features to please both groups.

Benefits for users

From the user's perspective, the benefits of USB are ease of use, fast and reliable data transfers, low cost, and power conservation. Table 1-1 compares USB with other interfaces.

Easy to use

Ease of use was a major design goal for USB. The features of the interface include:

One interface for many devices. USB is versatile enough for just about any standard peripheral function as well as devices with specialized functions. Instead of having a different connector and cable type for each peripheral function, one interface serves many.

Many ports. A typical PC has multiple USB ports, and hubs enable adding more ports.

Hot pluggable. Users can connect and disconnect a USB device whenever they want, whether or not the system and device are powered, without damaging the PC or device. The operating system detects when a device attaches.

Automatic configuration. When a user connects a USB device to a PC, the operating system detects the device and loads the appropriate software driver. The first time the device connects, the operating system may prompt the user to identify a driver, but other than that, installation is automatic. Users don't need to reboot before using a new device.

No user settings. USB devices don't have user-selectable settings such as port addresses and interrupt-request (IRQ) lines, so users have no jumpers to set or configuration utilities to run.

No power supply required (sometimes). The USB interface includes power-supply and ground lines that provide a nominal +5V from the PC or a hub. A device that requires up to 500 mA (USB 2.0) or 900 mA (USB 3.1) can draw all of its power from the bus instead of using a dedicated supply. Systems that support the *USB Power Delivery Rev. 2.0, v1.0* specification can provide up to 5A at voltages as high as 20V to devices.

Convenient cables. USB connectors are small and compact compared to connectors used by other interfaces such as RS-232. To ensure reliable operation, the USB specifi-

Table 1-1: USB is more flexible than other interfaces, which often target a specific use. (Part 1 of 2)

Interface	Type	Number of Connections (maximum)	Distance (maximum meters)	Speed (maximum bps)	Typical Use
USB 3.1	dual simplex serial	127 per bus	1 (5 m with 5 hubs)	10 G	Mass storage, video
USB 3.0	dual simplex serial	127 per bus	2 (10 m with 5 hubs)	5 G	Mass storage, video
USB 2.0	half duplex serial	127 per bus	5 (30 m with 5 hubs)	1.5 M, 12 M, 480 M	Keyboard, mouse, drive, speakers, printer, camera
CAN bus	serial	Varies with hardware	500 @ 125 kbs	1M @40 m	Automotive
eSATA	serial	2 (port multiplier supports 16)	2	6 G	Drives
Ethernet	serial	1024	500, varies with speed, longer using fiber	10 G	General network communications
IEEE-1394 (FireWire)	serial	64	100	3.2 G	Video, mass storage
IEEE-488 (GPIB)	parallel	15	20	8 M	Instrumentation
I^2C	synchronous serial	1007	Several meters, varies with load & speed	3.4 M	Embedded systems, general purpose
Microwire	synchronous serial	8	3	2 M	Embedded systems, general purpose
MIDI	serial current loop	2 (more with MIDI thru ports)	15	31.25 k	Music, show control
Parallel printer port	parallel	2 (8 with daisy-chain support)	3–10	16 M	Printers, scanners, disk drives
RS-232 (EIA/TIA-232)	asynchronous serial	2	15–30	20 k (higher with some hardware)	Embedded systems, general purpose

Table 1-1: USB is more flexible than other interfaces, which often target a specific use. (Part 2 of 2)

Interface	Type	Number of Connections (maximum)	Distance (maximum meters)	Speed (maximum bps)	Typical Use
RS-485 (TIA/EIA-485)	asynchronous serial	32 unit loads (up to 256 devices depending on hardware)	1200	10 M	Data acquisition and control systems
SPI	synchronous serial	Varies with hardware	Several meters, varies with load and speed	2 M or higher depending on hardware	Embedded systems, general purpose
Thunderbolt	full duplex serial	7	3 m (copper), 100 m (optical)	10 G (v1), 20 G (v2)	Mass storage, video

cation defines electrical requirements for cables and connectors. A cable segment can be as long as 5m depending on bus speed and connector type. With hubs, again depending on bus speed and connector type, a device can be as far as 30 m from its host computer. USB Type-C connectors bring two advances for user convenience: the connectors can attach either side up, and both ends of the cable are identical so users don't need to figure out which end goes where.

Wireless options. USB originated as a wired interface, but technologies are available for wireless communications with USB devices.

Multiple speeds

USB supports five bus speeds: low speed (1.5 Mbps), full speed (12 Mbps), high speed (480 Mbps), SuperSpeed (5 Gbps), and SuperSpeedPlus (10 Gbps). In PCs, USB 3.1 host controllers support all five speeds, USB 3.0 host controllers support all but SuperSpeedPlus, and USB 2.0 host controllers support low, full, and high speeds. Embedded systems that function as USB hosts can support fewer speeds depending in part on which devices the system supports.

The bus speed determines the rate that information travels on the bus. In addition to application data, the bus must carry status, control, and error-checking information, and multiple devices can share a bus. Thus, the throughput for an individual device's application data is somewhat less than the bus speed.

The USB 1.0 specification defined low and full speeds. Full speed was intended for most peripherals that had been using RS-232 (serial) and parallel ports. Full-speed to use low speed because the less stringent cable requirements allow more flexible cables. Low-speed devices may have lower manufacturing cost due in part to cheaper cables. High speed became an option with the release of USB 2.0, USB 3.0 defined SuperSpeed, and USB 3.1 defined SuperSpeedPlus.

Reliable

USB's reliability is due to both its hardware and protocols. The hardware specifications for USB drivers, receivers, and cables ensure an electrically quiet interface that reduces noise that could result in data errors. The USB protocols enable detecting errors in received data and notifying the sender so it can retransmit. Hardware performs the detecting, notifying, and retransmitting without software or user support.

Inexpensive

Because the host computer provides most of the intelligence to control the interface, components for USB devices are inexpensive. A device with a USB interface is likely to cost the same or less than an equivalent device with a different interface.

Power saving

Power-saving circuits and protocols reduce a device's power consumption while keeping the device ready to communicate when needed. Reducing power consumption saves money, helps the environment, and for battery-powered devices, allows a longer time between charges.

Benefits for developers

Many of the user advantages described above also make things easier for developers. For example, USB's cable standards and error checking mean that developers don't have to specify cable characteristics or develop error- checking protocols.

Other advantages help hardware designers who select components and design the circuits in devices and the programmers who write firmware embedded in the devices and software to communicate with devices.

Versatile

USB's four transfer types and five speeds make the interface feasible for many types of peripherals. USB has transfer types suited for exchanging large and small blocks of data with and without time constraints. For data that can't tolerate delays, the host computer can guarantee bandwidth. These abilities are especially welcome under Windows and other desktop operating systems where accessing peripherals in real time is often a challenge. Although the operating system, device drivers, and application software can introduce unavoidable delays, USB makes it as easy as possible to achieve transfers that are close to real time even on desktop systems.

Unlike other interfaces, USB doesn't assign specific functions to signal lines or make other assumptions about how the system will use the interface. For example, the status and control lines on the PC's parallel port were defined with the intention of communicating with line printers. USB makes no such assumptions and is suitable for just about any peripheral type.

USB classes define protocols for communicating with common peripherals such as printers, keyboards, and drives. Developers can program a device to conform to a class specification instead of having to reinvent everything from the ground up.

Operating system support

This book focuses on Windows programming for PCs, but other operating systems also have USB support, including Linux, Mac OSes, and Android. Some real-time kernels also support USB.

At the most basic level, an operating system (OS) that supports USB must do three things:

- Detect when devices are attached and removed from the system.
- Communicate with newly attached devices to find out how to exchange data with them.
- Provide a mechanism that enables software drivers to pass communications between the USB hardware and applications that want to access USB peripherals.

At a higher level, operating-system support may also include class drivers that enable applications to access specific device types. If the operating system doesn't include a driver for a device, the device vendor must provide the driver.

Microsoft continues to improve and add to the class drivers included with Windows. Supported device types include human interface devices (keyboards, mice, game controllers), speakers and other audio devices, drives, still-image and video cameras, scanners, and printers. Filter drivers can support device-specific features and abilities within a class. Applications use Application Programming Interface (API) functions or other software components to communicate with the drivers that access devices.

Devices that have vendor-specific functions can sometimes use a supported class such as the communications-device or human-interface device class. Other options for vendor-specific functions include Microsoft's WinUSB driver and generic drivers from other sources. Some chip companies offer generic drivers that developers can use with the provider's chips.

Writers of USB device drivers for Windows can use Microsoft's Windows Driver Frameworks (WDF) libraries to simplify the task of writing drivers.

Device support

Every USB device must include a hardware USB interface and must respond to requests that identify and configure the device. Some controllers perform some or all of these functions entirely in hardware while others require firmware support.

Many USB device controllers are based on popular processor architectures such as ARM Holdings' ARM, Intel Corporation's 8051, or Microchip Technology's PIC®. If you're already familiar with a chip architecture that has a USB-capable variant, you don't need to learn a new architecture. Other controllers provide a serial or parallel interface to any external processor with a compatible interface. Most chip companies provide example code to help you get started.

USB Implementers Forum

The USB Implementers Forum, Inc. (USB-IF) (*usb.org*) is the non-profit corporation founded by the companies that developed the USB specification.

The USB-IF's mission is to support the advancement and adoption of USB technology. To that end, the USB-IF offers information, tools, and testing support. The information includes specification documents, white papers, and FAQs. The tools include software and hardware to help in developing and testing products. Support for testing includes compliance tests to verify proper operation and compliance workshops where developers can have their products tested and certified to display a USB logo.

Addressing USB's limits

All of USB's advantages mean that the interface is a good candidate for a remarkable variety devices. A single interface can't handle every task, but USB can do the job in many situations that at first might seem challenging or impossible.

Interface restrictions

Limits of the USB interface include distance constraints, no support for peer-to-peer communications or broadcasting, and lack of support in older hardware and operating systems.

Distance. USB was designed as a desktop-expansion bus where devices are relatively close at hand. Other interfaces, including RS-485 and Ethernet, allow much longer cables. However, to extend the distance between a device and its host computer, a USB device can function as a bridge to a long-distance interface that connects to the end device.

Peer-to-Peer Communications. With a few exceptions, every USB communication is between a host computer and a device. The host is a PC or other computer that contains host-controller hardware. The device contains device-controller hardware. Hosts can't talk to each other directly, and devices can't talk to each other directly.

Other interfaces, such as Ethernet and Thunderbolt 2, allow direct device-to-device communication.

USB provides a partial solution with USB On-The-Go (OTG) hardware and protocols. An OTG device can function as both a device and a limited-capability host that communicates with other devices.

Two USB hosts can communicate with each other using a bridge cable that contains two USB devices with a shared buffer. USB 3.1 defines a host-to-host cable for Super-Speed and SuperSpeedPlus debugging and other uses. With driver support, this cable can support host-to-host communications.

Broadcasting. USB doesn't support sending data simultaneously to multiple devices. The host computer must send data to each device individually. Ethernet supports broadcasting to multiple devices.

Legacy Hardware. Older "legacy" computers and peripherals don't have USB ports, but the need to support legacy equipment is fading as these systems are retired.

If you need to connect a legacy peripheral to a USB port, a solution is an intelligent adapter that converts between USB and the older interface. Several sources have adapters for use with peripherals with RS-232, RS-485, and parallel ports. An adapter is useful only for devices that use protocols supported by the adapter's driver in the host computer. For example, most parallel-port adapters support communications only with printers, not with other parallel-port peripherals. RS-232 adapters work with most RS-232 devices.

If you want to use a USB device with a computer that doesn't support USB, a solution is to add USB capabilities to the computer. To do so, you need to add USB host-controller hardware and use an operating system that supports USB. The hardware is available on expansion cards that plug into a PCI slot or on a replacement motherboard.

If upgrading the PC to support USB isn't feasible, you might think an adapter would be available to translate a peripheral's USB interface to the PC's RS-232, parallel, or other interface. An adapter is rarely an option when the computer has the legacy interface because an adapter that contains the needed host-controller hardware and code is expensive to design and manufacture for its limited market.

Even on new systems, users may occasionally run applications on older operating systems such as DOS. Without a device driver, the operating system can't access a USB device. Although it's possible to write a USB device driver for DOS, few device vendors provide one. For mice and keyboards, the system's UEFI or BIOS typically provide support to ensure that the devices are usable any time, including from within DOS and from the setup screens that you can view on boot-up.

Developer challenges

For developers, challenges to USB are the complexity of the protocols, operating-system support for some applications, and for small-scale developers, the need to obtain a Vendor ID.

Protocol Complexity. A USB device must have the intelligence to respond to requests and other events on the bus. Device-controller chips vary in how much firmware support they require to perform USB communications. For controllers that need extensive firmware support, example code can provide a quick start.

On the host computer, applications communicate with class or device drivers that in turn communicate with the lower-level USB drivers that manage communications on the bus. While device-driver writers need some knowledge of USB protocols, device drivers insulate application programmers from having to be familiar with low-level protocols.

Evolving Support in the Operating System. The class drivers included with Windows and other OSes enable applications to communicate with many devices. Often, you can design a device to use one of the provided drivers. If not, you may be able to use or adapt a driver provided by a chip company or other source. If you need to provide your own driver, a third-party driver toolkit can help in developing the driver.

Fees. The USB-IF's website provides the USB specifications, related documents, software for compliance testing, and much more at no charge. Anyone can develop USB software without paying a licensing fee.

Every USB device must contain a Vendor ID and a Product ID that identifies the device to the operating system. To obtain the rights to use a Vendor ID, you can join the USB-IF, become a USB-IF non-member logo licensee, or buy a Vendor ID for a 1-time fee. Each option costs several thousand dollars, and the first two options have recurring fees. If you pay only the 1-time fee, you aren't authorized to use the USB logo. The owner of the Vendor ID assigns Product IDs to devices.

Devices that don't undergo compliance testing and don't display the USB-IF logo have lower-cost options. Some chip companies, including Future Technology Devices International Limited (FTDI) and Microchip Technology, will assign a range of Product IDs to a customer for use in products that use the company's Vendor ID, typically at no charge. Chips that perform all of their USB communications in hardware can use a Vendor ID and Product ID embedded in the hardware. An example is FTDI's USB device controllers.

Companies that sell products that implement a USB specification must sign an adopters agreement. The agreement grants a royalty-free, non-exclusive patent license to implement the specification. You must submit a signed agreement within one year after first sale of a product. See *usb.org* for current fees and agreements.

USB and Ethernet

For some devices, the choice is between USB and Ethernet. Ethernet's advantages include the ability to use very long cables, support for broadcasting, and use of familiar Internet protocols. However, Ethernet hardware is more complex and expensive than typical USB device hardware. Plus, USB is much more versatile, with four transfer types and defined class protocols for many device functions.

USB and Thunderbolt

Thunderbolt, developed by Intel in collaboration with Apple, is a high-speed data interface that also provides power. The original Thunderbolt interface has two 10-Gbps channels with each channel having dedicated wires for each direction. Thunderbolt 2 combines the channels into a single 20-Gbps channel.

Thunderbolt uses the same connector as the Mini DisplayPort video port. A Thunderbolt port on a PC can connect to a device with a Thunderbolt port or a Mini DisplayPort. Adapters enable using devices with other connector types.

The speed of a Thunderbolt channel is roughly the same as USB 3.1, while Thunderbolt 2's single channel is 2× faster. Thunderbolt can provide up to 10W of power, which is more than USB 3.1's 4.5 W but much less than *USB Power Delivery Rev. 2.0, v1.0*'s maximum of just under 100 W.

Thunderbolt has been available mainly on Macs and a few PCs, while all new PCs have USB. Thunderbolt, which targets storage and video, is less versatile than USB. Thunderbolt controllers and cables are more expensive than USB hardware. Thus, Thunderbolt has been popular mainly for applications where very high speed is essential.

Evolution of an interface

The main reason why new interfaces don't appear very often is that existing interfaces have the advantage of all of the peripherals that users don't want to scrap. The developers of the original IBM PC chose compatibility with the existing Centronics parallel interface and RS-232 serial-port interface to speed up the design process and enable users to connect to printers and modems already on the market. These interfaces proved serviceable for close to two decades. But as computers became more powerful and the number and kinds of peripherals increased, the older interfaces became a bottleneck of slow communications with limited options for expansion.

A break with tradition makes sense when the desire for enhancements is greater than the inconvenience and expense of change. This is the situation that prompted the development of USB.

And the interface hasn't stood still since its introduction. New versions of the USB specification and related documents take advantage of hardware advances and address new user needs.

The USB-IF releases the specifications that define the interface. Each specification is developed by a Promoter Group whose members are corporations involved in USB technology.

USB 1.0

The *Universal Serial Bus Specification Revision 1.0* was released in January, 1996. USB capability first became available on PCs with the release of Windows 95's OEM Service Release 2, available only to vendors installing Windows 95 on PCs they sold. The USB support in these versions was limited and buggy, and there weren't many USB peripherals available, so use of USB was limited in this era.

The situation improved with the release of Windows 98 in June, 1998. By this time, many more vendors had USB peripherals available, and USB began to take hold as a popular interface. Windows 98 Second Edition (SE) fixed bugs and further enhanced the USB support.

The USB 1.0 specification was a product of Compaq Computer Corporation, Digital Equipment Corporation, IBM PC Company, Intel Corporation, Microsoft Corporation, NEC Corporation, and Northern Telecom.

USB 1.1

The *Universal Serial Bus Specification Revision 1.1* (September, 1998) added one new transfer type (interrupt OUT). USB 1.1 replaced USB 1.0. The USB 1.1 specification was a product of Compaq Computer Corporation, Hewlett-Packard Company, Intel Corporation, Koninklijke Philips Electronics N.V., Lucent Technologies Inc, Microsoft Corporation, and NEC Corporation.

USB 2.0

As USB gained in popularity and PCs became more powerful, demand grew for a faster bus. Investigation showed that a bus 40× faster than full speed could remain backwards compatible with the low- and full-speed interfaces. April 2000 saw the release of the *Universal Serial Bus Specification Revision 2.0*, which added high speed at 480 Mbps. High speed made USB more attractive for peripherals such as printers, drives, and video cameras. Windows added support for USB 2.0 in Windows XP SP1 and Windows 2000 SP4. USB 2.0 replaced USB 1.1.

A USB 2.0 device other than a hub can support low speed, full speed, or high speed, and a high-speed device can support full speed when connected to a USB 1.1 bus. A USB 2.0 hub must support all three USB 2.0 speeds. The ability to communicate at any speed increases the complexity of the hubs but conserves bus bandwidth and eliminates a need to use different hubs for different speeds.

USB 2.0 is backwards compatible with USB 1.1. USB 2.0 devices can use the same connectors and cables as 1.1 devices, and a USB 2.0 device works when connected to a PC that supports USB 1.1 or USB 2.0 except for a few devices that function only at high speed and thus require USB 2.0 support.

When USB 2.0 devices first became available, there was confusion among users about whether all USB 2.0 devices supported high speed. To clarify, the USB-IF released naming and packaging recommendations that emphasize speed and compatibility rather than USB version numbers. A product that supports high speed should be labeled *Hi-Speed USB*, and messages on the packaging might include *Fully compatible with Original USB* and *Compatible with the USB 2.0 Specification*. For products that support low or full speed only, the recommended messages on packaging are *Compatible with the USB 2.0 Specification* and *Works with USB and Hi-Speed USB systems, peripherals and cables*. The recommendations advise avoiding references to low or full speed on consumer packaging.

To use high speed, a high-speed-capable device must connect to a USB 2.0, USB 3.0, or USB 3.1 host computer with only USB 2.0, USB 3.0, or USB 3.1 hubs between the host and device. USB 2.0, USB 3.0, and USB 3.1 hosts and hubs can also communicate with USB 1.1 devices.

The USB-IF releases revisions and additions to USB specifications in Engineering Change Notices (ECNs). Table 1-2 lists ECNs to the USB 2.0 specification. Twice a year, the USB-IF releases a new zip file containing the specification and all ECNs that apply to it. The main specification is *not* updated with the ECNs so when studying a section of the spec, be sure to check the ECNs for corrections or updates.

The USB 2.0 specification is a product of Compaq Computer Corporation, Hewlett-Packard Company, Intel Corporation, Koninklijke Philips Electronics N.V., Lucent Technologies Inc, Microsoft Corporation, NEC Corporation, STEricsson, and Texas Instruments.

USB 2.1

The USB 2.0 Link Power Management Addendum and the USB 3.1 specification define when a device must report its version as USB 2.1. A low-, full-, or high-speed device that supports the BOS descriptor (see Chapter 4) is a USB 2.1 device. A SuperSpeed or SuperSpeedPlus device that also supports one or more USB 2.0 speeds must declare itself as a USB 2.1 device when operating at a USB 2.0 speed.

Table 1-2: Engineering change notices (ECNs) correct, add to, and clarify the USB 2.0 specification.

Category	Title	Description
Connecting	Connect Timing Update	Allow devices with dead batteries to draw 500 mA on connect.
	Device Capacitance	Require detectable change in capacitance on VBUS on attachment.
	Pull-up/Pull-Down Resistors	Loosen tolerances for pull-up and pull-down resistors.
Connectors and Cables	Material Change	Allow alternate materials.
	Micro-USB connector	New connector type.
	Mini-B Connector	New connector type.
	Rounded Chamfer for the Mini-B Plug	Connector recommendation.
Power	5V Short Circuit Withstand Requirement Change	Change short circuit requirement to a recommendation.
	Link Power Management	Additional power-saving capabilities.
	Errata for Link Power Management ECN	Error corrections.
	Suspend Current Limit Changes	Loosen Suspend current requirements.
	USB 2.0 Phase-locked SOFs	Phase lock requirement for power management in isochronous transfers.
	USB 2.0 VBUS Max Limit	Increase VBUS maximum to 5.5V.
Descriptors and Requests	Interface Association Descriptor	New descriptor type for functions with multiple interfaces.
	USB TEST_MODE selector values	Add TEST_MODE Feature values.
	Unicode UTF-16LE for String Descriptors	Specify encoding for string descriptors.
Errors	Errata as of 12/7/2000	Error corrections and clarifications.
	Errata as of 5/28/2002	Error corrections and clarifications.
Interchip	Inter-Chip USB Supplement	Chip-to-chip interconnects without external cables, low and full speeds.
	Hi-Speed Interchip Electrical Specification	Chip-to-chip interconnects without external cables, high speed.
	High Speed Inter Chip Specification (HSIC) ECN	Interchip modifications and clarifications.

USB 3.0

The USB-IF released the *Universal Serial Bus 3.0 Specification Revision 1.0* in November, 2008. USB 3.0 defines a new architecture with two physical buses that operate in parallel. One pair of wires carries USB 2.0 traffic, and two additional pairs of wires carry USB 3.0 traffic.

USB 3.0's 5-Gbps SuperSpeed offers a more than 10× increase over USB 2.0's high speed. Plus, with a pair of wires for each direction, a SuperSpeed bus can carry data in both directions at the same time. SuperSpeed devices can also draw more bus current and use new protocols for more aggressive power saving and more efficient transfers.

USB 3.0 is backwards compatible with USB 2.0. USB 3.0 hosts and hubs support all four speeds. USB 2.0 cables fit USB 3.0 receptacles.

Unlike the USB 2.0 specification, which replaced USB 1.1, the USB 3.0 specification supplemented, but didn't replace, USB 2.0. SuperSpeed devices use many of the higher-level protocols defined in the USB 2.0 specification. Low, full, and high-speed devices continue to comply with USB 2.0 and can't take advantage of USB 3.0's features such as higher bus-current limits and larger data packets.

Windows 8 and Windows Server 2012 were the first Windows editions to have built-in support for USB 3.0.

The USB 3.0 specification is a product of Hewlett-Packard Company, Intel Corporation, Microsoft Corporation, NEC Corporation, STEricsson, and Texas Instruments.

USB 3.1

The *Universal Serial Bus 3.1 Specification Revision 1.0*, released in July, 2013, updates USB 3.0 with 10-Gbps SuperSpeedPlus bus speed plus new power-saving features and other enhancements that apply to both SuperSpeed and SuperSpeedPlus. A marketing term that you might see on products that support SuperSpeedPlus is *SuperSpeed USB 10Gbps*.

USB 3.1 replaces USB 3.0. A new product that operates at SuperSpeed should comply with USB 3.1 whether or not the product also operates at SuperSpeedPlus. Except for hubs, which must support SuperSpeedPlus, SuperSpeed-only USB 3.0 devices require few changes to comply with USB 3.1.

A device that supports SuperSpeedPlus must also support SuperSpeed, and a device that supports SuperSpeed must at minimum support at least one USB 2.0 speed. A USB 3.1 device doesn't have to fully function at a USB 2.0 speed, but the host must be able to detect the device and advise the user to move the device to a SuperSpeed or SuperSpeedPlus port.

Cables defined in the USB 3.1 specification have the same number of wires as USB 3.0 cables but with new requirements to ensure good performance at SuperSpeedPlus.

The USB 3.1 specification defines some new terms. *Gen 1* is the 5-Gbps SuperSpeed data rate. *Gen 2* is the 10-Gbps SuperSpeedPlus data rate. *Gen X* refers to features that apply to both Gen 1 and Gen 2.

Enhanced SuperSpeed refers to features or requirements that apply to both USB 3.0 and USB 3.1 buses. Note that Enhanced SuperSpeed does not mean SuperSpeedPlus only. For example, the statement *Enhanced SuperSpeed bulk and interrupt endpoints can support burst transactions* means that both SuperSpeed and SuperSpeedPlus endpoints can support burst transactions.

Thus **the terms Enhanced SuperSpeed and USB 3.1 refer to components that support SuperSpeed only as well as components that support SuperSpeedPlus.** In virtually all cases, the information also applies to USB 3.0 components. In the few cases in this book where something is specific to USB 3.0, I mention it.

The USB 3.1 specification is a product of Hewlett-Packard Company, Intel Corporation, Microsoft Corporation, Renesas Corporation, STEricsson, and Texas Instruments.

Embedded Host and On-The-Go

As USB became the interface of choice for all kinds of peripherals, developers of embedded systems wanted more flexibility in designing USB hosts that didn't have to meet all of the requirements for a USB host in a PC. Developers also saw a need for a way for USB peripherals to access other USB devices. For example, a user might want to attach a printer to a camera or connect a flash drive to a phone.

The *On-The-Go and Embedded Host Supplement to the USB 2.0 Specification* and *On-The-Go and Embedded Host Supplement to the USB Revision 3.0 Specification* define limited-capability hosts that embedded systems can implement to enable communicating with USB peripherals.

Bus components

USB communications require a host computer with USB support, a device with a USB port, and hubs, connectors, and cables as needed to connect the device to the host computer.

The host computer is a PC or a handheld device or other embedded system that contains USB host-controller hardware and a root hub. The host controller formats data for transmitting on the bus and translates received data to a format that operating-system components understand. The host controller also helps manage communications on the bus. The root hub has one or more connectors for attaching devices. The root hub and host controller together detect device attachment and removal,

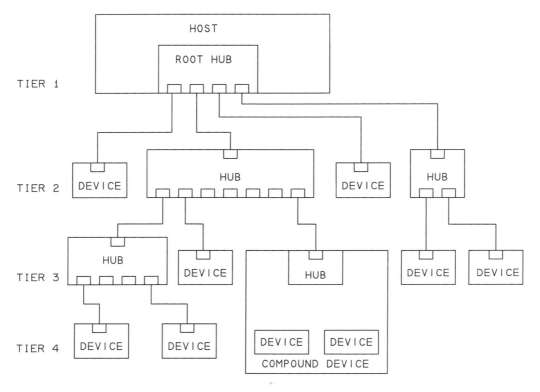

Figure 1-1. USB uses a tiered star topology. Each external hub has one upstream-facing port and one or more downstream-facing ports.

carry out requests from the host controller, and pass data between devices and the host controller. In addition to the root hub, a bus may have one or more external hubs.

Each device has hardware and firmware as needed to communicate with the host computer. The USB specifications define the cables and connectors that connect devices to their hubs.

Topology

The topology, or arrangement of connections, on the bus is a tiered star (Figure 1-1). At the center of each star is a hub, and each connection to the hub is a point on the star. The root hub is in the host. If you think of the bus as a stream with the host as the source, an external hub has one upstream-facing (host-side) connector for communicating with the host and one or more downstream-facing (device-side) connectors or internal connections to embedded devices. A typical hub has 2, 4, or 7 ports. When multiple hubs connect in series, the series forms a tier.

The tiered star describes only the physical connections. In programming, all that matters is the logical connection. Host applications and device firmware don't need to know or care whether the communication passes through one hub or five.

Up to five external hubs can connect in series with a limit of 127 peripherals and hubs including the root hub. However, bandwidth and scheduling limits can prevent a single host controller from communicating with this many devices. To increase the available bandwidth for USB devices, many PCs have multiple host controllers, each controlling an independent bus.

Bus speed considerations

A USB 1.1 host supports low and full speeds only. A USB 2.0 host adds high speed. A USB 3.0 host adds SuperSpeed, and a USB 3.1 host adds SuperSpeedPlus. Exceptions include On-The-Go devices and other hosts in embedded systems, which may support only the speeds needed to access specific peripherals.

A USB 3.1 hub contains both a USB 2.0 hub and a SuperSpeed/SuperSpeedPlus hub. The hub handles traffic at any speed. SuperSpeed and SuperSpeedPlus traffic uses the SuperSpeed/SuperSpeedPlus hub's circuits and wires, and other traffic uses the USB 2.0 hub's circuits and wires. A USB 3.0 hub is similar but doesn't support SuperSpeedPlus.

A SuperSpeed-capable device communicates at SuperSpeed only if the host and all hubs between the host and device are USB 3.1 hubs (Figure 1-2). Otherwise the device must use a slower speed. In a similar way, a SuperSpeedPlus-capable device communicates at SuperSpeedPlus only if the host and all hubs between the host and device are USB 3.1 hubs. On a USB 3.0 bus or with a USB 3.0 hub, a SuperSpeedPlus device communicates at SuperSpeed.

For compatibility with USB 2.0 hosts and hubs, a SuperSpeed or SuperSpeedPlus device that doesn't fully function at a USB 2.0 speed must at least respond to bus resets and standard requests at a USB 2.0 speed so the device can inform the host that the device requires a higher speed to perform its function.

A USB 2.0 high-speed-capable device communicates at high speed if the host and all hubs between are USB 2.0 or USB 3.1 hubs (Figure 1-3). For compatibility with USB 1.1 hosts and hubs, a high-speed device that doesn't fully function at full speed must at least respond to bus resets and standard requests at full speed so the device can inform the host that the device requires high speed to perform its function. Many

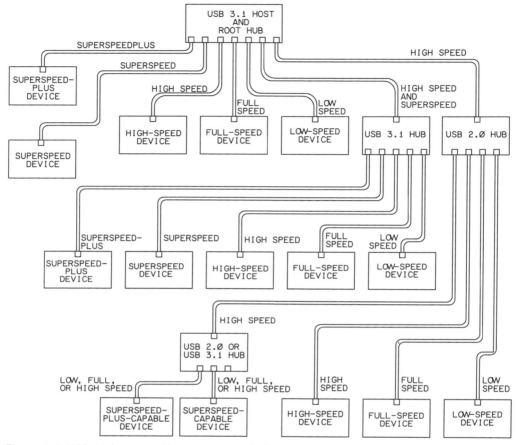

Figure 1-2. USB 3.1 hosts and hubs support all five speeds for downstream communications.

high-speed devices function, though more slowly, at full speed because adding support for full speed is generally easy and is required to pass USB-IF compliance tests.

A device that supports full or low speed communicates with its nearest hub at the supported speed. For any segments upstream from that hub, if all upstream hubs are USB 2.0 or higher, the device's traffic travels at high speed.

Terminology

In the world of USB, the words *function* and *device* have specific meanings. Also important is the concept of a USB port and how it differs from other ports such as RS-232.

Function

A USB *function* is a set of one or more related interfaces that expose a capability. Examples of functions are a mouse, a set of speakers, a data-acquisition unit, or a hub. A single physical device can contain multiple functions. For example, a device might provide both printer and scanner functions. A host identifies a device's functions by requesting a device descriptor and one or more interface descriptors from the device. The descriptors are data structures that contain information about the device.

Device

A *device* is a logical or physical entity that performs one or more functions. Hubs and peripherals are devices. The host assigns a unique address to each device on the bus. A *compound device* contains a hub with one or more permanently attached devices. The host treats a compound device in much the same way as if the hub and its functions were separate physical devices. The hub and embedded devices each have a unique address.

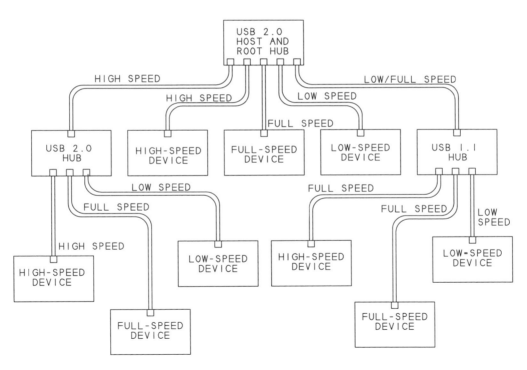

Figure 1-3. USB 2.0 hubs use high speed for upstream communications if the host and all hubs between are USB 2.0 or higher.

A USB 3.1 hub is a special case. The hub contains both a USB 2.0 hub function and a USB 3.1 hub function.

A *composite device* has one bus address but multiple, independent interfaces or groups of related interfaces that each provide a function. Each interface or group of related interfaces can use a different driver on the host. For example, a composite device could have interfaces for a printer and a drive. Composite devices are very common.

Port

In general terms, a hardware computer port is an addressable location that can connect to peripheral circuits. A port's circuits can terminate at a cable connector or be hard-wired to peripheral circuits. For USB, each downstream-facing connector on a hub represents a USB port. Host applications can't access USB ports directly but instead communicate with drivers assigned to the devices attached to ports. A USB host controller may reside at a series of port addresses the system's CPU accesses, but these ports are distinct from the ports on the bus.

Division of labor

The host and its devices each have defined responsibilities. The host bears most of the burden of managing communications, but a device must have the intelligence to respond to communications from the host and other events on the bus.

Host responsibilities

To communicate with USB devices, a computer needs hardware and software that support the USB host function. The hardware consists of a USB host controller and a root hub with one or more USB ports. The software support is typically an operating system that enables device drivers to communicate with lower-level drivers that access the USB hardware.

PCs have one or more hardware host controllers that each support multiple ports. The host is in charge of the bus. The host has to know what devices are on the bus and the capabilities of each device. The host must also do its best to ensure that all devices on the bus can send and receive data as needed. A bus may have many devices, each with different requirements, all wanting to transfer data at the same time. The host's job isn't trivial.

Fortunately, the host-controller hardware and drivers in Windows and other OSes do much of the work of managing the bus. Each device attached to the host must have an assigned device driver that enables applications to communicate with the device. System-level software components manage communications between the device driver and the host controller and root hub.

Applications don't have to know the hardware-specific details of communicating with devices. All the application has to do is send and receive data using standard operating-system functions or other software components. Often the application doesn't have to know or care whether the device uses USB or another interface.

The host must detect devices, manage data flow, perform error checking, provide and manage power, and exchange data with devices.

Detect devices

On power up, hubs make the host aware of all attached USB devices. In a process called enumeration, the host determines what bus speed to use, assigns an address, and requests additional information. After power up, whenever a device is removed or attached, a hub informs the host of the event, and the host enumerates any newly attached device and removes any detached device from its list of devices available to applications.

Manage data flow

The host manages traffic on the bus. Multiple devices may want to transfer data at the same time. The host controller divides the available time into intervals and gives each transmission a portion of the available time. A USB 2.0 host can send or receive data at one USB 2.0 speed at a time. A USB 3.1 host can simultaneously transmit SuperSpeed or SuperSpeedPlus data, receive SuperSpeed or SuperSpeedPlus data, and send or receive data at a USB 2.0 speed.

During enumeration, a device's driver requests bandwidth for any transfer types that must have guaranteed timing. If the bandwidth isn't available, the driver can request a smaller portion of the bandwidth or wait until the requested bandwidth is available. Transfers that have no guaranteed timing use the remaining bandwidth and must wait if the bus is busy with higher priority data.

Error checking

When transferring data, the host adds error-checking bits. On receiving data, the device performs calculations on the data and compares the result with received error-checking bits. If the results don't match, the device doesn't acknowledge receiving the data and the host knows it should retransmit. In a similar way, the host error-checks data received from devices. USB also supports a transfer type without acknowledgments for use with data such as real-time audio, which can tolerate occasional errors but needs a constant transfer rate.

If a transmission attempt fails after multiple tries, the host can inform the device's driver of the problem, and the driver can notify the application so it can take action as needed.

Provide and manage power

In addition to data wires, a USB cable has wires for a power supply and ground. The default power is a nominal +5 V. The host provides power to all devices on power up or attachment and works with the devices to conserve power when possible. Some devices draw all of their power from the bus.

A high-power USB 2.0 device can draw up to 500 mA from the bus. A high-power SuperSpeed or SuperSpeedPlus device can draw up to 900 mA from an Enhanced SuperSpeed bus. Ports on some battery-powered hosts and hubs support only low-power devices, which are limited to 100 mA (USB 2.0) or 150 mA (Enhanced SuperSpeed). To conserve power when the bus is idle, a host can require devices to enter a low-power state and reduce their use of bus current.

Hosts and devices that support *USB Power Delivery Rev. 2.0, v1.0* can negotiate for bus currents up to 5 A and voltages up to 20 V.

Exchange data with devices

All of the above tasks support the host's main job, which is to exchange data with devices. In some cases, a device driver requests the host to attempt to send or receive data at defined intervals, while in others the host communicates only when an application or other software component requests a transfer.

Device responsibilities

In many ways, a device's responsibilities are a mirror image of the host's. When the host initiates communications, the device must respond. But devices also have duties that are unique. The device-controller hardware typically handles much of the load. The amount of needed firmware support varies with the chip architecture. Devices must detect communications directed to the device, respond to standard requests, perform error checking, manage power, and exchange data with the host.

Detect communications

Devices must detect communications directed to the device's address on the bus. The device stores received data in a buffer and returns a status code or sends requested data or a status code. In almost all controllers, these functions are built into the hardware and require no support in code besides preparing the buffers to send or receive data. The firmware doesn't have to take other action or make decisions until the chip has detected a communication intended for the device's address. Enhanced SuperSpeed devices have less of a burden in detecting communications because the host routes Enhanced SuperSpeed communications only to the target device.

Respond to standard requests

On power up or when a device attaches to a powered system, a device must respond to standard requests sent by the host computer during enumeration and after enumeration completes.

All devices must respond to these requests, which query the capabilities and status of the device or request the device to take other action. On receiving a request, the device places data or status information in a buffer to send to the host. For some requests, such as selecting a configuration, the device takes other action in addition to responding to the host computer.

The USB specification defines requests, and a class or vendor may define additional requests. On receiving a request the device doesn't support, the device responds with a status code.

Error check

Like the host, a device adds error-checking bits to the data it sends. On receiving data that includes error-checking bits, the device performs the error-checking calculations. The device's response or lack of response tells the host whether to retransmit. The device also detects the acknowledgment the host returns on receiving data from the device. The device controller's hardware typically performs these functions.

Manage power

A device may have its own power supply, obtain power from the bus, or use power from both sources. A host can request a device to enter the low-power Suspend state, which requires the device to draw no more than 2.5 mA of bus current. Some devices support remote wakeup, which can request to exit the Suspend state. USB 3.1 hosts can place individual functions within a USB 3.1 device in the Suspend state. With host support, devices can use additional, less restrictive low-power states to conserve power and extend battery life.

Exchange data with the host

All of the above tasks support the main job of a device's USB port, which is to exchange data with the host computer. For most transfers where the host sends data to the device, the device responds to each transfer attempt by sending a code that indicates whether the device accepted the data or was too busy to accept it. For most transfers where the device sends data to the host, the device must respond to each attempt by returning data or a code indicating the device has no data to send. Typically, the hardware responds according to firmware settings and the error-checking result. Some transfer types don't use acknowledgments, and the sender receives no feedback about whether the receiver accepted transmitted data.

Devices send data only at the host's request. Enhanced SuperSpeed devices can send a packet that causes the host to request data from the device.

The controller chip's hardware handles the details of formatting the data for the bus. The formatting includes adding error-checking bits to data to transmit, checking for errors in received data, and sending and receiving the individual bits on the bus.

Of course, the device must also do whatever other tasks it's responsible for. For example, a mouse must be ready to detect movement and button clicks and a printer must use received data to generate printouts.

Bus speeds and data throughput

The data throughput, or rate of transfer of application data, between a device and host is less than the bus speed and isn't always predictable. Some of the transmitted bits identify, synchronize, and error-check the data, and the throughput also varies with the transfer type and how busy the bus is.

For time-sensitive data, USB supports transfer types that have a guaranteed rate or guaranteed maximum latency. Isochronous transfers have a guaranteed rate, where the host can request a specific number of bytes to transfer at defined intervals. The intervals can be as short as 1 ms at full speed or 125 μs at high speed, SuperSpeed, and SuperSpeedPlus. Isochronous transfers have no error correcting, however. Interrupt transfers have error correcting and guaranteed maximum latency. The device specifies a maximum interval, and when a driver has requested a data transfer, the host allows no more than the specified interval, or maximum latency, to elapse between transfer attempts. The requested maximum interval can have a range of 10–255 ms at low speed, 1–255 ms at full speed, and 125 μs – 4.096 s at high speed and Enhanced SuperSpeed.

Because all devices share the bus, a device has no guarantee that a particular rate or maximum latency will be available on attachment. If the bus is too busy to allow a requested transfer rate or maximum latency, the host refuses to complete the configuration process that enables the host to schedule transfers. The device's driver can then request a configuration or interface that requires less bandwidth. For the fastest transfers, the device driver and application software and device firmware should eliminate retries as much as possible. The device should have data ready to send when the host requests it and should be ready to accept data when the host sends it.

Of USB's four transfer types (control, bulk, interrupt, isochronous), the fastest on an otherwise idle bus are bulk transfers, with theoretical maximums of around 1.2 MB/s at full speed, 53 MB/s at high speed, 460 MB/s at SuperSpeed, and 1.1 GB/s at SuperSpeedPlus. Isochronous transfers can request the most bandwidth (1.023 MB/s at full speed, 24.576 MB/s at high speed, over 393 MB/s at SuperSpeed, and over 786 MB/s at SuperSpeedPlus). Low speed doesn't support bulk or isochronous transfers, and the maximum guaranteed bandwidth for a single low-speed transfer is 800 bytes/s.

Developing a device

Designing a USB device for PCs involves both getting the device up and running and providing software to communicate with the device.

Components

A USB device needs the following:

- A device-controller chip with a USB interface and a CPU or other intelligent hardware that communicates with the controller. The CPU can be in the controller chip or on a different chip.

- Program code, hardware, or a combination of these to carry out the USB communications in the device.

- Hardware and code to carry out the device's function (processing data, reading inputs, writing to outputs).

The host that communicates with the device needs the following:

- Host controller hardware and software (typically included with the OS).

- Device-driver software on the host to enable applications to communicate with the device. The driver may be included with the OS or provided by the device vendor, the chip company, or another source.

- Application software to enable users to access the device. For standard device types such as a mouse, keyboard, or disk drive, you don't need custom application software though you may want to write a test application.

Tools for developing

To develop a USB device, you need the following tools:

- A compiler or assembler to create the device firmware (the code that runs inside the device's controller chip).

- A mechanism for storing the assembled or compiled code in the controller's program memory.

- A compiler for writing and debugging host software, which may include a combination of a device driver, filter driver, and application code.

Also recommended are a monitor program for debugging device firmware and a protocol analyzer for viewing USB traffic.

Steps in developing a project

The steps in project development include initial decisions, enumerating, and exchanging data.

Selecting hardware and software

Before you can begin programming, you need to select device hardware and a host driver:

1. Specify the device's requirements. For the USB interface, define the required rate of data transfer and timing or bandwidth requirements. Consider what else your device needs to carry out its function. For example, a data logger might need an analog input. Chapter 3 has more about the capabilities of the different transfer types and how they relate to device requirements.

2. Decide whether the PC can access the device using a driver included with the operating system or a driver you provide. Chapter 7 has more about drivers.

3. Select a device controller chip. Chapter 6 has more about selecting chips.

Enumerating

To enable a host to enumerate your device, do the following:

1. Write or obtain device firmware to respond to standard USB requests from the host and other events on the bus. The requests ask for a series of descriptors, which are data structures that describe the device's USB capabilities. Chip companies generally provide example code that you can modify for a specific device. A few controllers can enumerate with no device firmware required.

2. For a Windows host, identify or create a device driver and INF (information) file to enable identifying the device and assigning a driver. The INF file is a text file that names the driver the device will use on the host computer. If your device fits a class supported by Windows, you may be able to use an INF file included with Windows. Other operating systems use different methods to match a driver to a device.

3. Build or obtain a development board or other circuit to test the chip and your firmware. Chip companies typically offer development boards for their chips.

4. Load the code into the device and attach the device to the bus. A Windows host will enumerate the device and add it to Device Manager.

Exchanging data

When the device enumerates successfully, you can begin to add components and code to carry out the device's function. If needed, write application code to communicate with and test the device. When the code is debugged, you're ready to test on your final hardware.

USB 3.1 essentials

USB 3.0 was a major update to the USB specification, and USB 3.1 builds on USB 3.0's foundation. This section describes what is new in USB 3.0 and USB 3.1.

Features

USB 3.1 incorporates many new features while continuing to support USB 2.0.

USB 3.1 replaces USB 3.0

USB 3.1 replaces USB 3.0 as the current specification for Enhanced SuperSpeed. USB 3.0 defined a new SuperSpeed bus that operates parallel to the USB 2.0 bus. USB 3.1 uses the same wires but adds support for SuperSpeedPlus. New designs, whether they support SuperSpeedPlus or just SuperSpeed, should comply with USB 3.1.

USB 3.1 doesn't replace USB 2.0

USB 2.0 remains the specification for low, full, and high speeds as well as features and protocols that apply to all speeds including transfer types, descriptors, and general bus topology.

Devices that don't support a USB 3.1 speed should continue to comply with USB 2.0. SuperSpeed and SuperSpeedPlus devices comply with USB 3.1 when operating at USB 3.1 speeds and comply with USB 2.0 when operating at a lower speed.

Devices that benefit

Devices that can benefit from Enhanced SuperSpeed include drives and video devices. High-resolution video displays that use USB for data are feasible. Power-hungry devices can benefit from higher current limits, and power-sensitive devices can benefit from new protocols.

Faster data transfers

The SuperSpeed bus has a signaling rate, or speed of the bits on the wires, of 5 Gb/s, which is over 10× faster than high-speed USB. SuperSpeedPlus doubles the signaling rate to 10 Gb/s. Unlike USB 2.0, SuperSpeed and SuperSpeedPlus use a pair of wires for each direction so data can travel in both directions at the same time. After encoding and other overhead, a SuperSpeed bus can carry around 460 MB/s of application data in each direction, and a SuperSpeedPlus bus can carry around 1.1 GB/s of application data in each direction.

Other Enhanced SuperSpeed features that can increase data throughput include these:

- Devices can asynchronously notify the host when they have data to send. The host doesn't have to use bandwidth polling devices that have nothing to send.
- Bulk transfers can use a streaming protocol for improved performance.

Some features remain the same

These features remain essentially unchanged in USB 3.1 compared to USB 2.0:

- Tiered star topology.
- Four transfer types (control, bulk, interrupt, isochronous).
- Use of descriptors to provide device information. USB 3.1 adds new descriptors and adds new information in some fields in descriptors defined in USB 2.0.
- Device classes and many class drivers.
- Low, full, and high-speed protocols and cabling.

Other enhancements

Besides the new bus speeds, other changes with USB 3.1 compared to USB 2.0 include these:

- Direct routing. Hubs route downstream traffic only to the receiving device rather than to every Enhanced SuperSpeed port.
- No polling. When a host requests data from an Enhanced SuperSpeed, non-isochronous endpoint that is busy or has no data, the endpoint returns Not Ready (NRDY). The host can then leave the endpoint alone until the device sends an Endpoint Ready (ERDY) notification indicating that the endpoint has data to send. Thus the host doesn't waste bus time polling endpoints that may have nothing to send.
- New, aggressive power-saving modes and protocols.
- More bus current available to devices.
- Support for bursts, where a host or device sends multiple data packets without waiting for each previous packet's acknowledgment.
- Streaming on bulk endpoints. Multiple, independent data streams can use the same endpoint with a dedicated buffer for each stream.

Compatibility

USB 3.1 is backwards compatible with USB 2.0. The statements below also apply to USB 3.0 except for lack of support for SuperSpeedPlus.

USB 2.0 devices work with USB 3.1 hosts

A USB 3.1 host has a USB 2.0 bus in parallel with an Enhanced SuperSpeed bus. USB 2.0 devices require no changes to work with USB 3.1 hosts.

USB 3.1 devices may work with USB 2.0 hosts

Every Enhanced SuperSpeed device must also support a USB 2.0 speed but doesn't have to fully function at that speed. A device that can't perform its function at the lower speed informs the host that the device requires SuperSpeed.

Changes in host software

The operating system must provide a driver for the USB 3.1 host controller. Class and device drivers that support isochronous transfers are likely to require changes to support SuperSpeed and SuperSpeedPlus.

USB 3.1's higher bus currents are available only on the USB 3.1 bus

Enhanced SuperSpeed devices should comply with USB 3.1 when operating at a Gen 1 or Gen 2 data rate and should comply with USB 2.0 when operating at a lower speed. Thus a high-power device that can operate at both a USB 3.1 speed and a USB 2.0 speed can draw 900 mA at the USB 3.1 speed but only 500 mA at the USB 2.0 speed.

USB 3.1 hubs support all speeds

A USB 3.1 hub contains an Enhanced SuperSpeed hub and a USB 2.0 hub that share power and ground lines and logic to control power to the bus. The hub enumerates as two devices, an Enhanced SuperSpeed hub on the USB 3.1 bus and a USB 2.0 hub on the USB 2.0 bus.

A USB 3.1 device communicates at one speed at a time

USB 3.1 devices communicate at the highest speed supported by the device, the host, and the hubs between them. An exception is upstream communications on hubs on some buses—a USB 2.0 hub connected to a USB 2.0 or higher host always communicates upstream at high speed.

Except for hubs, a device can't use the USB 3.1 and USB 2.0 buses at the same time.

Cables

USB 3.1 defines new cables and connectors.

At USB 2.0 speeds, devices can use USB 2.0 cables with USB 3.1 hosts and hubs

For traffic at USB 2.0 speeds, USB 2.0 cables fit USB 3.1 receptacles but don't have wires to carry USB 3.1 traffic.

USB 3.1 cables fit USB 2.0 hosts and hubs

The USB 3.1 Standard-A plug fits the USB 2.0 Standard-A receptacle so you can use a USB 3.1 cable to attach a USB 3.1 device to a USB 2.0 host or hub. The device will communicate at a USB 2.0 speed.

USB 3.1 cables don't fit USB 2.0 devices

A USB 3.1 cable with a USB 3.1 Standard-B or USB 3.1 Micro-B plug doesn't fit USB 2.0 receptacles.

USB 3.1 receptacles have additional requirements

For noise reduction, USB 3.1 has more requirements for receptacle back-shields, ground tabs, and grounding spring tabs.

USB 3.1 devices and hosts can use USB Type-C cables

The USB Type-C connector specification followed the release of USB 3.1. These connectors have many benefits including small form factor, support for advanced power delivery protocols, and the ability to insert them either side up. Any USB 3.1 or USB 2.0 host or device can be designed to use USB Type-C connectors and cables.

Maximum cable length

Maximum cable lengths for Enhanced SuperSpeed are shorter compared to USB 2.0. The USB 3.1 specification defines performance requirements but not maximum cable length. A practical limit for USB 3.1 cables is 1 m.

The USB Type-C specification provides practical maximum lengths for cables that use USB Type-C connectors: 1 m for SuperSpeedPlus, 2 m for SuperSpeed and USB 2.0 cables with micro-B plugs, and 4 m for other USB 2.0 cables.

Connecting two USB 3.1 hosts

USB 3.1 defines a new cable with a USB 3.1 Standard-A plug on each end. The cable is intended for debugging and other host-to-host applications with driver support. The cable includes Enhanced SuperSpeed data wires but no wires for VBUS, D+, or D-.

Power

USB 3.1 provides both more power and more power-saving options to devices.

More bus power available

A USB 3.1 host or hub can provide up to 900 mA to high-power SuperSpeed and SuperSpeedPlus devices and up to 150 mA to low-power SuperSpeed and SuperSpeedPlus devices.

When operating at low, full, or high speed, USB 2.0's limits apply: high power devices can draw up to 500 mA, and low power devices can draw up to 100 mA. *USB Power Delivery Rev. 2.0, v1.0* expands the options for power on both USB 2.0 and USB 3.1 systems.

2

Inside USB Transfers

This chapter looks at the elements that make up a USB transfer. You don't always need to know every detail about USB transfers to get a project up and running, but understanding how transfers work can help in deciding which transfer types a device should use and in writing and debugging device firmware.

Transfer basics

To send or receive data, the USB host initiates a USB transfer. Each transfer uses a defined format to send data, an address, error-detecting bits, and status and control information. The format varies with the transfer type and direction.

Essentials

Every USB communication (with one exception in USB 3.1) is between a host and a device. The host manages traffic on the bus, and the device responds to communications from the host. An endpoint is a device buffer that stores received data or data to transmit. Each endpoint address has a number, a direction, and a maximum number of data bytes the endpoint can send or receive in a transaction.

Each USB transfer consists of one or more transactions that can carry data to or from an endpoint. A USB 2.0 transaction begins when the host sends a token packet on the bus. The token packet contains the target endpoint's number and direction. An IN token packet requests a data packet from the endpoint. An OUT token packet precedes a data packet from the host. In addition to data, each data packet contains error-checking bits and a Packet ID (PID) with a data-sequencing value. Many transactions also have a handshake packet where the receiver of the data reports success or failure of the transaction.

For Enhanced SuperSpeed transactions, the packet types and protocols differ, but the transactions contain similar addressing, error-checking, and data-sequencing values along with the data.

USB supports four transfer types: control, bulk, interrupt, and isochronous. In a control transfer, the host sends a defined request to the device. On device attachment, the host uses control transfers to request a series of data structures called descriptors from the device. The descriptors provide information about the device's capabilities and help the host decide what driver to assign to the device. A class specification or vendor can also define requests.

Control transfers have up to three stages: Setup, Data (optional), and Status. The Setup stage contains the request. When present, the Data stage contains data from the host or device, depending on the request. The Status stage contains information about the success of the transfer. In a control read transfer, the device sends data in the Data stage. In a control write transfer, the host sends data in the Data stage, or the Data stage is absent.

The other transfer types don't have defined stages. Instead, higher-level software defines how to interpret the raw data. Bulk transfers are the fastest on an otherwise idle bus but have no guaranteed timing. Printers and drives use bulk transfers. Interrupt transfers have guaranteed maximum latency, or time between transaction attempts. Mice and keyboards use interrupt transfers. Isochronous transfers have guaranteed timing but no error correcting. Streaming audio and video use isochronous transfers.

Purposes for communication

USB communications fall into two general categories: communications that help to identify and configure the device and communications that carry out the device's purpose. During enumeration, the host learns about the device and requests a configuration. When enumeration is complete, the host can send and request data as needed to carry out the device's purpose.

During enumeration, the device's firmware responds to a series of standard requests from the host. The device must decode the requests, return requested information, and take other actions to carry out the requests.

Windows and other OSes perform enumeration with no application programming required. Under Windows, the first time a device attaches to a system, the Plug and Play (PnP) Manager must locate an INF file that identifies the name and location of one or more driver files to assign to the device. If the required files are available and the firmware functions correctly, the enumeration process is generally invisible to users. Chapter 9 has more about device drivers and INF files.

After the host has enumerated the device and assigned and loaded a device driver, application communications can begin. At the host, applications can use Windows API functions or other software components to read and write to the device. At the device, transferring data typically requires either placing data to send in an endpoint's transmit buffer or retrieving received data from an endpoint's receive buffer, and on completing a transaction, ensuring that the endpoint is ready for another transaction. Most devices also require firmware support for handling errors and other events.

Managing data on the bus

The host schedules the transfers on the bus. A USB 2.0 host controller manages traffic by dividing time into 1-ms frames at low and full speeds and 125-μs microframes at high speed. The host allocates a portion of each (micro)frame to each transfer. Each (micro)frame begins with a Start-of-Frame (SOF) timing reference.

An Enhanced SuperSpeed bus doesn't use SOFs, but the host schedules transfers within 125-μs bus intervals. A USB 3.1 host also sends timestamp packets once every bus interval to all Enhanced SuperSpeed ports that aren't in a low-power state.

Each transfer consists of one or more transactions. Control transfers always have multiple transactions because they have multiple stages, each consisting of one or more transactions. Other transfer types use multiple transactions when they have more data than will fit in a single transaction. Depending on how the host schedules the transactions and the speed of a device's response, the transactions in a transfer may all be in a single (micro)frame or bus interval, or the transactions may be spread over multiple (micro)frames or bus intervals.

Every device has a unique address assigned by the host, and all data travels to or from the host. Except for remote wakeup signaling, everything a USB 2.0 device sends is in response to receiving a packet sent by the host. Because multiple devices can share a data path on the bus, each USB 2.0 transaction includes a device address that identifies the transaction's destination.

Enhanced SuperSpeed devices can send status and control information to the host without waiting for the host to request the information. Every Enhanced SuperSpeed Data Packet and Transaction Packet includes a device address. Enhanced SuperSpeed buses also use Link Management Packets that travel only between a device and the nearest hub and thus don't need addressing information.

Elements of a transfer

Every USB transfer consists of one or more transactions, and each transaction in turn contains packets of information. To understand transactions, packets, and their contents, you also need to understand endpoints and pipes. So that's where we'll begin.

Endpoints: the source and sink of data

All bus traffic travels to or from a device endpoint. The endpoint is a buffer that typically stores multiple bytes and consists of a block of data memory or a register in the device-controller chip. The data stored at an endpoint may be received data or data waiting to transmit. The host also has buffers that hold received data and data waiting to transmit, but the host doesn't have endpoints. Instead, the host serves as the source and destination for communicating with device endpoints.

An *endpoint address* consists of an endpoint number and direction. The number is a value in the range 0–15. The direction is defined from the host's perspective: an IN endpoint provides data to send to the host and an OUT endpoint stores data received from the host. An endpoint configured for control transfers must transfer data in both directions so a control endpoint consists of a pair of IN and OUT endpoint addresses that share an endpoint number.

Every device must have endpoint zero configured as a control endpoint. Additional control endpoints offer no improvement in performance and thus are rare.

In other transfer types, the data flows in one direction though status and control information can travel in the opposite direction. A single endpoint number can support both IN and OUT endpoint addresses. For example, a device might have endpoint 1 IN for sending data to the host and endpoint 1 OUT for receiving data from the host.

In addition to endpoint zero, a full- or high-speed device can have up to 30 additional endpoint addresses (1–15, IN and OUT). A low-speed device can have at most two additional endpoint addresses which can be two IN, two OUT, or one in each direction.

Transaction types

Every USB 2.0 transaction begins with a packet that contains an endpoint number and a code that indicates the direction of data flow and whether the transaction is initiating a control transfer:

Transaction Type	Source of Data	Types of Transfers that Use the Transaction Type	Contents
IN	device	all	data or status information
OUT	host	all	data or status information
Setup	host	control	a request

As with endpoint directions, the naming convention for IN and OUT transactions is from the perspective of the host. In an IN transaction, data travels from the device to the host. In an OUT transaction, data travels from the host to the device.

A Setup transaction is like an OUT transaction because data travels from the host to the device, but a Setup transaction is a special case because it initiates a control transfer. Devices need to identify Setup transactions because these are the only transactions that devices must always accept. Any transfer type may use IN or OUT transactions.

In every USB 2.0 transaction, the host sends an *addressing triple* that consists of a device address, an endpoint number, and endpoint direction. On receiving an OUT or Setup packet, the endpoint stores the data that follows the packet, and the device hardware typically triggers an interrupt. Firmware can then process the received data and take any other required action. On receiving an IN packet, if the endpoint has data ready to send to the host, the hardware sends the data on the bus and typically triggers an interrupt. Firmware can then do whatever is needed to get ready to send data in the next IN transaction. An endpoint that isn't ready to send or receive data in response to an IN or OUT packet sends a status code.

For Enhanced SuperSpeed transactions, the protocol differs as described later in this chapter.

Pipes: connecting endpoints to the host

Before data can transfer, the host and device must establish a *pipe*. A pipe is an association between a device's endpoint and the host controller's software. Host software establishes a pipe with each endpoint address the host wants to communicate with.

The host establishes pipes during enumeration. If a user detaches a device from the bus, the host removes the no longer needed pipes. The host can also request new pipes or remove unneeded pipes by using control transfers to request an alternate configuration or interface for a device. Every device has a default control pipe that uses endpoint zero.

The configuration information received by the host includes an endpoint descriptor for each endpoint the device wants to use. Each endpoint descriptor contains an endpoint address, the type of transfer the endpoint supports, the maximum size of data packets, and, for interrupt and isochronous transfers, the desired service interval, or period of time between attempts to send or receive data.

Transfer types

Devices with varied requirements for transfer rate, response time, and error correcting can all use USB. Each of the four types of data transfers meets different needs. Each device can support the transfer types that are best suited for its purpose. Table 2-1 summarizes the features and uses of each type.

Control transfers are the only type with functions defined by the USB specification. Control transfers enable the host to read information about a device, set a device's address, and select configurations and other settings. With driver support, control transfers can also contain class- and vendor-specific requests that send and receive data for any purpose. All USB devices must support control transfers.

Bulk transfers are intended for applications where the rate of transfer isn't critical, such as sending a file to a printer or accessing files on a drive. For these applications, quick transfers are nice, but the data can wait if necessary. On a busy bus, bulk transfers have to wait, but on a bus that is otherwise idle, bulk transfers are the fastest. Low speed devices don't support bulk endpoints. Devices aren't required to support bulk transfers, but a specific device class can require them.

Interrupt transfers are for devices that must receive the host's or device's attention periodically, or with low latency, or delay. Other than control transfers, interrupt transfers are the only way low-speed devices can transfer data. Keyboards and mice use interrupt transfers to send keypress and mouse-movement data. Interrupt transfers can use any speed. Devices aren't required to support interrupt transfers, but a specific device class can require them.

Isochronous transfers have guaranteed delivery time but no error correcting. Data that uses isochronous transfers includes streaming audio and video. Isochronous is the only transfer type that doesn't support automatic re-transmitting of data received with errors, so occasional errors must be acceptable. Low-speed devices don't support isochronous endpoints. Devices aren't required to support isochronous transfers, but a specific device class can require them.

Table 2-1: Each of the USB's four transfer types is suited for different uses.

Transfer Type	Control	Bulk	Interrupt	Isochronous
Typical Use	Identification and configuration	Printer, scanner, drive	Mouse, keyboard	Streaming audio, video
Device support required?	yes	no	no	no
Low speed allowed?	yes	no	yes	no
Maximum packet size; maximum guaranteed packets/interval (Enhanced SuperSpeed).	512; none	1024; none	1024; 3 / 125 µs	1024; SuperSpeed: 48 / 125 µs SuperSpeedPlus: 96 / 125 µs
Maximum packet size; maximum guaranteed packets/interval (high speed).	64; none	512; none	1024; 3 / 125 µs	1024; 3 / 125 µs
Maximum packet size; maximum guaranteed packets/interval (full speed).	64; none	64; none	64: 1 / ms	1023; 1 / ms
Maximum packet size; maximum guaranteed packets/interval (low speed).	8; none	not allowed	8; 1 / 10 ms	not allowed
Direction of data flow	IN and OUT	IN or OUT	IN or OUT	IN or OUT
Reserved bandwidth for all transfers of the type	10% at low/full speed, 20% at high speed and Enhanced SuperSpeed	none	90% at low/full speed, 80% at high speed and Enhanced SuperSpeed (isochronous and interrupt combined)	
Message or Stream data?	message	stream	stream	stream
Error correction?	yes	yes	yes	no
Guaranteed delivery rate?	no	no	no	yes
Guaranteed latency (maximum time between transfer attempts)?	no	no	yes	yes

Stream and message pipes

In addition to classifying a pipe by the type of transfer it carries, the USB specification defines pipes as either stream or message. Control transfers use bidirectional message pipes; all other transfer types use unidirectional stream pipes.

Control transfers

In a control transfer's message pipe, a transfer begins with a transaction containing a request. Depending on the request, to complete the transfer, the host and device may exchange data and status information, or the device may just send status information. Each control transfer has at least one transaction that sends information in each direction.

If a device supports a received request, the device takes the requested action. If a device doesn't support the request, the device responds with a code to indicate that the request isn't supported.

Other transfers

The data in a stream pipe has no structure defined by the USB specification. The receiver just accepts or rejects the data that arrives. The device firmware or host software can process the data in whatever way is appropriate for the application.

Of course, even with stream data, the sending and receiving devices must agree on a data format. For example, the USB mass-storage specification defines structures the host can use for sending commands and receiving status information when communicating with drives.

Initiating a transfer

The USB 2.0 specification defines a transfer as one or more bus transactions that move information between a software client and its function. A transfer may be very short, sending as little as one byte of application data or no data (only status information), or very long, such as sending the contents of a large file.

Windows applications can access some USB devices by calling API functions to open a handle to the device and request data transfers. The operating system passes a request to transfer data to a device or class driver, which in turn passes the request to other system-level drivers and on to the host controller. The host controller initiates the transfer on the bus.

For devices in standard classes, a programming language can provide alternate ways to access a device. In many cases, the application doesn't have to know or care whether the device uses USB or another interface. For example, the .NET Framework includes Directory and File classes for accessing files on drives, including USB drives.

A vendor-supplied driver can also define API functions. For example, chip company FTDI provides a driver that provides functions for setting communications parameters and exchanging data with FTDI's controller chips.

For receiving data from a device, some drivers request the host controller to poll an endpoint at intervals, while other drivers don't initiate communications unless an application has requested data from the device.

USB 2.0 transactions

Figure 2-1 shows the elements of a typical USB 2.0 transfer. A lot of the terminology here begins to sound the same. There are transfers and transactions, stages and phases, data transactions and data packets. There are Status stages and handshake phases. Data stages have handshake packets and Status stages have data packets. It can take a while to absorb it all. Table 2-2 lists the elements that make up each of the four transfer types.

Each transfer consists of one or more transactions, and each transaction in turn consists of two or three packets. (Start-of-Frame markers transmit in single packets.) The USB 2.0 specification defines a transaction as the delivery of service to an endpoint. *Service* in this case can mean either the host's sending information to the device or the host's requesting and receiving information from the device. Setup transactions

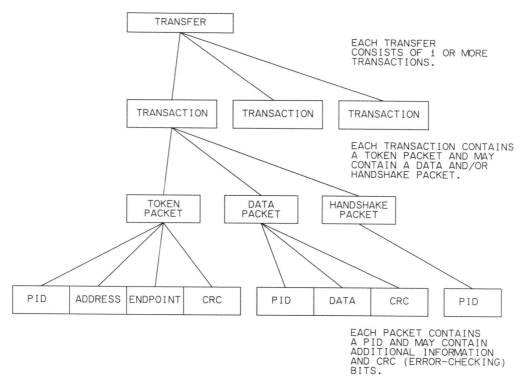

Figure 2-1. A USB 2.0 transfer consists of transactions. The transactions in turn contain packets, and the packets contain a packet identifier (PID) and sometimes additional information.

Table 2-2: Each USB 2.0 transaction has two or three phases. (Not shown are additional transactions required for split transactions, the PING protocol used in some transfers, and the PRE packet that precedes downstream, low-speed packets.)

Transfer Type	Number and Direction of Transactions		Phases (packets)
Control	Setup Stage	1 (SETUP)	Token
			Data
			Handshake
	Data Stage	Zero or more (IN or OUT)	Token
			Data
			Handshake
	Status Stage	1 (opposite direction of the transaction(s) in the Data stage or IN if there is no Data stage)	Token
			Data
			Handshake
Bulk	1 or more (IN or OUT)		Token
			Data
			Handshake
Interrupt	1 or more (IN or OUT)		Token
			Data
			Handshake
Isochronous	1 or more (IN or OUT)		Token
			Data

send control-transfer requests to a device. OUT transactions send other data or status information to the device. IN transactions send data or status information to the host.

Each USB 2.0 transaction includes identifying, error-checking, status, and control information as well as any data to be exchanged. A transfer may take place over multiple frames or microframes, but each USB 2.0 transaction completes within a frame or microframe without interruption. No other packets on the bus can break into the middle of a transaction. Devices must respond quickly with requested data or status information. Device firmware typically arms, or sets up, an endpoint's response to a received packet, and on receiving a packet, the hardware places the response on the bus.

A non-control transfer with a small amount of data may complete in a single transaction. Other transfers use multiple transactions with each carrying a portion of the data.

Transaction phases

Each transaction has up to three phases, or parts that occur in sequence: token, data, and handshake. Each phase consists of one or two transmitted packets. Each packet is a block of information with a defined format. All packets begin with a Packet ID (PID) that contains identifying information (Table 2-3). Depending on the transaction, the PID may be followed by an endpoint address, data, status information, or a frame number, along with error-checking bits.

In the token phase of a transaction, the host initiates a communication by sending a token packet. The PID indicates the transaction type, such as Setup, IN, OUT, or SOF.

In the data phase, the host or device may transfer any kind of information in a data packet. The PID includes a data-toggle or data PID sequencing value that guards against lost or duplicated data when a transfer has multiple data packets.

In the handshake phase, the host or device sends status information in a handshake packet. The PID contains a status code (ACK, NAK, STALL, or NYET). The USB 2.0 specification sometimes uses the terms *status phase* and *status packet* to refer to the handshake phase and packet.

The token phase has one additional use. A token packet can carry a Start-of-Frame (SOF) marker, which is a timing reference that the host sends at 1-ms intervals at full speed and at 125-μs intervals at high speed. This packet also contains a frame number that increments, rolling over on exceeding the maximum value. The number indicates the frame count so the eight microframes within a frame all have the same number. An endpoint can synchronize to the SOF packet or use the frame count as a timing reference. The SOF marker also keeps devices from entering the low-power Suspend state when the bus has no other USB traffic.

Low-speed devices don't see the SOF packet. Instead, the hub the device attaches to provides an End-of-Packet (EOP) signal, called the low-speed keep-alive signal, once per frame. As the SOF does for full- and high-speed devices, the low-speed keep-alive keeps low-speed devices from entering the Suspend state.

The PRE PID contains a preamble code that tells hubs that the next packet is low speed. On receiving a PRE PID, the hub enables communications with any attached low-speed devices. On a low- and full-speed bus, the PRE PID precedes all token, data, and handshake packets directed to low-speed devices. High-speed buses encode the PRE in the SPLIT packet, rather than sending the PRE separately. Low-speed packets sent by a device don't require a PRE PID.

In a high-speed bulk or control transfer with multiple data packets, before sending the second and any subsequent data packets, the host may send a PING PID to find out if the endpoint is ready to receive more data. The device responds with a status code.

Table 2-3: The PID provides information about a transaction. Content from *Universal Serial Bus Specification, Revision 2.0* and *USB 2.0 Link Power Management Addendum.* (Part 1 of 2)

Packet Type	PID Name	Value (binary)	Transfer types used in	Source	Bus Speed	Description
Token (identifies transaction type)	OUT	0001	all	host	all	Device and endpoint address for OUT transaction.
	IN	1001	all	host	all	Device and endpoint address for IN transaction.
	SOF	0101	Start of Frame	host	all	Start-of-Frame marker and frame number.
	SETUP	1101	control	host	all	Device and endpoint address for Setup transaction.
Data (carries data or status code)	DATA0	0011	all	host, device	all	Data toggle or data PID sequencing.
	DATA1	1011	all	host, device	all	Data toggle or data PID sequencing.
	DATA2	0111	isochronous	host, device	high	Data PID sequencing.
	MDATA	1111	isochronous, split transactions	host, device	high	Data PID sequencing.
Handshake (carries status code)	ACK	0010	control, bulk, interrupt	host, device	all	Receiver accepts error-free data packet.
	NAK	1010	control, bulk, interrupt	device	all	Receiver can't accept data or sender can't send data or has no data to transmit.
	STALL	1110	control, bulk, interrupt	device	all	A control request isn't supported or the endpoint is halted.
	NYET	0110	control write, bulk OUT, split transactions	device	high	Device accepts an error-free data packet but isn't ready for another, or a hub doesn't yet have complete-split data.

Table 2-3: The PID provides information about a transaction. Content from *Universal Serial Bus Specification, Revision 2.0* and *USB 2.0 Link Power Management Addendum*. (Part 2 of 2)

Packet Type	PID Name	Value (binary)	Transfer types used in	Source	Bus Speed	Description
Special	PRE	1100	control, interrupt	host	full	Preamble issued by a host to indicate that the next packet is low speed (low/full-speed segment only).
	ERR	1100	all	hub	high	Returned by a hub to report a low- or full-speed error in a split transaction (high-speed segment only).
	SPLIT	1000	all	host	high	Precedes a token packet to indicate a split transaction.
	PING	0100	control write, bulk OUT	host	high	Busy check for bulk OUT and control write data transactions after NYET.
	EXT	0000	–	host	all	Protocol extension token.

The SPLIT PID identifies a token packet as part of a split transaction as explained later in this chapter. The ERR PID is only for split transactions to enable a USB 2.0 hub to report an error in a downstream low- or full-speed transaction. The ERR and PRE PIDs have the same value but don't cause confusion because a hub never sends a PRE to the host or an ERR to a device. Also, ERR is only for high-speed segments and PRE never transmits on high-speed segments.

The *Link Power Management* addendum to the USB 2.0 specification defines the EXT PID. The host follows an EXT token packet with an extended token packet for a specific function. Chapter 17 has more about an extended token packet for use in power management.

Packet sequences

Every USB 2.0 transaction has a token packet. The host is always the source of this packet, which sets up the transaction by identifying the packet type, the receiving device and endpoint, and the direction of any data the transaction will transfer. For low-speed transactions on a full-speed bus, a PRE packet precedes the token packet. For split transactions, a SPLIT packet precedes the token packet.

Depending on the transfer type and whether the host or device has information to send, a data packet may follow the token packet. The direction specified in the token packet determines whether the host or device sends the data packet.

In all transfer types except isochronous, the receiver of the data packet (or the device if there is no data packet) returns a handshake packet containing a code that indicates the success or failure of the transaction. The absence of an expected handshake packet can indicate a more serious error or an unsupported Packet ID.

Timing constraints and guarantees

The allowed delays between the token, data, and handshake packets of a USB 2.0 transaction are very short, intended to allow only for cable delays and switching times plus a brief time to allow hardware to determine a response, such as data or a status code, in response to a received packet.

A common mistake in writing firmware is to assume that the firmware should wait for an interrupt before providing data to send to the host. Instead, before the host requests the data, the firmware must copy the data to send into the endpoint's buffer and arm the endpoint to send the data on receiving an IN token packet. The interrupt occurs when the transaction completes. After a successful transaction, the interrupt informs the firmware that the endpoint's buffer is ready to store data for the next transaction. If the firmware waits for an interrupt before providing the initial data, the interrupt never happens and data doesn't transfer.

A single transaction can carry data up to the maximum packet size the device specifies for the endpoint. A data packet with fewer than the maximum packet size's number of bytes is a *short packet*. A transfer with multiple transactions can take place over multiple frames or microframes, which don't have to be contiguous. For example, in a full-speed bulk transfer of 512 bytes, the maximum number of bytes in a single transaction is 64, so transferring all of the data requires at least eight transactions, which may occur in one or more frames.

A data packet that contains a Data PID and error-checking bits but no data bytes is a *zero-length packet* (ZLP). A ZLP can indicate the end of a transfer or successful completion of a control transfer.

Split transactions

A USB 2.0 hub communicates with a USB 2.0 host at high speed unless a USB 1.1 hub is between the host and hub. When a low- or full-speed device is attached to a USB 2.0 hub, the hub converts between speeds as needed. Speed conversion isn't all a hub does to manage multiple speeds. High speed is 40× faster than full speed and 320× faster than low speed. It doesn't make sense for the entire bus to wait while a hub exchanges low- or full-speed data with a device.

The solution is split transactions. A USB 2.0 host uses split transactions when communicating with a low- or full-speed device on a high-speed bus. What would be a single transaction at low or full speed usually requires two types of split transactions: one or more start-split transactions to send information to the device and one or more complete-split transactions to receive information from the device. The exception is isochronous OUT transactions, which don't use complete-split transactions because the device has nothing to send; the transaction completes with the start-split.

Transfers that use split transactions require more transactions to complete a transfer but make better use of bus time because they minimize the time spent waiting for a low- or full-speed device to transfer data. The components responsible for performing split transactions are the USB 2.0 host controller and a USB 2.0 hub that has an upstream connection to a high-speed bus segment and a downstream connection to a low- or full-speed bus segment. The transactions at the device are identical whether the host is using split transactions or not. At the host, device drivers and application software don't have to know or care whether the host is using split transactions because the protocol is handled at a lower level. Chapter 16 has more about how the host and hubs manage split transactions.

Ensuring successful transfers

USB 2.0 transfers use status and control codes and error-checking to help ensure that data gets to its destination as quickly as possible and without errors.

Status and control

The USB 2.0 specification defines handshake codes that indicate acceptance of received data, support or non-support of a control request, flow-control conditions, and an endpoint's HALT state.

A code indicates the success or failure of all transactions except those in isochronous transfers. In addition, in control transfers, the Status stage reports the success or failure of an entire transfer.

The handshake codes travel in the handshake or data packet of a transaction. The defined status codes are ACK, NAK, STALL, NYET, and ERR. The absence of an expected handshake code indicates an error. In all cases, the expected receiver of the handshake uses the information to help decide what to do next. Table 2-4 shows the status indicators and where they transmit in each transaction type.

ACK

ACK (acknowledge) indicates that a host or device has received data without error. Devices must return ACK in the handshake packets of Setup transactions if the token and data packets were received without error. Devices return ACK in the handshake

Table 2-4: The location, source, and contents of the handshake code depend on the type of transaction.

Transaction Type or PING Query	Data Packet		Handshake Packet	
	Source	Contents	Source	Contents
Setup	host	data	device	ACK
OUT	host	data	device	ACK, NAK, STALL, (high speed only) NYET, (from hub in complete split) ERR
IN	device	data, NAK, STALL, (from hub in complete split) ERR	host	ACK
PING (high speed only)	no data packet	–	device	ACK, NAK, STALL

packets of OUT transactions to complete the transaction and accept the received data. The host returns ACK in the handshake packets of IN transactions if the token and data packets were received without error.

NAK

NAK (negative acknowledge) means the device is busy or has no data to return. If the host sends data when the device is too busy to accept data, the endpoint returns NAK in the handshake packet. If the host requests data when the device has nothing to send, the endpoint returns NAK in the data packet. In either case, NAK indicates a temporary condition, and the host normally retries later up to a driver-defined limit.

Hosts never send NAK. Isochronous transactions don't use NAK because they have no handshake packet for returning a NAK. If a device or the host doesn't receive trans-mitted isochronous data, it's lost.

STALL

The STALL handshake can mean an unsupported control request, control request failed, or endpoint failed.

On receiving an unsupported control-transfer request, the device returns STALL in the Data or Status stage. The device also returns STALL if the device supports the request but for some reason can't take the requested action. For example, if the host sends a Set Configuration request to set the device configuration to 2, and the device supports only configuration 1, the device returns STALL. To clear this type of stall, the host sends another Setup packet to begin a new control transfer. The USB 2.0 specification calls this type of stall a *protocol stall*.

Another use of STALL is a response when the endpoint's Halt feature is set, which means that the endpoint is unable to send or receive data at all. The USB 2.0 specification calls this type of stall a *functional stall*.

Bulk and interrupt endpoints must support the functional stall. USB 2.0 control endpoints may support the functional stall but have little reason to do so. A control endpoint in a functional stall must continue to respond normally to other requests that monitor and control the stall condition. An endpoint that is capable of responding to these requests is capable of communicating and thus shouldn't be stalled. Isochronous transactions don't use STALL because they have no handshake packet for returning the STALL. Enhanced SuperSpeed control endpoints don't use the functional STALL.

On receiving a functional STALL, the host drops all pending requests to the device and doesn't resume communications until the host has sent a successful control request to clear the Halt feature on the device. Hosts never send STALL.

NYET

Only high-speed devices send NYET (*not yet*). High-speed bulk and control transfers support a protocol that enables the host to find out before sending data if an endpoint is ready to receive the data. At low and full speeds, when the host wants to send data in a control, bulk, or interrupt transfer, the host sends the token and data packets and receives a reply from the device in the transaction's handshake packet. If not ready for the data, the endpoint returns NAK and the host retries later. Retrying can waste a lot of bus time if the data packets are large and the device is often not ready.

High-speed bulk and control transfers with multiple data packets have a better way. After receiving a data packet, an endpoint can return a NYET handshake, which says the endpoint accepted the data but is not yet ready to receive another data packet. When the host thinks the endpoint might be ready, the host can send a PING token packet, and the endpoint returns either an ACK to indicate the device is ready for the next data packet or NAK or STALL if the endpoint isn't ready.

Sending a PING is more efficient than sending the entire data packet only to find out the device wasn't ready and having to resend later. Even after responding to a PING or OUT with ACK, an endpoint is allowed to return NAK on receiving the data packet that follows but should do so rarely. The host then tries again with another PING. The use of PING by the host is optional.

A USB 2.0 hub may return NYET in a complete-split transaction. Hosts and low- and full-speed devices never send NYET.

ERR

The ERR handshake is for use only by high-speed hubs in complete-split transactions. ERR indicates the device didn't return an expected handshake in the transaction the hub is completing with the host.

No response

Another type of status indication occurs when the host or a device expects to receive a handshake but receives nothing. This lack of response can occur if the receiver's error-checking calculation detected an error. On receiving no response, the sender knows it should retry. After multiple failures, the sender can take other action.

Reporting the status of control transfers

In control transfers, the data and handshake packets in the Status stage indicate the status of the transfer. Table 2-5 shows the status indicators for control transfers.

For control write transfers, the device returns the status of the transfer in the data packet of the Status stage. On accepting the request and receiving data in the Data stage (if present) without error, the device returns a ZLP. Or the device may return NAK (busy) or STALL (failure). The host returns ACK to complete the transfer. For an unsupported request, a device may return STALL in the Data stage to end the transfer.

For control read transfers, on receiving data in the Data stage without error, the host sends a ZLP in the data packet of the Status stage. The device responds with ACK (transaction complete), NAK (busy), or STALL (failure). A host may begin the Status stage before the device has sent all of the requested data packets, and if so, the device must abandon the Data stage and return a handshake code.

Error checking

The USB specifications define hardware requirements that ensure that errors due to line noise are rare. Still, a noise glitch or unexpectedly disconnected cable could corrupt a transmission. USB packets include error-checking bits that enable a receiver to identify just about any received data that doesn't match what was sent. For transfers that use multiple transactions, a data-toggle value keeps the transmitter and receiver synchronized to guard against missed transactions.

Error-checking bits

Token, data, and SOF packets include bits for use in error-checking. The bit values are calculated using a cyclic redundancy check (CRC) algorithm defined in the USB 2.0 specification. Hardware performs the calculations, which must be fast to enable the device to meet the specification's timing requirements.

Table 2-5: The Status stage of a control transfer indicates the success or failure of the transaction. (A device may also return STALL in the Data stage.)

Control Transfer Type	Status Stage			
	Data Packet Source	Data Packet Contents	Handshake Packet Source	Handshake Packet
Write (Host sends data in Data Stage or no Data stage)	Device	ZLP (success), NAK (busy), or STALL (failed)	Host	ACK
Read (Device sends data in Data Stage)	Host	ZLP	Device	ACK (success), NAK (busy), or STALL (failed)

The CRC is applied to the data to be checked. The sender, whether host or device, performs the calculation and sends the result along with the data. The receiver performs the identical calculation on the received data. If the results match, the data has arrived without error and the receiver returns ACK. If the results don't match, the receiver sends no handshake. The absence of the expected handshake tells the sender to retry. Hosts typically try a total of three times. On giving up, the host can notify the driver that requested the transfer.

The PID field in token packets uses a simpler form of error checking. The lower four bits in the field are the PID, and the upper four bits are the PID's complement. The receiver can check the integrity of the PID by complementing the upper four bits and ensuring that they match the PID. If not, the packet is corrupted and the receiver ignores the contents.

The data toggle

The data-toggle value enables detecting missed or duplicate data packets in control, bulk, and interrupt transfers. IN and OUT transactions have a data-toggle value in the data packet's PID field. DATA0 is a code of 0011_b, and DATA1 is 1011_b. In controller chips, a register bit often indicates the data-toggle state, so the data-toggle value is sometimes called the data-toggle bit. Each endpoint maintains its own data toggle.

Both the sender and receiver keep track of the data toggle. Host controllers handle data toggles at a low level that is invisible to applications and device drivers. Some device-controller chips handle the data toggles completely in hardware while others require some firmware control. *If you're debugging a device where the correct data is transmitting on the bus but the receiver is ignoring or discarding the data, the chances are good that the device isn't sending or expecting the correct data-toggle value.*

When the host configures a device on power up or attachment, the host and device each set their data toggles to DATA0 for all except some high-speed isochronous endpoints. On detecting an incoming data packet, the host or device compares the state of its data toggle with the received data toggle. If the values match, the receiver toggles its value and returns an ACK handshake packet. The ACK causes the sender to toggle its value for the next transaction.

The next received packet in the transfer should contain a data toggle of DATA1, and again the receiver toggles its bit and returns ACK. The data toggle on each end continues to alternate in each transaction except for control transfers as explained below.

If the receiver is busy and returns NAK, or if the receiver detects corrupted data and returns no response, the sender doesn't toggle its bit and instead tries again with the same data and data toggle.

If a receiver returns ACK but for some reason the sender doesn't see the ACK, the sender will think the receiver didn't get the data and will try again using the same data and data-toggle bit. In this case, the receiver of the repeated data ignores the data, doesn't toggle the data toggle, and returns ACK. If the sender mistakenly sends two packets in a row with the same data-toggle value, on receiving the second packet, the receiver ignores the data, doesn't toggle its value, and returns ACK. In both cases, the ACK re-synchronizes the data toggles.

Control transfers always use DATA0 in the Setup stage, use DATA1 in the first transaction of the Data stage, toggle the value in any additional Data-stage transactions, and use DATA1 in the Status stage. Bulk endpoints toggle the value in every transaction, resetting the data toggle only after completing a Set Configuration, Set Interface, or Clear Feature(ENDPOINT_HALT) request. Interrupt OUT endpoints behave the same as bulk OUT endpoints. Interrupt IN endpoints can behave the same as bulk IN endpoints, or to simplify processing with the risk of losing some data, the endpoint can toggle its data toggle in each transaction without checking for the host's ACK. Full-speed isochronous transfers always use DATA0. Isochronous transfers can't use the data toggle to correct errors because there is no packet for returning ACK or NAK and no time to resend missed data.

Data PID sequencing

Some high-speed isochronous transfers use DATA0, DATA1, and additional PIDs of DATA2 and MDATA. This use of the DATA and MDATA PIDs is called data PID sequencing. High-speed isochronous IN transfers with two or three transactions per microframe use DATA0, DATA1, and DATA2 encoding to indicate a transaction's position in the microframe:

IN Transactions per Microframe	Data PID		
	First Transaction	Second Transaction	Third Transaction
1	DATA0	–	–
2	DATA1	DATA0	–
3	DATA2	DATA1	DATA0

High-speed isochronous OUT transfers that have two or three transactions per microframe use DATA0, DATA1, and MDATA encoding to indicate whether more data will follow in the microframe:

OUT Transactions per Microframe	Data PID		
	First Transaction	Second Transaction	Third Transaction
1	DATA0	–	–
2	MDATA	DATA1	–
3	MDATA	MDATA	DATA2

Enhanced SuperSpeed transactions

Like USB 2.0, Enhanced SuperSpeed buses carry data, addressing, and status and control information. But Enhanced SuperSpeed has a dedicated data path for each direction, more support for power conservation, and other enhancements for greater efficiency. To support these differences, Enhanced SuperSpeed transactions use different packet formats and protocols.

Packet types

Enhanced SuperSpeed communications use two packet types when transferring data:

A Transaction Packet (TP) carries status and control information.

A Data Packet (DP) carries data and status and control information.

Two additional packet types perform other functions:

An Isochronous Timestamp Packet (ITP) carries timing information that devices can use for synchronization. The host multicasts an ITP following each bus-interval boundary to all links that aren't in a low-power state. The timestamp holds a count from zero to 0x3FFF and rolls over on overflow.

Table 2-6: Each Enhanced SuperSpeed packet has a 14-byte header followed by a Link Control Word.

Bits	Length (bits)	Use	
0–4	5	Type	Packet header
5–95	91	Fields specific to the packet type	
96–111	16	CRC	
112–127	16	Link Control Word	

A Link Management Packet (LMP) travels only in the link between a device's port and the hub the device connects to. The ports are called link partners. LMPs help manage the link.

Enhanced SuperSpeed doesn't use token packets because packet headers contain the token packet's information. Instead of data toggles, Enhanced SuperSpeed uses 5-bit sequence numbers that roll over from 31 to zero.

When TPs and DPs are both available to transmit, SuperSpeedPlus buses must transmit the TPs first.

Format

Each Enhanced SuperSpeed packet has a 14-byte header followed by a 2-byte Link Control Word (Table 2-6). The first five bits in the header are a Type field that identifies the packet as one of the four types described above. Every header also contains type-specific information and a 16-bit CRC. The Link Control Word (Table 2-7) provides information used in managing the transmission.

A DP consists of a Data Packet Header (DPH) followed immediately by a Data Packet Payload (DPP). The DPH (Table 2-8) consists of the 14-byte packet header and a Link Control Word. (SuperSpeedPlus non-deferred DPHs have two additional 16-bit fields, each containing a length field replica.) Note that the DPH's second field provides values for Gen 1 speed and "other speed," indicating that the specification may in the future support speeds other than SuperSpeed and SuperSpeedPlus.

The DPP contains the transaction's data, with the number of bytes specified in the Data Length field, and a 4-byte CRC. A DPP with less than the endpoint's maximum packet size bytes is a *short packet*. A DPP consisting of just the CRC and no data is a *zero-length Data Payload*.

For SuperSpeedPlus only, the DP specifies the transfer type, and non-periodic DPs specify an arbitration rate for use by the hub in scheduling SuperSpeedPlus traffic.

The other three packet types are always 128 bytes. In a TP, the Subtype field indicates the transaction's purpose (Table 2-9). All TPs have a device address that indicates the

Table 2-7: Each Enhanced SuperSpeed packet has a Link Control Word with information used in managing the transmission. Content from *Universal Serial Bus 3.1 Specification, Revision 1.0*.

Bit(s)	Name	Description
0–2	Header Sequence Number	Valid values are 0–7 in continuous sequence.
3–5	Reserved	–
6–8	Hub Depth	Valid only if Deferred is set. Identifies the hub that deferred the packet.
9	Delayed	Set to 1 if a hub resends or delays sending a Header Packet.
10	Deferred	Set to 1 if a hub can't send a packet because the downstream port is in a power-managed state.
11–15	CRC-5	Error checking bits.

source or destination of the packet. All TPs sent by the host contain a Route String that hubs use in routing the packet to its destination.

Transferring data

An Enhanced SuperSpeed transaction has one or two phases that each contain a DP or a TP.

In a non-isochronous IN transaction, the host sends an ACK TP to request data, and the device returns a DP, a NRDY TP, or a STALL TP. In an isochronous IN transaction, the host sends an ACK TP to request data, and the device returns a DP. For IN transactions, a SuperSpeedPlus host may issue simultaneous ACK TPs to different endpoints on devices operating at SuperSpeedPlus.

In a non-isochronous OUT transaction, the host sends a DP and the device returns an ACK, NRDY, or STALL TP. In an isochronous OUT transaction, the host sends a DP.

Sequence Numbers

Table 2-10 shows the contents of the ACK TP. In an IN transaction, on receiving an ACK TP with NumP = 1, the endpoint sends a DP with the DPH containing the Sequence Number of the received ACK TP. Except for isochronous transactions, on receiving the DP, the host acknowledges receiving the data by incrementing the Sequence Number and sending another ACK TP. If NumP > 0, the ACK TP also serves as a request for more data. In other words, instead of requiring separate transactions to ACK received data and then request more data, a single ACK TP can perform both functions.

At SuperSpeedPlus, a host can pipeline multiple isochronous IN transactions, sending an ACK TP before all of the data requested in the ACK TP has arrived.

Table 2-8: The Data Packet Header (DPH) provides the Data Packet (DP)'s length and other information. Following the DPH are the data and a CRC value. Content from *Universal Serial Bus 3.1 Specification, Revision 1.0.* (Part 1 of 2)

Field	Bits	Function
Type	5	Data Packet Header (01000_b)
Route String, Arbitration Rate, or Reserved	20	Gen 1: In downstream communications, used by hubs to route a packet to the correct port. Other speed: for downstream flowing packets, a Route String. For upstream-flowing asynchronous packets the lower 16 bits are the Arbitration Rate. Remaining bits are zero.
Device Address	7	The device that is the source or receiver of the DP.
Sequence Number	5	Identifies the DP.
Reserved	1	–
End of Burst (EOB) (non-isochronous IN), zero (non-isochronous OUT), or Last Packet Flag (LPF) (isochronous)	1	For non-isochronous IN endpoints, identifies the last packet in a burst. For non-isochronous OUT and control endpoints, zero. For isochronous endpoints, identifies the last packet in a service interval.
Direction	1	0 = host to device; 1 = device to host.
Endpoint Number	4	The endpoint that is the source or receiver of the DP.
Transfer Type (TT) or Reserved	3	Gen 1: reserved Other speed: 100_b control transfer 101_b isochronous transfer 110_b bulk transfer 111_b interrupt transfer 000_b unknown for ACKs and deferred DPs from SuperSpeed bus instances Other values reserved
Setup	1	Set by the host when the DP is a Setup packet.
Data Length	16	The number of data bytes in the Data Packet Payload.
Stream ID or Reserved	16	For bulk endpoints, can identify a stream.
Reserved	8	–
Support Smart Isochronous (SSI) or Reserved	1	Indicates support for smart isochronous scheduling.
Will Ping Again (WPA)/Reserved	1	If SSI = 1, the host will send a PING TP before servicing the endpoint again.
Data in this Bus Interval is done (DBI)/ Reserved	1	If SSI = 1, the host is finished with transactions with the endpoint in the current bus interval.

Table 2-8: The Data Packet Header (DPH) provides the Data Packet (DP)'s length and other information. Following the DPH are the data and a CRC value. Content from *Universal Serial Bus 3.1 Specification, Revision 1.0.* (Part 2 of 2)

Field	Bits	Function
Packets Pending (PP)	1	Indicates whether the host has another packet for the endpoint.
Number of Bus Intervals (NBI)/Reserved	4	If SSI = 1, WPA = 0, and DBI = 1, the host controller will next service the endpoint in (current bus interval + NBI value + 1).
CRC-16	16	Error checking.
Link Control Word	16	Link management.
Data Block	varies	Data specified in Data Length field.
CRC-32	32	Error checking for Data Block.

In an OUT transaction, the DP from the host contains a Sequence Number. The ACK TP that the device sends in response contains the Sequence Number of the next expected DP and serves as an implicit acknowledgment of receiving the previous DP.

In a control transfer, the Setup TP and the first DPH each use a Sequence Number of zero. (Note that this differs from USB 2.0, where the Data Stage begins with DATA1.) For any additional DPs, the Sequence Number increments, resetting to zero on rollover.

Bulk and interrupt endpoints increment the Sequence Number for every transaction, resetting to zero on rollover or after completing a Set Configuration, Set Interface, or Clear Feature(ENDPOINT_HALT) request. In isochronous transfers, the Sequence Number resets to zero at the start of a service interval and increments on each additional DP within the service interval. The endpoint descriptor specifies the length of a service interval and the maximum number of DPs per service interval.

On detecting an error in a received DP, the host or device sends an ACK TP with the Retry bit set and the Sequence Number of the packet that contained the error. The sender of the DP must then resend all sent DPs beginning with that Sequence Number.

For SuperSpeedPlus only, the ACK TP specifies the transfer type

Burst transactions

Enhanced SuperSpeed bulk and interrupt endpoints can support burst transactions where the host or device sends multiple DPs without waiting for ACK TPs to acknowledge previous received data. Every data payload in a burst except the last must equal the endpoint's maximum packet size.

Table 2-9: Hosts and devices use Transaction Packets (TPs) to send status and control information. Content from *Universal Serial Bus 3.1 Specification, Revision 1.0.*

Subtype	Source	Description
ACK	Host	Requests data from an IN endpoint and acknowledges a previously received DP.
	Device	Acknowledges data received on an OUT endpoint and specifies how many data packet buffers are available after receiving this packet.
NRDY	Device	On receiving a DP on an OUT endpoint, informs the host that the device has no buffer space to accept the data. On receiving an ACK TP on an IN endpoint, informs the host that the device can't return a DP. Valid for non-isochronous endpoints.
ERDY	Device	An endpoint is ready to send or receive DPs. Valid for non-isochronous endpoints.
STATUS	Host	The host has initiated the Status stage of a control transfer. Valid for control endpoints.
STALL	Device	The endpoint is halted or a requested control transfer is invalid or unsupported.
DEV_NOTIFICATION	Device	A change in a device or interface state has occurred. The highest four bits are the type of change: 0x0 reserved 0x1 function wake 0x2 latency tolerance message 0x3 bus interval adjustment message 0x4 host role request (OTG) 0x5 sublink speed (for devices not operating at SuperSpeed or SuperSpeedPlus 0x6–0xF reserved
PING	Host	Before initiating an isochronous transfer when a link is in a low-power state, requests all paths between the host and the isochronous endpoint to transition to the active state.
PING_RESPONSE	Device	Response to PING.

The NumP field in an ACK TP sets the number of DPs a device or host can receive in a burst. Valid values are zero or any value from one less than the value in the previous ACK packet to bMaxBurst + 1 in the endpoint companion descriptor. Note that bMax-Burst is zero-based, with zero indicating a maximum burst of 1 packet, while NumP indicates the actual number of packets a receiver can accept (which may be zero).

A Set Configuration, Set Interface, or Clear Feature(ENDPOINT_HALT) request resets the burst size of the associated endpoint(s).

Table 2-10: An ACK Transaction Packet (TP) can acknowledge received data and request new data. Content from *Universal Serial Bus 3.1 Specification, Revision 1.0.* (Part 1 of 2)

Number of Bits	Field Name	Description
5	Type	Transaction Packet (00100_b)
20	Route String or Reserved	Used by hubs in routing packets downstream.
7	Device Address	The address assigned during enumeration.
4	SubType	ACK (0001_b)
2	Reserved	–
1	Retry DP (rty)	If set, the host or device requests a resend due to not receiving a packet or receiving a corrupted packet.
1	Direction (D)	The direction of the endpoint sending or receiving the data: 0 = host to device; 1 = device to host.
4	Endpoint Number (EPT Num)	The endpoint sending or receiving the data.
3	Transfer Type (TT) or Reserved	Gen 1 speed: Reserved Other speed: 100_b control transfer 101_b isochronous transfer 110_b bulk transfer 111_b interrupt transfer 000_b unknown for ACKs and deferred DPs from SuperSpeed bus instances Other values reserved
1	Host Error (HE)	For host-to-device ACK TPs, indicates that host was unable to accept a valid DP.
5	Number of Packets (NumP)	The number of DPs the receiver can accept in a burst.
5	Sequence Number (Seq Num)	The sequence number of the next expected DP.
5	Reserved	–
1	TP Follows (TPF) or Reserved	Gen 1 speed: Reserved Other speed: 1 if the device will send a Device Notification TP following this TP.
16	Stream ID or Reserved	For bulk endpoints, can identify a stream.
8	Reserved	–
1	Support Smart Isochronous (SSI) or Reserved	Indicates support for smart isochronous scheduling.
1	Will Ping Again (WPA)/Reserved	If SSI = 1, the host will send a PING TP before servicing the endpoint again.

Table 2-10: An ACK Transaction Packet (TP) can acknowledge received data and request new data. Content from *Universal Serial Bus 3.1 Specification, Revision 1.0.* (Part 2 of 2)

Number of Bits	Field Name	Description
1	Data in this Bus Interval is done (DBI)/ Reserved	If SSI = 1, the host is finished with transactions with the endpoint in the current bus interval.
1	Packets Pending (PP)	Indicates whether the host has another packet for the endpoint.
4	Number of Bus Intervals (NBI)/Reserved	If SSI = 1, WPA = 0, and DBI = 1, the host controller will next service the endpoint in (current bus interval + NBI value + 1).
16	CRC-16	Error detecting.
16	Link Control Word	Defines link-level flow control.

Isochronous endpoints can support isochronous burst transactions, which consist of multiple DPs transferred in a service interval with each packet except the last required to be the endpoint's maximum packet size. Isochronous transactions never use ACK.

Timing constraints

Devices and hosts must respond quickly to received DPs and ACK TPs that request data. On receiving an ACK TP, STATUS TP, or DP, a device must begin to return a response within 400 ns. On receiving a DP, a host must begin to return an ACK TP within 3 µs. The maximum interval between DPs in a burst is 100 ns for Gen 1 and 50 ns for Gen 2. Thus, device hardware rather than firmware handles responding to received packets.

Notifying the host

To conserve bandwidth and to enable inactive links to transition to low-power states, Enhanced SuperSpeed hosts stop requesting to send or receive data from Enhanced SuperSpeed endpoints that are in the flow control condition. This condition indicates that the endpoint temporarily can't send or receive data. To request to resume communications, the endpoint sends an ERDY TP. A device can send the ERDY at any time without waiting for the host to request a packet. On receiving the ERDY, the host resumes communications with the endpoint.

An IN endpoint is in the flow control condition after responding to an ACK TP with a NRDY TP or a DP with the End of Burst (EOB) field set to 1 indicating that the packet is the last in a burst. The device sets EOB if the data payload is equal to the endpoint's maximum packet size and the endpoint is returning fewer than the number of packets requested in the previous ACK TP.

An OUT endpoint is in the flow control condition on responding to a DP with either a NRDY TP or an ACK TP with the NumP field set to zero, indicating that the endpoint can't accept any DPs.

Hosts retain the option to attempt communications with bulk endpoints in the flow-control condition before receiving ERDY.

Link Management Packets

Link Management Packets have these subtypes:

- **Set Link Function** defines a bit for use in testing.

- **U2 Inactivity Timeout** specifies the timeout for transitioning between low-power states.

- **Vendor Device Test** provides a mechanism for vendor-specific tests.

- **Port Capabilities** indicates if the port can be configured as an upstream-facing port, a downstream-facing port, or both. The ports in a link exchange this packet after initializing the link. For situations where both ports in a link support both port types, a tiebreaker field and protocol determines which port is upstream-facing and which is downstream-facing.

- **Port Configuration** contains a bit that is set to 1 to specify that the link speed for the upstream-facing port shall be 5 Gbps. A downstream-facing port operating at Gen 1 speed sends this packet to its link partner.

- **Port Configuration Response** accepts or rejects a received Port Configuration LMP.

3

A Transfer Type for Every Purpose

This chapter takes a closer look at USB's four transfer types: control, bulk, interrupt, and isochronous. Each type has features that make it suitable for specific purposes.

Control transfers

Control transfers have two uses. For all devices, control transfers carry the standard requests that the host uses to learn about and configure devices on attachment. Control transfers can also carry requests defined by a class or vendor for any purpose.

Availability

Every device must support control transfers using the default pipe at endpoint zero. A device may also have additional pipes for control transfers, but in reality there's no need for more than one. Even if a device needs to send a lot of control requests, hosts allocate bandwidth for control transfers according to the number and size of requests, not by the number of control endpoints so additional control endpoints offer no advantage.

Structure

Chapter 2 introduced control transfers and their Setup, Data, and Status stages. Each stage consists of one or more transactions.

Every control transfer must have a Setup stage and a Status stage. Not all transfers have Data stages, though a specific request can require a Data stage. Because every control transfer requires transferring information in both directions, the control transfer's message pipe uses both the IN and OUT endpoint addresses.

In a control write transfer, the data in the Data stage travels from the host to the device. Control transfers that have no Data stage are also considered to be control write transfers. In a control read transfer, the data in the Data stage travels from the device to the host. Figure 3-1 and Figure 3-2 show the stages of control read and control write transfers at low and full speeds on a low/full-speed bus. There are differences, described later in this chapter, for some high-speed transfers, low- and full-speed transfers with USB 2.0 hubs on high-speed buses, and Enhanced Super-Speed transfers.

In the Setup stage, the host begins a Setup transaction by sending information about the request. The token packet's SETUP PID identifies the transaction as a Setup transaction that begins a control transfer. The data packet contains eight bytes of information about the request including the request number, whether or not the transfer has a Data stage, and if so, in which direction the data will travel.

The USB 2.0 and USB 3.1 specifications define standard requests. Successful enumeration requires specific responses to some requests, such as the request that sets a device's address. For other requests, a device can return STALL to indicate that the device doesn't support the request. A STALL ends the transfer. A class may require a device to support class-specific requests, and devices can support requests defined by a vendor-provided driver.

When present, the Data stage consists of one or more transactions. Depending on the request, the host or peripheral may be the source of the data in these transactions, but all data packets in this stage are in the same direction.

The Status stage consists of one IN or OUT transaction where the device reports the success or failure of the transfer. The source of the Status stage's data packet is the receiver of the data in the Data stage. When a transfer has no Data stage, the device sends the Status stage's data packet. On completing or abandoning the current transfer, the host can begin a new control transfer.

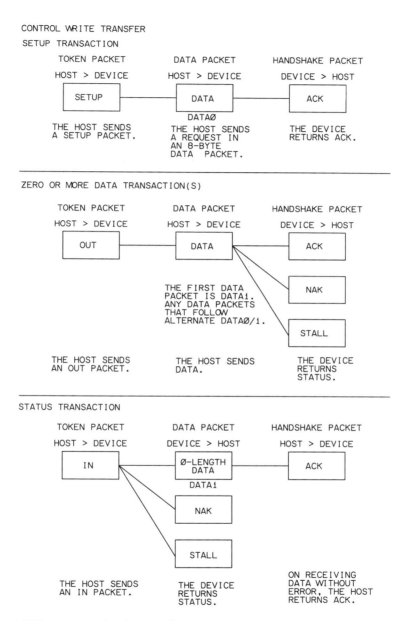

Figure 3-1. A USB 2.0 control write transfer contains a Setup transaction, zero or more Data transactions, and a Status transaction. Not shown are the PING protocol used in some high-speed transfers with multiple data packets and the split transactions used with low- and full-speed devices on a high-speed bus. Information source: *Universal Serial Bus Specification, Revision 2.0.*

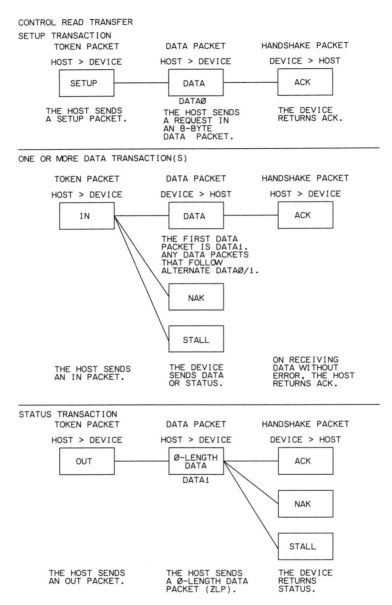

Figure 3-2. A USB 2.0 control read transfer contains a Setup transaction, one or more data transactions, and a status transaction. Not shown are the split transactions used with low- and full-speed devices on a high-speed bus. Information source: *Universal Serial Bus Specification, Revision 2.0.*

High speed differences

As described in Chapter 2, if a high-speed control write transfer has more than one data packet in the Data stage and the device returns NYET after receiving a data packet, the host may use the PING protocol before sending the next data packet.

If a host is performing a control transfer with a low- or full-speed device on a high-speed bus, the host uses split transactions for all of the transfer's transactions. To the device, the transaction is no different than a transaction with a USB 1.1 host. The USB 2.0 or USB 3.1 hub nearest the device initiates transactions with the device and returns data and status information to the host.

Enhanced SuperSpeed differences

On an Enhanced SuperSpeed bus, the Setup stage's Setup DP contains the eight bytes of Setup data. The Data Packet Header uses the following values:

    Sequence Number = 0
    Data Length = 8
    Setup = 1

Figure 3-3 shows the structure of an Enhanced SuperSpeed control write transfer. The host begins the transfer with a Setup DP, and on receiving the packet without error, the device responds with an ACK TP. If the transfer has a Data stage, the host sends one or more DPs, and the device accepts each DP with an ACK TP. If the transfer has multiple Data packets, the Sequence Numbers in the Data and ACK packets increment for each Data packet. In the Status stage, the host sends a STATUS TP, and the device returns ACK.

Figure 3-4 shows the structure of an Enhanced SuperSpeed control read transfer., which is identical to a control write transfer except for the Data stage. In the Data stage, the host sends one or more ACK TPs, and the device responds to each with a DP.

A device can control the flow of a control transfer by responding to the Setup DP with an ACK TP with NumP = 0 and Sequence Number = 0. The device then requests to start the Data and Status stages by sending an ERDY TP.

In the Data or Status stage, an endpoint can return a STALL or NRDY TP instead of ACK. A STALL ends the transfer. NRDY halts the transfer until the device returns ERDY.

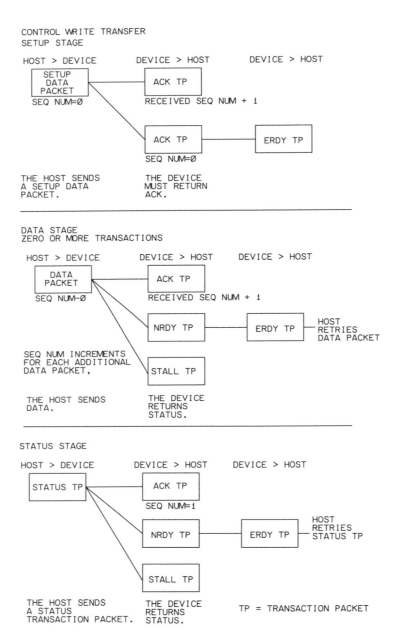

Figure 3-3. A Setup Data packet initiates an Enhanced SuperSpeed control write transfer. A Status TP initiates the Status stage. Information source: *Universal Serial Bus 3.1 Specification, Revision 1.0.*

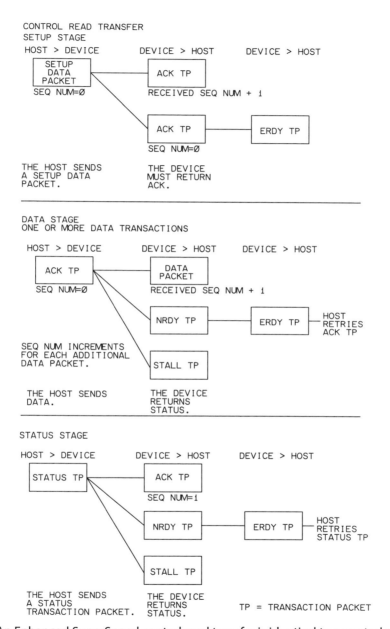

Figure 3-4. An Enhanced SuperSpeed control read transfer is identical to a control write transfer except for the Data stage. Information source: *Universal Serial Bus 3.1 Specification, Revision 1.0.*

Data size

In a control transfer's Data stage, the allowed maximum data packet size varies with bus speed:

Bus Speed	Maximum Data Packet Size
Low	8
Full	8, 16, 32, or 64
High	64
SuperSpeed/SuperSpeedPlus	512

These bytes include only the information transferred in the data packet (USB 2.0) or Data Packet Payload (Enhanced SuperSpeed), excluding PID and CRC bits.

In the Data stage, all data packets except the last must be the maximum packet size for the endpoint. The maximum packet size for the default control pipe is in the device descriptor that the host retrieves during enumeration. If a transfer has more data than will fit in one data transaction, the host sends or receives the data in multiple transactions.

For some control read transfers, the amount of data returned by the device can vary. If the amount is less than the requested number of bytes and is an even multiple of the endpoint's maximum packet size, the device should indicate when it has no more data to send by returning a ZLP (USB 2.0) or a zero-length Data Payload (Enhanced SuperSpeed) in response to a request for data after the device has sent all of its data.

Speed

The host must make its best effort to ensure that all control transfers complete as quickly as possible. A USB 2.0 host controller reserves a portion of the bus bandwidth for control transfers: 10% of each frame for low- and full-speed endpoints and 20% of each microframe for high-speed endpoints. An Enhanced SuperSpeed host reserves 20% of the bus bandwidth for control transfers. If the control transfers don't need all of the reserved bandwidth, other transfers can use what remains. If the bus has other unused bandwidth, control transfers can use more than the reserved amount. The host attempts to parcel out the available time as fairly as possible to all devices. A single frame, microframe, or bus interval can contain multiple transactions for the same transfer, or a transfer's transactions can be spread among multiple (micro)frames or bus intervals.

There are two opinions on whether control transfers are appropriate for transferring data other than enumeration and configuration data. Some believe control transfers should be reserved as much as possible for servicing the standard USB requests and performing other infrequent configuration tasks. This approach helps ensure that the transfers complete quickly by keeping the reserved bandwidth as open as possible. But the USB specifications don't forbid other uses for control transfers, and some see no problem in using control transfers for any purpose. Low-speed devices have no other option except periodic interrupt transfers that can waste bandwidth if data transfers are infrequent.

Control transfers aren't the most efficient way to transfer data. Each transfer has significant overhead. At low speed, a single control transfer with 8 data bytes uses over 1/3 of a frame's bandwidth, though the transfer's transactions may travel in multiple frames. In a control transfer with multiple data packets in the Data stage, the data may travel in the same or different (micro)frames or bus intervals. On a busy bus, all control transfers may have to share the reserved portion of the bandwidth.

The USB specifications define timing limits that apply to control requests except for class requests that specify a faster response. Where stricter timing isn't specified, in a transfer where the host requests data from the device, a device may delay as long as 500 ms before making the data available to the host. To find out if data is available, a USB 2.0 host sends a token packet to request the data. If the data is ready, the device returns the data in that transaction's data packet. Otherwise the device returns NAK to advise the host to retry later. The host keeps trying at intervals for up to 500 ms. Enhanced SuperSpeed devices can delay communications by setting NumP = 0 and Sequence Number = 0 in response to a Setup DP or by sending NRDY in response to requested or received data.

In a transfer where the host sends data to the device, if the host sends data at the maximum rate the device can accept the data, a USB 2.0 device can take up to 5 seconds to accept all of the data and complete the Status stage. Once begun, the Status stage must complete within 50 ms.

A device operating at Enhanced SuperSpeed must complete each of the following within 50 ms (though additional delays by the host may extend the time): time between Setup packet and first Data stage, time between consecutive Data stages, and time between last Data stage and Status stage. In a control transfer with no Data stage, the device must complete the transfer within 50 ms.

The host and its drivers aren't required to enforce the timing limits, but all devices should comply with the limits to ensure proper operation with any host. For USB 2.0 and Enhanced SuperSpeed hubs, the recommended average response time is under 5 ms.

Detecting and handling errors

If a USB 2.0 device doesn't return an expected handshake packet during a control transfer, the host retries. On receiving no response after a typical total of three tries, the host notifies the software that requested the transfer and stops communicating with the endpoint until the problem is resolved, such as by re-enumerating the device. The two retries include only those sent in response to no handshake at all. A NAK triggers a retry but doesn't increment the error count.

Control transfers use data toggles (USB 2.0) or Sequence Numbers (Enhanced Super-Speed) to protect against lost data. In the Data stage of a USB 2.0 control read trans-fer, on receiving data from the device, the host normally returns ACK and then sends an OUT token packet to begin the Status stage. If the device for any reason doesn't see the ACK returned after the transfer's final data packet, the device must interpret a received OUT token packet as evidence that the Status stage has begun.

Devices must accept all error-free Setup packets. If a new Setup packet arrives before a previous control transfer completes, the device must abandon the previous transfer and start the new transfer.

Device responsibilities

A USB 2.0 device has these responsibilities for transfers on a control endpoint:

- Send ACK in response to every Setup packet received without error.
- For supported control write requests, send ACK in response to received data in the Data stage (if present) and return a ZLP in the Status stage.
- For supported control read requests, send data in response to IN token packets in the Data stage and ACK the received ZLP in the Status stage.
- For unsupported requests, return STALL in the Data or Status stage.

For all but the Setup stage, one or more NAKs preceding ACK, ZLP, data, or STALL are acceptable up to the timing limit for the stage.

An Enhanced SuperSpeed device has these responsibilities for transfers on a control endpoint:

- Send an ACK TP in response to Setup data received without error in DPs.
- For supported control write requests, when there is a Data stage, send an ACK TP in response to received data in DPs. In the Status stage, send an ACK TP in response to a received STATUS TP.
- For supported control read requests, receive acknowledgments and requests to send data in ACK TPs and send data in DPs. In the Status stage, send an ACK TP in response to a received STATUS TP.
- For unsupported requests, return a STALL TP in the Data or Status stage.

For all but the Setup stage, one or more NRDY TPs preceding an ACK TP, data, or STALL TP are acceptable up to the timing limit for the stage.

Bulk transfers

Bulk transfers are useful for transferring data when time isn't critical. A bulk transfer can send large amounts of data without clogging the bus because the transfers defer to the other transfer types, waiting until time is available. Uses for bulk transfers include sending data to a printer and reading and writing to a drive. On an otherwise idle bus, bulk transfers are the fastest transfer type for large amounts of data.

Availability

Low speed doesn't support bulk transfers. Devices aren't required to support bulk transfers, but a specific device class may require them. For example, a mass-storage device must have a bulk endpoint in each direction.

Structure

A USB 2.0 bulk transfer consists of one or more IN or OUT transactions (Figure 3-5). All data travels in one direction. Transferring data in both directions requires a separate pipe and transfer for each direction.

A bulk transfer ends successfully when the expected amount of data has transferred or when a transaction contains less than the endpoint's maximum packet size, including zero data bytes. The USB 2.0 specification doesn't define a protocol for indicating the number of data bytes in a bulk transfer. When needed, the device and host can use a class-specific or vendor-defined protocol to pass this information. For example, a transfer can begin with a header that specifies the number of bytes to be transferred, or the device or host can use a class-specific or vendor-defined protocol to request a quantity of data.

High speed differences

To conserve bus time, a host may use the PING protocol in some high-speed bulk transfers. If a high-speed bulk OUT transfer has more than one data packet and the device returns NYET after receiving a packet, the host may use PING to find out when it's OK to send more data. In a bulk transfer on a high-speed bus with a low- or full-speed device, the host uses split transactions for all of the transfer's transactions.

Enhanced SuperSpeed differences

Figure 3-6 shows Enhanced SuperSpeed bulk IN and OUT transactions. In an IN transaction, the host sends an ACK TP to request one or more DPs and acknowledge previous data, if any, and the device sends DP(s), NRDY, or STALL. On receiving a DP, the host returns an ACK TP. If the host requests multiple DPs by setting NumP > 1, the

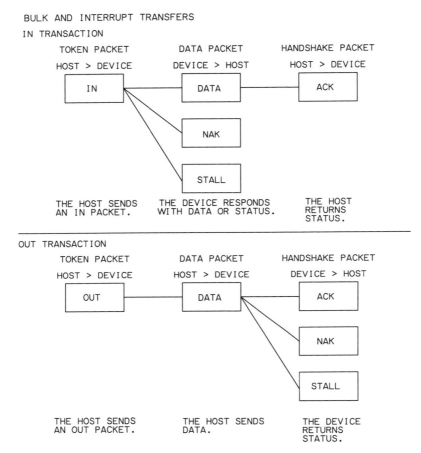

BULK AND INTERRUPT TRANSFERS

Figure 3-5. USB 2.0 bulk and interrupt transfers have identical structure, but different scheduling by the host. Not shown are the PING protocol used in some high-speed bulk OUT transfers with multiple data packets or the split transactions used with low- and full-speed devices on a high-speed bus. Information source: *Universal Serial Bus Specification, Revision 2.0.*

device doesn't have to wait for each ACK before sending the next packet. If NumP > 0 in an ACK TP that the host sends in response to received data, the packet also serves as a request for more data. In an OUT transaction, the host sends data in DPs, and the device acknowledges receiving data in ACK TPs or returns NRDY or STALL. After an endpoint has sent NRDY, a host can attempt to resume communications even if the endpoint hasn't sent ERDY.

Enhanced SuperSpeed bulk transfers can use a Stream Protocol to transfer multiple, independent data streams using a single endpoint. A class or other host driver can

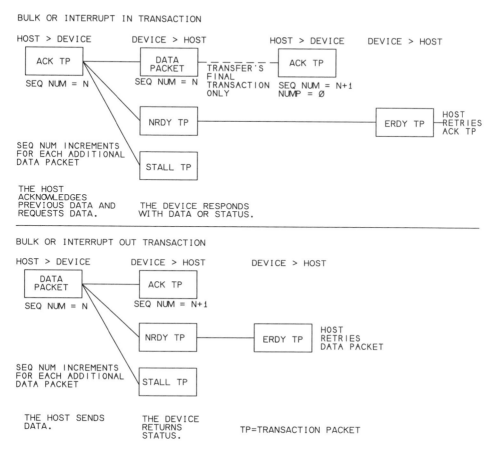

Figure 3-6. Enhanced SuperSpeed bulk and interrupt transfers use ACK TPs to request and acknowledge data. Information source: *Universal Serial Bus 3.1 Specification, Revision 1.0.*

define uses for the streams. Each stream has its own endpoint buffer. A CStream ID value identifies the current stream in Data Packet Headers and in ACK, NRDY, and ERDY TPs.

Data size

The allowed maximum data bytes in a bulk transaction's data packet vary with the bus speed:

Bus Speed	Maximum Data Packet Size
Full	8, 16, 32, or 64
High	512
SuperSpeed/SuperSpeedPlus	1024

These bytes include only the information transferred in the data packet (USB 2.0) or Data Packet Payload (Enhanced SuperSpeed), excluding PID and CRC bits.

During enumeration, the host reads the maximum packet size for each bulk endpoint from the device's descriptors. The amount of data in a transfer may be less than, equal to, or greater than the maximum packet size. If the data doesn't fit in a single packet, the host uses multiple transactions to complete the transfer.

Speed

The host controller guarantees that bulk transfers will complete eventually but doesn't reserve bandwidth for them. Control transfers are guaranteed to have 10% of the bandwidth at low and full speeds and 20% at high speed and Enhanced Super-Speed. Interrupt and isochronous transfers may use the rest. So if a bus is very busy, a bulk transfer can take a long time.

However, when the bus is otherwise idle, bulk transfers can use the most bandwidth of any type and have low overhead and thus are the fastest of all. When a full-speed bulk endpoint's maximum packet size is less than 64, some host controllers schedule no more than one packet per frame even if more bandwidth is available. Thus for best performance, a full-speed bulk endpoint should have a maximum packet size of 64.

At full speed on an otherwise idle bus, up to nineteen 64-byte bulk transfers can transfer up to 1,216 data bytes per frame, for a data rate of 1.216 MB/s. In theory, at high speed on an otherwise idle bus, up to thirteen 512-byte bulk transfers can transfer up to 6,656 data bytes per microframe, for a data rate of 53.248 MB/s. Real-world performance varies with the host-controller hardware and driver and the host architecture, including latencies when accessing system memory. Some high-speed hosts can transfer bulk data at around 50 MB/s. A SuperSpeed bus is capable of transferring around 460 MB/s in bulk transfers. A SuperSpeedPlus bus is capable of transferring around 1.1 GB/s in bulk transfers.

Detecting and handling errors

If a USB 2.0 device doesn't return an expected handshake packet, the host tries up to twice more. A host also retries on receiving NAK. The class or device driver determines whether the host eventually gives up on receiving multiple NAKs. For Enhanced SuperSpeed endpoints, a device uses NRDY and ERDY to cause the host to stop requesting to send or receive data when an endpoint isn't ready to receive data or has no data to send. Data toggles (USB 2.0) or Sequence Numbers (Enhanced SuperSpeed) detect lost or repeated data.

Device responsibilities

A USB 2.0 device has these responsibilities for transfers on a bulk endpoint:

- For OUT transfers, ACK data received in data packets.
- For IN transfers, return data in data packets in response to IN token packets.

One or more NAKs preceding ACK or data are acceptable up to the timing limit for the transfer, if any.

An Enhanced SuperSpeed device has these responsibilities for transfers on a bulk endpoint:

- For OUT transfers, send ACK TPs to acknowledge data received in DPs.
- For IN transfers, receive requests to send data and acknowledgments of received data in ACK TPs and send data in DPs.

One or more NRDY TPs preceding an ACK TP or data are acceptable up to the timing limit, if any, for the transfer.

Interrupt transfers

Interrupt transfers are useful when data has to transfer without delay. Typical applications include keyboards, pointing devices, game controllers, and hub status reports. Users don't want a noticeable delay between pressing a key or moving a mouse and seeing the result on screen. A hub needs to report the attachment or removal of devices promptly. Low-speed devices, which support only control and interrupt transfers, are likely to use interrupt transfers.

At low and full speeds, the bandwidth available for interrupt endpoints is limited, but high speed and Enhanced SuperSpeed loosen the limits.

Interrupt transfers are interrupt-like because they guarantee fast response from the host. For both bulk and interrupt endpoints, firmware typically uses interrupts to detect new received data. On a USB 2.0 bus, both bulk and interrupt endpoints must wait for the host to request data before sending data. Enhanced SuperSpeed bulk and interrupt endpoints can notify the host that they have data to send by sending an ERDY TP but still must wait for the host to request data packets.

Availability

All speeds allow interrupt transfers. Devices aren't required to support interrupt transfers, but a device class may require it. For example, a HID-class device must support interrupt IN transfers for sending data to the host.

Structure

A USB 2.0 interrupt transfer consists of one or more IN transactions or one or more OUT transactions. Transferring data in both directions requires a separate transfer and pipe for each direction.

On the bus, interrupt transactions are identical to bulk transactions (Figure 3-5 and Figure 3-6) with these differences:

- Interrupt transactions have guaranteed maximum latency and thus different scheduling by the host.
- The host doesn't use the PING protocol in high-speed interrupt transfers.
- Enhanced SuperSpeed interrupt transfers don't support Streams.
- On an Enhanced SuperSpeed bus, after receiving NRDY, a host must wait for ERDY before resuming communications with an interrupt endpoint. Waiting is optional for bulk endpoints.

An interrupt transfer ends successfully when the expected amount of data has transferred or when a transaction contains less than the endpoint's maximum packet size, including zero data bytes. The USB specification doesn't define a protocol for specifying the amount of data in an interrupt transfer. When needed, the device and host can use a class-specific or vendor-defined protocol to pass this information.

High speed differences

In an interrupt transfer on a high-speed bus with a low- or full-speed device, the host uses split transactions for all of the transfer's transactions. Unlike high-speed bulk OUT transfers, high-speed interrupt OUT transfers can't use the PING protocol when a transfer has multiple transactions.

Enhanced SuperSpeed differences

The host schedules ACK TPs to an IN endpoint until the device has sent all of the transfer's data, or the device returns a Data Packet Header with the End Of Burst bit set, or the device returns a NRDY or STALL TP. The host sends DPs to an OUT endpoint until the host has no more data to send or the device returns a NRDY or STALL TP. After receiving NRDY, the host must receive an ERDY TP to resume communications with the endpoint. To ensure fast response when a device is ready to communicate, the host's delay between receiving an ERDY and sending an ACK TP is at most 2× the service interval specified in the endpoint's descriptor.

The USB 3.1 specification advises that Enhanced SuperSpeed interrupt transfers are intended only for small amounts of data that must transfer within defined service intervals. In other words, to transfer large blocks of data, another transfer type such as bulk is a better choice.

Data size

The allowed maximum data bytes in an interrupt transaction's data packet varies with bus speed and the number of packets per microframe (high speed) or the number of packets per bus interval and the bMaxBurst value (Enhanced SuperSpeed):

Bus Speed	Maximum Data Packet Size	Maximum Guaranteed Packets / Interval
Low	1–8	1 / 10 frames
Full	1–64	1 / frame
High	1–1024	1 / microframe
	513–1024	2 / microframe
	683–1024	3 / microframe
SuperSpeed/SuperSpeedPlus	1–1024 and bMaxBurst = 0	1 / bus interval
	1024 and bMaxBurst > 0	3 / bus interval

These bytes include only the information transferred in the data packet (USB 2.0) or Data Packet Payload (SuperSpeed/SuperSpeedPlus), excluding PID and CRC bits. If a transfer's data doesn't fit in a single transaction, the host uses multiple transactions.

The USB 2.0 and USB 3.1 specifications require interrupt endpoints in a default interface to have a maximum packet size of 64 bytes or less. To use a larger maximum packet size, the device driver on the host must support selecting an alternate interface or configuration.

Speed

An interrupt transfer guarantees a maximum latency, or time between transaction attempts. In other words, there is no guaranteed transfer rate, just the guarantee that the host will make bandwidth available for a transaction attempt in each maximum latency period.

A low-speed endpoint can request only up to 8 bytes every 10 ms. Devices with endpoints that need to transfer more than 800 bytes/s shouldn't use low speed. A full-speed endpoint can request up to 64 bytes per frame, or 64 kB/s. A high-speed endpoint can request up to three 1024-byte packets per microframe for a maximum throughput of 24.576 MB/s. A high-speed endpoint that requests more than 1024 bytes per microframe is called a *high-bandwidth endpoint*. For hosts that don't support high-bandwidth interrupt endpoints, the maximum throughput is 8.192 MB/s. If the host's driver doesn't support alternate interfaces, the maximum is the 64 kB/s allowed for the default interface. An Enhanced SuperSpeed endpoint can request a burst of up to three 1024-byte packets per bus interval for a maximum data throughput of 24.576 MB/s, the same as for high speed.

The endpoint descriptor stored in the device specifies the maximum latency period. For low-speed devices, the maximum latency can be any value from 10–255 ms. For full speed, the range is 1–255 ms. For high speed and Enhanced SuperSpeed, the range is 125 µs to 4.096 s in increments of 125 µs. In addition, a high-speed or Enhanced SuperSpeed interrupt endpoint with a maximum latency of 125 µs can request 1, 2, or 3 transactions per interval.

The host can begin each transaction at any time up to the specified maximum latency since the previous transaction began. So, for example, on a full-speed bus with a 10-ms maximum latency, five transfers could take as long as 50 ms or as little as 5 ms. OHCI host controllers for low and full speeds schedule transactions using periods of 1, 2, 4, 8, 16, or 32 ms. So for a full-speed device that requests a maximum anywhere from 8 to 15 ms, an OHCI host will begin a transaction every 8 ms, while a maximum latency from 32 to 255 will cause a transaction attempt every 32 ms. However, devices shouldn't rely on behavior that is specific to a type of host controller and should assume only that the host complies with the specification. Chapter 8 has more about host-controller types.

Because the host is free to transfer data more quickly than the requested rate, interrupt transfers don't guarantee a precise rate of delivery. The only exceptions are when the maximum latency equals the fastest possible rate. For example, on a USB 1.1 host, a full-speed interrupt pipe configured for 1 transaction / ms will have reserved bandwidth for one transaction per frame.

A class driver or device driver for an interrupt IN endpoint can request the host controller to schedule an IN transaction in each interval. The HID-class driver is an example. Or a driver can request the host controller to schedule an IN transaction only when an application has requested data. The WinUSB driver is an example. For interrupt OUT data, the driver requests transactions only when an application or other software component has provided data to send.

Enhanced SuperSpeed interrupt and isochronous transfers combined can use no more than 90% of the total bandwidth. High-speed interrupt and isochronous transfers combined can use no more than 80% of a microframe. Full-speed isochronous transfers and low- and full-speed interrupt transfers combined can use no more than

90% of a frame. The section *More about time-critical transfers* below has more about the capabilities and limits of interrupt transfers.

Detecting and handling errors

If a device doesn't return an expected handshake packet, host controllers retry up to twice more. On receiving NAK, a USB 2.0 host may retry without limit. For example, a keyboard might sit idle for days before someone presses a key. A host driver can increment an error count on every incomplete transaction (those with no received handshake packet), reset the count when the device returns data or ACK, and stop communications to the endpoint if the error count reaches a defined number. These errors should be rare, yet a device that is NAKing for a long time might accumulate enough errors to cause the host to stop communicating. If you can't change the driver to cause it to reset the error counter and retry in this situation, a solution is for the device to send data periodically, defining a "no operation" code if needed, to reset the error counter.

Enhanced SuperSpeed endpoints use NRDY and ERDY as described in Chapter 2 to cause the host to stop requesting to send or receive data when an endpoint isn't ready to receive data or has no data to send and to enable an endpoint to request to resume communications.

Interrupt transfers can use data toggles (USB 2.0) or Sequence Numbers (Enhanced SuperSpeed) to ensure that all data is received without errors. A receiving endpoint that cares only about getting the most recent data can ignore the data toggle or Sequence Number.

Device responsibilities

Device responsibilities for interrupt endpoints are the same as for bulk endpoints.

Isochronous transfers

Isochronous transfers are streaming, real-time transfers that are useful when data must arrive at a constant rate or within a specific time limit and occasional errors are tolerable. At full speed and Enhanced SuperSpeed, isochronous transfers can transfer more data per frame or bus interval compared to interrupt transfers, but the transfer type doesn't support automatic resending of data received with errors.

Examples of uses for isochronous transfers include audio and video to be played in real time. Data that will eventually be consumed at a constant rate doesn't always require an isochronous transfer. For example, a host can use a bulk transfer to send a music file to a device. After receiving the file, the device can stream the music on request.

Nor does the data in an isochronous transfer have to be real-time data such as audio and video. An isochronous transfer is a way to ensure that any block of data has reserved bandwidth on a busy bus. Unlike with bulk transfers, a host guarantees that a configuration's requested isochronous bandwidth will be available, so the completion time is predictable.

Availability

Low speed doesn't support isochronous transfers. Devices aren't required to support isochronous transfers but a device class may require them. For example, many audio- and video-class devices use isochronous endpoints.

Structure

Isochronous means that the data has a fixed transfer rate, with a defined number of bytes transferring in every frame, microframe, or bus interval.

A USB 2.0 isochronous transfer consists of one or more IN transactions or one or more OUT transactions with bandwidth reserved for the transfer at equal intervals. Transferring data in both directions requires a separate transfer and pipe for each direction. High-speed and Enhanced SuperSpeed isochronous transfers are more flexible. They can request as many as 3 transactions per microframe (USB 2.0), 48 transactions per bus interval (SuperSpeed), or 96 transactions per bus interval (SuperSpeedPlus) or as little as 1 transaction every 32,768 microframes or bus intervals.

Figure 3-7 shows the packets in full-speed isochronous IN and OUT transactions. An isochronous transfer is one way. The transactions in a transfer must all be IN transactions or all OUT transactions. Transferring data in both directions requires a separate pipe and transfer for each direction.

The USB 2.0 specification doesn't define a protocol for specifying the amount of data in an isochronous transfer. When needed, the device and host can use a class-specific or vendor-defined protocol to pass this information.

Before requesting a device configuration that consumes isochronous bandwidth, the host controller determines whether the requested bandwidth is available by comparing the available unreserved bus bandwidth with the maximum packet size and requested transfer rate of the configuration's isochronous endpoint(s).

Every device with isochronous endpoints must have a default interface that requests *no* isochronous bandwidth so the host can configure the device even if the bus has no available reservable bandwidth. In addition to the default interface and an alternate interface that requests the optimum bandwidth for a device, a device can support additional alternate interfaces that have smaller isochronous data packets or transfer fewer isochronous packets per microframe. The device driver can then request to use an interface that transfers data at a slower rate if needed. Or the driver can try again later in the hope that the bandwidth will be available. After the host configures the device and selects an interface, the transfers are guaranteed to have the time they need.

Each transaction has overhead and must share the bus with other devices. The host can schedule a transaction anywhere within a scheduled (micro)frame or bus interval. Isochronous transfers may also synchronize to another data source or recipient, SOF packets (USB 2.0), or Isochronous Timestamp Packets (Enhanced SuperSpeed). For example, a microphone's input may synchronize to the output of speakers. The descriptor for an isochronous endpoint can specify a synchronization type and a usage value that indicates whether the endpoint contains data or feedback information used to maintain synchronization.

High speed differences

If a host is performing an isochronous transfer with a full-speed device on a high-speed bus, the host uses the split transactions introduced in Chapter 2 for all of the transfer's transactions. Isochronous OUT transactions use start-split transactions but don't use complete-splits because there is no status information to report back to the host. Isochronous transfers don't use the PING protocol.

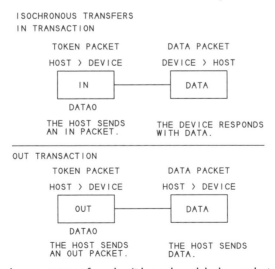

Figure 3-7. USB 2.0 isochronous transfers don't have handshake packets, so occasional errors must be acceptable. Not shown are the split transactions used with full-speed devices on a high-speed bus or the data PID sequencing in high-speed transfers with multiple data packets per microframe. Information source: *Universal Serial Bus Specification, Revision 2.0*.

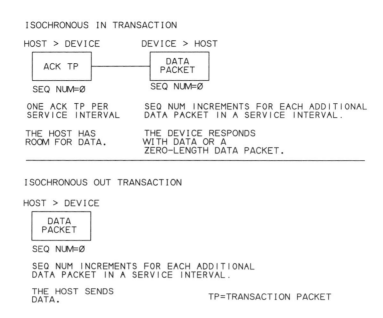

ISOCHRONOUS IN TRANSACTION

HOST > DEVICE   DEVICE > HOST

ACK TP   DATA PACKET

SEQ NUM=0   SEQ NUM=0

ONE ACK TP PER   SEQ NUM INCREMENTS FOR EACH ADDITIONAL
SERVICE INTERVAL   DATA PACKET IN A SERVICE INTERVAL.

THE HOST HAS   THE DEVICE RESPONDS
ROOM FOR DATA.   WITH DATA OR A
                       ZERO-LENGTH DATA PACKET.

ISOCHRONOUS OUT TRANSACTION

HOST > DEVICE

DATA PACKET

SEQ NUM=0

SEQ NUM INCREMENTS FOR EACH ADDITIONAL
DATA PACKET IN A SERVICE INTERVAL.

THE HOST SENDS
DATA.   TP=TRANSACTION PACKET

Figure 3-8. As with USB 2.0, Enhanced SuperSpeed endpoints don't acknowledge isochronous data packets. Information source: *Universal Serial Bus 3.1 Specification, Revision 1.0*.

Enhanced SuperSpeed differences

Figure 3-8 shows Enhanced SuperSpeed isochronous IN and OUT transactions. The first DP in a service interval has Sequence Number = 0. The Sequence Number increments with each DP that follows in the service interval. In an IN transaction, the host sends a single ACK TP to request one or more DPs in a service interval, and the device sends the packet(s). In an OUT transaction, the host sends data in DPs, and the device sends nothing. The endpoint descriptor specifies the length of a service interval and the number of DPs per service interval. For the last data packet in the service interval, the sender sets the last-packet flag in the Data Packet Header.

Data size

The allowed maximum data bytes in an isochronous transaction's data packet varies with bus speed and the number of packets per microframe (high speed) or the number of packets per bus interval and bMaxBurst (Enhanced SuperSpeed):

Bus Speed	Maximum Data Packet Size	Maximum Number of Packets / Interval
Full	0–1023	1 / frame
High	0–1024	1 / microframe
	513–1024	2 / microframe
	683–1024	3 / microframe
SuperSpeed	0–1024 and bMaxBurst = 0	3 / bus interval
	1024 and bMaxBurst > 0	48 / bus interval
SuperSpeedPlus	0–1024 and bMaxBurst = 0	3 / bus interval
	1024 and bMaxBurst > 0	96 / bus interval

These bytes include only the information transferred in the data packet (USB 2.0) or Data Packet Payload (Enhanced SuperSpeed), excluding PID and CRC bits.

If the data doesn't fit in a single packet, the host completes the transfer in multiple transactions. Within a USB 2.0 transfer, the amount of data in each transaction doesn't have to be the same and doesn't have to be the maximum packet size. For example, data at 44,100 samples / s could use a sequence of 9 packets containing 44 samples each, followed by 1 packet containing 45 samples.

SuperSpeed endpoints can support up to 3 burst transactions per service interval, with each burst consisting of up to 16 DPs. All but the last DP in a burst must be the endpoint's maximum packet size. In addition, each burst except the last must have an equal number of DPs, and the number of DPs in each burst except the last must be 2, 4, 8, or 16.

For example, with endpoint support for 16 DPs per burst, the quickest way to send 48 maximum-size DPs is in 3 bursts of 16 DPs each. With endpoint support for 3 bursts per service interval, all of the data can transfer within one service interval. But the sender also has the option to send the data in 6 bursts of 8 DPs each, 12 bursts of 4 DPs each, 24 bursts of 2 DPs each, or 48 non-burst DPs.

SuperSpeedPlus isochronous endpoints have twice the capacity of SuperSpeed endpoints, with support for up to 6 burst transactions per service interval, with each burst consisting of up to 16 DPs. SuperSpeedPlus hosts can use bursts of any size up to the maximum size supported by the endpoint.

Speed

A full-speed isochronous transaction can transfer up to 1023 bytes per frame, or up to 1.023 MB/s. A high-speed isochronous transaction can transfer up to 1024 bytes. A high-speed isochronous endpoint that requires more than 1024 bytes per microframe can request 2 or 3 transactions per microframe for a maximum data throughput of 24.576 MB/s. A SuperSpeed isochronous non-burst transaction can transfer up to 1024 bytes. A SuperSpeed isochronous burst transaction can have up to sixteen 1024-byte data packets. An endpoint can request up to 3 burst transactions per service interval for a maximum data throughput of 49,152 kB/service interval or over 393 MB/s. A SuperSpeedPlus isochronous endpoint can request up to 6 burst transactions per service interval for a maximum data throughput of 98,304 kB/service interval or over 786 MB/s.

Windows supports high-bandwidth isochronous endpoints, which request multiple transactions per microframe. High-speed and Enhanced SuperSpeed isochronous endpoints don't have to reserve bandwidth in every (micro)frame or service interval and thus can request less bandwidth than full-speed transfers. The minimum requested bandwidth is one byte every 4.096 seconds. However, any endpoint can transfer less data than the maximum reserved bandwidth by skipping available transactions or by transferring less than the maximum data per transfer. An Enhanced SuperSpeed isochronous IN endpoint that has no data to transmit responds to a request for data with a zero-length Data Payload.

Enhanced SuperSpeed interrupt and isochronous transfers combined can use no more than 90% of the total bus bandwidth. High-speed interrupt and isochronous transfers combined can use no more than 80% of a microframe. Full-speed isochronous transfers and low- and full-speed interrupt transfers combined can use no more than 90% of a frame.

The section *More about time-critical transfers* below has more about the capabilities of isochronous transfers.

Detecting and handling errors

The price for guaranteed on-time delivery of large blocks of data is no error correcting. Isochronous transfers are intended for uses where occasional errors are acceptable. For example, listeners may tolerate or not notice a short dropout in voice or music. In reality, under normal circumstances, a USB transfer should experience only infrequent errors due to line noise. The USB 3.1 specification estimates an error rate of less than one in every 10^{12} bits in the Enhanced SuperSpeed physical layer. Because isochronous transfers must keep to a schedule, the receiver can't request the sender to retransmit if the receiver is busy or detects an error. A receiver that suspects errors could ask the sender to resend the entire transfer, but this approach isn't efficient.

A device or host that doesn't receive an expected data packet or receives a data packet with an error can define what to do. The options include using the data as-is, skipping the data, or inserting a packet identical to the previous packet or other "dummy" data.

Device responsibilities

A USB 2.0 device has these responsibilities for transfers on an isochronous endpoint:

- For OUT transfers, accept received data in data packets.
- For IN transfers, return data in data packets in response to IN tokens.

An Enhanced SuperSpeed device has these responsibilities for transfers on a isochronous endpoint:

- For OUT transfers, accept data in DPs.
- For IN transfers, send data in DPs in response to requests in ACK TPs.

More about time-critical transfers

Just because an endpoint is capable of a rate of data transfer doesn't mean that a particular device and host will be able to achieve the rate. Several things can limit an application's ability to send or receive data at the rate that a device requests. The limiting factors include bus bandwidth, the capabilities of the device, the capabilities of the device driver and application software, and latencies in the host's hardware and software.

Bus bandwidth

When a device requests more interrupt or isochronous bandwidth than is available, the host refuses to configure the device. A high-speed interrupt endpoint can request up to three 1024-byte data packets in each microframe, using as much as 40% of the bus bandwidth. To help ensure that devices can enumerate without problems, the interrupt endpoints in default interfaces must specify a maximum packet size of 64 bytes or less. The device driver is then free to try to increase the endpoint's reserved bandwidth by requesting alternate interface settings or configurations.

However, many drivers don't support requesting alternate interface settings or configurations. For example, under Windows, the human interface device (HID) class driver doesn't support selecting an alternate interface. The WinUSB driver does enable applications to select alternate interface settings.

Isochronous endpoints might also request more bandwidth than is available. In particular, Enhanced SuperSpeed endpoints can request over half of the bus bandwidth, an amount that might not be available. To help ensure that devices will enumerate without problems, default interfaces must request no isochronous bandwidth. In other words, a default interface can transfer no isochronous data at all and typically includes no isochronous endpoints. After enumeration, the device driver can request isochronous bandwidth by requesting an alternate interface setting or a configuration with one or more isochronous endpoints.

A specific host might configure and communicate with a device that has non-compliant default interfaces, but future editions of the operating system might enforce this part of the specification and refuse to configure the device.

In general, a device that can operate using up to 30–40% of the bus bandwidth has a good chance of successful configuration even on a busy host.

Device capabilities

If the host has promised that the requested USB bandwidth will be available, there's still no guarantee that a device will be ready to send or receive data when needed.

To transfer data efficiently, a device should be ready to send and receive data on request. To send data, the device must write the data into the endpoint's buffer so the data is ready to send when requested by the host. Otherwise, in all but isochronous transfers, the endpoint returns NAK or NRDY and the host wastes time retrying. When receiving data, the device must read previously received data from the endpoint's buffer before new data arrives from the host. Otherwise the old data will be overwritten, or the endpoint will return NAK or NRDY and require the host to retry.

One way to help ensure that a device is always ready for a transfer is to use a device controller that supports multiple buffers as described in Chapter 6. Double or quadruple buffering gives the firmware extra time to load the next data to transfer or to retrieve received data.

Host capabilities

The capabilities of the device driver and application software on the host can also affect whether transfers occur as efficiently as possible and without losing data.

A device driver requests a transfer by submitting an I/O request packet (IRP) to a lower-level driver. For interrupt and isochronous transfers, the host controller attempts a scheduled transaction only if the host has an outstanding IRP for the endpoint. To ensure that no transfer opportunities are missed, drivers with large amounts of data to send or request typically submit a new IRP immediately on completing the previous one.

The application software that uses the data also has to be able to keep up with the transfers. For example, the Windows driver for HID-class devices places report data received in interrupt transfers in a buffer, and applications can use the ReadFile API function or .NET FileStream methods to retrieve reports from the buffer. If the buffer is full when a new report arrives, the driver discards the oldest report and replaces it with the newest one. If the application can't keep up with reading the buffer, some reports are lost. A solution is to increase the size of the buffer the driver uses to store received data or increase the size of the read buffer to enable reading multiple reports at once.

One way to help ensure that an application sends or receives data with minimal delay is to place the code that communicates with the device driver in its own program thread. The thread should have few responsibilities other than managing these communications.

Doing fewer, larger transfers rather than multiple, small transfers can also help. A host application can typically send or request a few large chunks of data more efficiently than sending or requesting many smaller chunks. Lower-level drivers manage the scheduling for transfers with multiple transactions.

Host latencies

Also affecting the performance of time-critical USB transfers under Windows is latencies due to how the OS handles multi-tasking. Windows wasn't designed as a real-time operating system that can guarantee a rate of data transfer with a peripheral.

With multi-tasking, multiple program threads run at the same time, and the OS grants a portion of the available time to each thread. Different threads can have different priorities, but under Windows, no thread has guaranteed CPU time at a defined rate such as once per ms. Latencies under Windows are often well under 1 ms, but in some cases a thread can keep other code from executing for over 100 ms. Newer Windows editions and newer system hardware tend to have improved performance over older editions and hardware.

A USB device and its software have no control over what other tasks the host CPU is performing and how fast the CPU performs them. If possible, the device should handle any critical, real-time processing so the timing of the host communications can be as non-critical as possible. For example, consider a full-speed device that reads a sensor once per ms. The device could attempt to send each reading to the host in a separate interrupt transfer, but if a transfer fails to occur for any reason, the data will never catch up. If the device instead collects a series of readings and transfers them using less frequent, larger transfers, the timing of the bus transfers is less critical. Data compression can also help by reducing the number of bytes that need to transfer.

4

Enumeration: How the Host Learns about Devices

Before applications can communicate with a device, the host computer needs to learn about the device and assign a driver. Enumeration is the exchange of information that accomplishes these tasks. The process includes assigning an address to the device, reading descriptors from the device, assigning and loading a driver, and selecting a configuration that specifies the device's power requirements and interfaces. The device is then ready to transfer data.

This chapter describes the enumeration process, including the structure of the descriptors that the host reads from the device during enumeration. Understanding enumeration is essential in creating the descriptors that will reside in the device and in writing firmware that responds to enumeration requests.

Events and requests

One of a hub's duties is to detect attachment and removal of devices on its down-stream-facing ports. Each hub has an interrupt IN endpoint for reporting these events to the host. On system boot-up, hubs inform the host if any devices are attached including additional downstream hubs and any devices attached to those hubs. After boot-up, a host continues to poll periodically (USB 2.0) or receives ERDY TPs (Enhanced SuperSpeed) that request communications to learn of any newly attached or removed devices.

On learning of a new device, the host sends requests to the device's hub to cause the hub to establish a communications path between the host and device. The host then attempts to enumerate the device by issuing control transfers containing standard USB requests to the device. All USB devices must support control transfers, standard requests, and endpoint zero. For a successful enumeration, the device must respond to requests by returning requested information and taking other requested actions.

From the user's perspective, enumeration is invisible and automatic but may display a message that announces the new device and whether the attempt to configure it succeeded. Sometimes on first use, the user needs to assist in selecting a driver or telling the host where to look for driver files. Under Windows, when enumeration is complete, the new device appears in the Device Manager. (Right-click **Computer**, click **Manage**, and in the **Computer Management** pane, select **Device Manager**.) On detaching, the device disappears from Device Manager. In a typical device, firmware decodes and responds to received requests for information. Some controllers can manage enumeration entirely in hardware except possibly for vendor-provided values in EEPROM or other memory. On the host side, the operating system handles enumeration.

Getting to the Configured state

The USB 2.0 specification defines six device states. During enumeration, a device moves through the Powered, Default, Address, and Configured states. (The other defined states are Attached and Suspend.) In each state, the device has defined capabilities and behavior.

Typical USB 2.0 sequence

The steps below are a typical sequence of events that occurs during enumeration of a USB 2.0 device under Windows. *Device firmware shouldn't assume that enumeration requests and events will occur in a particular order.* Different OSes and different OS editions might use a different sequence. To function successfully, a device must detect and respond to any control request or other bus event at any time as required by the

Item	Device	Endpoint	Interface	Status	Speed	Payload
Enter text here	Ent...	Ente...	Ente...	E...	E...	Enter text here
Reset (4.1 s)						
Suspended (104.9 ms)						
Reset (11.1 ms)						
High speed Detection Handshake				TIME...		
⊞ GetDescriptor (Device)	0 (14)	0		OK	FS	8 bytes (12 01 00 02 00 00 00 08)
Reset (10.6 ms)						
High speed Detection Handshake				TIME...		
⊞ SetAddress (14)	0 (14)	0		OK	FS	No data
⊞ GetDescriptor (Device)	14	0		OK	FS	18 bytes (12 01 00 02 00 00 00 08...
⊞ GetDescriptor (Configuration)	14	0		OK	FS	41 bytes (09 02 29 00 01 01 00 C0...
⊞ GetDescriptor (String lang IDs)	14	0		OK	FS	4 bytes (04 03 09 04)
⊞ GetDescriptor (String iProduct)	14	0		OK	FS	24 bytes (18 03 47 00 65 00 6E 00...
⊞ GetDescriptor (Device)	14	0		OK	FS	18 bytes (12 01 00 02 00 00 00 08...
⊞ GetDescriptor (Configuration)	14	0		OK	FS	9 bytes (09 02 29 00 01 01 00 C0 ...
⊞ GetDescriptor (Configuration)	14	0		OK	FS	41 bytes (09 02 29 00 01 01 00 C0...
⊞ SetConfiguration (1)	14	0		OK	FS	No data

Figure 4-1. To enumerate a newly attached device, the host sends a series of requests to obtain descriptors and set the device's bus address and configuration. (Screen capture from Ellisys USB Explorer analyzer.)

USB specifications. Figure 4-1 shows received requests and other events during a device enumeration.

1. The system has a new device. A user attaches a device to a USB port, or the system powers up with a device attached. The port may be on the root hub at the host or on a hub that connects downstream from the host. The hub provides power to the port, and the device is in the Powered state. The device is in the Attached state and can draw up to 100 mA from the bus.

2. The hub detects the device. The hub monitors the voltages on the signal lines (D+ and D-) at each of its ports. The hub has a pull-down resistor of 14.25k–24.8kΩ on each line. A device has a pull-up resistor of 900–1575Ω on D+ for a full-speed device or on D- for a low-speed device. High-speed-capable devices attach at full speed. On attaching to a port, the device connects to the bus by bringing the appropriate pull-up line high so the hub can detect that a device is attached. Except for some devices with weak or dead batteries, the device must connect within 1 s after detecting that VBUS is at least 0.8 V. A device can continue to draw 100 mA of bus current for 1 s after connecting regardless of whether the upstream bus segment is suspended. On detecting a device, the hub continues to provide power but doesn't yet transmit USB traffic to the device. Chapter 16 has more on how hubs detect devices.

3. The host learns of the new device. Each hub uses its interrupt endpoint to report events at the hub. The report indicates only whether the hub or a port (and if so, which port) has experienced an event. On learning of an event, the host sends the hub a Get Port Status request to find out more. Get Port Status and the other hub-class requests used during enumeration are standard requests that all hubs support. The information returned tells the host when a device is newly attached.

4. The hub detects whether a device is low or full speed. Just before resetting the device, the hub determines whether the device is low or full speed by detecting which signal line has a higher voltage when idle. The hub sends the information to the host in response to the next Get Port Status request. A USB 1.1 hub may instead detect the device's speed just after a bus reset. USB 2.0 requires speed detection before the reset so the hub knows whether to check for a high-speed-capable device during reset as described below.

5. The hub resets the device. When a host learns of a new device, the host sends the hub a Set Port Feature request that asks the hub to reset the port. The hub places the device's USB data lines in the Reset condition for at least 10 ms. Reset is a special condition where both D+ and D- are logic low. (Normally, the lines have opposite logic states.) The hub sends the reset only to the new device. Other hubs and devices on the bus don't see the reset.

6. The host learns if a full-speed device supports high speed. Detecting whether a device supports high speed uses two special signal states. In the Chirp J state, only the D+ line is driven, and in the Chirp K state, only the D- line is driven.

During the reset, a device that supports high speed sends a Chirp K. A high-speed-capable hub detects the Chirp K and responds with a series of alternating Chirp K and Chirp J. On detecting the pattern KJKJKJ, the device removes its full-speed pull-up and performs all further communications at high speed. If the hub doesn't respond to the device's Chirp K, the device knows it must continue to communicate at full speed. All high-speed devices must be capable of responding to control-transfer requests at full speed.

7. The hub establishes a signal path between the device and the bus. The host verifies that the device has exited the reset state by sending a Get Port Status request. A bit in the returned data indicates whether the device is still in the reset state. If necessary, the host repeats the request until the device has exited the reset state.

When the hub removes the reset, the device is in the Default state. The device's USB registers are in their reset states, and the device is ready to respond to control transfers at endpoint zero. The device communicates with the host using the default address of 0x00.

8. The host sends a Get Descriptor request to learn the maximum packet size of the default pipe. The host sends the request to device address 0x00, endpoint zero. Because the host enumerates only one device at a time, only one device will respond to communications addressed to device address 0x00 even if several devices attach at once.

The eighth byte of the device descriptor contains the maximum packet size supported by endpoint zero. The host may request 64 bytes but after receiving just one packet (whether or not it has 64 bytes), may begin the Status stage of the transfer.

On completing the Status stage, Windows may request the hub to reset the device as in step 5 above. The USB 2.0 specification doesn't require a reset here. The reset is a precaution that ensures that the device will be in a known state when the reset ends. Windows 8 and later skip the second reset for high-speed devices because these devices typically don't require a second reset. If enumeration fails without the second reset, Windows includes the reset on the next enumeration attempt.

9. The host assigns an address. When the reset is complete, the host controller assigns a unique address to the device by sending a Set Address request. The device completes the Status stage of the request using the default address and then implements the new address. The device is now in the Address state. All communications from this point on use the new address. The address is valid until the device is detached, a hub resets the port, or the system reboots. On the next enumeration, the host may assign a different address to the device.

10. The host learns about the device's abilities. The host sends a Get Descriptor request to the new address to read the device descriptor. This time the host retrieves the entire descriptor. The descriptor contains the maximum packet size for endpoint zero, the number of configurations the device supports, and other information about the device.

The host continues to learn about the device by requesting the configuration descriptor(s) specified in the device descriptor. A request for a configuration descriptor is actually a request for the configuration descriptor followed by all of its subordinate descriptors up to the number of bytes requested.

If the host requests 255 bytes, the device responds by sending the configuration descriptor followed by all of the configuration's subordinate descriptors, including interface descriptor(s), with each interface descriptor followed by any endpoint descriptors for the interface. Some configurations also have class- or vendor-specific descriptors.

One of the configuration descriptor's fields is the total length of the configuration descriptor and its subordinate descriptors. If the value is greater than 255, the device returns 255 bytes. Windows then requests the configuration descriptor again, this time requesting the number of bytes in the total length specified in the configuration descriptor.

Earlier Windows editions began by requesting just the configuration descriptor's nine bytes to retrieve the total length value, then requesting the complete descriptor set.

11. The host requests additional information from the device. The host then may request additional descriptors from the device. In every case, a device that doesn't support a requested descriptor should return STALL.

When the device descriptor reports that the device is USB 2.1 or higher, the host requests a BOS descriptor. If the device returns the BOS descriptor, the host uses the descriptor's total length value to request the BOS descriptor followed by its subordinate descriptor(s).

The host requests string descriptor zero, which contains one or more codes indicating what languages additional strings use.

If the device descriptor reports that the device contains a serial number string descriptor, the host requests that descriptor.

If the device descriptor indicates that the device contains a Product string descriptor, the host requests that descriptor.

For USB 2.0 and higher devices, if Windows doesn't have a record of previously retrieving a Microsoft-specific MS OS string descriptor, the OS may request that descriptor.

If a BOS descriptor or a Microsoft OS string descriptor indicates support for additional Microsoft-defined descriptors, the host may request these descriptors.

For USB 2.0 or higher devices operating at full speed with an upstream USB 1.1 hub, the host requests a device qualifier descriptor. A device that returns this descriptor is capable of operating at high speed if all upstream ports are USB 2.0 or higher.

12. The host assigns and loads a device driver (except for composite devices). After learning about a device from its descriptors, the host looks for the best match in a driver to manage communications with the device. Windows hosts use INF files to identify the best match. The INF file may be a system file for a USB class or a vendor-provided file that contains the device's Vendor ID and Product ID. Chapter 9 has more about INF files and selecting a driver.

For devices that have been enumerated previously, Windows may use stored information instead of searching the INF files. After the operating system assigns and loads a driver, the driver may request the device to resend descriptors or send other class-specific descriptors.

An exception to this sequence is composite devices, which can have different drivers assigned to multiple interfaces in a configuration. The host can assign these drivers only after enabling the interfaces, so the host must first configure the device as described below.

13. The host's device driver selects a configuration. After learning about a device from the descriptors, the device driver requests a configuration by sending a Set Configuration request with the desired configuration number. Many devices support only one configuration. When a device supports multiple configurations, many drivers just select the first configuration, but a driver can decide based on information the driver has about how the device will be used, or the driver can ask the user what to do. On receiving the request, the device implements the requested configuration. The device is now in the Configured state and the device's interface(s) are enabled.

For composite devices, the host can now assign drivers. As with other devices, the host uses the information retrieved from the device to find a driver for each active interface in the configuration. The device is then ready for use.

Hubs are also USB devices, and the host enumerates a newly attached hub in the same way as other devices. If the hub has devices attached, the host enumerates these after the hub informs the host of their presence.

Attached state. If the hub isn't providing power to a device's VBUS line, the device is in the Attached state. The absence of power may occur if the hub has detected an over-current condition or if the host requests the hub to remove power from the port. With no power on VBUS, the host and device can't communicate, so from their perspective, the situation is the same as when the device isn't attached.

Suspend State. A device enters the Suspend state after detecting no bus activity, including SOF markers, for at least 3 ms. In the Suspend state, the device should limit its use of bus power. Both configured and unconfigured devices must support this state. Chapter 17 has more about the Suspend state.

Enhanced SuperSpeed differences

Enumerating Enhanced SuperSpeed devices has some differences compared to USB 2.0:

- On detecting a downstream Enhanced SuperSpeed termination at a port, a hub initializes and trains the port's link. Enumeration then proceeds at SuperSpeed or SuperSpeedPlus with no need for further speed detecting.

- The host isn't required to reset the port after learning of a new device.

- The bus-current limits are 150 mA before configuration and 900 mA after configuration.

- The host sends a Set Isochronous Delay request to inform the device of the bus delay for isochronous packets.

- The host sends a Set SEL request to inform the device of the system exit latency (the amount of time required to transition out of a low-power state).

- Protocols for entering and exiting the Suspend state differ.

- For hubs, the host sends a Set Hub Depth request to set the hub-depth value.

Device removal

When a user removes a device from the bus, the hub disables the device's port. The host knows that the removal occurred after the hub notifies the host that an event has occurred, and the host sends a Get Port Status request to learn what the event was. The device disappears from Device Manager and the device's address becomes available to another newly attached device.

Tips for successful enumeration

Without successful enumeration, the device and host can't perform other communications. Most chip companies provide example enumeration code that can serve as a model even if your application doesn't exactly match the example application. If your controller interfaces to an external CPU, you may have to adapt code written for another chip.

In general, a device should assume nothing about what requests or events the host will initiate and should concentrate on responding to requests and events as they occur. The following tips can help avoid problems.

Don't assume requests or events will occur in a specific order. Some requests, such as Set Configuration, require the device to be in the Address or Configured state so the request is valid only after the device has accepted a Set Address request. But the host has some flexibility in what requests to issue and in what order during enumeration. A host might also reset or suspend the bus at any time, and a device that has been connected for at least 1 s must detect the event and respond appropriately.

Be ready to abandon a control transfer or end it early. On receiving a new Setup packet, a device must abandon any transfer in progress and begin the new one. On receiving an OUT token packet (USB 2.0) or STATUS TP (Enhanced SuperSpeed), the device must assume that the host is beginning the Status stage of the transfer even if the device hasn't sent all of the requested data in the Data stage.

Don't attempt to send more data than the host requests. In the Data stage of a control read transfer, a device should send no more than the amount of data the host has requested. If the host requests nine bytes, the device should send no more than nine bytes.

Send a zero-length data packet when required. In some cases, the device returns less than the requested amount of data, and the amount of data is an exact multiple of the endpoint's maximum packet size. On receiving a request for more data, the device should indicate that it has no more data by returning a ZLP (USB 2.0) or a zero-length Data Payload (Enhanced SuperSpeed).

Stall unsupported requests. A device shouldn't assume it knows every request the host might send. The device should return STALL in response to any request the device doesn't support.

Don't set the address too soon. In a Set Address request, the device should set its new address only after the Status stage of the request is complete.

Be ready to enter the Suspend state. A host can suspend the bus when the device is in any powered state. Except within 1 s after the device connects, the device must reduce its use of bus power when the bus is in the Suspend state.

Test under different host-controller types. Devices should be able operate with any host controller that complies with the specifications. For example, some full-speed host controllers schedule multiple stages of a control transfer in a single frame, while others don't. Devices should be able to handle either way. Chapter 8 has more about host controllers.

Descriptors

USB descriptors are the data structures that enable the host to learn about a device. Each descriptor contains information about the device as a whole or an element of the device.

All USB devices must respond to requests for the standard USB descriptors. The device must store the contents of its descriptors and respond to requests for the descriptors.

Types

Table 4-1 lists the descriptors defined in the USB 2.0 and USB 3.1 specifications. Except for compound devices, each device has one and only one device descriptor that contains information about the device and specifies the number of configurations the device supports. For each configuration, a device has a configuration descriptor with information about the device's use of power and the number of interfaces the configuration supports. For each interface, the device has an interface descriptor that specifies the number of endpoints. Each endpoint has an endpoint descriptor that contains information needed to communicate with the endpoint. An interface with no endpoint descriptors must use the control endpoint for all communications.

Table 4-1: The bDescriptorType field in a descriptor contains a value that identifies the descriptor type. Information source: *Universal Serial Bus Specification, Revision 2.0* and *Universal Serial Bus 3.1 Specification, Revision 1.0*.

bDescriptorType	Descriptor Type	Required?
0x01	device	Yes.
0x02	configuration	Yes.
0x03	string	No unless a class or vendor driver requires it. Optional descriptive text.
0x04	interface	Yes.
0x05	endpoint	Yes to use other than endpoint zero.
0x06	device_qualifier	Yes for devices that support both full and high speeds. Not allowed for other devices.
0x07	other_speed_configuration	Yes for devices that support both full and high speeds. Not allowed for other devices.
0x08	interface_power	No (proposed but never approved or implemented).
0x09	OTG	Yes for OTG devices.
0x0A	debug	No.
0x0B	interface_association	Yes for some composite devices.
0x0C	security	For wireless devices.
0x0D	key	
0x0E	encryption type	
0x0F	binary device object store (BOS)	Yes for Enhanced SuperSpeed devices, wireless devices, and devices that support link power management.
0x10	device capability	
0x11	wireless endpoint companion	For wireless devices.
0x30	SuperSpeed endpoint companion	Yes for endpoints in Enhanced SuperSpeed devices.
0x31	SuperSpeedPlus isochronous endpoint companion	Yes for SuperSpeedPlus isochronous endpoints that request more than 48 KB per service interval.

On receiving a request for a configuration descriptor, a device should return the configuration descriptor and all of the configuration's interface, endpoint, and other subordinate descriptors up to the requested number of bytes. There is no standard request to retrieve, for example, only an endpoint descriptor. Devices that support both full and high speeds support two additional descriptor types: device_qualifier and other_speed_configuration. These and their subordinate descriptors contain information about the device when using the speed not currently in use.

Enhanced SuperSpeed devices must provide a binary device object store (BOS) descriptor and at least two subordinate device capability descriptors: a SuperSpeed USB descriptor and a USB 2.0 Extension descriptor. Other devices and device functions may also use BOS and device capability descriptors. Every Enhanced SuperSpeed endpoint descriptor has a subordinate SuperSpeed endpoint companion descriptor.

A string descriptor can store text such as the vendor or device name or a serial number. Another descriptor may contain an index value that points to the string descriptor. The host reads string descriptors using Get Descriptor requests.

Class- and vendor-specific descriptors offer a structured way for a device or interface to provide more detailed information about a function. For example, if an interface descriptor specifies that the interface belongs to the HID class, the interface also has a HID class descriptor.

Standard descriptors begin with a bLength value that gives the descriptor's length in bytes followed by a bDescriptorType value that identifies the descriptor's type.

In a Get Descriptor request, the Setup stage's data packet passes wValue and wLength values to the device. The wValue field identifies the descriptor being requested. The wLength field is the number of bytes the host is requesting from the device. Chapter 5 has more about the Get Descriptor request.

Some class- or vendor-specific descriptors modify or extend other descriptors. In the descriptors returned in response to a request for a configuration and subordinate descriptors, a descriptor that extends or modifies a descriptor follows the descriptor being extended or modified. Like standard descriptors, these class- and vendor-specific descriptors begin with a bLength value followed by a bDescriptorType value.

For descriptors that don't modify or extend a standard descriptor, such as a request for a HID-class report descriptor, the host uses a Get Descriptor request that specifies the class- or vendor-specific descriptor type and the index of the request. The class specification or vendor defines the format for these descriptors.

Each descriptor below begins with bLength and bDescriptorType fields. The other fields vary with the descriptor type.

Multiple-byte values in descriptors travel on the bus in little-endian order (from least-significant byte (LSB) to most significant byte (MSB). For example, Vendor ID 0x0925 transmits as 0x25 followed by 0x09.

Device

The device descriptor is the first descriptor the host reads on device attachment. The descriptor contains information the host needs to retrieve additional information from the device. A host retrieves a device descriptor by sending a Get Descriptor request with the high byte of the Setup transaction's wValue field set to 0x01.

The descriptor (Table 4-2) provides information about the device, its configurations, and any classes the device belongs to.

bcdUSB is the USB specification version that the device and its descriptors comply with. The value is in BCD (binary-coded decimal) format. If you think of the version's value as a decimal number, the upper byte represents the integer, the next four bits are tenths, and the final four bits are hundredths. USB 1.1 is 0x0110 (*not* 0x0101); USB 2.0 is 0x0200; USB 2.1 is 0x0210; USB 3.0 is 0x0300; USB 3.1 is 0x0310.

A device with bcdUSB = 0x0210 or higher must support the BOS descriptor. A device or device wire adapter that complies with Wireless USB V1.0 should set bcdUSB to 0x0250.

bDeviceClass specifies the class for devices whose function is defined at the device level. Values from 0x01 to 0xFE are reserved for classes defined by USB specifications. Table 4-3 shows defined codes. Vendor-defined classes use 0xFF. Most devices specify their class or classes in interface descriptors. For these devices, bDeviceClass in the device descriptor equals 0x00 if the function doesn't use an interface association descriptor or 0xEF if the function uses an interface association descriptor.

bDeviceSubclass can specify a subclass within a class. A subclass can add support for additional features and abilities shared by a group of functions in a class. If bDevice-Class is 0x00, bDeviceSubclass must be 0x00. If bDeviceClass is in the range 0x01–0xFE, bDeviceSubclass equals 0x00 or a code defined for the device's class. Vendor-defined subclasses in standard classes use 0xFF.

bDeviceProtocol can specify a protocol for the selected class and subclass. For example, a USB 2.0 hub uses this field to indicate whether the hub is currently supporting high speed and if so, if the hub supports one or multiple transaction translators. If bDeviceClass is in the range 0x01–0xFE, the protocol is 0x00 or a code defined by the device's class.

bMaxPacketSize0 specifies the maximum packet size for endpoint zero. The host uses this information in the requests that follow the request for the device descriptor. For USB 2.0, the maximum packet size equals the field's value and must be 8 for low speed; 8, 16, 32, or 64 for full speed; and 64 for high speed. For Enhanced Super-Speed, the maximum packet size equals $2^{bMaxPacketSize0}$ and bMaxPacketSize0 must equal 9, which translates to a maximum packet size of 512.

idVendor is a Vendor ID assigned by the USB-IF to members of the USB-IF and others who pay an administrative fee. The host may have an INF file that contains this value, and if so, Windows may use the value to help select a driver for the device. Except for

Table 4-2: The device descriptor identifies the product and its manufacturer, sets the maximum packet size for endpoint zero, and can specify a device class. Information source: *Universal Serial Bus Specification, Revision 2.0.*

Offset (decimal)	Field	Size (bytes)	Description
0	bLength	1	Descriptor size in bytes (0x12)
1	bDescriptorType	1	The constant DEVICE (0x01)
2	bcdUSB	2	USB specification release number (BCD)
4	bDeviceClass	1	Class code
5	bDeviceSubclass	1	Subclass code
6	bDeviceProtocol	1	Protocol Code
7	bMaxPacketSize0	1	Maximum packet size for endpoint zero
8	idVendor	2	Vendor ID
10	idProduct	2	Product ID
12	bcdDevice	2	Device release number (BCD)
14	iManufacturer	1	Index of string descriptor for the manufacturer
15	iProduct	1	Index of string descriptor for the product
16	iSerialNumber	1	Index of string descriptor for the serial number
17	bNumConfigurations	1	Number of possible configurations

devices used only in-house where the user is responsible for preventing conflicts, every device descriptor must have a valid Vendor ID in this field.

idProduct is a Product ID that identifies the vendor's device. The owner of the Vendor ID assigns the Product ID. Both the device descriptor and the device's INF file on the host may contain this value, and if so, the host may use the value to help select a driver for the device. Each Product ID is specific to a Vendor ID, so multiple vendors can use the same Product ID without conflict.

bcdDevice is the device's release number in BCD format. The vendor assigns this value. The host may use this value to help select a driver for the device.

iManufacturer is an index that points to a string describing the manufacturer or zero if there is no manufacturer descriptor.

iProduct is an index that points to a string describing the product or zero if there is no string descriptor.

iSerialNumber is an index that points to a string containing the device's serial number or zero if there is no serial number. Serial numbers are useful if users may have more than one identical device on the bus and the host needs to remember which device is which even after rebooting or moving the devices to different ports. A serial

Table 4-3: The bDeviceClass field in the device descriptor can name a class the device belongs to. Information source: *usb.org*.

bDeviceClass	Description
0x00	The interface descriptor specifies the class and the function doesn't use an interface association descriptor. (See 0xEF below.)
0x02	Communications device (can instead be declared at the interface level)

0x09	Hub
	bDeviceSubclass = 0x00
	  bDeviceProtocol = 0x00: Full speed
	  bDeviceProtocol = 0x01: High speed with single Transaction Translator
	  bDeviceProtocol = 0x02: High speed with multiple Transaction Translators
	  bDeviceProtocol = 0x03: SuperSpeed/SuperSpeedPlus

0x0F	Personal healthcare device (declaring at the interface level preferred)
0xDC	Diagnostic device (can instead be declared at the interface level) bDeviceSubclass = 0x01 bDeviceProtocol = 0x01: USB2 Compliance Device

0xE0	Wireless Controller (Bluetooth only. All other protocols must be declared at the interface level.)
	bDeviceSubclass = 0x01
	  bDeviceProtocol = 0x01: Bluetooth programming interface
	  (should also be declared at the interface level)
	bDeviceSubclass = 0x04: Bluetooth AMP controller
	  (should also be declared at the interface level)

0xEF	Miscellaneous
	bDeviceSubclass = 0x01
	  bDeviceProtocol = 0x01: active sync
	  bDeviceProtocol = 0x02: Palm sync
	bDeviceSubclass = 0x02
	  bDeviceProtocol = 0x01: interface association descriptor
	  bDeviceProtocol = 0x01: wire adapter multifunction peripheral (Wireless USB)

0xFF	Vendor-specific (can instead be declared at the interface level)

number also enables a host to determine whether a device is the same one used previously or a new installation of a device with the same Vendor ID and Product ID. Devices with the same Vendor ID, Product ID, and device release number should not share a serial number. Mass-storage devices that use the bulk-only protocol must have serial numbers.

bNumConfigurations equals the number of configurations the device supports at the current operating speed.

Device_qualifier

Devices that support both full and high speeds must have a device_qualifier descriptor (Table 4-4). When a device switches speeds, the values of some fields in the device descriptor may change. The device_qualifier descriptor contains the values for these fields at the speed not currently in use. In other words, the contents of fields in the device and device_qualifier descriptors swap depending on which speed is in use. A host retrieves a device_qualifier descriptor by sending a Get Descriptor request with the high byte of the Setup transaction's wValue field equal to 0x06.

The Vendor ID, Product ID, device release number, manufacturer string, product string, and serial-number string don't change when the speed changes, so the device_qualifier descriptor doesn't include these fields.

Configuration

After retrieving the device descriptor, a host can retrieve the device's configuration, interface, and endpoint descriptors.

Each device has at least one configuration that specifies the device's features and abilities. Many devices need only a single configuration, but with driver support, a device with multiple uses or multiple options for power use can support multiple configurations. Only one configuration is active at a time. Each configuration requires a descriptor with information about the device's use of power and the number of interfaces supported (Table 4-5).

Each configuration descriptor has subordinate descriptors, including one or more interface descriptors and endpoint descriptors as needed. A host retrieves a configuration descriptor and its subordinate descriptors by sending a Get Descriptor request with the high byte of the Setup transaction's wValue field equal to 0x02 and the wLength field equal to wTotalLength.

The host selects a configuration with the Set Configuration request and reads the current configuration number with a Get Configuration request.

wTotalLength equals the number of bytes in the configuration descriptor and all of its subordinate descriptors.

bNumInterfaces equals the number of interfaces in the configuration. The minimum is 0x01.

bConfigurationValue identifies the configuration for Get Configuration and Set Configuration requests and must be 0x01 or higher. A Set Configuration request with a value of zero causes the device to enter the Not Configured state.

iConfiguration is an index to a string that describes the configuration. This value is zero if there is no string descriptor.

Table 4-4: In a device that supports both full and high speeds, the device_qualifier descriptor contains information about the device when operating in the speed not currently in use. Information source: *Universal Serial Bus Specification, Revision 2.0*

Offset (decimal)	Field	Size (bytes)	Description
0	bLength	1	Descriptor size in bytes (0x0A)
1	bDescriptorType	1	The constant DEVICE_QUALIFIER (0x06)
2	bcdUSB	2	USB specification release number (BCD)
4	bDeviceClass	1	Class code
5	bDeviceSubclass	1	Subclass code
6	bDeviceProtocol	1	Protocol Code
7	bMaxPacketSize0	1	Maximum packet size for endpoint zero
8	bNumConfigurations	1	Number of possible configurations
9	Reserved	1	For future use

bmAttributes has bit 6 = 1 if the device is self-powered and zero if bus powered. Bit 5 = 1 if the device supports the remote wakeup feature, which enables a device in the Suspend state to tell the host that the device wants to communicate. The other bits in the field are unused. Bits 4..0 must be zero. Bit 7 must equal 1 for compatibility with USB 1.0

bMaxPower specifies how much bus current a device requires. For USB 2.0, bMax-Power is in units of 2 mA. If the device requires 200 mA, bMaxPower = 100 (0x64). For SuperSpeed, bMaxPower is in units of 8 mA. The maximum bus current a device can request in this descriptor is 500 mA for USB 2.0 and 900 mA for Enhanced Super-Speed. If the requested current isn't available, the host will refuse to configure the device. A driver may then request an alternate configuration if available.

When a device and host support *USB Power Delivery Rev. 2.0, v1.0*, the host can retrieve a device's power needs from a different descriptor as described in Chapter 17.

Other_speed_configuration

The second descriptor unique to devices that support both full and high speeds is the other_speed_configuration descriptor (Table 4-6). The structure of the descriptor is identical to that of the configuration descriptor. The only difference is that the other-speed_configuration descriptor describes the configuration when the device is operating at the speed not currently in use. The descriptor has subordinate descriptors just as the configuration descriptor does.

Table 4-5: The configuration descriptor specifies the maximum amount of bus current the device will require and gives the total length of the subordinate descriptors. Information source: *Universal Serial Bus Specification, Revision 2.0* and *Universal Serial Bus 3.1 Specification, Revision 1.0.*

Offset (decimal)	Field	Size (bytes)	Description
0	bLength	1	Descriptor size in bytes (0x09)
1	bDescriptorType	1	The constant CONFIGURATION (0x02)
2	wTotalLength	2	The number of bytes in the configuration descriptor and all of its subordinate descriptors
4	bNumInterfaces	1	Number of interfaces in the configuration
5	bConfigurationValue	1	Identifier for Set Configuration and Get Configuration requests
6	iConfiguration	1	Index of string descriptor for the configuration
7	bmAttributes	1	Self/bus power and remote wakeup settings
8	bMaxPower	1	Bus power required in units of 2 mA (USB 2.0) or 8 mA (Enhanced SuperSpeed).

A host retrieves an other_speed_configuration descriptor by sending a Get Descriptor request with the high byte of the Setup transaction's wValue field equal to 0x07.

Interface association

An interface association descriptor (IAD) identifies multiple interfaces associated with a function (Table 4-7). In relation to a device and its descriptors, the term *interface* refers to a feature or function a device implements.

Most device classes specify the class at the interface level rather than at the device level. Assigning functions to interfaces enables a single configuration to support multiple functions. When two or more interfaces in a configuration are associated with the same function, the interface association descriptor tells the host which interfaces are associated. For example, a video-camera function may use one interface to control the camera and another to carry video data.

The *Interface Association Descriptors* ECN says that the descriptor must be supported by future implementations of devices that use multiple interfaces to manage a single device function. Devices that comply with the video and audio-class 2.0 specifications must use interface association descriptors. Class specifications that predate the IAD don't require it. For example, the audio 1.0 class specification defines a class-specific descriptor to associate audio interfaces in a function. Hosts that don't support the IAD ignore it. Windows began supporting the descriptor with Windows XP SP2. In

Table 4-6: The other_speed_configuration descriptor has the same fields as the configuration descriptor but contains information about the device when it operates in the speed not currently in use. Information source: *Universal Serial Bus Specification, Revision 2.0* and *Universal Serial Bus 3.1 Specification, Revision 1.0.*

Offset (decimal)	Field	Size (bytes)	Description
0	bLength	1	Descriptor size in bytes (0x09)
1	bDescriptorType	1	The constant OTHER_SPEED_CONFIGURATION (0x07)
2	wTotalLength	2	The number of bytes in the configuration descriptor and all of its subordinate descriptors
4	bNumInterfaces	1	Number of interfaces in the configuration
5	bConfigurationValue	1	Identifier for Set Configuration and Get Configuration requests
6	iConfiguration	1	Index of string descriptor for the configuration
7	bmAttributes	1	Self/bus power and remote wakeup settings
8	MaxPower	1	Bus power required in units of 2 mA (USB 2.0) or 8 mA (SuperSpeed/SuperSpeedPlus).

Enhanced SuperSpeed devices, every function with multiple interfaces must use an IAD.

To enable hosts to identify devices that use the Interface Association descriptor, the device descriptor should contain the following values:

bDeviceClass = 0xEF (miscellaneous device class)
bDeviceSubClass = 0x02 (common class)
bDeviceProtocol = 0x01 (interface association descriptor)

These codes together form the *Multi-interface Function Device Class Codes*.

A host retrieves an interface association descriptor as one of the subordinate descriptors sent in response to a request for a configuration descriptor. The IAD precedes the interface descriptors that the IAD specifies.

bFirstInterface identifies the interface number of the first of multiple interfaces associated with a function. The interface number is the value of bInterfaceNumber in the interface descriptor. The interface numbers of associated interfaces must be contiguous.

bInterfaceCount equals the number of contiguous interfaces associated with the function.

bFunctionClass is a class code for the function shared by the associated interfaces. For classes that don't specify a value to use, the preferred value is the bInterfaceClass

Table 4-7: The interface association descriptor can link multiple interfaces to a single function. Information source: *Universal Serial Bus 3.1 Specification, Revision 1.0.*

Offset (decimal)	Field	Size (bytes)	Description
0	bLength	1	Descriptor size in bytes (0x08)
1	bDescriptorType	1	The constant Interface Association (0x0B)
2	bFirstInterface	1	Number identifying the first interface associated with the function
3	bInterfaceCount	1	The number of contiguous interfaces associated with the function
4	bFunctionClass	1	Class code
5	bFunctionSubClass	1	Subclass code
6	bFunctionProtocol	1	Protocol code
7	iFunction	1	Index of string descriptor for the function

value from the descriptor of the first associated interface. Values from 0x01–0xFE are reserved for USB-defined classes. 0xFF indicates a vendor-defined class. Zero is not allowed.

bFunctionSubClass is a subclass code for the function shared by the associated interfaces. For classes that don't specify a value to use, the preferred value is the bInterfaceSubClass value from the descriptor of the first associated interface.

bInterfaceProtocol is a protocol code for the function shared by the associated interfaces. For classes that don't specify a value to use, the preferred value is the bInterfaceProtocol value from the descriptor of the first associated interface.

iFunction is an index to a string that describes the function. This value is zero if there is no string descriptor.

Interface

The interface descriptor provides information about a function or feature that a device implements. The descriptor contains class, subclass, and protocol information and the number of endpoints the interface uses (Table 4-8).

A configuration can have multiple interfaces that are active at the same time. The interfaces may be associated with a single function or they may be unrelated. Each interface has its own interface descriptor and subordinate descriptors. Each of these interfaces can also have one or more alternate interface settings. Interface settings are mutually exclusive; only one is active at a time. Each setting has an interface descriptor and subordinate descriptors as needed. Devices that use isochronous

Table 4-8: The interface descriptor specifies the number of subordinate endpoints and may specify a USB class. Information source: *Universal Serial Bus Specification, Revision 2.0.*

Offset (decimal)	Field	Size (bytes)	Description
0	bLength	1	Descriptor size in bytes (0x09)
1	bDescriptorType	1	The constant Interface (0x04)
2	bInterfaceNumber	1	Number identifying this interface
3	bAlternateSetting	1	A number that identifies a descriptor with alternate settings for this bInterfaceNumber.
4	bNumEndpoints	1	Number of endpoints supported not counting endpoint zero
5	bInterfaceClass	1	Class code
6	bInterfaceSubclass	1	Subclass code
7	bInterfaceProtocol	1	Protocol code
8	iInterface	1	Index of string descriptor for the interface

transfers must have alternate interface settings because the default interface can request no isochronous bandwidth.

A host retrieves interface descriptors as subordinate descriptors sent in response to a request for a configuration descriptor.

bInterfaceNumber identifies the interface. In a composite device, a configuration has multiple interfaces that are active at the same time. Each interface must have a descriptor with a unique value in this field. The first interface is 0x00.

bAlternateSetting identifies the default interface setting or an alternate setting. For each bInterfaceNumber, the device provides an interface descriptor with bAlternateSetting = 0x00. This interface is the default setting. A descriptor for an alternate setting has the same value in bInterfaceNumber, a unique value in bAlternateSetting, and different values as needed in the descriptor's final five bytes and different subordinate descriptors as needed.

For each bInterfaceNumber, only one bAlternateSetting is active at a time. The alternate settings enable the host to request an interface with different bandwidth or other requirements and capabilities. The Get Interface request retrieves the currently active bAlternateSetting. The Set Interface request selects the bAlternateSetting that a specific bInterfaceNumber should use.

bNumEndpoints equals the number of endpoints the interface supports in addition to endpoint zero. For a device that supports only endpoint zero, this field is zero.

bInterfaceClass is similar to bDeviceClass in the device descriptor, but for devices with a class specified by the interface. Table 4-9 shows defined codes. Values 0x01–0xFE are reserved for USB-defined classes. 0xFF indicates a vendor-defined class. Zero is reserved.

bInterfaceSubClass is similar to bDeviceSubClass in the device descriptor, but for devices with a class defined by the interface. If bInterfaceClass equals 0x00, bInterfaceSubclass must equal 0x00. If bInterfaceClass is in the range 0x01–0xFE, bInterfaceSubclass equals 0x00 or a code defined for the interface's class. 0xFF indicates a vendor-defined subclass.

bInterfaceProtocol is similar to bDeviceProtocol in the device descriptor, but for devices whose class is defined by the interface. The field can specify a protocol for the selected bInterfaceClass and bInterfaceSubClass. If bInterfaceClass is in the range 0x01–0xFE, bInterfaceProtocol must equal 0x00 or a code defined for the interface's class. The value 0xFF indicates a vendor-defined protocol.

iInterface is an index to a string that describes the interface. This value is zero if there is no string descriptor.

Endpoint

Each endpoint specified in an interface descriptor has an endpoint descriptor (Table 4-10). Endpoint zero never has a descriptor because every device must support endpoint zero, the device descriptor contains the maximum packet size, and the USB specifications define everything else about the endpoint. A host retrieves endpoint descriptors as subordinate descriptors sent in response to a request for a configuration descriptor.

Devices in the audio 1.0 class extend the endpoint descriptor with two additional bytes of audio-specific information. These bytes are the only allowed extension that changes the length of a standard descriptor type. Other specifications define separate, subordinate descriptors that return extended information. For example, USB 3.1 defines the endpoint companion descriptor to return endpoint information that is specific to Enhanced SuperSpeed.

bEndpointAddress specifies the endpoint number and direction. Bits 3..0 are the endpoint number. Low-speed devices can have a maximum of 3 endpoint numbers (usually in the range 0–2), while other devices can have 16 (0–15). Bit 7 is the direction, with OUT = 0 and IN = 1. Bits 6..4 are unused and must be zero.

bmAttributes sets bits 1..0 to specify the type of transfer the endpoint supports: 00_b=control, 01_b=isochronous, 10_b=bulk, 11_b=interrupt. Bits 7..6 are reserved and must be zeros. The functions of the remaining bits vary with the endpoint type and speed.

Table 4-9: The bInterfaceClass field in the interface descriptor can name a class the interface belongs to. Information source: *Universal Serial Bus Specification, Revision 2.0 and* USB-IF class specifications. (Part 1 of 2).

Class Code	Description
0x00	Reserved
0x01	Audio
0x02	Communications device: communication interface
0x03	Human interface device
0x05	Physical
0x06	Image bInterfaceSubclass = 0x01 bInterfaceProtocol = 0x01: Imaging device
0x07	Printer
0x08	Mass storage
0x09	Hub (must also be declared in the device descriptor)
0x0A	Communications device: data interface
0x0B	Smart Card
0x0D	Content Security bInterfaceSubclass = 0x01 bInterfaceProtocol = 0x01: Content security device
0x0E	Video
0x0F	Personal healthcare device (can instead be declared at the device level)

0x10	Audio/Video (AV):
	bInterfaceSubclass = 0x01
	  bInterfaceProtocol = 0x00: AVControl Interface
	bInterfaceSubclass = 0x02
	  bInterfaceProtocol = 0x00: AVData Video Streaming Interface
	bInterfaceSubclass = 0x03
	  bInterfaceProtocol = 0x00: AVData Audio Streaming Interface

0xDC	Diagnostic device (can instead be declared at the device level) bInterfaceSubclass= 0x01 bInterfaceProtocol = 0x01: USB2 compliance device

Table 4-9: The bInterfaceClass field in the interface descriptor can name a class the interface belongs to. Information source: *Universal Serial Bus Specification, Revision 2.0 and* USB-IF class specifications. (Part 2 of 2).

Class Code	Description

0xE0	Wireless controller
	bInterfaceSubclass = 0x01
	  bInterfaceProtocol = 0x01: Bluetooth programming interface
	  (should also be declared at the device level)
	  bInterfaceProtocol = 0x02: UWB Radio control interface (Wireless USB)
	  bInterfaceProtocol = 0x03: RNDIS
	  bInterfaceProtocol = 0x04: Bluetooth AMP controller
	  (should also be declared at the device level)
	bInterfaceSubclass = 0x02: Host and device wire adapters (Wireless USB)
	  bInterfaceProtocol = 0x01: Host wire adapter control/data interface
	  bInterfaceProtocol = 0x02: Device wire adapter control/data interface
	  bInterfaceProtocol = 0x03: Device wire adapter isochronous interface

0xEF	Miscellaneous
	bInterfaceSubclass = 0x01
	  bInterfaceProtocol = 0x01: active sync
	  bInterfaceProtocol = 0x02: Palm sync
	bInterfaceSubclass = 0x02
	  bInterfaceProtocol = 0x01: Interface Association Descriptor
	  bInterfaceProtocol = 0x02: Wire Adapter Multifunction Peripheral
	  programming interface
	bInterfaceSubclass = 0x03: Cable based association framework (Wireless USB)
	  bInterfaceProtocol = 0x01: Cable based association framework device
	bInterfaceSubclass = 0x04
	  bInterfaceProtocol = 0x01: RNDIS over Ethernet
	  bInterfaceProtocol = 0x02: RNDIS over WiFi
	  bInterfaceProtocol = 0x03: RNDIS over Maxim
	  bInterfaceProtocol = 0x04: RNDIS over WWAN
	  bInterfaceProtocol = 0x05: RNDIS for Raw IPv4
	  bInterfaceProtocol = 0x06: RNDIS for Raw IPv6
	  bInterfaceProtocol = 0x07: RNDIS for GPRS
	bInterfaceSubclass = 0x05: Machine vision device (USB3 Vision)
	  bInterfaceProtocol = 0x00: USB3 Vision Control Interface
	  bInterfaceProtocol = 0x01: USB3 Vision Event Interface
	  bInterfaceProtocol = 0x02: USB3 Vision Streaming Interface

0xFE	Application specific
	bInterfaceSubclass = 0x01: Device firmware upgrade
	bInterfaceSubclass = 0x02: IrDA bridge
	bInterfaceSubclass = 0x03: Test and measurement (USBTMC)
	  bInterfaceProtocol = 0x00: Complies with USBTMC spec
	  bInterfaceProtocol = 0x01: Complies with USBTMC USB488 subclass

0xFF	Vendor specific (can instead be declared at the device level)

Table 4-10: The endpoint descriptor provides information about an endpoint address. Information source: *Universal Serial Bus Specification, Revision 2.0.*

Offset (decimal)	Field	Size (bytes)	Description
0	bLength	1	Descriptor size in bytes (0x07)
1	bDescriptorType	1	The constant Endpoint (0x05)
2	bEndpointAddress	1	Endpoint number and direction
3	bmAttributes	1	Transfer type and supplementary information
4	wMaxPacketSize	2	Maximum packet size supported
6	bInterval	1	Service interval or NAK rate

For isochronous endpoints, bits 5..2 can indicate a synchronization type and usage type of data or feedback.

For Enhanced SuperSpeed interrupt endpoints, bits 5..4 indicate a usage type of Notification or Periodic. Interrupt endpoints have two primary uses with differing needs from the host. Some endpoints require quick response or frequent data transfers. For example, users don't want a noticeable delay before seeing the effect of pressing a key or moving a mouse. These endpoints should specify the Periodic usage. Other endpoints provide infrequent notifications or data where timing is less critical. An example is hub notifications that inform the host of device attachment, removal, or other events. The endpoints should specify the Notification usage. The host can use the Usage type in deciding whether to place a port in a low-power state that requires more time to exit. Any undefined bits are reserved.

wMaxPacketSize specifies the maximum number of data bytes the endpoint can transfer in a transaction. The allowed values vary with the device speed and type of transfer.

For USB 2.0, bits 10..0 are the maximum packet size with a range of 0–1024. For USB 1.1, the range is 0–1023. In USB 2.0, bits 12..11 indicate how many additional transactions per microframe a high-speed interrupt or isochronous endpoint supports: 00_b = no additional transactions (total of 1 / microframe), 01_b = one additional (total of 2 / microframe), 10_b = 2 additional (total of 3 / microframe), 11_b = reserved. In USB 1.1, these bits were reserved and zero. Bits 15..13 are reserved and zero.

For Enhanced SuperSpeed bulk endpoints, wMaxPacketSize is 1024. For Enhanced SuperSpeed interrupt and isochronous endpoints, the allowed values depend on the value of bMaxBurst in the SuperSpeed endpoint companion descriptor. If bMaxBurst = 0, wMaxPacketSize can be in the range 0–1024 for isochronous endpoints and 1–1024 for interrupt endpoints. If bMaxBurst > 0, wMaxPacketSize = 1024.

bInterval specifies the service interval for interrupt and isochronous endpoints. The service interval is a period within which the host must reserve time for an endpoint's transactions. The period is an integral number of frames (low and full speed), microframes (high speed), or bus intervals (Enhanced SuperSpeed). The allowed range and usage of bInterval varies with the device's speed, the transfer type, and the USB version.

For low-speed interrupt endpoints, bInterval is the maximum latency in ms in the range 10–255. For all full-speed interrupt endpoints and for full-speed isochronous endpoints on 1.1 devices, the interval equals bInterval in ms. For interrupt endpoints, the value may range from 1–255. For isochronous endpoints in USB 1.1 devices, the value must be 1. For isochronous endpoints in full-speed USB 2.0 devices, values 1–16 are allowed, and the interval is $2^{bInterval-1}$ in ms, allowing a range from 1 ms to 32.768 s.

For high-speed and Enhanced SuperSpeed endpoints, the value is in units of 125 µs. The value for interrupt and isochronous endpoints may range from 1–16, and the interval is calculated as $2^{bInterval-1}$, allowing a range from 125 µs to 4.096 s.

For high-speed bulk and control OUT endpoints, the field can contain a maximum NAK rate for use in compliance testing only. Devices typically set the field to zero. For other bulk transfers and control transfers, the value is reserved.

SuperSpeed endpoint companion

Every SuperSpeed and SuperSpeedPlus endpoint has a SuperSpeed endpoint companion descriptor (Table 4-11) to support Enhanced SuperSpeed capabilities. A USB 3.1 host retrieves endpoint companion descriptors as subordinate descriptors sent in response to a request for a configuration descriptor when the configuration has one or more endpoints.

bMaxBurst specifies the maximum number of packets the endpoint can send or receive in a burst minus one. A value of zero means one packet per burst. The maximum value is 15, indicating 16 packets per burst. A DP in a burst can transmit without waiting for an acknowledgment of the previous DP in the burst.

bmAttributes provides information specific to bulk and isochronous endpoints. For bulk endpoints, bits 4..0 are a MaxStreams value that indicates the maximum number of streams the endpoint supports. Zero means the endpoint doesn't use streams. For values 1–16, the number of streams equals $2^{MaxStreams}$ for a maximum value of 65,536.

For isochronous endpoints, if bit 7 = 0, bits 1..0 are a Mult value that indicates, along with bMaxBurst, the maximum number of packets in a service interval. The maximum number of packets equals:

$(bMaxBurst + 1) \times (Mult + 1)$

Table 4-11: An Enhanced SuperSpeed endpoint has a companion descriptor to provide a maximum burst value. Information source: *Universal Serial Bus 3.1 Specification, Revision 1.0.*

Offset (decimal)	Field	Size (bytes)	Description
0	bLength	1	Descriptor size in bytes (0x06)
1	bDescriptorType	1	The constant SUPERSPEED_USB_ENDPOINT_COMPANION (0x30)
2	bMaxBurst	1	The maximum number of packets the endpoint can send or receive as part of a burst - 1.
3	bmAttributes	1	For bulk endpoints, the maximum number of streams. For isochronous endpoints, the maximum number of packets in a service interval. Bit 7 indicates whether to use a SuperSpeedPlus isochronous endpoint companion descriptor.
4	wBytesPerInterval	2	For periodic interrupt and isochronous endpoints, the maximum number of bytes the endpoint expects to transfer per service interval.

Valid values for Mult are 0–2. The maximum allowed number of packets thus equals $(15 + 1) \times (2 + 1)$, or 48. With wMaxPacketSize = 1024, the throughput is 49,152 B/service interval.

SuperSpeedPlus endpoints that transfer more than 48 KB per service interval use a different method, detailed in the specification, to specify the maximum number of packets per service interval.

wBytesPerInterval is the maximum number of bytes a periodic interrupt or isochronous endpoint expects to transfer per service interval.

SuperSpeedPlus isochronous endpoint companion

As the name suggests, the SuperSpeedPlus isochronous endpoint companion descriptor (Table 4-12) contains information about an isochronous endpoint that operates above Gen 1 speed. An endpoint that requests more than 48 KB per service interval must return this descriptor following the endpoint companion descriptor. The descriptor specifies the total number of bytes the endpoint will transfer per service interval.

The maximum value for dwBytesPerInterval is 98,304 (1024 bytes/DP $\times$ 16 DPs/burst $\times$ 6 bursts per service interval.

Table 4-12: A SuperSpeedPlus isochronous endpoint may have a companion descriptor to provide additional information. Information source: *Universal Serial Bus 3.1 Specification, Revision 1.0.*

Offset (decimal)	Field	Size (bytes)	Description
0	bLength	1	Descriptor size in bytes (0x08)
1	bDescriptorType	1	The constant SUPERSPEED_ISOCHRONOUS _USB_ENDPOINT_COMPANION (0x31)
2	wReserved	2	Zero
4	dwBytesPerInterval	4	The total number of bytes the endpoint will transfer per service interval

String

A string descriptor (Table 4-13) contains descriptive text. Other descriptors can contain indexes to string descriptors that name the manufacturer, product, serial number, configuration, and interface. Class- and vendor-specific descriptors can contain indexes to additional string descriptors. Support for string descriptors is optional though a class specification may require them. A host retrieves a string descriptor by sending a Get Descriptor request with the high byte of the Setup transaction's wValue field equal to 0x03.

When the host requests a string descriptor, the low byte of wValue is an index value. An index value of zero has the special function of requesting language IDs, while other index values request strings.

wLANGID[0...n] is valid for string descriptor zero only. This field contains one or more 16-bit language ID codes that indicate the languages the strings are available in. U.S. English (0x0409) is likely to be the only code supported by an OS. The wLANGID value must be valid for any string to be valid. Devices that return no string descriptors must not return an array of language IDs. The USB-IF publishes a list of identifiers titled *Language Identifiers (LANGIDs).*

bString is valid for string descriptors 0x01 and higher and contains a string in Unicode UTF-16LE format. In this format, most characters are encoded as 16-bit code units with the low byte of the code unit transmitted first. For U.S. English, the low byte of the code unit is the character's ASCII code. For example, the character *A*, encoded as 0x0041, transmits as 0x41 followed by 0x00 (LSB first). Some rarely used characters are encoded as surrogate pairs consisting of two 16-bit code units. The strings are not null-terminated.

Table 4-13: A string descriptor identifies a supported language or stores a string of text. Information source: *Universal Serial Bus Specification, Revision 2.0.*

Offset (decimal)	Field	Size (bytes)	Description
0	bLength	1	Descriptor size in bytes (variable)
1	bDescriptorType	1	The constant String (0x03)
2	bSTRING or wLANGID	varies	For string descriptor zero, an array of one or more Language Identifier codes. For other string descriptors, a Unicode UTF-16LE string.

Binary device object store (BOS) and device capability

Some devices use additional descriptors to store information that is specific to a technology or a device function. To provide a standard way to provide this information, the Wireless USB specification introduced two new descriptor types: the binary device object store (BOS) and device capability descriptors. The *Universal Serial Bus 3.1 Specification, Revision 1.0* also contains the definitions for these descriptors. Other USB specifications and the Microsoft OS2 descriptors make use of the descriptors.

The binary device object store (BOS) descriptor (Table 4-14) functions as a base descriptor for one or more related device capability descriptors. A device capability descriptor (Table 4-15) provides information about a specific capability or technology.

The USB 3.1 specification defines these device capability descriptors:

- CONTAINER_ID provides a 128-bit universally unique identifier (UUID) that identifies the device instance. The descriptor is mandatory for USB 3.1 hubs and optional for other Enhanced SuperSpeed devices.

- PLATFORM defines a device capability specific to a particular platform or operating system. Microsoft OS 2.0 descriptors use this descriptor.

- PRECISION_TIME_MEASUREMENT indicates that a USB 3.1 hub or other device supports precision time measurement (PTM) capability. PTM uses measurements of link delays and propagation delays through a hub to provide more accurate timing of bus interval boundaries at devices. Hubs that support SuperSpeedPlus must provide this descriptor. The descriptor is optional for other Enhanced SuperSpeed devices including USB 3.0 hubs.

- SUPERSPEED_USB indicates which speeds the device supports up to and including SuperSpeed, the lowest speed that provides full functionality, and power-management capabilities. All Enhanced SuperSpeed devices must provide this descriptor.

- SUPERSPEED_PLUS describes features and capabilities for operating at SuperSpeedPlus. All SuperSpeedPlus devices must provide this descriptor.

Table 4-14: A binary device object store (BOS) descriptor provides a way to support descriptors that store additional information about a device. Information source: *Universal Serial Bus 3.1 Specification, Revision 1.0.*

Offset (decimal)	Field	Size (bytes)	Description
0	bLength	1	Descriptor size in bytes (0x05).
1	bDescriptorType	1	BOS (0x0F)
2	wTotalLength	2	The number of bytes in this descriptor and all of its subordinate descriptors
4	bNumDeviceCaps	1	The number of device capability descriptors subordinate to this BOS descriptor.

- USB 2.0 EXTENSION indicates that a device supports the Link Power Management protocol when operating at low, full, or high speed. All Enhanced SuperSpeed devices must provide this descriptor and must support Link Power Management when operating at high speed. The *USB 2.0 Link Power Management Addendum* to the USB 2.0 specification also defines this descriptor, and USB 2.0 devices that support Link Power Management provide this descriptor (and declare themselves as USB 2.1 devices).

The *USB Power Delivery Rev. 2.0, v1.0* specification defines these device capability descriptors:

- POWER_DELIVERY_CAPABILITY describes power delivery support and features.
- BATTERY_INFO_CAPABILITY describes battery features. Devices whose POWER_DELIVERY_CAPABILITY descriptor reports a battery as a power source support this descriptor.
- PD_CONSUMER_PORT_CAPABILITY describes power consumption features and capabilities. Devices whose POWER_DELIVERY_CAPABILITY descriptor reports they are capable of consuming power support this descriptor.
- PD_PROVIDER_PORT_CAPABILITY describes power providing features and capabilities. Devices whose POWER_DELIVERY_CAPABILITY descriptor reports they are capable of providing power support this descriptor.

The *Wireless Universal Serial Bus Specification* defines these device capability descriptors:

- Wireless_USB describes capabilities of Wireless USB devices.
- Wireless_USB_Ext describes capabilities of Wireless USB 1.1 devices.

The *Device Class Definition for Billboard Devices* defines a device capability descriptor for devices that support the billboard function

Table 4-15: A device capability descriptor can provide information that is specific to a technology or another aspect of a device or its function. Information source: *Universal Serial Bus 3.1 Specification, Revision 1.0.*

Offset (decimal)	Field	Size (bytes)	Description
0	bLength	1	Descriptor length in bytes (varies).
1	bDescriptorType	1	DEVICE CAPABILITY (0x10)
2	bDevCapabilityType	1	0x01 = Wireless_USB 0x02 = USB 2.0 EXTENSION 0x03 = SUPERSPEED_USB 0x04 = CONTAINER ID 0x05 = PLATFORM 0x06 = POWER_DELIVERY_CAPABILITY 0x07 = BATTERY_INFO_CAPABILITY 0x08 = PD_CONSUMER_PORT_CAPABILITY 0x09 = PD_PROVIDER_PORT_CAPABILITY 0x0A = SUPERSPEED_PLUS 0x0B = PRECISION_TIME_MEASUREMENT 0x0C = Wireless_USB_Ext 0x0D = Billboard 0x00, 0x0E–0xFF (reserved)
3	Capability-Dependent	varies	Capability-specific data and format.

A host retrieves a BOS descriptor and all of its subordinate device capability descriptors by sending a Get Descriptor request with the high byte of the Setup transaction's wValue field set to 0x0F and the wLength field equal to the descriptor's wTotalLength value. There is no request for reading only a device capability descriptor.

OTG descriptor

Devices that support OTG's Host Negotiation Protocol (HNP) or Session Request Protocol (SRP) have an OTG descriptor that indicates the supported protocols. Chapter 21 has more about this descriptor.

Microsoft OS descriptors

Microsoft OS descriptors enable storing Windows-specific information such as data that enables identifying a device that uses Microsoft's WinUSB driver. Placing the information in descriptors means the information is available on attachment instead of requiring access to an INF file or other resource on the PC.

Windows versions beginning with Windows XP SP1 support Microsoft OS 1 descriptors. Windows 8.1 and later support Microsoft OS 2 descriptors, which overcome some weaknesses and limits of the OS 1 descriptors. Chapter 15 has more about using Microsoft OS descriptors.

Updating descriptors to USB 2.0

To update descriptors for a USB 1.1 device to USB 2.0, all except some devices that have isochronous endpoints require just one change: in the device descriptor, bcdUSB must be 0x0200 or greater. A USB 2.0 device's default interface(s) must request no isochronous bandwidth so an interface that wants to do isochronous transfers must have at least one alternate interface setting, and the alternate interface descriptor will have at least one subordinate endpoint descriptor.

Updating descriptors to USB 3.1

To update descriptors for a USB 3.0 device to USB 3.1, many SuperSpeed-only devices require just one change: in the device descriptor, bcdUSB must be 0x0310.

Devices that support SuperSpeedPlus must have a SuperSpeedPlus USB device capability descriptor.

SuperSpeedPlus devices with isochronous endpoints that request more than 48 KB per service interval must have a SuperSpeedPlus Isochronous Endpoint Companion descriptor.

Hubs and devices that support PTM require a precision time measurement device capability descriptor.

5

Control Transfers: Structured Requests for Critical Data

Of USB's four transfer types, control transfers have the most complex structure. They're also the only transfer type to have functions defined by the USB specification. This chapter looks in greater detail at control transfers and the standard requests defined in the specification.

Elements of a control transfer

Control transfers enable the host and a device to exchange information about the device's capabilities and other class-specific or vendor-specific information. As Chapter 3 explained, a control transfer consists of a Setup stage, a Data stage (not used or optional for some transfers), and a Status stage. Each stage consists of one or more transactions.

The packet descriptions below apply to USB 2.0 transfers. Enhanced SuperSpeed transfers exchange the same information but use Enhanced SuperSpeed's packet structures and protocols as described in Chapter 3.

Multiple-byte values in control-transfer requests and responses travel on the bus in little-endian order, from least-significant byte (LSB) to most significant byte (MSB). For example, a wIndex value of 0x0001 transmits as 0x01 followed by 0x00.

Setup stage

The Setup stage consists of a Setup transaction, which identifies the transfer as a control transfer and transmits the request and other information that the device needs to complete the request.

Devices must return ACK for every Setup transaction received without error. An endpoint that is in the middle of another control transfer must abandon that transfer and acknowledge the new Setup transaction.

Token packet

Purpose: identifies the receiver and identifies the transaction as a Setup transaction.

Sent by: the host.

PID: SETUP.

Additional contents: device and endpoint addresses.

Data packet

Purpose: transmits the request and related information.

Sent by: the host.

PID: DATA0.

Additional contents: eight bytes in five fields:

bmRequestType specifies the direction of data flow, the type of request, and the recipient.

Bit 7 (Direction) names the direction of data flow for data in the Data stage. Host to device (OUT) or no Data stage is zero; device to host (IN) is 1.

Bits 6..5 (Request Type) specify whether the request is one of USB's standard requests (00_b), a request defined for a specific USB class (01_b), or a request defined by a vendor-specific driver for use with a particular product or products (10_b).

Bits 4..0 (Recipient) define whether the request is directed to the device (00000_b) or to a specific interface (00001_b), endpoint (00010_b), or other element (00011_b) in the device.

bRequest identifies the request.

wValue can pass request-specific information to the device. Each request can define the meaning of these two bytes in its own way. For example, in a Set Address request, wValue contains the device's address.

wIndex can pass request-specific information to the device. A typical use is to pass an index or offset such as an interface or endpoint number, but each request can define the meaning of these two bytes in any way. When passing an endpoint index, bits 3..0 specify the endpoint number, and bit 7 = 0 for a Control or OUT endpoint or 1 for an IN endpoint. When passing an interface index, bits 7..0 are the interface number. All undefined bits are zero.

wLength is two bytes that contain the number of data bytes in the Data stage that follows. For a host-to-device transfer, wLength is the exact number of bytes the host intends to transfer. For a device-to-host transfer, wLength is a maximum number of bytes to transfer, and the device may return this many bytes or fewer. If the field is zero, the transfer has no Data stage.

Handshake packet

Purpose: transmits the device's acknowledgment.

Sent by: the device.

PID: ACK.

Additional contents: none. The handshake packet consists of the PID alone.

Comments: If the device detects an error in the received Setup or Data packet, the device returns no handshake. The device's hardware typically handles the error checking and sending of the ACK with no firmware support needed.

Data stage

The Data stage, when present, consists of one or more IN or OUT transactions. A Data stage with IN transactions sends data to the host. An example is the Get Descriptor request, where the device sends a requested descriptor to the host. A Data stage with OUT transactions sends data to the device. An example is the HID-class request Set Report, where the host sends a report to a device. If wLength in the Setup transaction equals 0x0000, the transfer has no Data stage. For example, in the Set Configuration request, the host passes a configuration value to the device in the wValue field of the Setup stage's data packet, so the transaction has no need for a Data stage.

In the device descriptor, bMaxPacketSize0 specifies the maximum number of data bytes per packet. If all of the data can't fit in one packet, the stage uses multiple transactions. The transactions in the Data stage are all in the same direction. When the Data stage is present but there is no data to transfer, the data packet is a ZLP.

The host uses split transactions in the Data stage when the device is low or full speed and a hub between the device and host connects upstream at high speed. The host may use the PING protocol when the device is high speed, the Data stage uses OUT transactions, and the stage has more than one data transaction.

Each IN or OUT transaction in the Data stage contains token, data, and handshake packets.

Token packet

Purpose: identifies the receiver and identifies the transaction as an IN or OUT transaction.

Sent by: the host.

PID: If the request requires the device to send data to the host, the PID is IN. If the request requires the host to send data to the device, the PID is OUT.

Additional contents: the device and endpoint addresses.

Data packet

Purpose: transfers all or a portion of the data specified in the wLength field of the Setup transaction's data packet.

Sent by: the device if the token packet's PID is IN or the host if the token packet's PID is OUT.

PID: The first packet is DATA1. Any additional packets in the Data stage alternate DATA0/DATA1.

Additional contents: The host sends data or a ZLP. A device may send data, a ZLP, STALL (unsupported request or halted endpoint), or NAK.

Handshake packet

Purpose: the data packet's receiver returns status information.

Sent by: the receiver of the Data stage's data packet. If the token packet's PID is IN, the host sends the handshake packet. If the token packet's PID is OUT, the device sends the handshake packet.

PID: A device may return ACK (data received without error), NAK (endpoint busy), or STALL (unsupported request or halted endpoint). A high-speed device that is receiving multiple data packets may return NYET to indicate that the current transaction's data was accepted but the endpoint isn't yet ready for another data packet. A host can return only ACK.

Additional contents: none. The handshake packet consists of the PID alone.

Comments: If the receiver detected an error in the token or data packet, the receiver returns no handshake packet.

Status Stage

The Status stage completes the transfer. In some cases (such as after receiving the first packet of a device descriptor during enumeration), the host may begin the Status stage before the Data stage has completed, and the device must detect the token packet of the Status stage, abandon the Data stage, and complete the Status stage.

Token packet

Purpose: identifies the receiver and indicates the direction of the Status stage's data packet.

Sent by: the host.

PID: the opposite of the direction of the previous transaction's data packet. If the Data stage's PID was OUT or if there was no Data stage, the Status stage's PID is IN. If the Data stage's PID was IN, the Status stage's PID is OUT.

Additional contents: the device and endpoint addresses.

Data packet

Purpose: enables the receiver of the Data stage's data to indicate the status of the transfer.

Sent by: the device if the Status stage's token packet's PID is IN or the host if the Status stage's token packet's PID is OUT.

PID: DATA1

Additional contents: The host sends a ZLP. A device may send a ZLP (success), NAK (busy), or STALL (unsupported request or halted endpoint).

Comments: For most standard requests, a ZLP from the device indicates that the device has performed the requested action (if any). An exception is Set Address, where the device takes the requested action after the Status stage has completed.

Handshake packet

Purpose: The sender of the Data stage's data indicates the status of the transfer.

Sent by: the receiver of the Status stage's data packet. If the Status stage's token packet's PID is IN, the host sends the handshake packet; if the token packet's PID is OUT, the device sends the data packet.

PID: A device may return ACK (success), NAK (busy), or STALL (unsupported request or halted endpoint). The host returns ACK in response to a data packet received without error.

Additional contents: none. The handshake packet consists of the PID alone.

Comments: The Status stage's handshake packet is the final transmission in the transfer. If the receiver detected an error in the token or data packet, the receiver returns no handshake packet.

For any request that's expected to take many milliseconds to carry out, the request should define an alternate way to determine when the request has completed. Doing so ensures that the host doesn't waste a lot of time asking for an acknowledgment that will take a long time to appear. An example is the Set Port Feature(PORT_RESET) request sent to a hub. The reset signal lasts at least 10 ms. Rather than make the host wait this long for the device to complete the request, the hub acknowledges receiving the request when the hub first places the port in the reset state. When the reset is complete, the hub sets a bit that the host can retrieve at its leisure using a Get Port Status request.

Handling errors

A device might receive a request that firmware doesn't support. Or a device may be unable to respond because the endpoint is in the Halt condition, the firmware has crashed, or the device is no longer attached to the bus. A host may also decide to end a transfer early for any reason.

An example of an unsupported request is one that uses a request code that the device's firmware doesn't know how to respond to. Or a device may support the request but other information in the Setup stage doesn't match what the device expects or supports. On these occasions, a *Request Error* condition exists and the device notifies the host by returning STALL. Devices must respond to the Setup transaction with an ACK, so the STALL transmits in the Data or Status stage. When possible, the device should return STALL in the Data stage.

On failing to get a response or on detecting an error in received data or a Halt condition at the endpoint, the host abandons the transfer. The host then tries to re-establish communications with the endpoint by sending the token packet for a new Setup transaction. If a new token packet doesn't cause the device to recover, the host requests the device's hub to reset the device's port.

The host may also end a transfer early by beginning the Status stage before completing all of the Data stage's transactions. In this case, the device must respond to the Status stage in the same way as if all of the data had transferred.

Device firmware

USB 2.0 device firmware typically performs the steps below to support control transfers. The implementation details vary with the device architecture and programming language.

Control write requests with a data stage

To complete a control write request with a Data stage, the device must detect the request in the Setup stage, accept the data in the Data stage, and send a ZLP in the Status stage.

1. Device hardware detects a received Setup packet, stores the contents of the transaction's data packet, returns ACK, and triggers an interrupt.

2. On detecting the interrupt, the device decodes the request and ensures that endpoint zero is ready to accept data that arrives following an OUT token packet. The endpoint must also return ACK in response to a new Setup packet if the host decides to abandon the transfer. The endpoint should return a ZLP in response to an IN token packet, which indicates that the host is ending the transfer early.

3. The Data stage begins when the host sends an OUT token packet to endpoint zero. The endpoint stores the data that follows the token packet and returns ACK in the handshake packet. The hardware triggers an interrupt.

4. On detecting the interrupt, the device processes the received data as needed.

5. If the Data stage has additional data packets, steps 3 and 4 repeat for additional OUT transactions up to the wLength value in the Setup transaction.

6. To complete the transfer, the host sends an IN token packet, the device responds with a ZLP, and the host returns ACK.

Control write requests with no data stage

To complete a control write request without a Data stage, the device must detect the request in the Setup stage and send a ZLP in the Status stage.

1. The hardware detects a Setup packet, stores the contents of the transaction's data packet, returns ACK, and triggers an interrupt.

2. On detecting the interrupt, the device decodes the request, does what is needed to perform the requested action, and ensures that endpoint zero is ready to respond to an IN token packet. The endpoint must also return ACK in response to a new Setup packet if the host decides to abandon the transfer.

3. To complete the transfer, the host sends an IN token packet, the device responds with a ZLP, and the host returns ACK.

Control read requests

To complete a control read request, the device must detect the request in the Setup stage, send data in the Data stage, and acknowledge a received handshake in the Status stage.

1. The hardware detects a Setup packet, stores the contents of the transaction's data packet, returns ACK, and triggers an interrupt.

2. On detecting the interrupt, the device decodes the request and ensures that endpoint zero is ready to send the requested data on receiving an IN token packet. The endpoint must also return ACK in response to a new Setup packet if the host decides to abandon the transfer. The endpoint must return a ZLP in response to an OUT packet if the host begins the Status stage early.

3. The Data stage begins when the host sends an IN token packet to endpoint zero. The device hardware sends the data, detects the received ACK from the host, and triggers an interrupt.

4. On detecting the interrupt, a device that has more data to send ensures that the endpoint is ready to send the data on receiving another IN token packet, and steps 3 and 4 repeat.

5. On receiving an OUT token packet followed by a ZLP, the endpoint returns ACK to complete the transfer.

Standard requests

Table 5-1 summarizes the requests defined in the USB 2.0 and USB 3.1 specifications.

Table 5-1: The USB 2.0 and 3.1 specifications define these requests for control transfers. Information source: *Universal Serial Bus Specification, Revision 2.0* and *Universal Serial Bus 3.1 Specification, Revision 1.0*.

Request Code Request Name	Target	wValue	wIndex	Data Stage	
				Data Source	wLength; Contents
0x00 Get Status	device, interface, or endpoint	0x0000	0x0000 (device), interface, or endpoint	device	0x0002; status
0x01 Clear Feature	device, interface, or endpoint	feature	0x0000 (device), interface, or endpoint	none	0x0000
0x03 Set Feature	device, interface, or endpoint	feature	0x0000 (device), interface, or endpoint	none	0x0000
0x05 Set Address	device	device address	0x0000	none	0x0000
0x06 Get Descriptor	device	descriptor type and index	0x0000 or language ID	device	descriptor length; descriptor
0x07 Set Descriptor	device	descriptor type and index	0x0000 or language ID	host	descriptor length; descriptor
0x08 Get Configuration	device	0x0000	0x0000	device	0x0001; configuration
0x09 Set Configuration	device	configuration	0x0000	none	0x0000
0x0A Get Interface	interface	0x0000	interface	device	0x0001; alternate setting
0x0B Set Interface	interface	interface	interface	none	0x0000
0x0C Synch Frame	endpoint	0x0000	endpoint	device	0x002; frame number
0x30 Set SEL	device	0x0000	0x0000	host	0x0006; exit latency values
0x31 Set Isochronous Delay	device	Delay in ns	0x0000	none	0x0000

Get Status

Purpose: The host requests the status of the features of a device, interface, or endpoint.

Request number (bRequest): 0x00

Source of data: device

Data length (wLength): 0x0002

wValue: 0x0000

wIndex: For a device, 0x0000. For an interface, the interface number. For an endpoint, the endpoint number.

Data packet in the Data stage: the device, interface, or endpoint status.

Supported states: Default: undefined. Address: OK for address zero, endpoint zero. Otherwise the device returns STALL. Configured: OK.

Behavior on error: The device returns STALL if the target interface or endpoint doesn't exist.

Comments: For requests directed to devices operating at USB 2.0 speeds, two status bits are defined. Bit zero is the Self-Powered field: 0 = bus-powered, 1 = self-powered. The host can't change this value. Bit 1 is the Remote Wakeup field. The default on reset is zero (disabled). Enhanced SuperSpeed devices support the Self-Powered bit and use bits 2–4 for power-management options. Bit 2 = 1 means the device is enabled to initiate U1 entry. Bit 3 = 1 means the device is enabled to initiate U2 entry. Bit 4 = 1 means the device is enabled to send Latency Tolerance Messages.

For a request directed to the first interface in a function on a USB 3.1 bus, bit 0 = 1 if the function supports remote wakeup, and bit 1 = 1 if the host has enabled the function for remote wakeup. For requests directed to an interface on a USB 2.0 bus, all bits are reserved.

For requests directed to an endpoint, only bit zero is defined. Bit 0 = 1 indicates a Halt condition.

See Set Feature and Clear Feature for more about Remote Wakeup and Halt. All non-assigned bits are reserved.

Clear Feature

Purpose: The host requests to disable a feature on a device, interface, or endpoint.

Request number (bRequest): 0x01

Source of data: no Data stage

Data length (wLength): 0x0000

wValue: the feature to disable

wIndex: For a device feature, 0x0000. For an interface feature, the interface number. For an endpoint feature, the endpoint number.

Supported states: Default: undefined. Address: OK for address zero, endpoint zero. Otherwise the device returns a STALL. Configured: OK.

Behavior on error: If the feature, device, or endpoint specified doesn't exist, or if the feature can't be cleared, the device responds with STALL. Behavior is undefined if wLength > 0x0000.

Comments: For USB 2.0, this request can clear the DEVICE_REMOTE_WAKEUP and ENDPOINT_HALT features. The request does not clear the TEST_MODE feature.

For Enhanced SuperSpeed, this request can clear the ENDPOINT_HALT, LTM_ENABLE, U1_ENABLE, and U2_ENABLE features. (To clear the FUNCTION_SUS-PEND feature, see Set Feature.)

Clear Feature(ENDPOINT_HALT) resets a bulk, interrupt, or isochronous data toggle to DATA0 (USB 2.0) or Sequence Number to zero (Enhanced SuperSpeed) and resets an Enhanced SuperSpeed bulk endpoint's burst size.

Hubs support additional features.

See also Set Feature and Get Status.

Set Feature

Purpose: The host requests to enable a feature on a device, interface, or endpoint.

Request number (bRequest): 0x03

Source of data: no Data stage

Data length (wLength): 0x0000

wValue: the feature to enable

wIndex: The low byte equals 0x00 for a device, the interface number for an interface, or the endpoint number for an endpoint. For an Enhanced SuperSpeed FUNCTION_SUSPEND request, the high byte can request the Suspend state (bit 0 = 1) or normal operation (bit 0 = 1) and remote wakeup enabled (bit 1 = 1) or disabled (bit 1 = 0). To set the TEST MODE Feature, the high byte of wIndex = the test selector value.

Supported states: For features other than TEST_MODE: Default: undefined. Address: OK for address zero, endpoint zero. Otherwise the device returns STALL. Configured: OK. High speed must support the TEST_MODE feature in the Default, Address, and Configured states.

Behavior on error: If the endpoint or interface specified doesn't exist, the device responds with STALL.

Comments: USB 2.0 and Enhanced SuperSpeed devices may use these features: ENDPOINT_HALT applies to endpoints. Bulk and interrupt endpoints must support the Halt condition. Events that cause a Halt condition are transmission errors and the device's receiving a Set Feature request to halt the endpoint. DEVICE_REMOTE_WAKEUP applies to devices. When the host has set this feature, a device in the Suspend state can request the host to resume communications. TEST_MODE causes an upstream-facing port to enter a test mode. OTG devices use the b_hnp_enable, a_hnp_support, and a_alt_hnp_support features in role swapping. Wireless USB devices use WUSB_DEVICE.

Enhanced SuperSpeed devices can support additional features: FUNCTION_SUSPEND can place a function in the Suspend state and enable or disable remote wakeup. U1_ENABLE and U2_ENABLE enable low-power states. LTM_ENABLE enables sending Latency Tolerance Messages for power management. LDM_ENABLE is used in Precision Time Measurement. OTG devices use B3_NTF_HOST_REL and B3_RSP_ENABLE in role swapping.

Hubs support additional features.The Get Status request tells the host what features, if any, are enabled. Also see Clear Feature.

Set Address

Purpose: The host specifies an address to use in future communications with the device.

Request number (bRequest): 0x05

Source of data: no Data stage

Data length (wLength): 0x0000

wValue: new device address. Allowed values are 0x0001–0x007F. Each device on the bus, including the root hub, has a unique address.

wIndex: 0x0000

Supported states: Default, Address.

Behavior on error: not specified.

Comments: When a hub enables a port after power-up or attachment, the port uses the default address of 0x0000 until completing a Set Address request from the host.

This request is unlike most other requests because the device doesn't carry out the request until the device has completed the Status stage of the request by sending a ZLP. The host sends the Status stage's token packet to the default address, so the device must detect and respond to this packet before changing its address.

After completing this request, all communications use the new address.

A device using the default address of 0x0000 is in the Default state. After completing a Set_ Address request to set an address other than 0x0000, the device enters the Address state.

A device must send the handshake packet within 50 ms after receiving the request and must implement the request within 2 ms after completing the Status stage.

Get Descriptor

Purpose: The host requests a specific descriptor.

Request number (bRequest): 0x06

Source of data: device

Data length (wLength): the number of bytes to return. If the descriptor is longer than wLength, the device returns up to wLength bytes. If the descriptor is shorter than wLength, the device returns the entire descriptor. If the descriptor is shorter than wLength and is an even multiple of the endpoint's maximum packet size, the device returns a ZLP in response to a request for more data after the device has sent the descriptor. The host detects the end of the data on receiving either the requested amount of data or a data packet containing less than the maximum packet size (including a ZLP).

wValue: High byte: descriptor type. Low byte: descriptor index, to specify which descriptor to return when there are multiple descriptors of the same type.

wIndex: for string descriptors, Language ID. Otherwise 0x0000.

Data packet in the Data stage: the requested descriptor.

Supported states: Default, Address, Configured.

Behavior on error: A device that doesn't support the specified descriptor should return STALL.

Comments: Hosts can request the following standard descriptor types: device, device_qualifier, configuration, other_speed configuration, BOS, and string. On receiving a request for a configuration or other_speed configuration descriptor, the device should return the requested descriptor followed by all of its subordinate interface, endpoint, endpoint companion, and class-specific descriptors, up to the number of bytes requested. A class or vendor can define additional descriptors that the host can request, such as the HID-class report descriptor. See also Set Descriptor.

Set Descriptor

Purpose: The host adds a descriptor or updates an existing descriptor.

Request number (bRequest): 0x07

Source of data: host

Data length (wLength): The number of bytes the host will transfer to the device.

wValue: high byte: descriptor type. (See Get Descriptor). Low byte: a descriptor index that specifies which descriptor the device is sending when it has multiple descriptors of the same type.

wIndex: For string descriptors, Language ID. Otherwise 0x0000.

Data packet in the Data stage: descriptor length.

Supported states: Address and Configured.

Behavior on error: A device that doesn't support the request or the specified descriptor should return STALL.

Comments: This request makes it possible for the host to add new descriptors or change an existing descriptor. Few devices support this request, which can enable errant code to place incorrect information in a descriptor. See also Get Descriptor.

Get Configuration

Purpose: The host requests the value of the current device configuration.

Request number (bRequest): 0x08

Source of data: device

Data length (wLength): 0x0001

wValue: 0x0000

wIndex: 0x0000

Data packet in the Data stage: Configuration value

Supported states: Address (returns zero), Configured

Behavior on error: not specified.

Comments: A device that isn't configured returns 0x00 in the Data stage. See also Set Configuration.

Set Configuration

Purpose: The host requests the device to use the specified configuration.

Request number (bRequest): 0x09

Source of data: no Data stage

Data length (wLength): 0x0000

wValue: The low byte specifies a configuration. If the value matches a configuration supported by the device, the device implements the requested configuration. A value of 0x00 indicates not configured, and the device should enter the Address state and wait for a new Set Configuration request to be configured.

wIndex: 0x0000

Supported states: Address, Configured.

Behavior on error: If wValue isn't equal to 0x0000 or a configuration supported by the device, the device returns STALL.

Comments: After completing a Set Configuration request specifying a supported configuration, the device enters the Configured state. Many standard requests require the device to be in the Configured state. See also Get Configuration. This request resets bulk, interrupt, and isochronous data toggles to DATA0 (USB 2.0) and resets Sequence Numbers to zero (Enhanced SuperSpeed) and resets the burst size of Enhanced SuperSpeed bulk endpoints.

Get Interface

Purpose: For interfaces that have alternate, mutually exclusive settings, the host requests the currently active interface setting.

Request number (bRequest): 0x0A

Source of data: device

Data length (wLength): 0x0001

wValue: 0x0000

wIndex: interface number (bInterfaceNumber)

Data packet in the Data stage: the current setting (bAlternateSetting)

Supported states: Configured

Behavior on error: If the interface doesn't exist, the device returns STALL.

Comments: The wIndex value is the bInterfaceNumber value of an interface descriptor and indicates which interface the request applies to. In the Data stage, the device returns a bAlternateSetting value, which identifies which alternate interface setting the device is currently using. Each alternate interface has an interface descriptor and subordinate descriptors as needed. Many interfaces support only one interface setting. See also Set Interface.

Set Interface

Purpose: For interfaces that have alternate, mutually exclusive, settings, the host requests the device to use a specific interface setting.

Request number (bRequest): 0x0B

Source of data: no Data stage

Data length (wLength): 0x0000

wValue: alternate setting to select (bAlternateSetting)

wIndex: interface number (bInterfaceNumber)

Supported states: Configured

Behavior on error: If the requested interface or setting doesn't exist, the device returns STALL.

Comments: This request resets bulk, interrupt, and isochronous data toggles to DATA0 (USB 2.0) and resets Sequence Numbers to zero (Enhanced SuperSpeed) and resets the burst size of Enhanced SuperSpeed bulk endpoints. See also Get Interface.

Synch Frame

Purpose: The device sets and reports an endpoint's synchronization frame.

Request number (bRequest): 0x0C

Source of data: host

Data length (wLength): 0x0002

wValue: 0x0000

wIndex: endpoint number

Data packet in the Data stage: frame number

Supported states: Default: undefined. Address: The device returns STALL. Configured: OK.

Behavior on error: An endpoint that doesn't support the request should return STALL.

Comments: In isochronous transfers, a device endpoint may request data packets that vary in size according to a sequence. For example, an endpoint may send a repeating sequence of 8, 8, 8, 64 bytes. The Synch Frame request enables the host and endpoint to agree on which frame will begin the sequence. On receiving a Synch Frame request, an endpoint returns the number of the frame that will precede the beginning of a new sequence

This request is rarely used because there is rarely a need for the information it provides.

Set SEL

Purpose: For Enhanced SuperSpeed devices, sets system exit latencies for power management.

Request number (bRequest): 0x30

Source of data: host

Data length (wLength): 0x0006

wValue: 0x0000

wIndex: 0x0000

Contents of data packet in the Data stage: exit latency values.

Supported states: Address, Configured.

Behavior on error: A device that doesn't support the request should return STALL.

Comments: Chapter 17 has more on Enhanced SuperSpeed power management.

Set Isochronous Delay

Purpose: For Enhanced SuperSpeed devices, provides a calculated delay value in ns indicating the amount of time between when a host begins to transmit an isochronous packet and when a device begins to receive the packet.

Request number (bRequest): 0x31

Source of data: host

Data length (wLength): 0x0000

wValue: Delay (ns)

wIndex: 0x0000

Supported states: Default, Address, Configured.

Behavior on error: a device that doesn't support the request should return STALL.

Comments: the wValue field can range from 0x0000 to 0xFFFF.

Other requests

In addition to the requests defined in the USB 2.0 and USB 3.1 specifications, a device may respond to class-specific and vendor-specific control requests.

Class-specific requests

A class can define mandatory and optional requests. Class drivers on the host should support mandatory requests and may support optional requests. Some requests are unrelated to the standard requests while other requests build on standard requests by defining class-specific fields. An example of a request that's unrelated to standard requests is the Get Max LUN request supported by some mass-storage devices. The host uses this request to find out the number of logical units the interface supports. An example of a request that builds on an existing request is the Get Port Status request for hubs. This request is structured like the standard Get Status request but bits 4..0 = 00011_b indicate that the request applies to a port on a hub rather than the device, an interface, or an endpoint. The wIndex field contains the port number.

Vendor-defined requests

Implementing a vendor-defined request in a control transfer requires all of the following:

- Vendor-defined fields as needed in the Setup and Data stages of the request. Bits 6..5 in the Setup stage's data packet are set to 10_b to indicate a vendor-defined request.

- In the device, code that detects the request number in the Setup packet and knows how to respond.

- In the host, a vendor-provided device driver that supports the request. The driver can expose a function that enables applications to initiate the request.

6

Chip Choices

This chapter is a guide to selecting USB device-controller hardware. Available controllers include microcontrollers and high-end processors with built-in USB support, USB interface chips, and special-function chips. Chapter 21 discusses controllers for use in embedded hosts and OTG devices.

Components of a USB device

Every USB device must have the intelligence to detect and respond to requests and other events at the USB port. A processor with embedded firmware or an application-specific integrated circuit (ASIC) can perform these functions in a device.

Device-controller chips vary in how they implement USB communications and in how much firmware support the communications require. Some controllers require little more than the ability to access buffers to provide and retrieve USB data. Other controllers require device firmware to handle more of the protocols including managing the sending of descriptors to the host, setting data-toggle values, and ensuring that endpoints return appropriate handshake packets. In general, low-level firmware isn't portable among chips with different architectures, but chip companies provide example firmware for common tasks and applications.

Some device controllers are microcontrollers that include a processor and on-chip program and data memory or an interface to these components in external memory. Other device controllers must interface to an external processor that handles non-USB tasks and communicates with the USB controller as needed. These chips are sometimes called USB interface chips to distinguish them from microcontrollers with USB capabilities.

For high-volume products and products that require fast performance, an option is a custom-designed ASIC. Several sources offer synthesizable VHDL and Verilog source code for ASICs that function as USB controllers.

Inside a USB 2.0 controller

A typical USB 2.0 controller contains a USB transceiver, a serial interface engine, buffers to hold USB data, and registers to store configuration, status, and control information relating to USB communications.

The transceiver

The USB transceiver is the hardware interface between the device's USB connector and the circuits that control USB communications. The transceiver is typically embedded in the controller chip, but some controllers allow interfacing to an external transceiver. Another term for the transceiver is PHY (physical layer).

The serial interface engine

The circuits that interface to the transceiver form a unit called the serial interface engine (SIE). The SIE handles sending and receiving data in transactions. The SIE doesn't interpret or use the data but just places provided data on the bus and stores any data received. A typical SIE does all of the following:

- Detects incoming packets.
- Sends packets.
- Detects and generates Start-of-Packet, End-of-Packet, Reset, and Resume signaling.
- Encodes and decodes data for the bus using NRZI encoding with bit stuffing.
- Checks and generates CRC values.
- Checks and generates Packet IDs.
- Converts between USB's serial data and parallel data in registers or memory.

The UTMI+ Low Pin Interface (ULPI) is an 8- or 12-line interface that connects a PHY to an SIE. The interface, a product of the non-profit ULPI Working Group, evolved from the previous USB 2.0 Transceiver Macrocell Interface (UTMI) and UTMI+ interfaces.

Buffers

USB controllers use buffers to store received data and data that's ready to transmit on the bus. In some controllers, such as PLX Technology's USB 3380, a processor accesses the buffers by reading and writing to registers, while others, such as Cypress Semiconductor's EZ-USB series, reserve a portion of data memory for the buffers.

To enable faster transfers, some chips have double buffers that can store two full sets of data in each direction. While one block is transmitting, firmware can write the next block of data into the other buffer so the data is ready to go as soon as the first block finishes transmitting. In the receive direction, the extra buffer enables a new transaction's data to arrive before the firmware has retrieved the data from the previous transaction. The hardware automatically switches, or ping-pongs, between the two buffers. Some controllers, such as the Cypress EZ-USB FX2LP, support quadruple buffers, while the SuperSpeed Cypress EZ-USB FX3 can use configurable data buffers of any available size in system memory.

Configuration, status, and control Information

USB controller chips typically contain registers that hold information about what endpoints are enabled, the number of bytes received, the number of bytes ready to transmit, Suspend-state status, error-checking information, and other status and control information. The number of registers, their contents, and how to access the registers vary with the chip architecture. These differences are one reason why low-level firmware for USB communications isn't portable between chip families.

Clock

USB communications require a timing source, typically provided by a crystal oscillator. Because USB's low speed allows more variation in clock speed, low-speed devices can sometimes use a less expensive ceramic resonator. Some controllers have on-chip oscillators and don't require an external timing source.

Other device components

In addition to a USB interface, the circuits in a typical USB device include a CPU, program and data memory, other I/O interfaces, and other features such as timers and counters. These circuits may be in the controller chip or separate components.

CPU

The CPU, or processor, may use a general-purpose architecture such as the 8051 or ARM, or the CPU may have an architecture developed specifically for USB applications. An interface-only USB controller can communicate with any CPU that has a compatible interface.

Program memory

The program memory holds the code that the CPU executes, including code for USB communications and whatever other tasks the chip is responsible for. This memory may be in the microcontroller or in a separate chip.

The program storage may use ROM, flash memory, EEPROM, MTP memory, or RAM. All except RAM (unless battery-backed) are nonvolatile: the memory retains its data after powering down. Chips that can access memory off-chip may support a MB or more of program memory.

Another name for the code stored in program memory is firmware. The term suggests that the memory is nonvolatile and not as easily changed as program code that can be loaded into RAM, edited, and re-saved on disk. This book uses the term firmware to refer to a controller's program code, with the understanding that the code may reside in a variety of memory types, some more volatile than others.

ROM (read-only memory) must be mask-programmed at the factory and can't be erased. ROM is practical only for product runs in the thousands.

Flash memory is electrically erasable and thus is popular for use during project development and for final code storage in low-volume projects or devices that might require firmware updates in the field. Current flash-memory technology enables 10,000 erase/reprogram cycles. Wear leveling and other memory-management techniques can dramatically extend the life of a memory block.

EEPROM (electrically erasable programmable ROM) tends to have longer access times than flash memory but is useful for storing data that changes occasionally such as configuration data. Cypress' EZ-USB controllers can store firmware in EEPROM and load the firmware into RAM on powering up. EEPROMs are available with parallel interfaces and with synchronous serial interfaces such as Microwire, I2C, and SPI. Current EEPROM technology enables around 1 million erase/reprogram cycles.

MTP (multi-time-programmable) memory is a newer technology similar to flash memory and is most cost-effective for small amounts of data such as configuration data.

RAM (random-access memory) can be erased and rewritten endlessly, but the stored data disappears when the chip powers down. RAM can store program code if using battery backup or if the code loads from a PC into RAM on each power up. Cypress Semiconductor's EZ-USB controllers can use RAM for program storage with special hardware and driver code that loads code from the host computer into the chip on power up or attachment. RAM loaded in this way has no limit on the number of erase/rewrite cycles. For battery-backed RAM, the limit is the battery life. Access time for RAM is fast.

Data memory

Data memory provides temporary storage during program execution. The contents of data memory may include data received from the USB port, data to be sent to the USB port, values for use in calculations, or anything else the chip needs to remember or keep track of. Data memory is RAM.

Other I/O

To do useful work, virtually every USB controller has an interface to the world outside itself in addition to the USB port. An interface-only chip must have a local bus or other interface to the device's CPU. Most chips also have a series of general-purpose input and output (I/O) pins that can connect to other circuits. A chip may have built-in support for other interfaces, such as an asynchronous serial interface for RS-232, synchronous serial interfaces, or Ethernet. Some chips have dedicated interfaces for special purposes such as accessing drives or audio or video components.

Other features

A device-controller chip may have features such as hardware timers, counters, analog-to-digital and digital-to-analog converters, and pulse-width-modulation (PWM) outputs. Just about anything that you can find in a general-purpose microcontroller is available in a USB device controller.

Simplifying device development

Project development will be easier and quicker if you can find a controller chip with all of the following:

- A chip architecture and compiler you're familiar with.
- Excellent hardware documentation.
- Well-documented, bug-free example firmware for an application similar to yours.
- A development system that enables easy downloading and debugging of firmware.

Also helpful is the ability to use a class driver included with the operating system or a well-documented and bug-free driver provided by the chip company or another source.

These are not trivial considerations. The right choices will save many hours and much aggravation.

Device requirements

In selecting a device controller for a project, these are some of the areas to consider.

Bus speed. A device's rate of data transfer depends on the supported speeds on the device and bus, the transfer type. and how busy the bus is. As a device designer, you don't control how busy a user's bus will be, but you can select a speed and transfer type that give the best possible performance for your application.

If a product requires only low-speed interrupt and control transfers, a low-speed chip might save money in circuit-board design, components, and cables. But low-speed devices can transfer only up to eight data bytes per transaction, and the USB specification limits the guaranteed bandwidth for an interrupt endpoint to 800 bytes per second, much less than the bus speed of 1.5 Mbps. Plus, implementing low speed's slower edge rates increases the manufacturing cost of low-speed controller chips, so you may find a full-speed chip that can do the job at the same or lower price.

Compared to low and full speeds, circuit-board design for high-speed and Enhanced SuperSpeed devices is more critical and can add to the cost of a product. If possible, devices that support high speed should also support full speed in case they are attached to a USB 1.1 host or hub. Enhanced SuperSpeed devices should also support a USB 2.0 speed, and SuperSpeedPlus devices must support SuperSpeed.

Endpoints. Each endpoint address supports a transfer type and direction. A device that uses only control transfers needs just the default endpoint. Interrupt, bulk, or isochronous transfers require additional endpoint addresses. Not all chips support all transfer types. Not every controller supports the maximum possible number of endpoint addresses, but few devices need the maximum.

Firmware upgrades. To enable firmware upgrades in the field, a device should store program code in flash memory, in EEPROM, or in RAM loaded from the host on attachment. The USB specification for the device firmware upgrade class defines a protocol for loading firmware from a host to a device. Chapter 7 has more about this class.

Cables. One reason why mice are almost certain to be low-speed devices is the less stringent cable requirements that allow thinner, more flexible cables. However, a cable on a low-speed device has a maximum length of 3 m, while full- and high-speed cables (except those with Micro-B or USB Type-C connectors) can be 5 m.

Other needs. Additional considerations are the amount and type of other I/O, the size of program and data memory, on-chip timers, and other special features that a particular application might require.

Documentation and example code

Most chip companies supplement their data sheets with technical manuals, application notes, example code, and other documentation. The best way to get a head start on writing firmware is to begin with example code.

Example code can be useful even if it doesn't perfectly match your desired application. Enumeration code is useful for any device and also provides a model for performing control transfers for other purposes. Get Descriptor can serve as a model for other control read transfers. Set Address can serve as a model for control write transfers with no Data stage. Example code for control write transfers with a Data stage is harder to find. The only standard, not-class-specific USB request with a host-to-device Data stage is the rarely supported Set Descriptor. One possible source for example code is the communications device class's Set Line Coding request, where the host sends serial-port parameters in the Data stage.

From the firmware's point of view, bulk and interrupt transfers are identical (except for Enhanced SuperSpeed's support for streams in bulk transfers) so code for either type of transfer can serve as a model for any firmware that uses bulk or interrupt transfers. For example, HID-class code for exchanging reports via interrupt transfers can serve as a model for bulk transfers in a different device type.

Chip and tool vendors vary in the amount and quality of documentation and example code provided. You might also find code examples from other sources.

Host driver

If your device fits a class supported by the operating system(s) that the device's USB hosts use, you don't need to write or obtain a device driver. For example, applications can access a HID-class device using standard API functions that communicate with the HID drivers included with Windows.

Some chip companies provide a generic driver that you can use to exchange data with devices. Cypress Semiconductor, Microchip Technology, and Silicon Laboratories all provide general-purpose drivers. Devices for Windows systems also have the option of using Microsoft's generic WinUSB driver. Windows, Linux, and Mac OS can use the open-source libusb generic driver. Chapter 7 and Chapter 8 have more about classes and device drivers.

Development boards

Ease of debugging also makes a big difference in how easy it is to get a project up and running. Products that can help include development boards and software offered by chip companies and other sources. A protocol analyzer can save much debugging time. Chapter 18 has more about protocol analyzers.

Boards from chip companies

Chip manufacturers offer development boards and debugging software to make it easier for developers to test and debug new designs (Figure 6-1). A development

Figure 6-1. This PICDEM Explorer board supports a variety of microcontrollers available on Plug-in Modules (PIMs) that attach to a socket on the board.

board enables you to load a program from a PC into a chip's program memory or circuits that emulate the chip's hardware.

Typical debugging software provided with development boards is a monitor program that runs on a PC and enables you to control program execution and view the results. Common features include the ability to step through a program, set breakpoints, and view the contents of the chip's registers and memory. You can run the monitor program and a test application at the same time. You can see exactly what happens inside the chip when it communicates with your application.

USB's timing requirements can limit what you can do with breakpoints. For example, if you halt execution during enumeration, the host will give up trying to communicate, and you'll need to restart the enumeration process. But even so, a monitor program can provide a useful window to the firmware in action. Microchip's MPLAB X IDE is an example of host software that supports debugging functions.

JTAG ports can enable monitoring and controlling of components during development.

The Silicon Laboratories C8051F34x controllers include a dedicated 2-wire debugging interface that uses no additional memory or port bits on the chip. With these chips, you can debug without needing to assign other chip resources to debugging.

Boards from other sources

Inexpensive printed-circuit boards from a variety of vendors can serve as an alternative to the development kits offered by chip companies. You can also use these boards as the base for one-of-a-kind or small-scale projects, saving the time and expense of designing and making a board for the controller chip.

If you just want to access I/O pins, a board programmed with firmware that supports I/O can give a quick start. Phidgets Inc. is one source for modules that have analog and digital I/O ports, driver support, and example code in a variety of program languages (Figure 6-2). The company offers a variety of ready-to-use I/O devices including sensors, relays, switches, motors, remote control, RFID modules, and displays, or you can interface your own components to the I/O ports.

Phidgets use the HID-class host driver included in virtually all OSes. For Windows, Phidgets provides a DLL that manages communications with the HID driver and exports functions for accessing the modules. Similar driver support is available for Apple OS, Linux, and mobile OSes. Example applications in over a dozen programming languages show how to communicate with the modules, source code included.

One of many modules offered, the 1018 Phidget Interface Kit board has 8 digital inputs, 8 analog inputs, and 8 digital outputs. The board contains a Cypress CY7C64215 enCoRe III full-speed USB controller, a Microchip MCP23S17 16-Bit I/O expander, and a Microchip MCP3008 10-bit ADC.

Another option for digital I/O is the modules from FTDI described later in this chapter.

Some development boards can store and run firmware that you provide, much like manufacturers' development boards but with advantages that may include lower cost, a more compact design, or other features.

The BeagleBone Black (Figure 6-3) is an example of a low-cost, community-supported development platform that can run Linux and other OSes. The board uses a Texas Instruments Sitara ARM Cortex-A8 processor, which has two high-speed OTG ports. On the BeagleBone Black board, one OTG port is configured as a dedicated host port with a Standard-A receptacle, and one OTG port is configured as a dedicated device port with a Mini-B receptacle.

The Linux gadget driver can configure the device port to perform a specific function. The Multifunction Composite Gadget (g_multi) implements a composite USB device

Figure 6-2. The Phidget Interface Kit (top) attaches to a USB host that can monitor and control I/O modules and other components (bottom).

with mass storage, virtual serial port, and Ethernet bridge functions. Chapter 21 has more about host ports on embedded systems.

USB microcontrollers

If you have a favorite CPU family, the chances are good that a USB-capable variant is available. For common applications such as keyboards, drives, and interface converters, application-specific controllers include hardware to support a particular application. Chapter 7 has more about controllers for specific applications.

The following descriptions of a selection of USB controllers with embedded CPUs will give an idea of the range of chips available. The chips described are a sampling, and

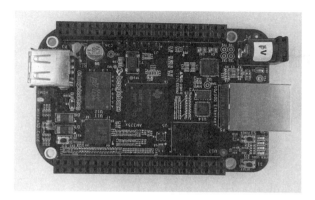

Figure 6-3. The BeagleBone Black can function as a USB device and as a USB host.

new chips are being released all the time, so for any new project, check the latest offerings.

Microchip PIC18

Microchip Technology's PIC microcontrollers are popular due to their low cost, wide availability, large selection, good performance, and low power consumption. One of Microchip's many offerings is the PIC18F46J50 low- and full-speed controller.

Architecture

The PIC18F46J50 is a member of Microchip's high-performance, low-cost, 8-bit PIC18 series. Firmware resides in 64 KB of flash memory. The chip also has 3.8 KB of RAM. A bootloader routine can upgrade firmware via the USB port.

The chip has 35 I/O pins with capabilities that include a 13-channel 10-bit analog-to-digital converter, two Enhanced USART modules, two synchronous serial ports that can be configured to use I²C or SPI, an 8-bit parallel port, a charge time measurement unit (CTMU) for touch sensing, and two modules that can function as capture or compare registers or pulse-width-modulation (PWM) outputs, and two analog comparators.

The USB module and CPU can use separate clock sources, enabling the CPU to use a slower, power-saving clock.

USB controller

The USB controller supports all four transfer types and up to 30 endpoint addresses plus the default endpoint. The endpoints share 3.8 KB of memory designated as USB RAM. Transfers can use double buffering. For isochronous transfers, USB data can transfer directly to and from a streaming parallel port.

For each enabled endpoint address, the firmware must reserve RAM for a data buffer and a Buffer Descriptor (BD). The Buffer Descriptor consists of four registers. Firmware can access the registers' contents as a structure, a single 32-bit value, or a byte array (Listing 6-1).

The status register contains status information and the two highest bits of the endpoint's byte count. The byte-count register plus the two bits in the status register contain the number of bytes sent or ready to send in an IN transaction or the number of bytes expected or received in an OUT transaction. The address-low and address-high registers contain the starting address for the endpoint's data buffer in USB RAM.

The microcontroller's CPU and the USB SIE share access to the buffers and buffer descriptors. A UOWN bit in the buffer descriptor's status register determines whether the CPU or SIE owns a buffer and its buffer descriptor. The SIE has ownership when the endpoint has data that is ready to transmit or the endpoint is waiting to receive data on the bus. When the SIE has ownership, firmware shouldn't attempt to access the buffer or buffer descriptor except to read the UOWN bit. When readying an endpoint to perform a transfer, the last operation the firmware should perform is to update the status register to set UOWN, which passes ownership to the SIE. When a transaction completes, the SIE clears the UOWN bit, passing ownership back to the CPU for firmware control.

Each endpoint number also has a control register that can enable a control endpoint, an IN endpoint, an OUT endpoint, or a pair of IN and OUT endpoints with the same endpoint number. Other bits in the register can stall the endpoint and disable hand-shaking (for isochronous transactions).

Additional registers store the device's bus address and status and control information for USB communications and interrupts.

This chip is just one example of dozens of Microchip's microcontrollers with USB support. Also available are 16- and 32-bit controllers and controllers with different options for I/O and memory.

Programming support

The Microchip Libraries for Applications include USB Framework firmware libraries and demo projects for USB communications. The firmware is written for Microchip's MPLAB XC compilers. The Framework handles general USB tasks and some class-specific tasks. The files may require only minor changes and additions for a specific application. Provided example projects include joystick, keyboard, mouse, custom HID, mass storage, virtual serial port, audio, and vendor-defined device. You can run the example code on Microchip development boards or other hardware.

```
// A Buffer Descriptor holds 4 bytes.
// This union enables firmware to access the bytes in different ways.

typedef union __BDT
{
    struct                  // Four 8-bit variables.
    {
        BD_STAT STAT;       // Status byte structure
        BYTE CNT;           // Byte count, bits 0-7
        BYTE ADRL;          // Endpoint address in RAM, low byte
        BYTE ADRH;          // Endpoint address in RAM, high byte
    };

    struct                  // The endpoint address in RAM
    {
        unsigned :8;
        unsigned :8;
        BYTE* ADR;          // Address pointer
    };

    DWORD Val;              // One 32-bit value.

    BYTE v[4];              // 4-byte array.

} BDT_ENTRY;
```

Listing 6-1: Firmware for Microchip's controllers can use structures to represent the contents of an endpoint's Buffer Descriptor. (Part 1 of 2)

```
// This union represents the Buffer Descriptor Table's 8-bit status
// register in a variety of ways.

typedef union _BD_STAT
{
    BYTE Val;           // Byte variable

    struct              // Bit values if the CPU owns the buffer.
    {
        unsigned BC8:1;         // Byte count, bit 8
        unsigned BC9:1;         // Byte count, bit 9
        unsigned BSTALL:1;      // Buffer stall enable
        unsigned DTSEN:1;       // Data toggle synchronization enable
        unsigned INCDIS:1;      // Address increment disable
        unsigned KEN:1;         // Buffer descriptor keep enable
        unsigned DTS:1;         // Data toggle synchronization value
        unsigned UOWN:1;        // USB ownership
    };

    struct              // Bit values if the USB module owns the buffer.
    {
        unsigned BC8:1;         // Byte count, bit 8
        unsigned BC9:1;         // Byte count, bit 9
        unsigned PID0:1;        // PID, bit 0
        unsigned PID1:1;        // PID, bit 1
        unsigned PID2:1;        // PID, bit 2
        unsigned PID3:1;        // PID, bit 3
        unsigned :1;
        unsigned UOWN:1;        // USB Ownership
    };

    struct              // The 4-bit PID
    {
        unsigned :2;
        unsigned PID:4;
        unsigned :2;
    };
} BD_STAT;
```

Listing 6-1: Firmware for Microchip's controllers can use structures to represent the contents of an endpoint's Buffer Descriptor. (Part 2 of 2)

A free edition of the compiler offers unrestricted use but with optimization features enabled for 60 days only. Other C compiler options are the CCS C compiler from CCS, Inc. and the HI-TECH C compiler from HI-TECH Software.

Cypress EZ-USB

Controllers in Cypress Semiconductor's EZ-USB family support a variety of options for storing firmware, including the ability to load firmware from the host on every power-up or attachment.

Architecture

The EZ-USB controllers include the full/high speed FX2LP and the SuperSpeed FX3. The FX2LP uses an 8051-compatible instruction set, while the FX3 has a 32-bit ARM9 core.

In EZ-USB controllers, all of the code and data memory is in internal RAM. The chips have no non-volatile memory for storing vendor firmware. However, the controllers can load firmware from external memory or a USB host. If no external source of firmware is provided, the controller enumerates as a vendor-defined device that uses a host driver provided by Cypress to download firmware to the device.

The FX3's USB port can operate as a device port that supports SuperSpeed, high speed, and full speed or as an OTG port that also supports high, full, and low speeds when operating as a host.

The controller has a GPIF II general programmable interface that can communicate with an external processor, FPGA, or image sensors. The interface can use an 8-, 16-, 24-, or 32-bit data bus. The chip also has UART, I2C, SPI, and I2S (Integrated Interchip Sound) serial interfaces and 256 KB or 512 KB of RAM for firmware and data.

The FX2LP supports full and high speeds, has 16 KB of RAM, and doesn't have the host/OTG port or I2S and SPI interfaces.

USB controller

The EZ-USB family's many options for storing firmware make the chips very flexible but also make the USB architecture and protocols more complex.

On the FX3, on power-on reset or device reset, three PMODE pins determine the source of firmware to load and run. Depending on the states of the pins, the controller's embedded bootloader may attempt to read firmware from the GPIF II, I2C, SPI, or USB interface (Table 6-1). For example, an external processor or FPGA may provide firmware via the GPIF II interface, a serial EEPROM containing firmware may use I2C, a serial EEPROM or flash memory may use SPI, or a USB host may send firmware to the USB port.

Table 6-1: The EZ-USB FX3's PMODE inputs determine the source for loading firmware.

PMODE Bit			Boot Source
2	**1**	**0**	
float	0	0	GPIF II, Sync ADMux
float	0	1	GPIF II, Async ADMux
float	1	1	USB
float	0	float	GPIF II, Async SRAM
float	1	float	I2C, on failure, USB
1	float	float	I2C
0	float	1	SPI, on failure, USB

To load firmware using USB, the FX3's embedded bootloader first enumerates the device as a full- or high-speed USB device with a Cypress Vendor ID and Product ID. To load vendor firmware, a driver provided by Cypress uses vendor-defined requests to initiate sending new firmware to the device. Additional requests cause the device firmware to emulate detach and reattach by electrically disconnecting and reconnecting to the bus. On reconnecting, the device enumerates using the newly loaded firmware.

The firmware must be embedded in a defined structure that begins with the signature "CY" in ASCII text and contains a checksum and other information.

The GPIF II interface can use any of three modes. The synchronous ADMux interface uses a clock input to the FX3 to control synchronous data transfers. The asynchronous ADMux interface (multiplexed address and data lines) uses read and write strobes rather than a clock to control data transfers. The asynchronous SRAM interface uses the industry-standard SRAM bus.

The FX2LP supports fewer firmware sources: the controller can load firmware from external EEPROM or a USB host or use internal ROM. Instead of using PMODE pins, the controller determines the source of the firmware by examining the initial bytes in an external EEPROM, if present, and the state of the chip's EA (external access) input.

Programming support

Firmware development for the FX3 can use the free, open-source GNU Toolchain and Eclipse IDE. The FX3 software development kit (SDK) includes libraries of firmware APIs and sample code for many USB device classes. The libraries support USB operation as a device, host, and OTG device. For efficient task management, the libraries incorporate functions of the Express Logic ThreadX real-time OS (RTOS), which user

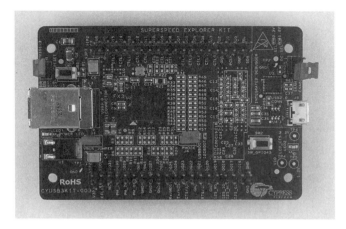

Figure 6-4. Cypress Semiconductor's FX3 SuperSpeed Explorer Kit is an inexpensive way to get started with SuperSpeed projects.

programs can use at no additional cost. A JTAG port enables debugging with an external JTAG probe.

The SDK's Control Center application enables loading firmware and programming EEPROMs for both the FX3 and FX2LP.

For creating host applications, the FX3 SDK provides a generic USB device driver, a .NET managed class library, and sample code. The SDK has similar host support for Linux and Apple OS.

An excellent guide to programming the FX3 is *SuperSpeed Device Design By Example* by John Hyde. Cypress offers an inexpensive FX3 SuperSpeed Explorer kit (Figure 6-4).

For the FX2LP, Cypress provides a firmware framework that uses a C compiler and IDE from Keil Software. For host applications to access the device, the support is similar to what is available for the FX3.

ARM processors

For high-end applications, many developers turn to ARM processors, which have a fast, efficient, 32- and 64-bit RISC architecture. ARM Holdings licenses intellectual property (IP) cores to chip companies for use in their chips. The ARM family includes a range of cores with different capabilities.

The Texas Instruments Sitara ARM Cortex-A8 in the BeagleBone Black and the Cypress EX-USB FX3 controller described above are examples of ARM-based USB device controllers.

Another example is Atmel's AT91SAM7S321. The chip has a full-speed USB device port, 32 KB of flash memory for firmware, and 8 KB of RAM. Other I/O includes an 8-channel, 10-bit ADC and synchronous and asynchronous serial ports. Programming can use the free GNU GCC compiler or a compiler from IAR Systems. NXP Semiconductors also has ARM-based device controllers.

Controllers that interface to CPUs

With a controller that interfaces to an external CPU, just about any CPU can communicate over USB. Interface chips communicate with the CPU over a local data bus that may use a serial or parallel interface. For fast transfers with external memory, a chip may support direct memory access (DMA), which can read or write blocks of data without CPU intervention. An interrupt pin can signal the CPU when the controller has received USB data or is ready for new data to send.

Table 6-2 compares a selection of interface chips. The following descriptions give an idea of the range of products available. The chips described are a sampling, and new chips are being released all the time, so for new projects, check the latest offerings.

Maxim MAX3420E

Maxim's MAX3420E is a full-speed USB interface chip with hardware support for SPI communications with an external CPU.

Architecture

The CPU that interfaces to the MAX3420E must have an SPI master interface, which can be hardware supported or implemented entirely in firmware. The SPI bus has clock and select outputs on the CPU and either one data line in each direction or one bidirectional data line. An interrupt output on the MAX3420E notifies the CPU when a USB event has occurred that requires the CPU's attention.

The CPU communicates with the MAX3420E by accessing a series of registers that configure the chip's operation and enable reading and writing to USB endpoints and general-purpose I/O bits. To access a register, the CPU writes a command byte on the SPI bus. The command byte contains the register number and direction of data flow. Following the command byte, the CPU clocks one or more data bytes to or from the specified register.

The chip has four general-purpose inputs and four general-purpose outputs.

USB controller

In addition to control endpoint zero, the chip supports two 64-byte double-buffered interrupt or bulk OUT endpoints, two 64-byte double-buffered interrupt or bulk IN

Table 6-2: These USB interface chips interface to an external CPU.

Company	Chips	CPU Interface	Bus Speed
FTDI	FT231X	Asynchronous serial	Full
	FT240X	Parallel	Full
	FT2232H, FT4232H	Asynchronous serial and parallel	High, full
Maxim	MAX3420E	SPI	Full
PLX Technology	NET2282	PCI	High, full
	USB 3380	PCI Express	SuperSpeed, high, full

endpoints, and one additional 64-byte interrupt or bulk IN endpoint. A separate 8-byte buffer holds Setup data received in control transfers.

Programming support

Maxim provides example C code for communicating with the MAX3420E over SPI, including enumerating and performing other USB transfers.

An evaluation board connects to a Keil Software board that has a Philips LPC2138 ARM7 processor with two SPI ports. The Keil ULINK JTAG unit enables loading code and debugging. Keil provides a free evaluation version of the compiler. The evaluation board also contains a MAX3421E USB host and peripheral controller, which can use the same setup for testing and debugging.

PLX Technology USB 3380

For SuperSpeed devices, PLX Technology has the USB 3380 PCI Express Gen 2 to USB 3.0 SuperSpeed peripheral controller. As the name suggests, the controller converts between the PCI Express I/O bus and USB.

Architecture

The PCI Express interface has differential pairs for data and a reference clock. The USB 3380 uses internal RAM to store data received on the PCI Express interface for transmitting via USB and data received on the USB interface for transmitting via PCI Express. A DMA controller manages the flow of data between RAM and the PCI Express interface. A series of registers contain USB configuration data and status and control information. The chip also has four general-purpose I/O pins.

The chip can interface to an external processor and can also operate standalone using the embedded 8051 microcontroller. An interface to serial EEPROM enables storing configuration data and device firmware.

For USB 2.0 designs, PLX Technology's 2282 PCI to high-speed USB 2.0 controller has a similar architecture and can use the same software as the 3380.

USB controller

The USB 3380's USB controller supports SuperSpeed, high speed, and full speed. In addition to endpoint zero and eight endpoint addresses for general device use, six endpoint addresses have dedicated functions for accessing the chip's registers.

Programming support

An SDK includes example C firmware for several USB device types. An evaluation board, configured as a PCI Express Gen 2 card, contains a USB 3.0 device port.

FTDI interface chips

Future Technology Devices International (FTDI) offers USB controllers that are useful for devices accessed as USB virtual serial ports as well as other devices that don't fit a defined USB class and that use only bulk or isochronous transfers.

Architecture

FTDI's chips take a different approach to USB design. The chips handle enumeration and other USB communications entirely in hardware. An external processor uses a UART, I²C, SPI, or parallel interface to connect to the chip.

For example, the FT231X USB UART chip interfaces to an asynchronous serial (UART) port at the device's CPU. The FT231X handles all of the USB-specific protocols. To send data to the host computer, the CPU's firmware writes data to the FT231X's asynchronous serial port. On receiving the data, the FT231X makes the data available for reading by the host on the USB port. When the host computer sends data to the FT231X's USB port, the FT231X makes the data available at the asynchronous serial port, where the CPU can read it.

Additional FTDI chips function in a similar way but support other interfaces to the CPU. On the FT240X USB FIFO, the CPU interface is a bidirectional parallel port. Other controllers support I²C and SPI. All of these controllers support full-speed USB, can detect a USB charging port, and can switch from data-transfer to charging mode.

The FT2232H is a high-speed version with two ports that can each function as a UART or parallel port, and the FT4232H is high speed with four ports.

USB controller

Both the FT231X and FT240X have a 512-byte transmit and receive buffers. The chips use bulk transfers by default with one endpoint for each direction. A driver for isochronous transfers is also available.

For easy prototyping, FTDI has modules (Figure 6-5) that each consist of a circuit board with a controller chip, USB connector, and related circuits mounted on a dual in-line package (DIP) that fits breadboards or PC boards.

Figure 6-5. For easy prototyping with FTDI's controllers, use modules such as the UMFT231XA USB to full-handshake UART development module and the UMFT240XA USB to 8-bit 245 FIFO development module.

Silicon Laboratories offers a similar series of controllers and also has a HID-class USB to UART bridge and a USB to I²S digital audio bridge controller.

Programming support

On the host computer, the chips use a driver provided by FTDI. The driver enables applications to access a chip as a USB virtual serial port or by using a driver-defined API.

Many USB/RS-232 adapters contain FTDI chips. If you have an existing device that communicates with a PC using RS-232, the FT231X offers a quick way to upgrade to USB. In most cases, using an FT231X to convert an RS-232 device to USB requires no changes to device firmware or host application software. The host accesses the device in the same way as if the device connected via an RS-232 serial port.

Host software can access an FT240X as a USB virtual serial port even though the chip doesn't have an asynchronous serial port. The host doesn't need to know what lies beyond the device's USB port.

FTDI's controllers contain on-chip EEPROM or MTP memory that can store vendor-specific values for a Vendor ID, Product ID, serial-number string, other descriptive strings, and values that specify whether the device is bus- or self-powered. The controller uses default values for items that don't have stored user values. FTDI provides a utility that programs the information into the on-chip memory. By default, the chips use FTDI's Vendor ID and Product ID. On request, FTDI will grant the right for your device to use their Vendor ID with a Product ID that FTDI assigns to you, or you can use your own Vendor ID and Product ID.

The chips also support a Bit Bang mode, where the chip operates as a standalone USB device without requiring a connection to a device CPU. A host computer can monitor and control I/O bits on the chip to control LEDs, relays, or other circuits and read switches and logic-gate outputs.

7

Device Classes

This chapter is an introduction to the defined USB classes, including how to determine if a new design can fit a defined class.

Purpose

Most USB devices have much in common with other devices that perform similar functions. Mice send data about mouse movements and button clicks. Drives transfer files. Printers receive data to print and inform the host when they're out of paper.

When devices provide or request similar services, it makes sense to define protocols for all of the devices to use. A class specification can serve as a guide for programmers who write device firmware or drivers for host systems. OSes can provide class drivers, eliminating the need for vendors to provide drivers for devices in supported classes.

When a device in a supported class has features or abilities not included in a class driver, a device often can use the class driver along with a vendor-provided filter driver to support the added features and abilities.

If a device fits a class that the target OS doesn't support, the device vendor can provide a class driver and device firmware that is compatible with the class. Then if a future edition of the operating system supports the class, the device is likely to be able to use the system-provided driver.

Approved specifications

The USB-IF sponsors device working groups that develop class specifications that cover most common device functions. Table 7-1 shows the classes with specifications approved by the USB-IF. The hub class is defined in the main USB 2.0 and USB 3.1 specifications rather than in a separate document. Every host must support the hub class because the host requires a root hub to do any communications.

Some classes are defined by companies or organizations other than the USB-IF. For example, Bluetooth USB specifications are available from the Bluetooth Special Interest Group. Chapter 4 listed all of the class codes that can appear in device and interface descriptors.

Windows provides drivers for many classes. As OS and class specifications have evolved, the number of supported classes has increased, and the support for many classes has become more robust. For some classes, such as the device firmware upgrade class, Windows hasn't provides a driver even though the specification has been available for many years.

Elements of a class specification

A class specification defines the number and type of required and optional endpoints for devices in the class. The specification may also define formats for data to be transferred including application data and status and control information. Some class specifications also define uses for the data being transferred. For example, the HID class has usage tables that define how to interpret data sent by keyboards, mice, and joysticks. Some classes use USB to transfer data in a format defined by another specification. An example is the SCSI commands used by mass-storage devices.

A class specification can define values for fields in standard descriptors and may also define class-specific descriptors, interfaces, and control requests. For example, the device descriptor for a hub includes a bDeviceClass value of 0x09 to indicate that the device belongs to the hub class. The hub must have a class-specific hub descriptor with bDescriptorType = 0x29. Hubs must also support class-specific requests. When the host sends a Get Port Status request to a hub with a port number in the Index field, the hub responds with status information for the port. A class may also require a device to support specific endpoints or comply with tighter timing for standard requests. Chapter 4 showed how the device or interface descriptor declares a class.

Table 7-1: These device types have approved USB class specifications.

Class	Class Code	Descriptor Where Class Is Declared	Windows Support?
Audio	0x01	Interface	yes
Audio/Video	0x21	Interface	no
Billboard	0x11	Device or BOS	no
Communication (CDC)	0x02	Device or interface	yes
Content security	0x0D	Interface	no
Device firmware upgrade (DFU)	0xFE, bInterfaceSubclass = 0x01	Interface (subclass of Application Specific Interface)	no
Hub	0x09	Device	yes
Human interface (HID)	0x03	Interface	yes
IrDA bridge	0xFE, bInterfaceSubclass = 0x02	Interface (subclass of Application Specific Interface)	no
Mass storage	0x08	Interface	yes
Personal healthcare	0x0F	Interface (preferred) or device	no
Printer	0x07	Interface	yes
Smart card	0x0B	Interface	yes
Still image capture	0x06	Interface	yes
Test and measurement	0xFE, bInterfaceSubclass = 0x03	Interface (subclass of Application Specific Interface)	no
Video	0x0E	Interface	yes

Defined classes

The following sections introduce the classes defined by the USB-IF. The descriptions can serve as a guide to deciding whether a new design can use a defined class and if so, what device controllers to consider and what host drivers are available. For more information about a class, consult the class specification.

Audio

The audio class encompasses devices that send or receive encoded voice, music, or other sounds. Audio functions are often part of a device that also supports video, storage, or other functions. Devices in the audio class can use isochronous transfers for audio streams or bulk transfers for data encoded using the MIDI (Musical Instrument Digital Interface) protocol.

Version 2.0 of the audio class specification retains much of the framework defined in version 1.0 but is not backwards compatible. In other words, an audio 2.0 device can't use an audio 1.0 host driver. Version 2.0 adds full support for high speed, requires use of the interface association descriptor, and defines new capabilities and controls.

Documentation

The audio specification consists of the main class specification and supporting documents for audio data formats, terminal types, and MIDI devices. The MIDI standard is available from the MIDI Manufacturers Association (*midi.org*).

Overview

Each audio function in a device has an Audio Interface Collection that consists of one or more interfaces. The interfaces include one AudioControl (AC) interface, zero or more AudioStreaming (AS) interfaces and zero or more MIDIStreaming (MS) interfaces (Figure 7-1). In other words, every Audio Interface Collection has an AudioControl interface, while AudioStreaming and MIDIStreaming interfaces are optional.

In audio 2.0 devices, an interface association descriptor (IAD) specifies the interfaces that belong to a collection. In audio 1.0 devices, a class-specific AC interface header descriptor contains this information.

An AudioControl interface can enable accessing controls such as volume, mute, bass, and treble. An AudioStreaming interface transfers audio data in isochronous transfers and may also carry control data related to the streaming data. A MIDIStreaming interface transfers MIDI data.

MIDI is a standard for controlling synthesizers, sound cards, and other electronic devices that generate music and other sounds. A MIDI representation of a sound includes values for pitch, length, volume, and other characteristics. A pure MIDI hard-

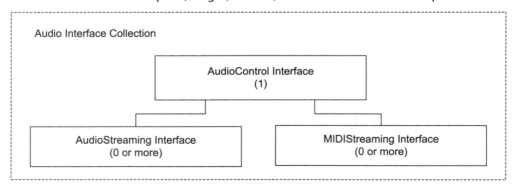

Figure 7-1. Each audio function has an Audio Interface Collection that contains one or more interfaces.

ware interface carries asynchronous data at 31.25 kbps. A USB interface that carries MIDI data uses the MIDI data format but instead of using an asynchronous interface, the MIDI data travels on the bus in bulk transfers.

A device can have multiple Audio Interface Collections that are active at the same time, with each collection controlling an independent audio function.

Descriptors

Each audio interface uses standard and class-specific descriptors to enable the host to learn about the interface, its endpoints, and what kinds of data the endpoints transfer. The specification defines a variety of class-specific descriptors that provide information specific to audio functions. Audio 1.0 endpoint descriptors have two additional bytes that follow the 7 bytes defined for endpoint descriptors in the USB 2.0 specification. Audio 2.0 endpoint descriptors use the standard 7-byte structure.

Class-specific requests

The audio class provides optional class-specific requests for setting and getting the state of audio controls and exchanging generic data.

Chips

Some USB controllers have built-in support for audio functions. The support may include codec functions, analog-to-digital converters (ADCs), digital-to-analog converters (DACs), and support for Sony/Philips Digital Interface (S/PDIF) encoding for transmitting audio data in digital format.

Texas Instruments has a variety of USB audio chips. The PCM2903C is a stereo audio codec with a full-speed USB port and 16-bit ADC and DAC and S/PDIF support. The chip has an AudioControl interface, an AudioStreaming interface for each direction, and a HID interface that reports the status of three parameters. The USB protocol controller requires no vendor-provided firmware. The PCM2705C is a 16-bit stereo DAC with a full-speed USB interface. The chip can accept data sampled at 48, 44.1, and 32 kHz and supports digital attenuation and mute. The TUSB3200A USB streaming controller contains an 8052-compatible microcontroller that supports up to seven IN endpoints and seven OUT endpoints. The audio support includes a codec port interface, a DMA controller with four channels for streaming isochronous data packets to and from the codec port, and a phase lock loop (PLL) and adaptive clock generator (ACG) to support synchronization modes.

Host support

Windows supports USB Audio 1.0 and Microsoft's Universal Audio Architecture (UAA), which provides audio support and defines requirements for devices that will use the OS's audio drivers. All devices that are compatible with the USB audio class system driver (*usbaudio.sys*) are UAA compliant.

For programmers, the Microsoft Media Foundation provides APIs for programming audio functions. For programming high-performance games, XAudio2 has APIs for generating audio with low latency. Both Media Foundation and XAudio2 are included in the Windows SDK and use unmanaged code.

XMOS's xCORE-USB microcontroller family supports USB Audio 2.0, and XMOS provides a driver for Windows. Thesycon Systemsoftware & Consulting GmbH (yes, that spelling is correct!) has a USB Audio 2.0 Class Driver for Windows.

Audio/Video

The audio/video (AV) class specifies methods for communicating with USB video displays and other devices that have audio and video functions. Uses for the AV class include connecting monitors to PCs and smart phones and connecting media players and smart phones to TVs.

Documentation

The specification's documents include an AV function definition, format definitions, and an XML schema that defines the format for the AV Description Document.

Overview

USB has had a defined audio class since 1998 and a video class since 2003. The AV class specification, released in 2011, encompasses both audio and video.

The class has a modular architecture that can accommodate basic, low-resolution devices as well as devices that are feature-rich and high resolution. The class supports robust synchronizing of audio and video and compressed and uncompressed data.

SuperSpeed, and especially SuperSpeedPlus, have the bandwidth to support displays with resolutions comparable to what is available with dedicated video interfaces such as DisplayPort and HDMI.

An AV-class display appears to the USB host as a USB/DisplayPort or USB/HDMI adapter with audio routed through the USB audio class using dedicated endpoints. The host driver can support content-security functions using high-bandwidth digital content protection (HDCP).

Every AV device has an XML document called the AV Description Document (AVDD). The AVDD conforms to the AVSchema, which is an XML document that specifies the syntax and structure of the AVDD's contents. XML is better suited to the long, complex descriptors of AV devices compared to the format used by other USB descriptors.

The AVDD contains AVControls that provide access to the device's descriptors and audio, video, and other functions. Each AVControl has one or more Properties that the host may access. For example, an AVControl for a video function might provide Properties for brightness and contrast.

To get and set Properties and receive notifications, the host issues AVControl Sequences. Most AVControl Sequences have two phases: the host sends a Command Message, and the device executes the received command and returns a Response Message. Notify Control Sequences have a single phase where the device sends a notification to the host. AVControl Sequences use bulk transfers.

Descriptors

Like other USB devices, an AV device returns a set of descriptors in response to Get Descriptor requests. However, in the AV class, these descriptors typically support a subset of device capabilities and are intended for use only during boot-up or other times when the complete AV driver isn't available. The specification calls these descriptors Legacy View descriptors.

A device declares an AV function in one or more interface descriptors. The AVControl interface descriptor is the top-level descriptor for the AV function. Interface descriptors for AV devices don't conform to the standard interface descriptor format and thus use class-specific codes in the bDescriptorType field. In the AVControl interface descriptor, bDescriptorType = 0x21 to specific the AVCONTROL_IF descriptor type. An interface association descriptor associates any additional interfaces with the function.

The device's complete descriptor set is in the AVDD. Every AV device has an AVDD Info Control with a Property that holds the length of the AVDD and an AVDD Content Control with a Property that holds the complete AVDD in XML format.

To retrieve the AVDD, the host first issues a Get Control Sequence to the AVDD Info Control, and the device returns the length of the AVDD. The host then issues a Get Control Sequence to the AVDD Content Control, and the device returns the AVDD in XML format.

Class-specific requests

The class has no class-specific control requests.

Chips

Fresco Logic has device controller silicon with AV class support.

Host support

Windows doesn't provide a driver for the AV class. A source for USB computer monitors is Lilliput Electronics Co., Ltd, which provides a vendor-specific driver.

Billboard

For a device that has no USB function but supports Alternate Modes as defined in the *USB Power Delivery Rev. 2.0, v1.0* specification, the billboard class enables the host to identify the device.

Documentation

The class specification is *Universal Serial Bus Device Class Definition for Billboard Devices*. Revision 1.0 was released in 2014.

Overview

A device that supports one or more Alternate Modes and doesn't have another USB function must support the billboard class to identify the device. A billboard device can be a USB device or a Device Container that supports one or more USB functions and a billboard function.

A standalone billboard device has only a control endpoint.

Chapter 20 has more about Alternate Modes.

Descriptors

A billboard capability descriptor lists supported Alternate Modes and may provide a string for each mode. The descriptor is a device capability descriptor that follows a BOS descriptor (see Chapter 4).

Class-specific Requests

The class has no class-specific requests.

Chips

Just about any general-purpose device controller that supports *USB Power Delivery Rev. 2.0, v1.0* can support the class. The device must have a USB Type-C connector.

Host Support

The host must support *USB Power Delivery Rev. 2.0, v1.0* protocols and the device's Alternate Mode(s).

Communications

The communications device class (CDC) encompasses a wide range of devices that perform telecommunications, networking, and other communication functions including virtual serial ports.

Communications data typically uses an application-specific protocol such as V.250 for modem control or Ethernet for network data.

Documentation

Documentation for the communications class consists of a main class specification and additional specifications for some subclasses.

A derivative of the Hayes AT modem command set is codified in the V.250 *serial asynchronous automatic dialing and control* recommendation available from the International Telecommunication Union (*itu.int*). The Ethernet standard, IEEE 802.3, is available from the IEEE (*ieee.org*). The Remote Network Driver Interface Specification (RNDIS) defines a protocol for using USB and other buses to configure network interfaces and carry Ethernet-framed data. Remote NDIS is based on NDIS, which defines a protocol to manage communications with network adapters and higher-level drivers. NDIS and Remote NDIS are from Microsoft.

Overview

A communications device is responsible for device management, call management if needed, and data transmission. Device management includes controlling and configuring a device and notifying the host of events. Call management involves establishing and terminating phone calls or other connections. Not all devices require call management. Data transmission is the sending and receiving of application data such as phone conversations or files sent over a modem or network.

The communications device class supports a number of models for communicating.

These models are targeted mainly for phone communications:

- Public switched telephone network (PSTN) devices include voice modems, telephones, and serial-emulation (virtual serial port) devices. Some devices that exchange Ethernet-framed data use the PSTN model with a vendor-specific protocol.

- Asynchronous transfer mode (ATM) devices include ADSL modems.

- ISDN devices include terminal adapters for ISDN lines.

- Wireless mobile communications (WMC) devices include cell phones and other multi-function devices.

These models are targeted for network communications:

- Ethernet emulation model (EEM) devices exchange Ethernet-framed data. EEM devices use a single pair of bulk endpoints. Each EEM packet is preceded by a 2-byte header. EEM isn't intended for devices that use routing or Internet connectivity.

- Ethernet control model (ECM) devices, which include cable modems, exchange Ethernet-framed data. Class-specific requests and notifications manage the interface.

- Network control model (NCM) devices build on ECM with improvements that support higher data rates. NCM devices can transfer multiple Ethernet frames in a single bulk transfer.
- Mobile broadband interface model (MBIM) devices extend NCM with support for more efficient transfers. Instead of Ethernet frames, MBIM devices transfer raw IP packets. The model is intended for mobile broadband networking devices. With alternate interface settings, a device can support both NCM and MBIM.

Notifications, which announce events such as ring detect and network connect or disconnect, can travel to the host in an interrupt or bulk pipe. Most devices use interrupt pipes. Each notification consists of an 8-byte header followed by a variable-length data field. Some device types don't require notifications.

Descriptors

A CDC device's descriptors can specify the communications class at the device or interface level. If specified at the device level, all of the device's interfaces belong to the communications function. In the device descriptor, bDeviceClass = 0x02 to specify CDC (Figure 7-2). In a composite device, an interface association descriptor (IAD) specifies which interfaces belong to the communication function.

Every communications device must have an interface descriptor with bInterfaceClass = 0x02 to indicate a Communication interface that handles device management and call management. The bInterfaceSubClass field specifies a communication model. Table 7-2 shows defined values for the subclasses. The bInterfaceProtocol field can name a protocol supported by a subclass. Table 7-3 shows defined values for protocols.

Following the Communication interface descriptor is a class-specific Functional descriptor consisting of a Header Functional descriptor followed by one or more descriptors (also called Functional descriptors) that provide information about a communication function. Table 7-4 shows defined values for these descriptors.

One of these descriptors, the Union Functional descriptor, has the special function of defining a relationship among interfaces that form a functional unit. The descriptor designates one interface as the master or controlling interface, which can send and receive certain messages that apply to the entire group. For example, a Communication interface can be a master interface for a group consisting of a Communication interface and a Data interface. The interfaces that make up a group can include communications-class interfaces as well as other related interfaces such as audio or HID.

If the Communication interface has a bulk or interrupt endpoint for event notifications, the endpoint has a standard endpoint descriptor.

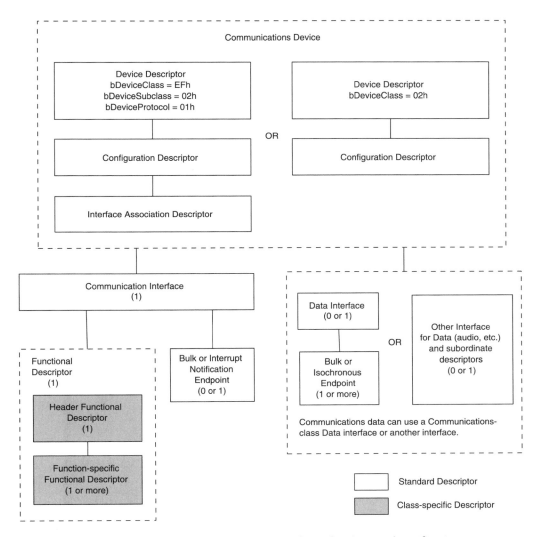

Figure 7-2. A communications device provides interfaces for data and notifications.

A communication-class device can also have an interface descriptor with bInterface-Class = 0x0A to indicate a Data interface. A Data interface can have bulk or isochronous endpoints for carrying application data. Each of these endpoints has a standard endpoint descriptor. Some devices use other class or vendor-specific interfaces for application data. For example, a phone might use an audio interface to send and receive voice data.

Table 7-2: In the Communication interface descriptor for a communication device, the bInterfaceSubClass field indicates the communication model the device supports. Information source: *Universal Serial Bus Class Definitions for Communications Devices Revision 1.2.*

bInterface-SubClass	Model	Application
0x00	RESERVED	none
0x01	PSTN Direct Line Control Model	Telephone modem with the host providing any data compression and error correction. The device or host may provide modulation/demodulation of the modem data
0x02	PSTN Abstract Control Model	Telephone modem with the device providing any data compression, error correction, and modulation/demodulation of the modem data
0x03	PSTN Telephone Control Model	Telephone
0x04	ISDN Multi-Channel Control Model	ISDN device with multiple, multiplexed channels
0x05	ISDN CAPI Control Model	ISDN device with support for COMMON-ISDN-API (CAPI) commands and messages
0x06	ECM	Cable modem
0x07	ATM	ADSL modem
0x08	WMC wireless handset control model	Logical handset
0x09	WMC device management model	AT commands only
0x0A	WMC mobile direct line model	Migrates some functions of wireless terminal adapters to the USB host
0x0B	WMC OBEX model	Data exchange protocol
0x0C	EEM	Device that exchanges Ethernet-framed data
0x0D	NCM	Device that benefits from fast transfers of Ethernet-framed data
0x0E	MBIM	Mobile broadband networking device
0x0F–0x7F	Reserved	Future use
0x80–0xFE	Vendor specific	Vendor defined

A virtual serial-port device, also called virtual COM-port device, provides serial port emulation. Applications can use serial-port functions to access the device in the same way as if the device connected directly to an RS-232 port on the PC. The device may also have an asynchronous serial interface that communicates with other circuits, but the device doesn't have to have an asynchronous interface at all. The USB host doesn't know how the device uses the virtual serial port data.

Table 7-3: In the descriptor for a Communication interface, the bInterfaceProtocol field can indicate a protocol the communications model supports. Information source: *Universal Serial Bus Class Definitions for Communications Devices Revision 1.2.*

Code	Description
0x00	Class-specific protocol not required
0x01	AT commands (specified in ITU V.250)
0x02–0x06	AT commands used by WMC devices
0x07	Ethernet Emulation Model (EEM)
0x08–0xFD	Future use
0xFE	External protocol. The commands are defined by a command set functional descriptor.
0xFF	Vendor specific

A virtual serial port device can use bInterfaceSubClass = 0x02 to specify the abstract control model and bInterfaceProtocol = 0x01 to specify AT commands. For compatibility with the Windows driver, the interface should specify this subclass even if the device doesn't use AT commands. The Communication interface has an interrupt endpoint, and the Data interface has a bulk endpoint for each direction.

For improved performance, some virtual serial-port devices use vendor-specific drivers and thus don't belong to the communication device class. My book *Serial Port Complete* has more about USB virtual serial-port devices.

A CDC device that functions as a Remote NDIS device consists of a Communication interface and a Data interface. In the Communication interface, bInterfaceSubClass = 0x02 to specify the abstract control model and bInterfaceProtocol = 0xFF to specify a vendor-specific protocol. The Communication interface has an interrupt endpoint, and the Data interface has two bulk endpoints. Each endpoint has an endpoint descriptor.

Class-specific requests

Class-specific requests get and set status and control information. The supported requests vary with the subclass and the device.

Chips

Many communications devices, including virtual serial-port devices, can use just about any general-purpose device controller that supports full speed or higher. FTDI's USB UART controllers, introduced in Chapter 6, can implement virtual serial ports but don't belong to the communications class because the controllers use a vendor-provided driver.

Table 7-4: A Functional descriptor consists of a Header functional descriptor followed by one or more function-specific descriptors. Information source: *Universal Serial Bus Class Definitions for Communications Devices Revision 1.2.*

bInterfaceSubClass	Functional Descriptor Type
0x00	Header
0x01	Call Management
0x02	Abstract Control Management
0x03	Direct Line Control Management
0x04	Telephone Ringer
0x05	Telephone Call and Line State Reporting Capabilities
0x06	Union
0x07	Country Selection
0x08	Telephone Operational Modes
0x09	USB Terminal
0x0A	Network Channel Terminal
0x0B	Protocol Unit
0x0C	Extension Unit
0x0D	Multi-channel Management
0x0E	CAPI Control Management
0x0F	Ethernet Networking
0x10	ATM Networking
0x11	Wireless Handset Control
0x12	Mobile Direct Line Model (MDLM)
0x13	MDLM Detail
0x14	Device Management Model
0x15	OBEX
0x16	Command Set
0x17	Command Set Detail
0x18	Telephone Control Model
0x19	OBEX Service Identifier
0x1A–0x7F	Reserved (future use)
0x80–0xFE	Vendor specific

SMSC/Microchip Technology and Asix Electronics Corporation have USB Ethernet bridge controllers that convert between USB and Ethernet at speeds up to Gigibit Ethernet.

Host support

The Windows modem driver (*usbser.sys*) is compatible with modems and other devices that use the abstract control model, including virtual serial port devices. Under Windows, a CDC virtual serial port must have an INF file that contains the device's Vendor ID and Product ID. Chapter 9 has an example.

Windows provides drivers for remote NDIS and WMC. Windows 8 added an MBIM driver.

Vendors that offer drivers for subclasses that Windows doesn't support or enhanced drivers for other subclasses include Belcarra Technologies Corporation, Jungo Ltd., MCCI, and Thesycon.

Content security

The content security class specifies ways to control access to files, music, video, or other data transmitted on the bus. The class supports two content security methods (CSMs): digital transmission content protection (DTCP) and high-bandwidth digital content protection (HDCP).

Documentation

The class documentation consists of a framework specification and an implementation specification for each content security method. The DTCP specification and license information are available from the Digital Transmission Licensing Administrator (*dtcp.com*). The HDCP specification and license information are available from Digital Content Protection LLC (*digital-cp.com*).

Overview

The class defines a protocol for activating and deactivating a content security method and for associating a content security method to a channel. A channel represents a relationship between an interface or endpoint and one or more CSMs. Only one CSM can be active on a channel at a time.

DTCP and HDCP prevent unauthorized copying of audio and video content via USB and other buses. CSM-2 implements DTCP, which a content provider can use to specify whether copying is allowed, identify authorized users, and specify an encryption method. CSM-5 implements HDCP, which uses an authentication protocol that establishes shared secrets that prevent eavesdropping by unauthorized devices.

Content providers who wants to use DTCP or HDCP must sign a license agreement and pay an annual—not trivial—fee.

Descriptors

In an interface descriptor, bInterfaceClass = 0x0D declares the content security class. The class has class-specific descriptors, and each CSM defines a string descriptor.

Class-specific requests

Two class-specific requests apply to all CSM interfaces. The Get_Channel_Settings request enables the host to learn what CSM is assigned to a channel. The Set_Channel_Settings request enables the host to assign a CSM to a channel or deactivate a previously assigned CSM. Each CSM has additional control requests.

Chips

For a device using content security, the choice of a USB controller depends mainly on the capabilities needed to exchange the content being protected. Adding a content-security function requires only the occasional use of the control endpoint and for CSM-2, two interrupt endpoints.

Host support

Windows doesn't include a driver for the content security class.

Device firmware upgrade

The device firmware upgrade (DFU) class defines a protocol for sending firmware enhancements and patches to a device. After receiving the firmware upgrade, the device re-enumerates using its new firmware.

Documentation

The *Device Firmware Upgrade* specification defines the class.

Overview

To perform a firmware upgrade as described in the specification, a device must have two complete sets of descriptors: run time and DFU mode. The run-time descriptors are for normal operation and include descriptors that inform the host that the device is capable of firmware upgrades. The DFU-mode descriptors are for use when a device is upgrading its firmware. For example, a keyboard using its run-time descriptors enumerates as a HID-class device and sends keypress data to the host. During a firmware upgrade, the device suspends normal operations as a keyboard and uses the DFU-mode descriptors to communicate with the DFU driver on the host.

The upgrade process has four phases. In the device-enumeration phase, the device sends its run-time descriptors to the host and operates normally. In the reconfiguration phase, the host sends a Dfu_Detach request and then resets and re-enumerates the device, which returns its DFU-mode descriptors. In the transfer phase, the host sends the firmware upgrade to the device. The manifestation phase begins when the host has completed the transfer.

When the device has finished loading the new firmware, device settings determine whether the host resets the device or the device initiates a reset by emulating detach and re-attach. On re-enumerating, the device uses its new, upgraded firmware. During the upgrade process, the device transitions through defined states.

An upgrade file stored on the host contains the firmware for the upgrade followed by a DFU suffix value that the host can use to help ensure that the firmware is valid and appropriate for a particular device. The suffix contains an error-checking value, a signature consisting of the ASCII text *DFU*, and optional values for the Vendor ID, Product ID, and product release number to identify devices the firmware is appropriate for. The suffix is for the host's use only; the host doesn't send the suffix to the device.

To ensure that the host will load the correct driver for the firmware-upgrade process, the device should use different Product IDs in its run-time and DFU-mode device descriptors.

DFU communications use only the control endpoint.

Descriptors

The DFU function is defined at the interface subclass level. In a device that supports DFU, both the run-time and DFU-mode descriptors include a standard interface descriptor with bInterfaceClass = 0xFE to indicate an Application Specific class and bInterfaceSubClass = 0x01 to indicate the device firmware upgrade class. In DFU mode, the DFU interface must be the only active interface in the device.

Both descriptor sets include a Run-time DFU Functional descriptor that specifies whether the device can communicate on the bus immediately after the manifestation phase, how long to wait for a reset after receiving a DFU_Detach request, and the maximum number of bytes the device can accept in a control write transfer during a firmware upgrade.

Class-specific requests

The class defines seven control requests that control the DFU process and request status information.

Chips

The choice of USB controller depends mainly on the requirements of the device in run-time mode. The device must have enough memory and other resources to store and implement the upgraded firmware. STMicroelectronics has a Windows driver and firmware examples for use with STMicroelectronics' microcontrollers.

Host support

Windows doesn't provide a driver for this class.

Human interface

The human interface device (HID) class includes keyboards, pointing devices, and game controllers. For all of these devices, the host receives data that corresponds to human input such as keypresses and mouse movements. The host must respond quickly enough so users don't notice a delay between an action and the expected response.

Barcode readers can function as HID keyboards with the barcode data emulating keypresses. Other devices with HID interfaces include uninterruptible power supply (UPS) units that can inform the host computer of power loss and configuration utilities for display monitors. Some devices that perform vendor-specific functions can also use the HID class.

All HID data travels in reports, which are structures with defined formats. Usage tags in a report tell the host or device how to use received data. For example, a Usage Page value of 0x09 indicates a button, and a Usage ID value tells which button, if any, was pressed.

To support keyboards and mice, Windows and other OSes have included HID drivers from the earliest editions that have supported USB. For this reason, the HID class has been popular for devices with vendor-specific functions. A HID can exchange data for any purpose but can use only control and interrupt transfers.

Documentation

In addition to the main HID specification, several documents define Usage-tag values for different device types. The *HID Usage Tables* document has values for keyboards, pointing devices, various game controllers, displays, telephone controls, and more.

These device types have their own documents:

Class Definition for Physical Interface Devices (PID) defines values for force-feedback joysticks and other devices that require physical feedback in response to inputs.

The *Monitor Control* specification defines values for user controls and power management for display monitors. The HID interface controls the display's settings only, not the images to display.

Usage Tables for HID Power Devices defines values for UPS devices and other devices where the host monitors and controls batteries or other power components.

Point of Sale (POS) Usage Tables defines values for barcode readers, weighing devices, and magnetic-stripe readers.

Additional Usage tables are available from the Gaming Standards Association (*gamingstandards.com*) and in Intel's *Open Arcade Architecture Device Data Format Specification* (*usb.org*).

In the main HID specification, the main change from version 1.0 to 1.1 was enabling the host to send reports in interrupt OUT transfers as allowed by the USB 1.1 specification. In a HID 1.0 interface, the host must send all reports in control transfers.

Chapters 11–13 have more information about HID device and host programming.

Overview

HIDs communicate by exchanging data in reports using control and interrupt transfers. Input and Output reports can use control or interrupt transfers. Feature reports use control transfers. A report descriptor defines the size of each report and Usage values for the report data.

Descriptors

In a HID's interface descriptor, bInterfaceClass = 0x03. The bInterfaceSubClass field indicates whether the HID supports a boot protocol, which a host can use instead of the report protocol defined in the device's report descriptor. Mice and keyboards support boot protocols to enable using the device before the host has loaded the full HID drivers.

Following the interface descriptor is a class-specific HID descriptor, which contains the size of the report descriptor. The report descriptor contains information about the data in the HID reports. An optional, rarely used, physical descriptor can describe the part(s) of the human body that activate a control.

Class-specific requests

The HID class specification defines six control requests to enable sending and receiving reports, setting and reading the idle rate (how often the device sends a report if the data is unchanged), and setting or reading the currently active protocol (boot or report). To obtain a report descriptor or physical descriptor, the host sends a Get Descriptor request to the interface with the high byte of wValue set to 0x22 to request a report descriptor or 0x23 to request a physical descriptor.

Chips

For devices with a human interface, low speed is fast enough to act on received user input with no detectable delay. Some HIDs use low speed because the device needs a flexible or inexpensive cable. A HID can use any speed, however.

Alcor Micro Corporation is a source for controllers with support for interfacing to keyboard matrixes. Cypress Semiconductor's CY7C638xx series supports both USB and PS/2 interfaces to make it easy to design a dual-interface keyboard or mouse.

Code Mercenaries offers programmed chips for use in pointing devices, keyboards, and joysticks. The MouseWarrior series has interfaces for sensors and buttons and supports USB, PS/2, asynchronous serial, and Apple Desktop Bus (ADB). The KeyWarrior series supports USB, PS/2, and ADB and has interfaces to keyboard matrixes and optional support for keyboard macros. The JoyWarrior series supports a variety of game-controller inputs. Phidgets modules, described in Chapter 6, use the HID driver for sensors, motor control, and other functions.

Host support

To communicate with vendor-defined HIDs, applications can use API functions and .NET classes. To send and receive reports, applications can use .NET's FileStream class, ReadFile and WriteFile, and API functions in the HIDClass Support Routines.

For system keyboards and pointing devices, Windows has exclusive access to Input and Output reports. Attempts to retrieve the reports via API functions trigger the error message *Access Denied*. Applications typically don't need to read the reports that describe keypresses and mouse movements and button clicks. Instead, the operating system reads the reports, and applications use higher-level methods to access the data. For example, a button on a form in a .NET application has a click event that can contain code to execute when a user clicks the button. If a system has multiple keyboards or pointing devices, the application treats them all as a single virtual keyboard or pointing device.

Other options for accessing HIDs include DirectX's DirectInput and the Raw Input API. DirectInput provides fast, more direct access to keyboard, mouse, and game-controller data. Raw input offers a way to read HID data, including keyboard and mouse data, from specific devices, including a specific keyboard when multiple keyboards are attached.

IrDA bridge

The IrDA (Infrared Data Association) interface defines hardware requirements and protocols for exchanging data over short distances via infrared energy. A USB IrDA bridge converts between USB and IrDA data and enables a host to use USB to monitor, control, and exchange data over an IrDA interface.

Documentation

The specification for USB IrDA bridges is *IrDA Bridge Device Definition*. The IrDA specifications are available from *irda.org*.

Overview

The data in an IrDA link uses the Infrared Link Access Protocol (IrLAP), which defines the format of the IrDA frames that carry data, addresses, and status and control information. The IrLAP Payload consists of the address, control, and optional information, or data, fields in an IrLAP frame. In addition to the IrLAP Payload, each frame contains an error-checking value and markers for the beginning and end of the frame.

A USB IrDA bridge uses bulk pipes to exchange data with the host. The host and bridge place status and control information in headers with formats defined in the IrDA bridge specification. On receiving data from the IrDA link, the IrDA bridge extracts the IrLAP Payload, adds a header, and passes the data and header to the host. The header can contain values for the IrDA link's Media_Busy and Link_Speed parameters. On receiving IrDA data from the host, the IrDA bridge removes the header added by the host. The header can specify new values for Link_Speed and the number of beginning-of-frame markers. The bridge then places the IrDA Payload in an IrDA frame for transmitting.

Descriptors

An IrDA-bridge function is defined at the interface subclass level. In the interface descriptor, bInterfaceClass = 0xFE to indicate an application-specific interface and bInterfaceSubclass 0x02 to indicate an IrDA bridge device. A class-specific descriptor contains IrDA-specific information such as the maximum number of bytes in an IrDA frame and supported baud rates.

Class-specific requests

The class defines five control requests:

Request	bRequest	Description
Receiving	0x01	Is the device currently receiving an IrLAP frame?
Check_Media_Busy	0x03	Is infrared traffic present?
Set_IrDA_Rate_Sniff	0x04	Accept frames at any speed or at a single speed.
Set_IrDA_Unicast_List	0x05	Accept frames from the named addresses only.
Get_Class_Specific_Descriptors	0x06	Return the class-specific descriptor.

Chips

To support the IrDA bridge function, a device must have a USB port with bulk endpoints and an IrDA interface. USB controllers can interface to IrDA transceivers and encoder/decoder circuits via asynchronous serial ports. The Texas Instruments TUSB3410 is an 8052 microcontroller with a full-speed USB port and on-chip IrDA encoder/decoder for serial communications via an external IrDA transceiver.

Host support

Windows supports IrDA via the *irda.sys* driver and the *irsir.sys* miniport driver for UART-based adapters but doesn't provide a driver for the USB IrDA bridge function.

Mass storage

The mass storage class is for devices that support a file system for storing data. The class includes hard drives as well as CD, DVD, and flash-memory drives. Cameras can use the mass-storage class to enable accessing picture files in a camera's memory.

Under Windows, devices that use the mass-storage driver appear as drives in Windows Explorer, and the file system enables users to copy, move, and delete files in the devices.

Mass-storage communications is a complex topic. My book *USB Mass Storage* has more about USB protocols, file systems, and the SCSI commands that access storage media.

Documentation

The USB mass-storage specifications include an overview and separate documents for individual protocols and features.

The bulk-only transport (BOT) specification defines a protocol supported by most mass-storage devices. The release of USB 3.0 prompted the development of new protocols to take advantage of Enhanced SuperSpeed's dual simplex interface. The *USB Attached SCSI (UAS)* standard from *t10.org* defines a transport protocol that offers faster mass-storage transfers at SuperSpeed and improved efficiency at lower speeds. The USB-IF's *USB Attached SCSI Protocol (UASP)* specifies how to implement the UAS standard.

The *Lockable Storage Devices Feature Specification* defines a protocol to address security and privacy concerns for media contents. With host support, a lockable storage device can require a user-provided passphrase before allowing a host to access the device's media.

Each mass-storage media type uses an industry-standard command-block set to enable controlling devices and reading status information.

Generic SCSI media uses the mandatory commands from *SCSI Primary Command (SPC) Set* and *SCSI Block Command (SBC) Set* from *t10.org*.

Drives with a Serial ATA (SATA) interface can use a bridge controller to communicate over USB.

Overview

Mass-storage devices use bulk transfers to exchange data. Control transfers send class-specific requests and can clear Stall conditions on bulk endpoints. For exchanging other information, virtually all devices use the BOT protocol.

In the BOT protocol, a successful data transfer has two or three stages: command transport, data transport (if needed), and status transport. In the command-transport

Table 7-5: The CBW contains a command block and other information about the command.

Name	Bits	Description
dCBWSignature	32	The value 0x43425355, which identifies the structure as a CBW.
dCBWTag	32	A tag that associates this CBW with the CSW the device will send in response.
dCBWDataTransferLength	32	The number of bytes the host expects to transfer in the data-transport stage.
bmCBWFlags	8	Specifies the direction of the data-transport stage. Bit 7 = 0 for an OUT (host-to-device) transfer. Bit 7 = 1 for an IN (device-to-host) transfer. All other bits are zero. If there is no data-transport stage, bit 7 is ignored.
Reserved	4	Zero
bCBWLUN	4	For devices with multiple LUNs, specifies the LUN the command block is directed to. Otherwise the value is zero.
Reserved	3	Zero
bCBWCBLength	5	The length (1–16) of the command block in bytes
CBWCB	128	The command block for the device to execute.

stage, the host sends a command in a structure called a Command Block Wrapper (CBW). In the data-transport stage, the host or device sends the requested data. In the status-transport stage, the device sends status information in a structure called a Command Status Wrapper (CSW). Some commands have no data-transport stage.

Table 7-5 shows the fields in the CBW. The meaning of the command-block value in the CBWCB field varies with the command set specified by the interface descriptor's bInterfaceSubClass field.

On receiving a CBW, a device must check that the structure is valid and has meaningful content. A CBW is valid if it is received after a CSW or reset, has 31 bytes, and has the correct value in dCBWSignature. The contents are considered meaningful if no reserved bits are set, bCBWLUN contains a supported LUN value, and bCBWCBLength and CBWCB are valid for the interface's subclass.

Table 7-6 shows the fields in the CSW. On receiving a CSW, the host must check that the structure is valid and has meaningful content. A CSW is valid if it has 13 bytes, has the correct value in dCSWSignature, and has a dCSWTag value that matches dCBWTag of a corresponding CBW. The contents are considered meaningful if bCSWStatus equals 0x02 or if bCSWStatus equals either 0x00 or 0x01 and dCSWDataResidue is less than or equal to dCBWDataTransferLength.

Table 7-6: The CSW contains status and related information about a command.

Name	Bits	Description
dCBWSignature	32	The value 0x53425355, which identifies the structure as a CSW.
dCBWTag	32	The value of the dCBWTag in a CBW received from the host.
dCSWDataResidue	32	For OUT transfers, the difference between dCBWDataTransferLength and the number of bytes the device processed. For IN transfers, the difference between dCBWDataTransferLength and the number of bytes the device sent.
bCSWStatus	8	0x00 = command passed 0x01 = command failed 0x02 = phase error

Descriptors

In an interface descriptor, bInterfaceClass = 0x08 specifies the mass-storage class.

The bInterfaceSubClass field specifies the supported command-block set. Most new designs should set the field to 0x06 (generic SCSI media). The host then determines the specific device type by issuing a SCSI INQUIRY command. The device's response specifies a peripheral device type (PDT). The SCSI Primary Commands (SPC) specification defines PDT codes. The code for hard drives and flash drives is 0x00. The bInterfaceProtocol field indicates the supported transport protocol. Most new designs should set the field to 0x50 (bulk only).

Every BOT mass-storage device must have a serial number in a USB string descriptor. The serial number must be at least 12 digits using Unicode characters in the range 0–9 and A–F. The final 12 digits must be unique to the Vendor ID and Product ID pair. A serial number enables the operating system to retain properties such as the drive letter and access policies after a user moves a device to another port or attaches multiple devices with the same Vendor ID and Product ID.

A device that supports BOT or UAS must have a bulk endpoint for each direction.

Lockable storage devices have additional descriptors to support the locking capability.

Class-specific requests

The BOT protocol has two defined control requests: Bulk Only Mass Storage Reset (reset the device) and Get Max Lun (get the number of logical units, or partitions, that the device supports). All other commands and status information travel in bulk transfers.

Lockable storage devices support additional requests for locking functions.

Chips

The device controller must have a bulk endpoint for each direction and sufficient memory for the needed storage. Genesys Logic; LucidPort Technology, Inc.; Prolific Technology; Texas Instruments, and VIA Labs, Inc have USB/SATA bridge controllers.

Host support

Windows supports BOT and bInterfaceSubClass codes 0x02, 0x05, and 0x06. The USB storage port driver (*usbstor.sys*) manages communications between the lower-level USB drivers and the Windows storage-class drivers. When a device is formatted using a supported file system, the operating system assigns a drive letter to the device and the device appears in Windows Explorer.

Windows 8 and higher have USB 3.0 UASP drivers for use with PCs and devices that support UASP.

One point of confusion relating to the mass-storage support under Windows is the difference between removable devices and removable media. All USB drives are removable devices because they're easily attached and detached from the PC. A removable device may have removable or non-removable media. CD and DVD drives have removable media. A hard drive has non-removable media because you can't easily remove the disk from the drive. Windows Autoplay applies to devices with removable media. Autoplay enables the operating system to run a program, play a movie, or perform other actions when a disk or other removable media is inserted. To support AutoPlay, some devices with non-removable media declare themselves to be devices with removable media.

Personal healthcare

The personal healthcare device class encompasses devices that help to maintain health and wellness, manage disease, and enable independent living for the elderly. Devices in the class include heart-rate and blood-pressure monitors, glucose meters, pulse oximeters, motion sensors, and pill monitors.

Documentation

The class doesn't define protocols for data or messaging. Instead, devices may use data and messaging standards defined in the ISO/IEEE 11073-20601 Base Exchange Protocol.

Overview

A device may send data that is episodic (at irregular or infrequent intervals) or continuous. A device may collect and store data before transmitting the data to the host, and a device may collect data when detached from the host. For example, a jogger might wear a monitor while out for a run and upload the data on returning home.

Devices may support host-to-device communications to receive configuration data and other episodic data from a host.

Descriptors

The preferred location for the class code is in the interface descriptor, but declaring the class in the device descriptor is allowed. The function must have at least one bulk endpoint in each direction. An interrupt IN endpoint and additional endpoints are optional. Several class-specific descriptors provide class-specific information.

Class-specific requests

Set Feature and Clear Feature requests can turn on and off the class-specific Meta-Data Message Preamble feature. A Get Status request can request a bitmap of endpoints that have data.

Chips

Just about any device that is full speed or higher can support the required endpoints.

Host support

Windows doesn't provide a driver for this class.

Printer

The printer class is for devices that convert received data into text, images, or both on paper or other media. The most basic printers print lines of text in a single font. Most laser and inkjet printers understand one or more page description languages (PDLs) and can print text in any font as well as images.

Documentation

The USB Printing Devices specification defines protocols for printers of all types. The IEEE-1284 standard (*ieee.org*) describes the interface used by parallel-port printers and defines the format for the Device IDs that USB printers use.

Printer languages include ESC/P documented in the *Epson ESC/P Reference Manual*, Printer Job Language (PJL), documented in HP's *Printer Job Language Technical Reference Manual*, Printer Command Language (PCL), documented in HP's *PCL 5 Printer Language Technical Reference Manual*, and PostScript, documented in Adobe's *PostScript Language Reference*.

Overview

Printer data uses a bulk OUT pipe. The host obtains status information via control requests or an optional bulk IN pipe.

Descriptors

In the interface descriptor, bInterfaceClass = 0x07 to specify the printer class. The interface descriptor's bInterfaceProtocol field contains a value that names a type of printer interface:

bInterfaceProtocol	Type
0x01	Unidirectional
0x02	Bidirectional
0x03	IEEE-1284.4-compatible Bidirectional

With all three interface protocols, the host uses the bulk OUT endpoint to send data to the printer. With the unidirectional protocol, the host retrieves status information by sending a class-specific Get Port Status request. With the bidirectional protocol, the host can retrieve status information using Get Port Status or the bulk IN pipe, which can provide more detailed information. The IEEE-1284.4-compatible bidirectional protocol is similar to the bidirectional protocol but with added support to enable communications with individual functions in a multifunction peripheral.

Class-specific requests

The printer class has three class-specific requests.

In response to a GET_DEVICE_ID request, the device returns a Device ID in the format specified by the IEEE-1284 standard. The first two bytes of the Device ID are the length in bytes, most significant byte first. Following the length is a string containing a series of keys and their values in this format:

```
key: value {,value};
```

All Device IDs must contain the keys MANUFACTURER, COMMAND SET, and MODEL, or their abbreviated forms (MFG, CMD, and MDL). The COMMAND SET key names any PDLs the printer supports, such as Hewlett Packard's Printer Control Language (PCL) or Adobe Postscript. Additional keys, which may be vendor-defined, are optional.

Here is an example Device ID:

```
MFG:My Printer Company;
MDL:Model 5T;
CMD:MLC,PCL,PML;
DESCRIPTION:My Printer Company Laser Printer 5T;
CLASS:PRINTER;
REV:1.3.2;
```

In response to the GET_PORT_STATUS request, the device returns a byte that emulates the Status-port byte on a parallel printer port. Three bits in the byte contain status information:

Bit	Name	Meaning When 1	Meaning When 0
3	Not error	no error	error
4	Select	printer selected	printer not selected
5	Paper empty	out of paper	not out of paper

A printer that can't obtain the status byte should respond with 0x18 to signify *no error, printer selected, not out of paper*. Parallel-port printers use two additional status bits, Busy and Ack, for flow control. These bits don't apply to USB printers.

On receiving a Soft_Reset request, a device should flush all buffers, reset the interface's bulk pipes to their default states, and clear all Stall conditions. In a Soft_Reset request, the bmRequestType value in the Setup transaction should equal 0x21 to signify a class-specific request that is directed to an interface and has no Data stage. However, version 1.0 of the printer-class specification incorrectly listed the bmRequestType for Soft_Reset as 0x23. To be on the safe side, devices should respond to hosts that use a bmRequestType of 0x23 with this request, and hosts should try the incorrect value on receiving a STALL in response to this request using the correct value.

Chips

Just about any device controller that supports full speed or higher will have the one or two bulk endpoints for a printer function. For converting parallel-port printers to USB, Prolific Technology has the PL-2305 USB-to-IEEE-1284 Bridge Controller. The chip's IEEE-1284 parallel port can interface to an existing parallel port on a printer or other peripheral.

Host support

Windows includes drivers that handle tasks for both Postscript and non-Postscript printers. A printer manufacturer can customize a driver for a specific printer by providing a printer data file, which is a text file with customization information. The Windows Driver Kit (WDK) has information on how to create printer data files.

For application programmers, .NET supports the Windows Presentation Foundation (WPF) subsystem with enhanced printing support.

Smart card

Smart cards are the familiar plastic cards used for phone and gift cards, keyless entry, access to toll roads and transit, storing medical and insurance data, and other uses that require storing modest amounts of information with easy and portable access. Alternate terms for smart card are chip card and integrated circuits card (ICC).

Each card contains a module with memory and often a CPU. Many cards allow updating of their contents, for example to change a monetary value or an entry code. Some cards have exposed electrical contacts, while others communicate using embedded antennas.

To access a smart card, you establish a connection to a chip card interface device (CCID), typically by inserting the card into a slot or waving a contactless card near a reader with a wireless interface. Another term for CCID is smart-card reader. Some CCIDs can write to cards as well as read them. USB enters the picture because some CCIDs have USB interfaces for communicating with USB hosts.

An ICC device (ICCD) is a smart card that has a built-in CCID function and USB interface. An ICCD uses a vendor-specific USB connector. Another term for ICCD is USB-ICC. If you're thinking that some of these terms are confusingly alike, you're not alone. Table 7-7 summarizes.

Documentation

CCIDs and ICCDs each have a specification document: *Device Class: Smart Card: CCID* and *Device Class: Smart Card: ICCD*. The ISO/IEC 7816 standard (available from *iso.org*) defines physical and electrical characteristics and commands for communicating with smart cards.

Overview

Every CCID must have a bulk endpoint in each direction. All readers with removable cards must also have an interrupt IN endpoint.

The host and device exchange messages on the bulk pipes. A CCID message consists of a 10-byte header followed by message-specific data. The specification defines commands that the host can use to send data and status and control information in messages. Every command requires at least one response message from the CCID. A response contains a message code and status information and may contain additional requested data. The device uses the interrupt endpoint to report errors and the inserting or removal of a card.

An ICCD may have an interrupt IN endpoint, a pair of bulk endpoints, or both endpoint types or may use the control endpoint only.

Descriptors

In an interface descriptor in a CCID or ICCD, bInterfaceClass = 0x0B to declare the CCID class. For ICCDs, bInterfaceProtocol specifies a protocol that indicates what endpoints the device uses. Following the interface descriptor is a class-specific CCID

Table 7-7: Smart card terminology can be a challenge to master.

Term	Meaning
Smart card Chip card ICC	The card.
CCID Smart card reader	A device that communicates with cards. May have a USB interface.
ICCD USB-ICC	A card with a built-in CCID function and USB interface.

Class descriptor with bDescriptorType = 0x21. The class descriptor contains parameters such as the number of slots, slot voltages, supported protocols, supported clock frequencies and data rates, and maximum message length. CCIDs and ICCDs use the same class-specific descriptor, but ICCDs ignore some fields.

Class-specific requests

CCIDs have defined control requests for aborting a transfer, getting clock frequencies, and getting data rates. ICCDs can use class-specific requests to transfer data and other information.

Chips

Some USB controllers have support for CCID functions built in. Chip companies that offer USB controllers with support for smart card readers include Alcor Micro Corporation and Microchip.

Host support

Under Windows, *Wudfusbcciddriver.dll* manages USB smart card readers. Applications can use DeviceIoControl API functions to communicate with CCIDs.

Still image capture

The still image capture class encompasses digital still cameras, scanners, and other devices that receive still-image data (in other words, not video). The main job of a typical still-image device's USB interface is to transfer image data from the device to the host. Some devices can receive image data from the host as well. If all you need is a way to transfer image files from a camera, another option is to use the mass-storage class.

Documentation

The still-image class specification uses features and commands from *ISO 15740 picture transfer protocol (PTP) for digital still photography devices*, which defines a protocol for exchanging images with and between digital still photography devices. The specification is available from *iso.org*.

The USB-IF's *Media Transfer Protocol* (MTP) specification is an extension of PTP for use with digital cameras, portable media players, mobile phones, and other devices that have significant storage capacity and that fulfill their primary purpose while not connected to the bus. For example, a digital camera stores images, and users typically attach the camera to the bus only to transfer images. MTP isn't limited to still images; it can carry video and other data formats.

Overview

A still-image device has one bulk IN endpoint and one bulk OUT endpoint for transferring both image data and non-image data and one interrupt IN endpoint for event data.

In the bulk and interrupt pipes, information travels in structures called containers. The container types are Command Block, Data Block, Response Block, and Event Block. The bulk OUT pipe carries Command and Data Blocks. The bulk IN pipe carries Data and Response Blocks. The interrupt IN pipe carries Event Blocks.

On the bulk pipes, the host communicates by using a protocol with three phases: Command, Data, and Response. A short packet indicates the end of a phase. In the Command phase, the host sends a Command Block that names an operation defined in ISO 15740. The Command Block contains an operation code that determines if the operation requires a data transfer and if so, the direction of data transfer. In a data transfer, the data travels in a Data Block in the Data phase. The first four bytes of the Data Block are the length in bytes of the data being transferred. Some operations have no Data phase. The final phase is the Response phase, where the device sends a Response Block containing completion information.

On the interrupt pipe, an Event Block can contain up to three Event Codes with status information such as a low-battery warning or a notification that a memory card has been removed. The Check Device Condition Event Code requests the host to send a class-specific Get_Extended_Event_Data request for more information about an event.

A device using the bulk-only protocol cancels a transfer by stalling the bulk endpoints. The host then sends a class-specific Get_Device_Status request and uses the Clear_Feature request to clear the stalled endpoints. The host cancels a transfer by sending a class-specific Cancel_Request request. A device is ready to resume data transfers when it returns OK (ISO 15740 Response Code 0x2001) in response to a Get_Device_Status request.

Descriptors

In an interface descriptor, bInterfaceClass = 0x06 to indicate a still-image device, bInterfaceSubclass = 0x01 to indicate an image interface, and bInterfaceProtocol = 0x01 to indicate a still-image capture function. The interface must have descriptors for the bulk IN, bulk OUT, and interrupt IN endpoints.

Class-specific requests

The class defines four control requests. Cancel_Request requests to cancel the ISO 15740 transaction named in the request. Get_Extended_Event_Data (optional) requests extended information regarding an event or vendor condition. Device_Reset_Request requests the device to return to the Idle state. The host can use this request after a bulk endpoint has returned a STALL or to clear a vendor-specific condition. Get_Device_Status requests information needed to clear halted endpoints. The host uses this request after a device has canceled a data transfer.

Chips

Just about any USB controller that supports full speed or higher will have the three endpoints required by the still-image class.

Host support

Windows provides the Windows Image Acquisition (WIA) API for communicating with devices in the still-image class. Applications communicate with devices by using ReadFile, WriteFile, and DeviceIoControl API functions. The *usbscan.sys* driver adds USB support to WIA.

Cameras that use PTP require no vendor-provided driver components though a vendor can provide a minidriver to support vendor-specific features and capabilities. For scanners, the vendor must provide a microdriver, which is a helper DLL that translates between the driver's communications and a language the scanner understands, or a minidriver that works with the provided drivers to enable communications with the device.

Test and measurement

The test-and-measurement class (USBTMC) is suitable for instrumentation devices where the data on the bus doesn't need guaranteed timing. These devices typically contain components such as ADCs, DACs, sensors, and transducers.

Before USB, many test-and-measurement devices used the IEEE-488 parallel interface, also known as the General Purpose Interface Bus (GPIB). The USB488 subclass of the test-and-measurement class defines protocols for communicating using IEEE 488's data format and commands.

Documentation

The class specifications include the main USBTMC specification and a document for the USB488 subclass. The IEEE 488 standards are available from *ieee.org*.

Overview

A USBTMC device requires a bulk OUT endpoint and a bulk IN endpoint. An interrupt IN endpoint is required for devices in the USB488 subclass and otherwise is optional for returning event and status information.

The bulk pipes exchange messages consisting of a header followed by data. The bulk OUT endpoint receives command messages. The bulk IN endpoint sends response messages. The header for a command message contains a message ID, a bTag value that identifies the transfer, and message-specific information. The header for a response message contains a message ID and bTag values of the command that prompted the response, followed by message-specific information.

Descriptors

The interface subclass specifies the USBTMC function. In the interface descriptor, bInterfaceClass = 0xFE to indicate an application-specific interface and bInterfaceSubClass = 0x03 to indicate USBTMC. There are no class-specific descriptors.

Class-specific requests

The class defines eight control requests for controlling and requesting the status of an interface or transfer and requesting information about the interface's attributes and capabilities.

Chips

USBTMC devices can use just about any device controller that supports full speed or higher.

Host support

Windows doesn't include a driver for this class. National Instruments provides a driver for use with the company's hardware. Other options for test-and-measurement devices that use bulk transfers include the mass-storage class, the WinUSB or libusb driver, and vendor-specific drivers. A HID-class device can perform test and measurement functions using control and interrupt transfers. For an existing device with an IEEE-488 interface, a quick solution is to use a commercial IEEE-488/USB converter.

Agilent Technologies, Inc. provides a USBTMC driver for Linux under the GNU Free Documentation License.

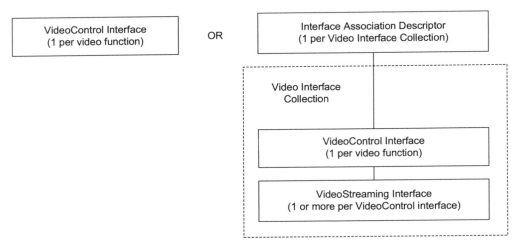

Figure 7-3. A video interface consists of a VideoControl interface and zero or more VideoStreaming interfaces.

Video

The USB video class (UVC) supports digital camcorders, webcams, and other devices that send, receive, or manipulate transient or moving images. The class also supports transferring still images from video devices.

Documentation

Multiple documents make up the video specification. The main class specification defines standard and class-specific descriptors and class-specific control requests for video devices. The video media transport terminal specification defines descriptors and protocols for video cameras and other devices that stream data stored in sequential media. Other specifications define descriptors and protocols for specific payload formats. Additional documents include an FAQ and implementation examples.

Overview

Figure 7-3 shows the elements that make up a video function in a USB device. Every function must have a VideoControl interface, which provides information about inputs, outputs, and other components of the function. Most functions also have one or more VideoStreaming interfaces that enable transferring video data. A Video Interface Collection consists of a VideoControl interface and its associated VideoStreaming interfaces. A device can have multiple, independent VideoControl interfaces and Video Interface Collections.

The VideoControl interface uses the control endpoint and may use an interrupt IN endpoint. Each VideoStreaming interface has one isochronous or bulk endpoint for video data and an optional bulk endpoint for still-image data.

Descriptors

The video class defines an extensive set of descriptors that enable devices to provide detailed information about the device's abilities. Each Video Interface Collection must have an interface association descriptor that specifies the interface number of the first VideoControl interface and the number of VideoStreaming interfaces associated with the function.

The VideoControl Interface. The VideoControl interface (Figure 7-4) has a standard interface descriptor with bInterfaceClass = 0x0E to indicate the video class. The descriptor's iFunction field must reference a string descriptor that contains a function name in U.S. English. (Other languages are optional.) A class-specific VideoControl interface descriptor consists of a VideoControl interface header descriptor followed by one or more Terminal and/or Unit descriptors.

A Terminal is the starting or ending point for information that flows into or out of a function. A Terminal may represent a USB endpoint or another component such as a CCD sensor, display module, or composite-video input or output. The defined Terminal types are generic Input and Output Terminals plus two special-purpose types. A Media Transport Terminal can stream sequential data to or from a USB host. A Camera Terminal controls features of a video-capture device that has controllable lenses or sensor characteristics.

A Unit transforms data flowing through a function. A Selector Unit routes a data stream to an output. A Processing Unit controls video attributes. An Encoding Unit controls attributes of a video encoder. An Extension Unit performs a vendor-defined function.

If the interface has an interrupt endpoint, the endpoint has a standard endpoint descriptor followed by a class-specific endpoint descriptor.

The VideoStreaming Interface. Each VideoStreaming interface (Figure 7-5) has a standard interface descriptor. Following this descriptor, an interface with an IN endpoint has a class-specific VideoStreaming Input Header descriptor, and an interface with an OUT endpoint has a class-specific VideoStreaming Output Header descriptor.

Following the Header descriptor is a Payload Format descriptor for each supported video format. For frame-based formats, the Payload Format descriptor is followed by one or more Video Frame descriptors that describe the dimensions of the video frames and other characteristics specific to a format. Some devices that support still-image capture have a Still Image Frame descriptor. A Payload Format can also

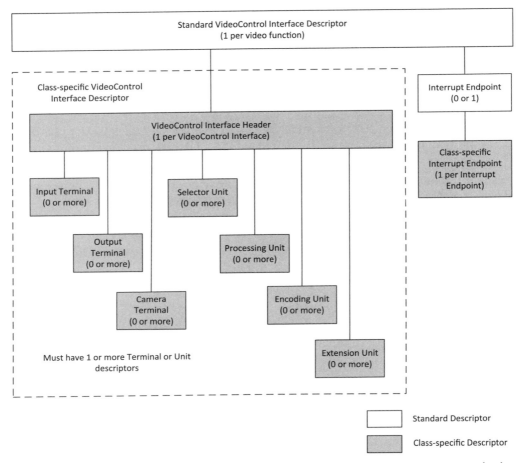

Figure 7-4. The VideoControl interface provides information about inputs, outputs, and other components of a video function.

have a Color Matching descriptor to describe a color profile. Each VideoStreaming interface has one isochronous or bulk endpoint descriptor for video data and an optional bulk endpoint descriptor for still-image data.

Class-specific requests

Class-specific control requests enable setting and reading the states of controls in VideoControl and VideoStreaming interfaces.

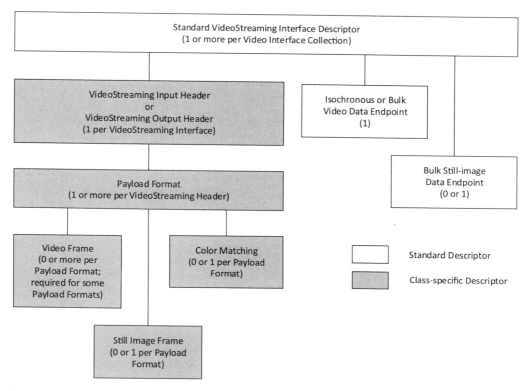

Figure 7-5. A VideoStreaming interface has an endpoint for video data and an optional endpoint for still-image data.

Chips

Video typically requires significant bus bandwidth so controllers used in video applications are likely to support high speed, SuperSpeed, or SuperSpeedPlus. Chip companies that offer USB controllers with video-class support include Alcor Micro, Genesys Logic, and Realtek Semiconductor Corp.

Host support

Windows XP SP2 introduced a driver compatible with the video class version 1.0 (*usb-video.sys*). Windows 7 supports version 1.1 of the class, and Windows 8 supports version 1.5, including H.264 video codec support for more efficient compression. Vendors of video-class devices that use the video-class driver don't need to provide any driver software but can provide a Control or Streaming extension to support vendor-specific functions or features.

Applications can access video devices using the DirectShow API documented in the Windows SDK.

The Linux UVC project provides kernel support for some video-class devices.

Classes defined by other specifications

Some USB class codes are defined by an organization other than the USB-IF or a document that is not primarily a class specification.

Bluetooth

USB/Bluetooth adapters convert between Bluetooth's short-range RF wireless interface and USB. The Bluetooth specification from Bluetooth Special Interest Group (SIG), Inc. (*bluetooth.org*) defines protocols for communicating with these devices. An adapter can be a separate device connected internally or externally, an element on a motherboard, or a subsystem on a chip.

The specification defines two controller types. A Primary Controller has two USB interfaces, one with bulk and interrupt endpoints and one with isochronous endpoints. Using two interfaces enables the USB host to select an alternate isochronous interface without interrupting pending bulk or interrupt transfers. An Alternate MAC/PHY (AMP) Controller has one interface with bulk and interrupt endpoints.

USB Bluetooth devices use these values in the device or interface descriptor:

Descriptor Field	Value	Description
Class	0xE0	wireless controller
Subclass	0x01	RF controller
Protocol	0x01	Bluetooth Primary Controller
	0x04	Bluetooth AMP Controller

Another option for USB/Bluetooth adapters is to use a USB/serial port adapter that interfaces to a serial port/Bluetooth adapter. The host then uses protocols defined in the Bluetooth UART transport layer.

Wireless USB

The USB-IF's Wireless USB specification defines a Device Wire Adapter that provides a USB Series-A connector for attaching a device and a wireless interface for communicating with a Wireless USB host.

Device Wire Adapters use these values in interface descriptors:

Descriptor Field	Value	Description
bInterfaceClass	0xE0	wireless controller
bInterfaceSubclass	0x02	Wireless USB wire adapter
bInterfaceProtocol	0x02	Device Wire Adapter control/data streaming interface
	0x03	Device Wire Adapter transparent RPipe interface (optional)

Chapter 20 has more about wireless options.

USB3 Vision

Machine-vision devices perform functions such as inspecting, tracking, and sorting items in production lines; guiding surgical robots; and detecting explosives. The USB3 Vision specification defines protocols for machine vision devices that use USB 3.0.

The Automated Imaging Association (AIA) (*visiononline.org*) sponsors the USB3 Vision standard committee and publishes the specification.

USB3 Vision devices use these values in interface descriptors:

Descriptor Field	Value	Description
bInterfaceClass	0xEF	Miscellaneous
bInterfaceSubclass	0x05	USB3 Vision
bInterfaceProtocol	0x00	Device control
	0x01	Device events (optional)
	0x02	Device streaming

A USB3 Vision devices use bulk endpoints for streaming data to the host, device control, and optional event messages.

A USB3 Vision camera must have an XML device description file that describes the camera's features. The file uses syntax defined in the GenICam standard (*geni-cam.org*).

Because machine vision applications often involve high movement or force, the USB 3 Vision specification defines a series of connectors that use locking screws to provide a secure connection.

Implementing non-standard functions

Some devices perform functions that don't have an obvious match to a USB class. Other functions might fit a class such as test and measurement or device firmware upgrade, but the lack of a driver in Windows and other OSes might prompt a different approach. Many legacy serial- and parallel-port devices perform vendor-specific functions. Host-to-host communications is another function that doesn't fit a defined class. USB is flexible enough to accommodate all of these needs.

Choosing a driver

Class drivers that are suitable for some devices with vendor-defined functions include HID, CDC, and mass storage. HIDs are limited to control and interrupt transfers but can transfer data for any purpose. A CDC virtual-serial-port device can exchange data in bulk transfers but require a vendor-provided INF file. Mass storage is an option for devices that transfer data in files.

For standard but unsupported classes such as test and measurement and device firmware upgrade, you might be able to obtain a class driver from a third party.

Using a generic driver

A generic driver can be a solution for devices that don't fit a standard class. Generic drivers typically enable applications to request control, interrupt, bulk, and/or isochronous transfers using a driver-specific API.

Microsoft's WinUSB, detailed in Chapters 14–15, and the open-source libusb driver are two options. Other sources for generic drivers include Andrew Pargeter & Associates, Jungo Ltd., and Thesycon. Many of these drivers have toolkits that generate the required INF file and include example application code. As Chapter 6 explained, some chip companies also provide generic drivers for use with their chips.

Converting from RS-232

The RS-232 serial port was included on the very first PCs and persisted for many years on PCs and peripherals. Just about any device that uses RS-232 can use USB instead. There are several approaches to making the switch.

Some RS-232 devices fit into a defined USB class. Modems are CDC devices. The HID class provides usages for pointing devices, uninterruptible power supplies, and point-of-sale devices.

For many other devices, controllers such as FTDI's USB UART series introduced in Chapter 6 provide a quick way to upgrade a design to USB. The chip can convert an existing RS-232 device to USB with minimal design changes and in most cases no changes to host software or device firmware.

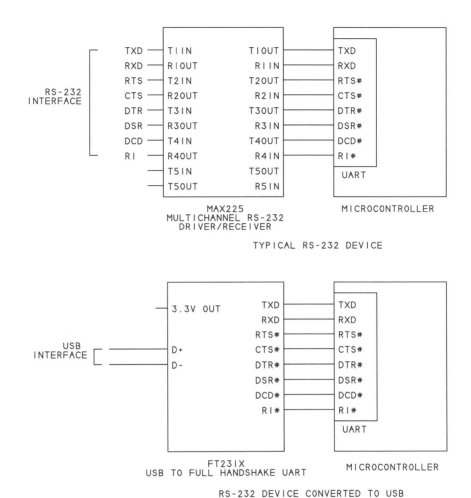

Figure 7-6. FTDI's FT231X USB UART can convert devices with RS-232 interfaces to USB. A driver provided by FTDI causes the device to appear as a COM-port device to host applications.

Figure 7-6 shows an example. A typical device with an RS-232 interface contains a UART that converts between the serial data used in RS-232 communications and the parallel data the CPU uses. The signals on the line side of the UART connect to drivers and receivers that translate between RS-232 voltages and the 5 V logic used by the UART. The line side of the converter connects to a cable to the remote computer with an RS-232 interface. To convert from RS-232 to USB, you replace the RS-232 converter with an FT231X or similar converter chip. On the host computer, FTDI's driver enables applications to access the device using the same functions used for RS-232 communications.

Many RS-232/USB adapter modules contain little more than an FT231X or similar chip, an RS-232 interface chip, and connectors for RS-232 and USB. An RS-232 device with an external adapter gives users the choice of using USB or RS-232.

When using a USB/RS-232 adapter, devices that use the status and control signals in unconventional ways and with critical timing requirements may require modifications to device hardware or firmware or application software.

Converting from the parallel port

Another port that PCs had from the beginning was the parallel port, which many devices besides printers used. For parallel-port printers, adapter modules are available to enable connecting to a PC via USB.

Devices with other functions may require redesigning for USB, possibly using the WinUSB driver or a generic or custom driver. The device will need new application software to communicate with the driver. A peripheral-side parallel-port interface has 8 bidirectional data pins, 5 status outputs, and 4 control inputs. Thus a USB controller with 17 I/O bits can emulate a parallel port. The device will need vendor-specific firmware to translate between the USB and parallel-port data, plus a host driver and new application software.

Connecting two PCs

Because every PC has a USB port, some applications might want to use the interface to communicate between PCs. But with one exception, every USB communication must be between a host and a device, not between two hosts (or two devices).

If both PCs have Ethernet ports, one solution is to forget about USB and use Ethernet. Use a crossover cable to connect the PCs directly or connect the PCs via a hub or router.

If Ethernet ports aren't an option, a USB host-to-host bridge cable can do the job. The cable incorporates two USB device controllers, which may reside in a single chip. Each controller functions as a USB device, with each device attaching to a different PC. The devices exchange data via a shared buffer (Figure 7-7). When a PC sends data to its attached device, the device writes the data to the shared buffer. The other device in the bridge retrieves the data from the buffer and sends it on to its attached PC.

Prolific Technology's PL-25A1 USB2.0 Host-to-Host Bridge Controller is a single chip designed for this type of host-to-host application. The chip contains an 8032 micro-

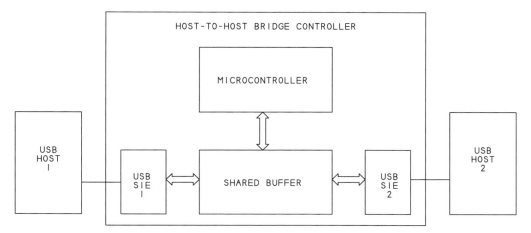

Figure 7-7. To enable two USB hosts to communicate with each other, two USB serial interface engines can share a buffer. Each SIE copies received USB data into the shared buffer, and the other device retrieves the data from the buffer and sends the data to the other host.

controller and two USB SIEs that access a common buffer. Typically, the drivers for bridge cables cause each PC to see the other as a network-connected computer.

Another way to achieve a network connection via USB is to use USB/Ethernet adapters.

A different approach for host-to-host communications is to use two FTDI FT231X or similar USB UARTs and cross-connect the asynchronous interfaces in a null-modem configuration. Each PC then has a virtual serial port that communicates with a virtual serial port on the other PC.

The exception to the host-and-device rule is the USB 3.1 Standard-A to USB 3.1 Standard-A cable. With host driver support, Enhanced SuperSpeed devices can use this cable to communicate with each other. Chapter 20 has more about the cable.

8

How the Host Communicates

This chapter explains how Windows manages communications with USB devices.

Device drivers

A device driver is a software component that enables applications to access a hardware device. The hardware device may be a printer, modem, keyboard, video display, data-acquisition unit, or just about anything controlled by circuits the CPU can access. Under Windows, every USB device must have an assigned device driver.

The layered driver model

USB communications under Windows use a layered driver model where each driver in a stack, or series, performs a portion of the communication task. At the top of the stack is a device driver called a client driver, which the operating system has assigned to the device. Another term for client driver is function driver. USB class drivers and vendor-specific device drivers are client drivers. Applications access a USB device by communicating with the client driver. The client driver in turn communicates with

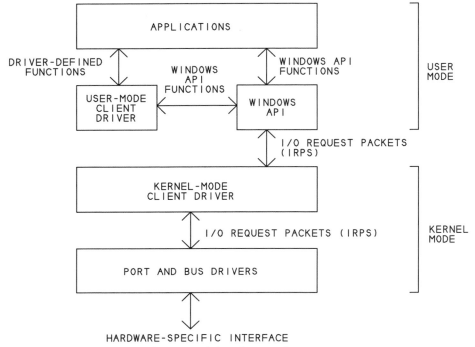

Figure 8-1. USB uses a layered driver model under Windows.

lower-level bus and port drivers that access the hardware. One or more filter drivers can supplement a client driver or bus driver.

Dividing communications into layers is efficient because devices that have tasks in common can use the same driver for those tasks. For example, it makes sense to have one set of drivers that handle tasks common to all USB devices. An operating system can provide these drivers so device vendors don't have to do so with much duplication of effort.

User and kernel modes

Under Windows, program code runs in either user mode or kernel mode. Each mode allows a different level of privilege in accessing memory and other system resources. Figure 8-1 shows the major components of user and kernel modes in USB communications. Applications run in user mode. A USB device must have a kernel-mode client driver, which can also have a supplementary user-mode driver.

User mode has limited access to memory and other system resources. Applications and user-mode client drivers can't access memory that the operating system has designated as protected. Limiting access to memory in this way enables a system to run multiple applications at the same time. If an application crashes, other applications shouldn't be affected.

Kernel-mode code has unrestricted access to system resources, including the ability to execute memory-management instructions and control access to I/O ports. A kernel-mode driver can allow any application to use a device or allow a single application to have exclusive use. Other abilities that Windows reserves for kernel-mode drivers include DMA transfers and responding to hardware interrupts.

The specifics vary with the driver, but in general, applications can communicate with kernel-mode drivers using a combination of Windows API functions, other functions exposed by a user-mode driver, or the properties, methods, and events of classes in the .NET Framework. To communicate with a USB device, an application often doesn't have to know anything about the USB protocol or even whether a device uses USB at all.

Kernel-mode drivers communicate using structures called I/O request packets (IRPs) supported by the operating system. Each IRP requests a single input or output action. A kernel-mode client driver for a USB device uses IRPs to communicate with the bus drivers that handle USB communications.

Drivers create *device objects* to handle I/O requests. A DEVICE_OBJECT structure represents a device object. A physical device object (PDO) represents a device to a bus driver. A functional device object (FDO) represents a device to a client driver. A filter device object (filter DO) represents a device to a filter driver.

The Windows PnP manager requests the bus driver to create a PDO for each device on a bus. For each PDO, the PnP manager may load and call client and filter drivers that in turn create FDOs and filter DOs.

Inside the layers

The components involved in accessing USB devices include applications, user-mode client drivers, kernel-mode client drivers, and bus drivers.

Applications

Before an application can communicate with a device, several things must happen. On power up or device attachment, the operating system enumerates the device as described in Chapter 4. To identify which driver to use, Windows compares the retrieved descriptors with the information in the system's INF files. Chapter 9 has more about INF files. When enumeration is complete and the driver is loaded, applications can access the device.

Some drivers cause the host to continuously request data from a device whether or not an application has requested data. For example, a host requests keypress data at intervals from a keyboard. Other drivers access a device only when requested by an application or other program code.

The Windows API

Applications written in Visual C# and other languages can access many devices by calling Windows API functions. The supported functions vary with the driver, but an application typically opens communications with CreateFile, exchanges data using a combination of ReadFile or ReadFileEx, WriteFile or WriteFileEx, and DeviceIoControl, and closes communications with CloseHandle. Microsoft's Windows software development kit (SDK) documents these functions.

Although the names suggest that the functions are for use with files, ReadFile and WriteFile (and their variants ReadFileEx and WriteFileEx) can communicate with drivers that access many device types via handle-based operations. The functions accept pointers to buffers to store data being read or data to be written. Depending on the driver, a call to ReadFile might request data from a device or return data that a driver has already requested and stored in the driver's buffer.

DeviceIoControl offers another way to transfer data. Included in each DeviceIoControl request is a control code that identifies a specific command. For example, the code IOCTL_STORAGE_GET_MEDIA_TYPES requests the types of media a mass-storage device supports. Because a function call sends codes to a specific driver, multiple drivers can use the same codes.

Using .NET's classes

For easier and safer programming, Microsoft's .NET Framework provides classes that eliminate the need to call many API functions from application code. Instead, applications communicate with a Common Language Runtime (CLR) component that in turn may call API functions. The CLR simplifies application programming by handling memory management and other low-level tasks. Instead of using ReadFile and WriteFile to access files on drives, applications can use methods in .NET's Directory and File classes. The CLR works with other components in the .NET Framework to translate the application code to API calls that access the files.

The .NET classes don't implement every API function, however. For example, .NET doesn't provide methods for exchanging Feature reports with HID-class devices.

User-mode client drivers

A user-mode client driver can define a driver-specific API that applications can use to access devices. The driver is in a dynamic link library (DLL). An example of a user-mode USB driver is *winusb.dll*, which exposes routines for accessing devices that use the WinUSB kernel-mode driver. These routines make up the WinUSB API. In a similar way, *hid.dll* is a user-mode driver that exposes HID API routines for accessing devices that use the HID kernel-mode class driver.

A user-mode driver translates between the driver-defined functions and the Windows API. For example, when an application calls the Hid_GetFeature API function, the user-mode HID driver calls a DeviceIoControl API function that causes the kernel-mode HID driver to request a HID Feature report from a device.

Kernel-mode client drivers

A kernel-mode client driver manages communications between user-mode code and lower-level USB drivers. Kernel-mode client drivers must conform to Microsoft's Windows Driver Model (WDM). These drivers have the extension *.sys*. (Other driver types may also use this extension.) Examples of kernel-mode client drivers are *winusb.sys* (WinUSB) and *hidclass.sys* (HID).

A kernel-mode client driver can be a class driver included with Windows or a vendor-provided driver. The driver manages communications that are specific to a device or a class of devices. A class driver may also communicate with a miniclass driver that manages communications with a subset of devices in a class.

A client driver or miniclass driver can have one or more upper and lower filter drivers (Figure 8-2). An upper-level filter driver can monitor and modify communications between applications and a client driver. A lower-level filter driver can monitor and modify communications between a client driver and the bus drivers.

For composite devices, Windows loads the USB common-class generic parent driver (*usbccgp.sys*) between the bus drivers and the client drivers for the device's interfaces. The generic parent driver handles synchronization, PnP, and power-management functions for the device as a whole and manages communications between the lower-level USB drivers and client drivers for the composite device's interfaces.

User-mode programmers have a choice of programming languages, including Visual Basic, C#, and C/C++. For kernel-mode drivers, C has the needed capabilities, including portability to multiple Windows platforms. The Windows Driver Kit (WDK) provides C header files that define data types and constants for drivers to use. While C++ is feasible for some kernel-mode drivers, Microsoft documents problems and risks

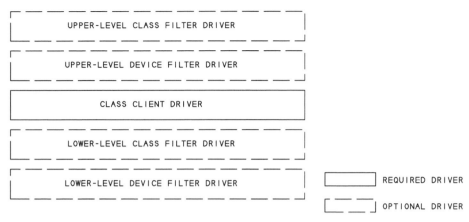

Figure 8-2. A client driver can have one or more filter drivers that monitor or modify communications with devices.

including issues with memory management, creating and using libraries, and using static and global variables.

USB communications use IRPs that contain structures called USB Request Blocks (URBs). The URBs enable a driver to configure devices and transfer data. The WDK documents the defined URBs. A kernel-mode client driver requests a transfer by creating an URB and submitting it in an IRP handled by a lower-level driver. The bus and host-controller drivers manage the details of scheduling transactions on the bus. For interrupt and isochronous transfers, if there is no outstanding IRP for an endpoint when its scheduled time arrives, the host controller skips the transaction.

In USB communications, an URB requests a USB transfer that can consist of one or more transactions. The lower-level drivers schedule the transfer's transactions without requiring further communications with the client driver.

If you're using an existing client driver (rather than writing your own), you need to understand how to access the driver's application-level interface, but you don't have to concern yourself with IRPs and URBs. If you're writing a client driver, you need to provide the IRPs that communicate with the system's USB drivers.

Low-level host drivers

Windows and other OSes provide the low-level USB drivers that manage the host controller and root hub. Microsoft provides little documentation for these drivers. Application and device-driver writers don't have to know how they work. If you want to know more about how to implement low-level USB communications, one source

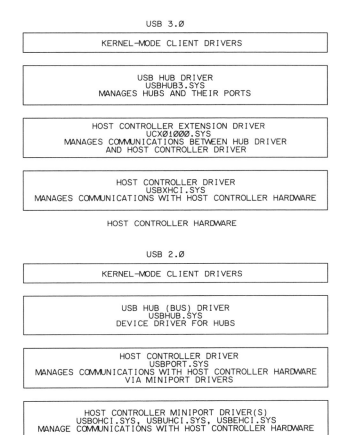

Figure 8-3. USB communications under Windows involve a hub, or bus, driver, a host controller driver, and a driver for each host-controller type.

of information is the source code and other documentation from the Linux USB Project. Another resource is the book *USB: The Universal Serial Bus* by Benjamin David Lunt.

USB 3.0 drivers

On a USB 3.0 host, Windows provides a hub, or bus, driver, a host-controller extension driver, and a host-controller driver (Figure 8-3). Presumably, the drivers for USB 3.1 will be similar.

The hub driver (*usbhub3.sys*) manages the hubs and their ports. The driver also enumerates the devices on the bus and creates a PDO for each device.

The host-controller extension driver (*ucx01000.sys*) provides an interface between the hub driver and the host-controller driver.

The host-controller driver (*usbxhci.sys*) manages the Extensible Host Controller Interface (xHCI) host-controller hardware. The xHCI host controller handles all speeds from low speed through SuperSpeedPlus.

USB 2.0 drivers

On a USB 2.0 host, Windows provides a hub, or bus, driver, a port driver, and with some exceptions, a miniport driver for a low- and full-speed host controller and a miniport driver for a high-speed host controller.

The hub driver (*usbhub.sys*) identifies devices on the bus, creates PDOs for the devices, and acts as a client driver for the bus as a whole.

The port driver (*usbport.sys*) manages tasks that are common to all host controllers.

Miniport drivers (*usbehci.sys* for high speed and *usbohci.sys* or *usbuhci.sys* for low and full speeds) each manage communications with a different type of host-controller hardware.

Host controller types

To access high-speed devices, USB 2.0 hosts use a host controller that conforms to the Enhanced Host Controller Interface (EHCI) standard. An EHCI controller handles high-speed communications only. The EHCI specification says that a host that supports EHCI must also support low and full speeds except for the unusual situation where every port has a permanently attached high-speed device.

To support low and full speeds, most USB 2.0 hosts use an integrated hub that performs the function of a host controller for low- and full-speed devices.

USB 1.1 hosts use an Open Host Controller Interface (OHCI) or Universal Host Controller Interface (UHCI) host controller to support low and full speeds. USB 2.0 hosts have the option to use a companion OHCI or UHCI controller for low and full speeds but most use an embedded hub instead. The USB-IF's website has links to the specifications.

In general, users and application programmers don't have to know or care which host controller is communicating with a device. To ensure the best performance, Windows notifies the user if a device can achieve a higher speed on a different port.

For information about which host-controller types a Windows PC has, in Device Manager, look under **Universal Serial Bus controllers**. To view a driver's name, right-click a host controller's entry and select **Properties** > **Driver** > **Driver Details.** One of the drivers listed should have *xhci, ehci, ohci*, or *uhci* in the name. Chapter 9 has more about Device Manager.

Host controller differences

Developers shouldn't assume a device works fine based on tests with one host-controller type. Different host controllers may manage bus traffic differently while still conforming to the USB specifications.

For example, an OHCI controller can schedule more than one stage of a control transfer in a single frame, while a UHCI controller always schedules each stage in a different frame. Developers who use UHCI hosts were sometimes surprised when their devices failed when connected to an OHCI host. The failure occurs because the device isn't expecting to see multiple stages of a control transfer in a frame.

Writing drivers

To support vendor-specific functions, a device can use a vendor-specific kernel-mode driver or a vendor-specific user-mode driver that communicates with a kernel-mode driver provided by the operating system or a vendor.

Microsoft provides the Windows Driver Foundation (WDF) framework to help in writing WDM drivers. When developing a WDF driver, you start with a functioning driver that provides default processing for PnP, power-management, and device I/O events. To support device-specific behavior, you add code that overrides the default processing. The framework hides much of the driver's complexity and helps produce a stable product.

This section will show you the options for creating drivers for devices that need vendor-provided drivers.

Kernel mode

Writing a kernel-mode client driver requires the WDK, which includes a C compiler, a linker, build utilities, and documentation including example source code. The WDK is a free download from Microsoft.

Kernel-mode drivers can use the Kernel-Mode Driver Framework (KMDF) library included in the WDK. The KMDF isolates the driver code from the details of creating and passing IRPs and managing PnP and power functions.

A KMDF driver creates a framework driver object to represent the driver and a framework device object for each device. Instead of creating and passing IRPs, KMDF drivers perform driver functions via properties, methods, and events of the framework device objects. Instead of handling PnP and power management directly, the framework manages these functions with callback functions, providing event notifications as needed.

The framework defines additional object types to represent resources that drivers can use. USB communications use objects that represent USB devices, interfaces, and pipes. Other framework objects can represent files, timers, strings, and other resources.

User mode

User-mode drivers can use the User-Mode Driver Framework (UMDF) library included in the WDK. UMDF drivers communicate using the Windows API instead of kernel-mode functions. Developers of UMDF drivers can program in C++ and debug with user-mode debuggers.

An example of an application that might use a UMDF driver is a device that uses the WinUSB kernel-mode driver but needs to support multiple open handles to a device interface. The provided user-mode WinUSB driver component limits interfaces to one open handle at a time, while a vendor-provided UMDF driver can allow multiple open handles.

Testing tools

The WDK provides a debugging engine for kernel-mode debugging. The debugger integrates with Visual Studio, the Microsoft Windows Debugger (WinDbg), and other debugging environments.

Using GUIDs

A Globally Unique Identifier (GUID) is a 128-bit value that uniquely identifies a class or other entity. Windows uses GUIDs in identifying two types of device classes. A *device setup GUID* identifies a device setup class. Devices in same device setup class install in the same way. A *device interface GUID* identifies a device interface class, which provides a mechanism for applications to communicate with a driver assigned to devices in the class. In many cases, devices that belong to a particular device setup class also belong to the same device interface class. Some SetupDi_ API functions accept either type of GUID, but the different GUID types provide access to different types of information for different purposes.

The conventional format for a GUID uses five sets of hex values separated by hyphens.

This is the GUID for the HIDCLASS device setup class:

```
745a17a0-74d3-11d0-b6fe-00a0c90f57da
```

Battery Devices
Biometric Device
Bluetooth Devices
CD-ROM Drives
Disk Drives
Display Adapters
Human Interface Devices (HID)
Imaging Device
IrDA Devices
Keyboard
Modem
Mouse
Multimedia
Network Adapter
Printers
Sensors
Smart Card Readers
USB Device (devices that don't belong to another class)
Windows CE USB ActiveSync Devices
Windows Portable Devices (WPD)
USB Bus Devices

Figure 8-4. Windows defines device setup GUIDs for many functions that USB devices can support.

This is the GUID for the HID device interface class:

```
4d1e55b2-f16f-11cf-88cb-001111000030
```

Driver writers and others who need to provide a custom GUID can generate one using the *guidgen* utility provided with Visual Studio and also available as a free download from Microsoft. The utility uses an algorithm that makes it extremely unlikely that someone else will create an identical GUID. To create a GUID in Visual Studio Professional edition or above, select **Tools** > **Create GUID.**

Device setup GUIDs

A device setup GUID identifies devices that Windows sets up and configures in the same way, using the same class installer and co-installers. The WDK provides the system file *devguid.h,* which defines device setup GUIDs for many classes. Figure 8-4 shows some of the device functions that have defined device setup GUIDs.

Most devices should use a device setup class that corresponds to the device's function, such as Printers or Disk Drives. A single device can belong to multiple setup classes, such as Human Interface Devices and Mouse. A device whose function doesn't fit a defined class can use the USB Device class or a vendor-defined class. The USB Bus Devices class is for hubs and host controllers that use system-supplied drivers. Each device setup GUID corresponds to a Class key in the system registry. Each Class key has a subkey for each instance of a device in the class. Chapter 9 has more about Class keys.

Applications can use device setup GUIDs to retrieve information and perform various installation functions on devices. In the downloadable WDK Samples, the Device Console utility (*devcon.exe*) shows how to use device setup GUIDs to detect and retrieve information about devices and perform functions such as enabling, disabling, restarting, updating drivers for, and removing devices. These functions are the same as those performed by the Device Manager. The sample includes C++ source code.

Device interface GUIDs

A class or device driver can register one or more device interface classes to enable applications to learn about and communicate with devices that use the driver. Each device interface class has a device interface GUID.

Using a device interface GUID and SetupDi_ functions, an application can find all attached devices in a device interface class. On detecting a device, the application can obtain a device path name to pass to the CreateFile function. CreateFile returns a handle that the application can use to access the device. Applications can also use device interface GUIDs to request to be notified when a device is attached or removed. Chapter 10 has more about using GUIDs for this purpose.

Device interface GUIDs are useful for finding devices that use the WinUSB driver, devices with vendor-specific drivers, and HID-class devices that perform vendor-specific functions.

Unlike device setup GUIDs, device interface GUIDs aren't defined in one file. A driver package may define a device interface GUID in a C header file or a Visual C# variable or constant. An application that uses the WinUSB driver can define a device interface GUID to identify a specific device. Applications can use the HidD_GetHidGuid function to retrieve the device interface GUID for the HID class.

For devices that perform standard peripheral functions, applications have other ways to find and gain access to devices. For example, to access a drive, the .NET Framework's Directory class includes a GetLogicalDrives method that enables applications to find all of the logical drives on a system (whether or not they use USB). A vendor-specific driver can also define an API to enable applications to access devices without having to provide a GUID.

9

Matching a Driver to a Device

On detecting a newly attached USB device, the host needs to decide what driver to assign to the device. This chapter shows how Windows uses the Device Manager and system registry to store information about devices and their drivers and how Windows selects a driver for a device.

Using Device Manager

Windows Device Manager displays information about all installed devices and presents a user interface for enabling, disabling, and uninstalling devices and updating or changing a device's assigned driver.

Viewing devices

You can open Device Manager in any of several ways: enter **devmgmt** in the Windows Search box; navigate to **Programs** > **Administrator Tools** > **Computer Management** and select **Device Manager**; or navigate to **Programs** > **Windows System** > **Control Panel** and select **Device Manager**. To save clicks and keystrokes, create a

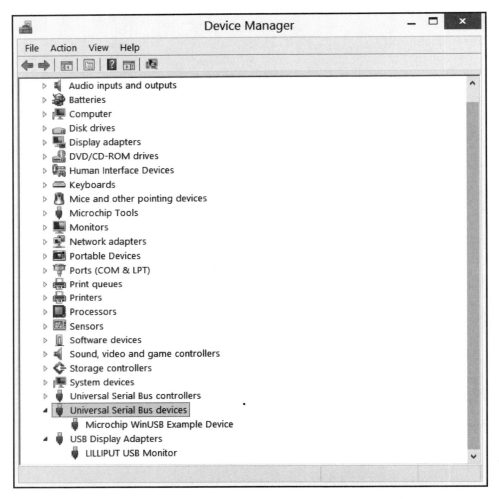

Figure 9-1. In Device Manager, you can view devices grouped by type, or function. Devices that don't fit a supported function such as keyboards or disk drives can use the *Universal Serial Bus devices* type.

shortcut that points to *devmgmt.msc* in *%SystemRoot%\System32* where *%System-Root%* is the Windows directory.

Device Manager's View menu offers options for viewing device information. Viewing devices by type (Figure 9-1) groups devices according to their functions. Viewing devices by connection (Figure 9-2) shows the physical connections from each host controller and root hub, through any additional hubs, to the attached devices.

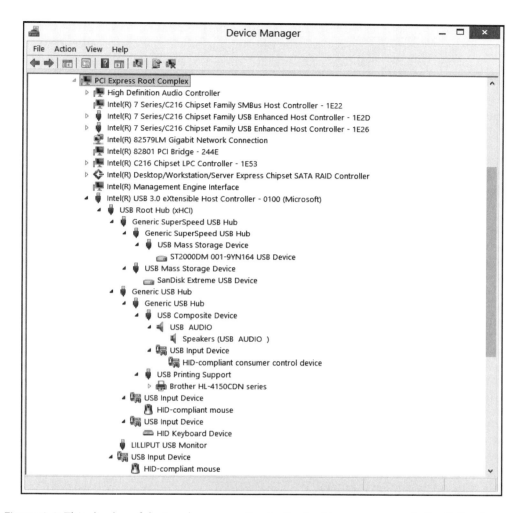

Figure 9-2. This display of devices by connection in Device Manager expands the listing for an xHCI host controller to show attached devices.

By default, Device Manager shows only attached USB devices. To view devices that have been removed but whose drivers are still installed, click **View** and check **Show Hidden Devices**.

Property pages

Each listing in Device Manager has property pages that provide additional information about a device and an interface for configuring the device and its driver. To view the property pages, double-click the device's entry or right-click the entry and select

Properties. You can request to enable or disable the device or view, update, roll back, or uninstall the device's driver. The Details page provides access to additional information including hardware IDs, any filter drivers or coinstallers the device uses, and power capabilities. A driver can also provide custom property pages.

Device information in the registry

The system registry is a database that Windows maintains for storing critical information about the hardware and software installed on a system. The registry stores information about USB devices that have been installed, including devices not currently attached.

After enumerating a new device, Windows stores information about the device in the registry. The registry obtains some of its information from the bus drivers, which in turn obtain the information from the devices. Other information comes from the INF file that the operating system selects when assigning a driver to a device.

You can view the registry's contents using the Windows Registry Editor utility. (Search on **regedit**.) You can also use the Registry Editor to edit the registry's contents, but making registry changes this way is seldom necessary. The Windows SDK documents API functions that enable applications to read and write to the registry. During device installation, the operating system may add or change device information in the registry. A request to uninstall a device via the Device Manager or another application also results in registry changes.

The system registry is so important that Windows maintains multiple backup copies if the current copy becomes unusable. The Windows System Restore utility (search on *recovery*) can restore the registry to an earlier state.

Registry Editor displays registry data using a tree structure. Each node on the tree is a registry key. Each key can have entries with assigned values and subkeys that in turn may have entries and subkeys.

Information about the system's hardware and installed software is under the HKEY_LOCAL_MACHINE\SYSTEM key. Information about USB devices is in subkeys of this key and includes the hardware key, the class key, the driver key, and the service key.

The hardware key

The hardware key, also called the instance key or device key, stores information about an instance of a specific device. Hardware keys for USB devices are under the Enum\USB key:

```
HKEY_LOCAL_MACHINE\System\CurrentControlSet\Enum\USB
```

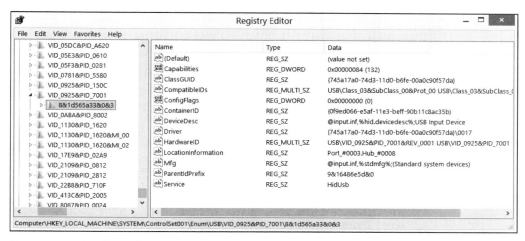

Figure 9-3. A hardware key contains information about an instance of a device with a specific Vendor ID and Product ID. This listing is for a vendor-defined HID-class device.

Under the USB key are subkeys that each contain a Vendor ID and Product ID for a USB device. Under each device's subkey are one or more hardware keys that each contain information about an instance of a device with that Vendor ID and Product ID.

Figure 9-3 shows a hardware key for a device with a Vendor ID of 0x0925 and Product ID of 0x7001. Table 9-1 lists some of the entries under the hardware key.

A device without a USB serial number string descriptor gets a new hardware key every time the device attaches to a port the device hasn't been attached to previously. If you physically remove the device from the bus and attach a different device with identical descriptors to the same port, the operating system doesn't know the difference and thus doesn't create a new hardware key. Devices with USB serial numbers have one hardware key per physical device without regard to what port the device attaches to.

Each hardware key has a Device Parameters subheading with additional information about the device instance such as a device interface GUID and whether selective suspend is enabled.

The class key

The class key stores information about a device setup class and the devices that belong to it. The class keys are under this registry key:

```
HKEY_LOCAL_MACHINE\System\CurrentControlSet\Control\Class
```

Table 9-1: These are some of the entries in a USB device's hardware key.

Key	Description	Source of Information
ClassGUID	GUID of the device's setup class	INF file
DeviceDesc	Device Description	INF file, Models section, device description entry
HardwareID	ID string containing the device's Vendor ID and Product ID	Device descriptor
CompatibleIDs	ID string(s) containing the device's class and (optional) subclass and protocol	Device and interface descriptors
Mfg	Device manufacturer	INF file, Manufacturer section, manufacturer name entry
Driver	Device's driver key	System registry, under CurrentControlSet\Control\Class
Location Information	Hub and port number	Hub and port where attached
Service	Name of the device's Service key	System registry under HKLM\System\ CurrentControlSet\Services

A class key's name is the device setup GUID for the class. A hardware key's ClassGUID value names the class key for a device instance.

Figure 9-4 shows the class key for the HID class. The key contains the Class name from the header file that defines the GUID and an IconPath value that specifies the location of the icon to use in the Device Manager and other windows that display setup

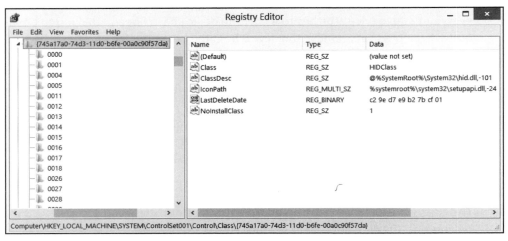

Figure 9-4. The class key for the HID class includes a friendly name for the class and an index to an icon.

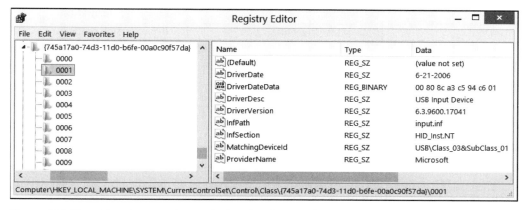

Figure 9-5. The driver keys under each class key have information about the drivers assigned to instances of devices in the class.

information. Applications can retrieve the index of the mini-icon for a class by calling SetupDiGetClassBitmapIndex. A vendor-specific class installer or co-installer can provide a vendor-specific icon.

Optional entries in the class key can affect what users see on device installation. If NoInstallClass is present and not equal to zero, users don't need to manually install devices in the class. If SilentInstall is present and not equal to zero, the PnP manager will install devices in the class without displaying dialog boxes or requiring user interaction. If NoDisplayClass is present and not equal to zero, the Device Manager doesn't display an item for the class.

UpperFilters and LowerFilters entries can specify upper filter and lower filter drivers that apply to all devices in the class.

The driver key

Under the class key, each device setup GUID has one or more driver keys, also called software keys, that each correspond to an instance of the driver. In the system registry, each driver key has a 4-digit, base-10 value (0000, 0001, and so on).

Figure 9-5 shows the key for a HID-class device. Table 9-2 lists some of the entries for a driver key. A driver key's MatchingDeviceId holds the hardware ID or compatible ID used to match an INF file to a device. The InfPath and InfSection entries contain the name and section of the INF file that in turn names the driver's files.

Table 9-2: The driver key contains information about the driver assigned to a device.

Key	Description	Source of Information
DriverDate	Date of the driver file	INF file, Version section, DriverVer directive
DriverDesc	Driver description	INF file
DriverVersion	Driver version	INF file, Version section, DriverVer directive
InfPath	Name of the INF file for the instance	INF file name
InfSection	Name of the driver's DDInstall section	INF file
InfSectionExt	"Decorated" extension used in INF file (.NTamd64, etc.)	INF file
MatchingDeviceID	The hardware or compatible ID used to assign the driver	Device descriptors and INF file
ProviderName	The provider of the driver	INF file, Provider string

The services key

Under the services key is information about a driver, including the path to the driver's file and optional driver-specific parameters. Services keys are in this branch:

`HKEY_LOCAL_MACHINE\System\CurrentControlSet\Services`

Services keys exist for each host controller type and hubs as well as classes such as storage (USBSTOR) and printers (usbprint) and HID functions (HidBatt, HidServ, HidUsb). Figure 9-6 shows the Services key for HidUsb.

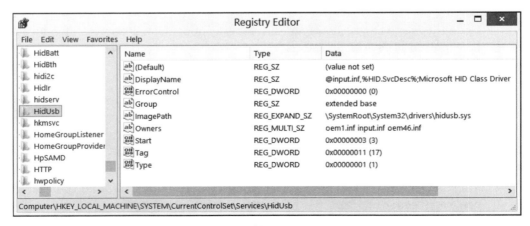

Figure 9-6. The service key names a driver's file.

Using INF files

A device-setup information file, or INF file, is a text file that contains information about one or more devices in a device setup class. The file tells system Setup components what driver or drivers to use and contains information about the device and its drivers to store in the registry. Windows includes INF files for devices that use drivers provided with the operating system.

The files are in *%SystemRoot%\inf*. By default, the INF folder is hidden. If you don't see it in Windows Explorer, select **View** and check **Hidden items** and **File name extensions**.

A vendor that provides a driver for a device must also provide an INF file. A vendor may also provide an INF file for use with a system-provided driver or request to have vendor-specific information added to a system INF file. During first enumeration of a device with a vendor-provided INF file, Windows copies the INF file to *%SystemRoot%\inf*.

On first attachment, after retrieving descriptors from a USB device, Windows looks for a match between the information in the descriptors and the information in the system's INF files.

Driver signing requirements

In looking for a match, Windows considers whether the catalog (*.cat*) file associated with a driver or embedded in the driver is digitally signed. A digital signature enables Windows to verify that the driver files haven't been modified since the driver was signed and to identify the source, or publisher, of the driver.

INF files are considered to be elements of device drivers. Any change in an INF file, including editing or adding a Product ID, device release number, or string, requires a new digital signature for the catalog file that names the INF file.

As Chapter 18 explains, obtaining a digital signature for a driver intended for distribution requires passing tests and a paying a fee. Fortunately, many USB devices can use system drivers or other digitally signed drivers and INF files. Chapter 18 shows how you can generate a test certificate to use on a single PC for development and testing at no cost.

If you need to provide an INF file, you can begin with an example and customize it as needed. The WDK documentation includes a detailed reference on INF files and many examples. Listing 9-1 shows an INF file for a virtual serial port device that uses the USB CDC driver.

```
; USB CDC Virtual Serial Port Setup File

[Version]
Signature="$Windows NT$"
Class=Ports
ClassGuid={4D36E978-E325-11CE-BFC1-08002BE10318}
Provider=%MFG%
CatalogFile=%MFGFILENAME%.cat
DriverVer=11/12/2014

[Manufacturer]
%MFG%=Models,NTamd64

[DestinationDirs]
DefaultDestDir=12

; Vendor ID and Product ID

[Models]
%DESCRIPTION%=DDInstall,USB\VID_0925&PID_2030

[Models.NTamd64]
%DESCRIPTION%=DDInstall,USB\VID_0925&PID_2030

; For all OSes

[SourceDisksNames]
[SourceDisksFiles]
[FakeModemCopyFileSection]

[Service_Inst]
DisplayName=%SERVICE%
ServiceType=1
StartType=3
ErrorControl=0
ServiceBinary=%12%\usbser.sys
```

Listing 9-1: This INF file is for a USB virtual serial-port device that uses the *usbser.sys* driver. (Part 1 of 2).

```
; For 32-bit OSes

[DDInstall.NTx86]
include=mdmcpq.inf
CopyFiles=FakeModemCopyFileSection
AddReg=DDInstall,NTx86.AddReg

[DDInstall.NTx86.AddReg]
HKR,,DevLoader,,*ntkern
HKR,,NTMPDriver,,%DRIVERFILENAME%.sys
HKR,,EnumPropPages32,,"MsPorts.dll,SerialPortPropPageProvider"

[DDInstall.NTx86.Services]
include=mdmcpq.inf
AddService=usbser, 0x00000002, Service_Inst

; For 64-bit OSes

[DDInstall.NTamd64]
include=mdmcpq.inf
CopyFiles=FakeModemCopyFileSection
AddReg=DDInstall.NTamd64.AddReg

[DDInstall.NTamd64.AddReg]
HKR,,DevLoader,,*ntkern
HKR,,NTMPDriver,,%DRIVERFILENAME%.sys
HKR,,EnumPropPages32,,"MsPorts.dll,SerialPortPropPageProvider"

[DDInstall.NTamd64.Services]
include=mdmcpq.inf
AddService=usbser, 0x00000002, Service_Inst

; Strings

[Strings]
MFGFILENAME="lvrcdc"
DRIVERFILENAME="usbser"
MFG="Lakeview Research"              ; Device Manager Provider property
DESCRIPTION="USB Virtual Serial Port" ; Device Mgr Friendly Name property
SERVICE="USB to Serial Driver"
```

Listing 9-1: This INF file is for a USB virtual serial-port device that uses the *usbser.sys* driver. (Part 2 of 2).

File structure

The contents of an INF file follow these rules.

- The information is arranged in sections, with each section containing zero or more entries. The section name is in square brackets [ ]. Some of the sections (Version, Manufacturer) are standard sections that every INF file contains. Other sections use names defined in other sections. For example, the Models section references a DDInstall section that provides information for use in device installation.

- A leading semicolon (;) indicates a comment.

- Text enclosed in percent symbols (%MFG%) is a token that references a string. For example, you might have the entry:

  `Provider=%MFG%`

  with an entry in the Strings section that defines the string:

  `MFG="Lakeview Research"`

- Windows defines Dirid values that can refer to system paths. The Dirid for the Windows directory (typically \windows) is 10. Other ways to represent the Windows directory are the environment variables %SystemRoot% and %windir%. The system32 directory (%SystemRoot%\system32) is Dirid 11. The system32\drivers directory (%SystemRoot%\system32\drivers) is Dirid 12.

- Some section names use extensions to specify which operating systems and CPUs the item applies to. For example, a section with an NTx86 extension applies only to systems with x86-based CPUs running Windows XP and later:

  `[DDInstall.NTx86]`

The NTamd64 extension means the section applies to 64-bit CPUs based on the x86 architecture. A section name with this type of extension is called a *decorated* section name.

Inside an INF file

The contents of an INF file vary depending on the device or devices, the driver(s), and the target Windows version(s). Listing 9-1's INF file for a USB virtual serial port is an example of what kinds of information an INF file provides.

The Version section and its the Signature entry are required. "$Windows NT$" means all versions of Windows.

The Class entry names the device setup class for the device. ClassGuid is the device setup GUID for the named class.

Provider contains a token (%MFG%) that references a string naming the provider of the INF file. In Device Manager, the string displays as the device's Provider.

CatalogFile is the catalog file for the INF file or its driver package with the %MFGFILE-NAME% token providing the filename minus the *.cat* extension.

DriverVer is the most recent date of any file in the driver package, including an INF file. If you change an INF file, don't forget to update the DriverVer value.

The Manufacturer section is required in INF files for devices and their drivers. The values following the token are the name used by the Models sections (called Models in the example) and zero or more TargetOSVersion extensions for Models sections that apply to a specific OS version (NTamd64 in the example).

The DestinationDirs section names the target destination directory for INF files that specify copying, deleting, or renaming files. The example INF file requires this section because the file contains a CopyFiles directive.

In the Models sections, Models and Models.NTamd64 each name an INF-file section (DDInstall) that provides installation information about the device or devices that the INF file supports. The %DESCRIPTION% token references a string that describes the device. In Device Manager's Properties for the device, the string displays as the Friendly Name property.

Each entry in the Models section also contains the device's hardware ID (USB\VID_0925&PID_2030 in the example). An entry can contain multiple hardware IDs separated by commas. Windows-provided INF files may support multiple manufacturers with Models sections for each manufacturer, for example, MyCompany and MyCompany.NTamd64 and similar for additional manufacturers.

SourceDisksNames, SourceDisksFiles, and FakeModemCopyFileSection require no entries in the example INF file because the file doesn't specify files to be copied from distribution media.

The Service_Inst section provides information about the *usbser.sys* driver. DisplayName references a string that describes the driver. ServiceType = 1 specifies that the driver is a kernel-mode device driver. StartType = 3 specifies that the driver starts on demand, including device enumeration. ErrorControl = 0 specifies ignoring errors if the driver doesn't load or initialize. ServiceBinary names the path to the driver.

The DDInstall.NTx86 sections apply to 32-bit OSes. Windows provides the *mdmcpq.inf* file for modems that use the *usbser.sys* driver. For devices other than modems that use *usbser.sys*, including USB virtual serial ports, Microsoft recommends providing an include directive for *mcpq.inf* and a CopyFiles entry that names the FakeModemCopyFileSection in *mdmcpq.inf*. (In *mdmcpq.inf*, the FakeModemCopyFileSection's single entry is *usbser.sys*.)

The AddReg entry instructs the OS to add the information in the DDInstall.NTx86.AddReg section to the system registry.

In the DDInstall.NTx86.AddReg section, a series of HKR entries adds information to the driver's registry key. Each entry specifies a subkey followed by a value for the subkey.

In the DDInstall.NTx86.Services section, the include directive specifies including *mdmcpq.inf*. The AddService directive specifies the *usbser* driver with 0x00000002 assigning the service as the device's PnP function driver. Service_Inst references the INF file's Service_Inst section that holds information about the driver.

Following these sections in the example are three similar DDInstall.NTamd64 sections for use on 64-bit OSes.

The Strings section defines the strings referenced in the INF file.

With edits, another USB virtual serial-port device that uses the *usbser.sys* driver can use Listing 9-1's INF file. In the Version section, in the DriverVer entry, replace the date with the date of your INF file. In the Models sections, replace 0925 and 2030 with your device's Vendor ID and Product ID in hexadecimal. In the Strings section, replace the MFGFILENAME string with the name of your catalog file minus the *.cat* extension and replace the MFG string with your vendor name.

Using device identification strings

To identify possible drivers for a device, Windows searches the system's INF files for a device identification string that matches a string created from information in the device's descriptors. Types of device identification strings include device ID, hardware ID, and compatible ID.

Device ID

A device ID is a string that identifies a device using information obtained from the device's bus driver. For USB devices, the information includes the Vendor ID, Product ID, revision number, and other values as appropriate from the device's descriptors. The PnP manager uses the device ID to create the registry subkey that holds the hardware keys for device instances. A device ID uses the same format as a hardware ID.

Hardware ID

A hardware ID identifies a device, a device interface, or a HID collection using the Vendor ID, Product ID, and revision number or other class-specific information.

When assigning a driver, a hardware ID in an INF file is the best match. A hardware ID for a USB device has this form:

USB\Vid_xxxx&Pid_yyyy&Rev_zzzz

The values in xxxx, yyyy, and zzzz are four characters each, with *xxxx* = idVendor, *yyyy* = idProduct, and *zzzz* = bcdDevice from the device descriptor. The *xxxx* and *yyyy* values are hexadecimal, and *zzzz* is in BCD format.

For example, a device with Vendor ID = 0x0925, Product ID = 0x1234, and bcdDevice = 0x0310 has this device ID:

`USB\Vid_0925&Pid_1234&Rev_0310`

An INF file may omit the bcdDevice value:

`USB\Vid_xxxx&Pid_yyyy`

Composite devices can specify a driver for each function so they have a device ID for each interface that represents a function. A device ID for an interface has this format:

`USB\Vid_xxxx&Pid_yyyy&Rev_zzzz&MI_ww`

The 2-character value in ww equals bInterfaceNumber in the interface descriptor for one of the device's interfaces.

A HID-class device whose report descriptor contains more than one top-level collection can have a device ID for each collection. (See Chapter 12 for more about HID collections.) A device ID for a collection has this format with *bb* indicating the collection number:

`USB\Vid_xxxx&Pid_yyyy&Rev_zzzz&MI_ww&Colbb`

Devices in some classes use other formats.

For CDC devices, the hardware ID can contain a value that specifies the subclass. This device ID specifies CDC subclass 0x08:

`USB\Vid_0925&Pid_0902&Rev_0210&Cdc_08`

For mass-storage devices, the USB mass-storage driver (*usbstor.sys*) creates a hardware ID for a drive, for example:

`USBSTOR\ST3000DM001-1CH166_____CC44`

The ID has an 8-character vendor identifier (ST3000DM), a 16-character product identifier (001-1CH166_____), and a 4-character revision level (CC44).

For printers, the USB printer driver creates a hardware ID, for example:

`USBPRINT\BrotherHL-4150CDN_se922A`

The ID contains the manufacturer's name and model using a maximum of 20 characters (BrotherHL-4150CDN_se) and a 4-character checksum (922A).

For keyboards, mice, game controllers, and other system HIDs, Windows uses special-purpose hardware IDs, for example, HID_DEVICE_SYSTEM_KEYBOARD and HID_DEVICE_SYSTEM_MOUSE. Vendor-provided INF files should not contain these hardware IDs, which begin with HID_DEVICE_SYSTEM_.

To specify a HID Usage Page and Usage, Windows uses device IDs with the format HID_DEVICE_UP:p(4)_U:u(4) where

p(4) is a 4-character hex value specifying the Usage Page and

u(4) is a 4-character hex value specifying the Usage.

For example, this hardware ID applies to devices with a Usage Page of 0x0C (Consumer) and Usage of 0x01 (Consumer Control):

```
HID_DEVICE_UP:000C_U:0001
```
Vendor-provided INF files should not contain Usage Page hardware IDs.

Compatible ID

A compatible ID identifies a device by class and optional subclass and protocol codes.

If a device has no device-specific installation requirements and the system's INF files include an appropriate compatible ID, the device vendor doesn't have to provide an INF file with a hardware ID. A vendor-provided INF file should not contain a compatible ID.

A compatible ID may have any of these forms:

```
USB\Class_aa&SubClass_bb&Prot_cc
USB\Class_aa&SubClass_bb
USB\Class_aa
```

The values *aa*, *bb*, and *cc* match values in the device descriptor or an interface descriptor and are two characters each: *aa* is bDeviceClass or bInterfaceClass, *bb* is bDeviceSubclass or bInterfaceSubclass, and *cc* is bDeviceProtocol or bInterfaceProtocol. The values are hexadecimal.

For example, the system INF file for printers (*printer.inf*) contains this compatible ID for devices in the printer class:

```
USB\Class_07
```

The *Usbstor.sys* driver provides compatible IDs for many types of mass-storage devices. For example, devices in the generic SCSI media subclass using the bulk-only protocol can use this compatible ID:

```
USB\CLASS_08&SUBCLASS_06&PROT_50
```

Obtaining identification strings from an INF file

In an INF file, each entry in a Models section has one or more device identification strings. A vendor-provided INF file should contain one or more hardware IDs. A system-provided INF file may contain hardware IDs and compatible IDs.

Finding a match

In looking for the best match between the information retrieved from a device and the information in INF files, Windows assigns a rank to every possible match with a lower numeric value indicating a better match. Signed drivers get more favorable ranks, and 64-bit Windows editions require signed drivers.

The best match is a device ID that matches a hardware ID in a signed driver's INF file. An installer that can't find any match starts the Found New Hardware wizard and gives the user a chance to point to a location to look for the INF file.

For composite devices, the compatible ID USB\COMPOSITE loads the USB common class generic parent driver. This driver creates device and compatible IDs for each interface, and the installer assigns a driver to each interface.

To speed up searching, when using a new INF file to install a device, Windows creates a precompiled INF (PNF) file. The PNF file contains much of the same information as the INF file but in a format that enables quicker searching.

When to provide an INF file

Many devices that use the system's class drivers can use an INF file that Windows provides for the class. These are provided INF files for supported USB classes:

Class	INF File	Driver
Audio	*wdma_usb.inf*	*usbaudio.sys*
Bluetooth	*bth.inf*	*bthusb.sys*
CDC modem	*mdmcpq.inf, mdm*.inf* (for specific models)	*usbser.sys*
HID	*input.inf*	*hidclass.sys, hidusb.sys*
Hub	*usb.inf*	*usbhub.sys*
Mass storage	*usbstor.inf*	*usbstor.sys*
Printer	*usbprint.inf*	*usbprint.sys*
Still image	*sti.inf*	*usbscan.sys*
Video	*usbvideo.inf*	*usbvideo.sys*

In addition, the *winusb.inf* file enables installing devices that use the WinUSB driver.

Because Windows prefers—and may require—signed drivers, if you provide an unsigned driver for a device in a supported class, Windows won't use your driver and instead will select a compatible ID from the class's INF file. CDC USB virtual COM ports must provide their own INF files even if they use the system-supplied drivers. A device with a vendor-provided driver must have an INF file.

Some INF files provided with Windows contain vendor-specific information in the Models section. When a device passes WHQL tests, Microsoft can add the device's sections to an existing system INF file or add a vendor-specific INF file to the files distributed with Windows.

Tools and diagnostic aids

Microsoft provides tools to help in creating and testing INF files. The INF File Syntax Checker (ChkINF) tests a file's structure and syntax. Log files record events that occur during device installation.

ChkINF, included in the WDK, is a Perl script that requires a Perl interpreter, available free from *activeware.com* and other sources. The script runs from a command prompt and creates an HTML page that annotates an INF file with errors and warnings.

During device installation, the PnP manager and the Windows Setup and Device Installer Services (SetupAPI) log events and errors to a text file. The log can be very helpful when debugging problems with device installations. The file, *setupapi.dev.log*, is in *%SystemRoot%\inf*.

Tips for using INF files

Here are some tips for using INF files during and after product development:

Use a unique Vendor ID and Product ID pair

Firmware that you make available outside of a controlled environment must use a Vendor ID assigned by the USB-IF. My example code uses the Vendor ID of 0x0925, which is assigned to my company, Lakeview Research. The owner of the Vendor ID is responsible for ensuring that each product and version has a unique Vendor ID/Product ID pair. Borrowing someone else's Vendor ID can lead to conflicts if the owner of the ID uses the same values for a different device.

Finding INF files

On installing a device with a new INF file, Windows copies the INF file to *%SystemRoot%\inf* and may rename the file *oem*.inf* and create a *.pnf* file named *oem*pnf*, where * is a number. Using numbered *oem* file names eliminates conflicts if multiple vendors provide INF files with the same name.

To find INF files that contain a specific Vendor ID and Product ID, open Windows Explorer and navigate to *%SystemRoot%\inf*. Select **Search**, **Advanced Options** and verify that **File Contents** is checked. In the Search box, enter **VID_xxxx&PID_yyyy**, where **xxxx** is the device's Vendor ID and **yyyy** is the Product ID.

Removing device information

During project development, if you change information in a device's descriptors, you may find that Windows is using device information from a previous enumeration. To cause Windows to forget what it knows about a device, with the device installed, right-click its entry in Device Manager and select **Uninstall**. You can then detach and reattach the device, and installation will start fresh in searching for a driver.

What the user sees

What the user sees on attaching a USB device varies with the Windows edition, the contents of the device's INF file, the driver's location, whether the driver has a co-installer and is digitally signed, and whether the device has been attached and enumerated previously and has a serial number.

Device and class installers

Device and class installers are DLLs that provide functions relating to device installation. Windows provides default installers for devices in supported device setup classes. A device vendor can provide a device co-installer that works along with a class co-installer to support operations specific to one or more devices in a class. A device co-installer can add information to the registry, request additional configuration information from the user, provide device-specific Property pages for the Device Manager to display, and perform other tasks relating to device installation. The WDK includes the Driver Install Frameworks (DIFx) tools for creating Windows Installer packages.

Searching for a driver

On boot up or device attachment, after retrieving a device's descriptors, Windows searches for a hardware key that matches information in the descriptors. On success, the operating system can assign a driver to the device. The hardware key's Driver entry points to the driver key, which names the INF file. The hardware key's Service entry points to the service key, which has information about the driver files.

On first attachment, no matching hardware key exists so Windows searches for a match in the INF files. On finding none, the New Device Wizard starts. For signed drivers, an installation program can use the SetupCopyOEMInf API to copy the provided INF file to the INF folder on the user's system. On finding a matching INF file, Windows copies the file to *%SystemRoot%\inf* (if the file isn't already present), loads the driver(s) specified in the file if necessary, and adds the appropriate keys to the system registry. The device then displays in Device Manager.

After installing a device, when installing additional devices that are identical except for the serial number, Windows behaves differently depending on whether the driver is digitally signed. When the driver is signed, Windows uses administrator privileges to install the driver for additional devices after the first device, even if the current user doesn't have these privileges. If the driver is unsigned, Windows uses the privileges of the current user in deciding whether to install the driver for additional devices.

When re-attaching a previously attached device, whether Windows finds a driver key can depend on whether the device's descriptors include a USB serial number string. If the device doesn't have a serial number, Windows uses the previous hardware key only if the device is re-attached to a port where the device had been attached previously. If the device has a serial number, Windows uses the previous hardware key no matter which port the device attaches to.

10

Detecting Devices

This chapter shows how applications can obtain information about an attached device, request a handle for communicating with a device, and detect when a device is attached or removed. Many of these tasks involve using Windows API functions and the device interface GUIDs introduced in Chapter 8. Because many .NET programmers aren't familiar with calling API functions, I begin with a short tutorial on the topic.

A brief guide to calling API functions

You can do a lot of programming without ever calling a Windows API function. Microsoft's .NET Framework provides classes that support common tasks including creating user interfaces, accessing files, manipulating text and graphics, accessing common peripheral types, networking, security functions, and exception handling. Internally, a class's methods are likely to call API functions, but the classes offer a safer, more secure, and more modular, object-oriented way for programmers to accomplish the tasks. Languages that can use the .NET Framework include Visual Basic, Visual C#, and Visual C++.

But .NET's classes don't handle every task. Some applications must do things that require calling API functions. A .NET application can use .NET classes wherever possible and use API calls for functions not supported by .NET. The code examples in this book use Visual C#. The examples in this chapter assume the following using statements:

```
using Microsoft.Win32.SafeHandles;
using System;
using System.Management;
using System.Runtime.InteropServices;
```

Managed and unmanaged code

Managed code is program code that accesses properties, methods, and events of the .NET Framework's classes. Managed code compiles to Microsoft Intermediate Language (MSIL) code, which consists of instructions that are not specific to a CPU. The .NET common language runtime (CLR) environment compiles MSIL code to native code for the target CPU.

Because all .NET languages use the same CLR, components written in different .NET languages can easily interoperate. For example, a Visual Basic application can call a function written in Visual C# without worrying about differences in calling conventions. The CLR also simplifies programming by implementing garbage collection to remove no-longer-needed objects from memory. In contrast, Windows API functions are unmanaged code whose DLLs contain compiled machine code that executes directly on the target CPU.

A Visual C++ application can compile to managed code, unmanaged code, or a combination. The language incorporates a technology that enables managed code to call API functions in the same way that unmanaged code does.

For .NET languages other than Visual C++, managed code can call API functions by using methods of the System.Runtime.InteropServices namespace. The namespace supports the Platform Invocation Services, also known as PInvoke or P/Invoke. The process of calling unmanaged functions from managed code is called *Interop*.

The DLLs

The DLLs included with Windows are typically stored in *%SystemRoot%\system32*. The operating system searches this folder when an application calls a function defined in a DLL. Header files and documentation for Windows API functions are in the Windows Driver Kit (WDK) and Windows Software Development Kit (SDK):

Function	DLL	Header File
Find devices	setupapi.dll	setupapi.h
Access devices that support handle-based operations	kernel32.dll	kernel32.h

A header file contains declarations in C for a DLL's functions and defines any constants, variables, structures, and other components that the functions access. The declarations enable applications to call the functions and pass parameters to them.

A Visual C# application must translate the declarations in the header files from C to Visual C# syntax and data types. Translating from C is more complicated than substituting one keyword for another because some variables and structure types don't have one-to-one equivalents in .NET. The .NET code may also requires marshaling to enable passing data safely between managed and umanaged code.

Marshaling

Visual C# applications must take special care to ensure that any data passed to an unmanaged function survives the trip from managed to unmanaged code, and back if needed. The .NET Framework provides the Marshal class to help. Marshaling means doing whatever is needed to make the data available.

The class provides methods for allocating memory for variables to be passed to unmanaged code, copying data between unmanaged and managed memory, and converting between managed and unmanaged data types. For example, the PtrToStringAuto method accepts a pointer to a string in unmanaged memory and returns the string being pointed to. This example retrieves a string from a pointer (IntPtr pDevicePathName) returned by an API function:

```
String devicePathName =
    Marshal.PtrToStringAuto(pDevicePathName);
```

The MarshalAs attribute can define an array's size to enable passing an array in a structure in unmanaged code. This example declares an array (Reserved), which consists of seventeen Int16 values. The array is an element in a structure that an API function passes:

```
[MarshalAs(UnmanagedType.ByValArray, SizeConst = 17)]
    internal Int16[] Reserved;
```

The MarshalAs attribute marshals Reserved into the array as an UnmanagedType.ByValArray. The SizeConst field sets the number of elements in the array (17 in the example).

By allocating memory that the garbage collector won't touch, marshaling can ensure that an unmanaged function can access data that an application passes and the application can access data returned by the unmanaged function. This example allocates memory for a buffer:

```
Dim bufferSize As Int32 = 168;
IntPtr detailDataBuffer = Marshal.AllocHGlobal(bufferSize);
```

An application can use marshaling to store data in a buffer to be passed to an unmanaged function. In this example, the application writes a value to the first location in the buffer.

```
Marshal.WriteInt32(detailDataBuffer, 8);
```

The application can then pass the buffer's pointer to an API function that will fill the rest of the buffer with data. When the function returns, the application can access the contents of the buffer.

The Marshal.FreeHGlobal method frees allocated memory when the application no longer needs to access the memory:

```
Marshal.FreeHGlobal(unManagedBuffer);
```

To ensure that code to free memory or other resources executes, place the code in the Finally block of a Try...Catch...Finally statement. For brevity, the examples in this book omit Try...Catch statements.

Declaring a function

Every API function requires a declaration to specify the function's location and parameters. This is a declaration for the function HidD_GetNumInputBuffers, which applications can use to learn the number of Input reports that the driver for a HID-class device can store:

```
[DllImport("hid.dll", SetLastError=true)]
internal static extern Boolean HidD_GetNumInputBuffers
    (SafeFileHandle HidDeviceObject,
     ref Int32 NumberBuffers);
```

The declaration contains this information:

- A DllImport attribute that names the file that contains the function's executable code (*hid.dll*). The optional SetLastError field is set to true to enable retrieving error codes using the GetLastWin32Error method.
- The function's name (HidD_GetNumInputBuffers).
- The parameters the function will pass to the operating system (HidDeviceObject, NumberBuffers).
- The data types of the values passed (SafeFileHandle, Int32).

- Whether the function passes parameters by value or by reference. The default is by value. To pass by reference, precede the parameter name with ref. The function passes HidDeviceObject by value and NumberBuffers by reference.

- The data type of the value returned for the function (Boolean). A few API routines have no return value.

The extern modifier indicates that the function being declared resides in a different file.

Using a NativeMethods class

Microsoft recommends placing declarations for unmanaged code in a class called NativeMethods. The class is declared as internal, and the class's methods should be declared as static and internal.

To declare the class, use:

```
internal static class NativeMethods
{
    // Unmanaged function example:

[DllImport("hid.dll", SetLastError=true)]
internal static extern Boolean HidD_GetNumInputBuffers
    (SafeFileHandle HidDeviceObject,
    ref Int32 NumberBuffers);

    // Additional unmanaged functions here...
}
```

When calling an umanaged function, specify the NativeMethods class:

```
NativeMethods.HidD_GetHidGuid(ref myGuid);
```

Calling a function

After declaring a function and any parameters to be passed, an application can call the function. This is a call to the HidD_GetNumInputBuffers function declared above:

```
Boolean success = NativeMethods.HidD_GetNumInputBuffers
    (hidDeviceObject,
    ref numberOfInputBuffers);
```

The hidDeviceObject parameter is a SafeFileHandle returned previously by the CreateFile function, and numberOfInputBuffers is an Int32 variable. If the function returns with success = true, numberOfInputBuffers contains the number of Input buffers.

Managing data

Understanding how to pass data to API functions and how to use data returned by API functions requires understanding .NET's data types and how the CLR passes them to unmanaged code. The explanations below provide a background to understand the example code in this and later chapters.

Data types

The header files for API functions use many data types that the .NET Framework doesn't support. To specify a variable's type for an API call, in many cases you can use a .NET type of the same length. For example, a DWORD is a 32-bit integer, so a .NET application can declare a DWORD as an Int32. GUIDs can use .NET's System.Guid type. For pointers, .NET provides the IntPtr type, whose size adjusts as needed to 32 or 64 bits depending on the platform. IntPtr.Zero is a null pointer.

A parameter defined in C as a HANDLE can use an IntPtr, but a safer and more reliable option for many handles is a SafeHandle object. With an IntPtr, in some situations, an exception can leak a handle, and a finalizer can corrupt a handle still in use in an asynchronous operation. Recycling of IntPtr handles can also expose data that belongs to another resource. SafeHandle objects don't have these vulnerabilities.

The SafeHandle class is abstract. To use a SafeHandle object, you can use one of the provided classes derived from SafeHandle or derive a new class from SafeHandle.

Passing variables

Every parameter passed to a function has both an element type and a passing mechanism. The element type is *value* or *reference,* and the passing mechanism is *by value* or *by reference*. The element type helps to determine the effect of the passing mechanism.

A value type contains data. For example, a Byte variable assigned a value of 3 consists of one byte with the value 00000011_b. Value types include all numeric data types; the Boolean, Char, and Date types; structures, even if their members are reference types; and enumerations.

A reference type contains a reference, or pointer, that specifies the location of the variable's data in memory. For example, an array variable contains the location where the array's contents are stored. Reference types include Strings; arrays, even if their elements are value types; classes; and delegates.

Whether to pass a parameter by value or by reference depends on what information the function expects, the element type being passed, and in some cases whether the type is *blittable* (defined below). Sometimes multiple ways can achieve the same result.

Passing a value type by value passes a copy of the variable's value. If the called function changes the value of the variable or its members, the calling function doesn't see the change. For example, when calling the WinUsb_ReadPipe function to read data from a device, the application passes an UInt32 variable that contains the maximum number of bytes requested from the device. The called function uses the passed value but doesn't have to return the value to the calling application so the application can pass the variable, which is a value type, by value.

Passing a value type by reference passes a pointer to the variable's data. If the called function changes the variable or its members, the calling application sees the changes. An example, again using WinUsb_ReadPipe, is passing a UInt32 variable by reference to hold the number of bytes the function returns. The called function writes a value to the variable, and when the function returns, the calling application sees the value written.

Passing a reference type by value also passes a pointer to the variable's data, but the effect varies depending on whether the type is *blittable*. A blittable type is a .NET data type that managed and unmanaged code represent in the same way. Blittable types include Byte, SByte, Int16, UInt16, Int32, UInt32, Int64, UInt64, IntPtr, UIntPtr, Single, Double, and IntPtr as well as SafeHandles used as IN parameters.

When an application passes a blittable, reference type by value to an unmanaged function, the application passes a reference to the original variable. To prevent the garbage collector from moving the variable while the function executes, the CLR pins the variable in memory. The calling routine sees changes to the variable's value but doesn't see changes to the variable's instance. Passing a reference to the original variable in this way reduces overhead and improves performance compared to passing the variable by value.

An example of passing a blittable, reference type by value is passing a Byte array in a call to WinUsb_ReadPipe, which will fill the array with data read from the device. Because a Byte array is a reference type and a Byte is a blittable type, if the application passes the array by value, the called function receives a pointer to the original array. The function writes the data to the array, and when the function returns, the calling application can access the new data.

For non-blittable types, the CLR converts the data to a format the function accepts and passes a pointer to the converted data.

The calling application doesn't see changes the called function makes to the variable's instance, only changes to its value. Thus if the called function sets the variable to Nothing/null, the calling application doesn't see the change.

Passing a reference type by reference passes a pointer that points to a pointer to the variable's data. The calling application sees changes to the variable and to the variable's instance. The examples in this book don't use this passing mechanism.

Passing structures

Some API functions pass and return structures that can contain multiple items of different types. The header files for the functions contain declarations for the structures in C syntax.

A .NET application can usually declare an equivalent structure or class that contains the items in the structure. To ensure that the managed and unmanaged code agree on the layout and alignment of the structure's members, a structure's declaration or class definition can set the StructLayout attribute to LayoutKind.Sequential.

```
[StructLayout(LayoutKind.Sequential)]
```

The Visual C# compiler always specifies LayoutKind.Sequential for value types, which include structures but not classes, so specifying LayoutKind.Sequential is optional for structures.

The optional CharSet field can determine whether strings are converted to ANSI or Unicode before being passed to unmanaged code. CharSet.Auto selects 8-bit ANSI or 16-bit Unicode characters depending on the target platform. A DllImport attribute can also use the CharSet field.

```
[StructLayout(LayoutKind.Sequential, CharSet=CharSet.Auto)]
```

Some structures are difficult or impractical to duplicate in Visual C#. A solution is to use a generic buffer of the expected size. The application can fill the buffer before passing it and extract returned data from the buffer as needed.

The optional Pack field sets the alignment of data fields in a structure. The fields in the structure start on offsets that are multiples of the Pack value in bytes. For example, setting Pack = 4 aligns the fields on 4-byte boundaries:

```
[StructLayout(LayoutKind.Sequential, Pack=4)]
```

Setting Pack = 0 uses the default value, which is 8 for all except unmanaged structures, which typically have a default of 4.

Finding a device

Windows provides a series of SetupDi_ API functions that enable applications to find all devices in a device interface class and to obtain a device path name for each device. The CreateFile function can use the device path name to obtain a handle for accessing the device. As Chapter 8 explained, these functions can be useful in finding HID-class devices that perform vendor-specific functions and devices that use WinUSB and vendor-specific drivers.

Obtaining a device path name requires these steps:

1. Obtain the device interface GUID.

2. Request a pointer to a device information set with information about all installed and present devices in the device interface class.

3. Request a pointer to a structure that contains information about a device interface in the device information set.

4. Request a structure containing a device interface's device path name.

5. Extract the device path name from the structure.

The application can then use the device path name to open a handle for communicating with the device.

Table 10-1 lists the API functions that applications can use to perform these tasks.

The following code shows how to use API functions to find a device and obtain its device path name. For a complete Visual C# application that demonstrates how to use these functions, visit *janaxelson.com*.

Obtaining the device interface GUID

As Chapter 8 explained, for many drivers, applications can obtain a device interface GUID from a C header file or other declaration provided with a driver. The device's INF file should contain the same GUID. As Chapter 15 explains, WinUSB devices have the option to store the GUID in device firmware.

For the HID class, Windows provides an API function to obtain the GUID defined in *hidclass.h*.

Definitions

```
[DllImport("hid.dll", SetLastError=true)]
internal static extern void HidD_GetHidGuid
   (ref Guid HidGuid);
```

Use

```
Guid myGuid = Guid.Empty;
NativeMethods.HidD_GetHidGuid(ref myGuid);
```

For other GUIDs, you can specify a a constant GUID value as a string and convert the string to a System.Guid object:

Definitions

```
private const String DeviceInterfaceGuid =
 "{ecceff35-146c-4ff3-acd9-8f992d09acdd}";
```

Use

```
var myGuid = new Guid(DeviceInterfaceGuid);
```

Table 10-1: Applications use these functions to find devices and obtain device path names to enable accessing devices.

API Function	DLL	Purpose
HidD_GetHidGuid	hid	Retrieve the device interface GUID for the HID class.
SetupDiDestroyDeviceInfoList	setupapi	Free resources used by SetupDiGetClassDevs.
SetupDiGetClassDevs	setupapi	Retrieve a device information set for the devices in a specified class.
SetupDiGetDeviceInterfaceDetail	setupapi	Retrieve a device path name.
SetupDiEnumDeviceInterfaces	setupapi	Retrieve information about a device in a device information set.

Requesting a pointer to a device information set

The SetupDiGetClassDevs function can return a pointer to an array of structures containing information about all devices in the device interface class specified by a GUID.

Definitions

```
[DllImport("setupapi.dll", SetLastError=true,
   CharSet = CharSet.Auto)]
internal static extern IntPtr SetupDiGetClassDevs
   (ref Guid classGuid,
   IntPtr enumerator,
   IntPtr hwndParent,
   Int32 flags);
```

Use

```
internal const Int32 DIGCF_PRESENT = 2;
internal const Int32 DIGCF_DEVICEINTERFACE = 0X10;

var deviceInfoSet = new IntPtr();

deviceInfoSet = NativeMethods.SetupDiGetClassDevs
   (ref myGuid,
   IntPtr.Zero,
   IntPtr.Zero,
   NativeMethods.DIGCF_PRESENT |
      NativeMethods.DIGCF_DEVICEINTERFACE);
```

How it works

For HID-class devices, the ClassGuid parameter is the HidGuid value returned by HidD_GetHidGuid. For other drivers, the application can pass a reference to the appropriate GUID. The example passes null pointers for Enumerator and hwndParent. The Flags parameter uses system constants defined in *setupapi.h*. The flags in the example cause the function to look for device interfaces that are currently attached and enumerated members of the class identified by the ClassGuid parameter.

The returned deviceInfoSet value is a pointer to a device information set that contains information about all attached and enumerated devices in the specified device interface class. The device information set contains a device information element for each device in the set, or array. Each device information element contains a handle to a device's devnode (a structure that represents the device) and a linked list of device interfaces associated with the device.

When finished using the device information set, the application should free the resources used by calling SetupDiDestroyDeviceInfoList as shown later in this chapter.

Identifying a device interface

A call to SetupDiEnumDeviceInterfaces retrieves a pointer to a structure for a device interface in the previously retrieved deviceInfoSet array. The call passes an array index to a device interface. To retrieve information about all devices in an array, an application can increment the index until the function returns zero, indicating that the array has no more interfaces.

In some cases, such as when looking for a HID-class device with a specific Vendor ID and Product ID, the application may need to request more information before deciding whether a retrieved device interface is the desired one.

Definitions

```
internal struct SP_DEVICE_INTERFACE_DATA
{
    internal Int32 cbSize;
    internal Guid InterfaceClassGuid;
    internal Int32 Flags;
    internal IntPtr Reserved;
}

[DllImport("setupapi.dll", SetLastError = true)]
internal static extern Boolean SetupDiEnumDeviceInterfaces
    (IntPtr DeviceInfoSet,
    IntPtr DeviceInfoData,
    ref Guid InterfaceClassGuid,
    Int32 MemberIndex,
    ref SP_DEVICE_INTERFACE_DATA DeviceInterfaceData);
```

Use

```
Int32 memberIndex = 0;
var myDeviceInterfaceData =
    new NativeMethods.SP_DEVICE_INTERFACE_DATA();
myDeviceInterfaceData.cbSize =
 Marshal.SizeOf(myDeviceInterfaceData);

Boolean success = NativeMethods.SetupDiEnumDeviceInterfaces
    (deviceInfoSet,
     IntPtr.Zero,
     ref myGuid,
     memberIndex,
     ref myDeviceInterfaceData);
```

How it works

In the SP_DEVICE_INTERFACE_DATA structure, the cbSize parameter is the size of the structure in bytes. The Marshal.SizeOf method returns the structure's size. The myGuid and deviceInfoSet parameters are values retrieved previously.

The DeviceInfoData parameter can be a pointer to an SP_DEVINFO_DATA structure that limits the search to a particular device instance or a null pointer. The memberIndex parameter is an index to a structure in the deviceInfoSet array. The myDeviceInterfaceData parameter is a pointer to the SP_DEVICE_INTERFACE_DATA structure that the function returns. The function returns true on success.

Requesting a structure with the device path name

The SetupDiGetDeviceInterfaceDetail function returns a structure that contains a device path name for a device interface identified in an SP_DEVICE_INTERFACE_DATA structure.

When calling this function for the first time, you don't know the size in bytes of the DeviceInterfaceDetailData structure to pass in the DeviceInterfaceDetailDataSize parameter. Yet the function won't return the structure unless the function call passes the correct size. The solution is to call the function twice. The first time, GetLastError returns the error *The data area passed to a system call is too small,* but the Required-Size parameter contains the correct value for DeviceInterfaceDetailDataSize. The second call can pass the returned size value, and the function will return the structure.

The code below doesn't pass a structure for the DeviceInterfaceDetailData parameter. Instead, the code reserves a generic buffer, passes a pointer to the buffer, and extracts the device path name from the buffer. The code thus doesn't require a structure declaration, but I've included one to show the contents of the returned buffer.

Definitions

```
internal struct SP_DEVICE_INTERFACE_DETAIL_DATA
{
   internal Int32 cbSize;
   internal String DevicePath;
}

[DllImport("setupapi.dll", SetLastError = true,
   CharSet = CharSet.Auto)]
internal static extern Boolean SetupDiGetDeviceInterfaceDetail
   (IntPtr DeviceInfoSet,
   ref SP_DEVICE_INTERFACE_DATA DeviceInterfaceData,
   IntPtr DeviceInterfaceDetailData,
   Int32 DeviceInterfaceDetailDataSize,
   ref Int32 RequiredSize,
   IntPtr DeviceInfoData);
```

Use

```
Int32 bufferSize = 0;
IntPtr detailDataBuffer = IntPtr.Zero;

NativeMethods.SetupDiGetDeviceInterfaceDetail
   (deviceInfoSet,
   ref myDeviceInterfaceData,
   IntPtr.Zero,
   0,
   ref bufferSize,
   IntPtr.Zero);

detailDataBuffer = Marshal.AllocHGlobal(bufferSize);

Marshal.WriteInt32
   (detailDataBuffer,
   (IntPtr.Size == 4) ? (4 + Marshal.SystemDefaultCharSize) : 8);

NativeMethods.SetupDiGetDeviceInterfaceDetail
   (deviceInfoSet,
   ref MyDeviceInterfaceData,
   detailDataBuffer,
   bufferSize,
   ref bufferSize,
   IntPtr.Zero);
```

How it works

After calling SetupDiGetDeviceInterfaceDetail, bufferSize contains the value to pass in the DeviceInterfaceDetailDataSize parameter in the next call. Before calling the function again, the code needs to take care of a few things.

The second function call returns a pointer (detailDataBuffer) to an SP_DEVICE_INTER-FACE_DETAIL_DATA structure in unmanaged memory. The Marshal.AllocGlobal method uses the returned bufferSize value to allocate memory for the structure.

The Marshal.WriteInt32 method stores a value in the cbsize member of detail-DataBuffer. The "?" conditional operator selects the correct value for 32- and 64-bit systems.

The second call to SetupDiGetDeviceInterfaceDetail passes the pointer to detail-DataBuffer and sets the deviceInterfaceDetailDataSize parameter equal to the buffer-Size value returned previously in RequiredSize.

When the function returns after the second call, detailDataBuffer points to a structure containing a device path name.

Extracting the device path name

In detailDataBuffer, the first four bytes are the cbSize member. The string containing the device path name begins at the fifth byte.

```
String devicePathName = "";
var pDevicePathName = new IntPtr(detailDataBuffer.ToInt64() + 4);

devicePathName = Marshal.PtrToStringAuto(pDevicePathName);
Marshal.FreeHGlobal(detailDataBuffer);
```

How it works

The pDevicePathName variable points to the string in the buffer, and Marshal.PtrTo-StringAuto retrieves the string from the buffer. When program code is finished using the buffer, Marshal.FreeHGlobal frees the memory previously allocated for the buffer.

Closing communications

When finished using the deviceInfoSet pointer returned by SetupDiGetClassDevs, the application should call SetupDiDestroyDeviceInfoList to free resources.

Definitions

```
[DllImport("setupapi.dll", SetLastError = true)]
internal static extern Int32 SetupDiDestroyDeviceInfoList
    (IntPtr deviceInfoSet);
```

Table 10-2: Applications can use CreateFile to request a handle to a device and CloseHandle to free the resources used by a handle.

API Function	DLL	Purpose
CloseHandle	kernel32	Free resources reserved by CreateFile. To close handles for the SafeHandle and derived classes, use the Close method, which calls CloseHandle internally.
CreateFile	kernel32	Retrieve a handle for communicating with a device.

Use

```
NativeMethods.SetupDiDestroyDeviceInfoList(deviceInfoSet);
```

Obtaining a handle

An application can use a retrieved device path name to obtain a handle that enables communicating with the device. Table 10-2 shows API functions related to requesting a handle.

Requesting a communications handle

After retrieving a device path name, an application is ready to open communications with the device. The CreateFile function requests a handle to an object, which can be a file or another resource managed by a driver that supports handle-based operations. For example, applications can request a handle to use in exchanging reports with HID-class devices. For devices that use the WinUSB driver, CreateFile obtains a handle the application uses to obtain a WinUSB device handle for accessing a device.

The call to CreateFile can pass a SECURITY_ATTRIBUTES structure that can limit access to the handle or IntPtr.Zero if the function doesn't need to limit access.

Definitions

```
internal const Int32 FILE_ATTRIBUTE_NORMAL = 0X80;
internal const Int32 FILE_FLAG_OVERLAPPED = 0X40000000;
internal const Int32 FILE_SHARE_READ = 1;
internal const Int32 FILE_SHARE_WRITE = 2;
internal const UInt32 GENERIC_READ = 0X80000000;
internal const UInt32 GENERIC_WRITE = 0X40000000;
internal const Int32 OPEN_EXISTING = 3;
```

```
[DllImport("kernel32.dll", SetLastError = true,
   CharSet = CharSet.Unicode)]
internal static extern SafeFileHandle CreateFile
   (String lpFileName,
   UInt32 dwDesiredAccess,
   Int32 dwShareMode,
   IntPtr lpSecurityAttributes,
   Int32 dwCreationDisposition,
   Int32 dwFlagsAndAttributes,
   IntPtr hTemplateFile);
```

Use

```
SafeFileHandle deviceHandle = NativeMethods.CreateFile
   (devicePathName,
   (NativeMethods.GENERIC_WRITE | NativeMethods.GENERIC_READ),
     NativeMethods.FILE_SHARE_READ |
       NativeMethods.FILE_SHARE_WRITE,
     IntPtr.Zero,
     NativeMethods.OPEN_EXISTING,
     NativeMethods.FILE_ATTRIBUTE_NORMAL |
       NativeMethods.FILE_FLAG_OVERLAPPED,
     IntPtr.Zero);
```

How it works

The function passes a pointer to the devicePathName string returned by SetupDiGet-DeviceInterfaceDetail.

dwDesiredAccess requests read/write access to the device.

dwShareMode allows other processes to access the device while the handle is open.

lpSecurityAttributes is a null pointer (or a pointer to a SECURITY_ATTRIBUTES structure).

dwCreationDisposition must be OPEN_EXISTING for devices. For use with the WinUSB driver, the dwFlagsAndAttributes parameter must use FILE_FLAG_OVER-LAPPED. The FILE_ATTRIBUTE_NORMAL attribute indicates that no other attributes such as hidden, read-only, or encrypted are set.

The example passes IntPtr.Zero for the unused hTemplate parameter.

The function returns a SafeFileHandle object.

Closing the handle

When finished communicating with a device, the application should free the resources reserved by CreateFile.

```
deviceHandle.Close();
```

How it works

SafeFileHandle objects support the Close method, which marks the handle for releasing and freeing resources. The method calls the CloseHandle API function internally.

Detecting device attachment and removal

Applications often find it useful to know when a specific target device has been attached or removed. On detecting when a device is attached, the application can begin communicating with the device. On detecting when a device has been removed, the application can stop attempting to communicate until detecting reattachment.

Using WMI

Windows Management Instrumentation (WMI) provides services that support system management operations such as detecting device arrival and removal and getting information about available devices. The System.Management namespace provides classes that support WMI operations.

The routines that follow use a variable to hold the state of the target device:

```
private Boolean _deviceReady;
```

Adding a handler for newly arrived devices

To create a handler that executes when a device becomes available:

1. Create a ManagementScope object that sets the scope, or namespace, for the management operations.

2. Create a WMI event query that defines the search criteria for the desired devices.

3. Create a ManagementEventWatcher to watch for the specified devices within the specified scope.

The routines that follow create and implement a handler for newly arrived devices.

Use

```
private ManagementEventWatcher deviceArrivedWatcher;
```

```
private void AddDeviceArrivedHandler()
{
    const Int32 pollingIntervalSeconds = 3;
    var scope = new ManagementScope("root\\CIMV2");
    scope.Options.EnablePrivileges = true;

    var q = new WqlEventQuery();
    q.EventClassName = "__InstanceCreationEvent";
    q.WithinInterval = new TimeSpan(0, 0, pollingIntervalSeconds);
    q.Condition = @"TargetInstance ISA 'Win32_USBControllerdevice'";
    deviceArrivedWatcher = new ManagementEventWatcher(scope, q);
    deviceArrivedWatcher.EventArrived += DeviceAdded;
    deviceArrivedWatcher.Start();
}
private void DeviceAdded(object sender, EventArrivedEventArgs e)
{
    FindDevice();

    // Perform other actions as needed.
}
```

How it works

deviceArrivedWatcher is an instance of the ManagementEventWatcher class that will listen for WMI events that signify the arrival of a new device.

The AddDeviceArrivedHandler routine creates and starts the handler for detecting new devices.

pollingIntervalSeconds sets the frequency of checking for new devices.

scope is a ManagementScope object that sets the namespace for management operations. The default namespace for WMI queries is "root\\CIMV2".

The Options.EnablePrivileges property is set to true to enable all user privileges for the management operations.

The WqlEventQuery object q represents a WMI event query for the search.

EventClassName names the WMI class for the query. The "__InstanceCreationEvent" class reports an event when a new instance is added to the specified namespace. Note the leading double underscore in __InstanceCreationEvent.

The WithinInterval property sets the polling interval for the queries. A TimeSpan structure sets the interval in hours, minutes, and seconds.

The Condition property @"TargetInstance ISA 'Win32_USBControllerdevice'" configures the query to get all events. The prepended "@" ensures that the single quotes in the string are interpreted as-is.

deviceArrivedWatcher subscribes to event notifications using the specified ManagementScope and WqlEventQuery. If you get a *cannot resolve* error for the ManagementEventWatcher object, go to **Project** > **Add Reference** and add **System.Management**.

DeviceAdded is the application-specific routine that executes when the EventArrived event occurs.

The Start method starts the ManagementEventWatcher and delivers notifications using the EventArrived event.

On event notification, the DeviceAdded routine can perform any desired action, such as looking for a specific device.

Detecting the target device

The example above calls the FindDevice routine on an event notification. The routine can use a ManagementObjectSearcher to look for a device with a specific Vendor ID and Product ID.

Use

```
void FindDevice()
{
   const String deviceIdString = @"USB\VID_0925"&PID_150C";

   _deviceReady = false;

   var searcher = new ManagementObjectSearcher ("root\\CIMV2",
      "SELECT PNPDeviceID FROM Win32_PnPEntity");

   foreach (ManagementObject queryObj in searcher.Get())
   {
      if (queryObj["PNPDeviceID"].ToString().Contains
        (deviceIdString))
      {
         _deviceReady = true;
      }
   }
}
```

How it works

deviceIdString is a PNPDeviceID, which is a string that contains the Vendor ID (0925) and Product ID (150C) of the desired device. The prepended "@" ensures that the backslash in the string is interpreted as-is and not as an escape character.

searcher is a ManagementObjectSearcher object that specifies a ManagementScope for the query ("root\\CIMV2") and a query to execute ("SELECT PNPDeviceID FROM

Win32_PnPEntity"). The query searches the PNPDeviceID properties of the WMI class Win32_PnPEntity. This class represents the properties of Plug and Play (PnP) devices, which include USB devices.

A foreach loop searches the results for a PNPDeviceID that contains the target string and sets _deviceReady true if found.

The ManagementObjectSearcher can search for properties other than the PNPDeviceID. Here are some examples.

To search the Description property for "winusb", use:

```
var searcher = new ManagementObjectSearcher ("root\\CIMV2",
    "SELECT Description FROM Win32_PnPEntity");

foreach (ManagementObject queryObj in searcher.Get())
{
    if (queryObj["Description"].ToString().ToLower().Contains
       ("winusb"))
    {
        _deviceReady = true;
    {
}
```

To search for any device that uses the WinUSB ClassGUID, use:

```
const String classGuid = "88bae032-5a81-49f0-bc3d-a4ff138216d6";

var searcher = new ManagementObjectSearcher ("root\\CIMV2",
    "SELECT ClassGUID FROM Win32_PnPEntity");

foreach (ManagementObject queryObj in searcher.Get())
{
        if (queryObj["ClassGUID"].ToString().Contains(classGUID))
        {
            _deviceReady = true;
        {
}
```

To search all properties, use an asterisk to specify the properties to search:

```
var searcher = new ManagementObjectSearcher ("root\\CIMV2",
    "SELECT * FROM Win32_PnPEntity");
```

An enum structure can hold device properties of interest in the Win32_PnPEntity class:

```
private enum WmiDeviceProperties
{
    Caption,
    Description,
    Manufacturer,
    Name,
    CompatibleID,
    PNPDeviceID,
    DeviceID,
    ClassGUID,
    Availability
}
```

A foreach loop can step through the enum's members and display the properties for a found device:

```
foreach (WmiDeviceProperties wmiDeviceProperty
    in Enum.GetValues(typeof(WmiDeviceProperties)))
{
   Console.WriteLine(wmiDeviceProperty.ToString() + ": {0}",
    queryObj[wmiDeviceProperty.ToString()]);
}
```

Adding a handler for removed devices

In a similar way, Management functions can detect when a target device is no longer available. This routine creates a handler for removed devices.

Use

```
private ManagementEventWatcher deviceRemovedWatcher;

private void AddDeviceRemovedHandler()
{
   const Int32 pollingIntervalSeconds = 3;
   var scope = new ManagementScope("root\\CIMV2");
   scope.Options.EnablePrivileges = true;

   var q = new WqlEventQuery();
   q.EventClassName = "__InstanceDeletionEvent";
   q.WithinInterval = new TimeSpan(0, 0, pollingIntervalSeconds);
   q.Condition = @"TargetInstance ISA 'Win32_USBControllerdevice'";
   deviceRemovedWatcher = new ManagementEventWatcher(scope, q);
   deviceRemovedWatcher.EventArrived += DeviceRemoved;
   deviceRemovedWatcher.Start();
```

```
private void DeviceRemoved(object sender, EventArgs e)
{
    FindDevice();

    // Perform other actions as needed.
}
```

How it works

The routine is similar to the AddDeviceArrivedHandler routines but uses the "__InstanceDeletionEvent" and calls a DeviceRemoved routine.

deviceRemovedWatcher is an instance of the ManagementEventWatcher class that will listen for WMI events that signify the removal of a device.

The DeviceRemoved routine calls the FindDevice routine to find out if the target device is available.

11

Human Interface Devices: Capabilities

The human interface device (HID) class has wide support on host systems to enable using keyboards, mice, and similar devices. For this reason, and because the HID class also supports exchanging data for application-specific purposes, many special-purpose devices use the HID class.

Chapter 7 introduced the HID class. This chapter shows how to determine whether a design can use the class, introduces HID-specific requests, and discusses HID firmware options. Chapter 12 describes the reports that HIDs use to exchange information, and Chapter 13 shows how to access HIDs from applications.

What is a HID?

The name *human interface device* suggests that HIDs interact directly with people, and many HIDs do just that. A mouse detects when someone moves it or presses a key. A host may send data that translates to an effect that a user senses on a joystick. Besides keyboards, mice, and joysticks, devices with HID interfaces include remote controls, telephone keypads, game controls such as data gloves and steering wheels, barcode readers, and UPS units. Devices with virtual control panels on the host can use a HID interface to send control-panel data to the device. A virtual control panel can be cheaper to implement than physical controls on a device.

A HID doesn't have to have a human interface. The device just needs to be able to function within the limits of the HID class specification. These are the major abilities and limits of HID-class devices:

• All data exchanged resides in fixed-length structures called reports. The host sends and receives data by sending and requesting reports in control or interrupt transfers. The report format is flexible and can handle just about any type of data, and a single device can support multiple reports, but each defined report has a fixed length.

• A HID must have an interrupt IN endpoint for sending Input reports.

• A HID can have at most one interrupt IN endpoint and one interrupt OUT endpoint.

• The interrupt IN endpoint enables the HID to send information to the host at unpredictable times. For example, there's no way for the host computer to know when a user will press a key on the keyboard, so the host's driver uses interrupt transactions to poll the device periodically to obtain new data.

• The rate of data exchange is limited. As Chapter 3 explained, a host can guarantee a low-speed interrupt endpoint a maximum data transfer rate of 800 B/s. For full-speed endpoints, the maximum is 64 kB/s. High-speed and Enhanced Super-Speed endpoints support faster rates, but to comply with the USB 2.0 and USB 3.0 specifications, the endpoints in the default interface should request no more than 64 kB/s. Under Windows and other OSes, supporting an alternate HID interface requires a vendor-provided driver, which eliminates the advantage of using the OS-provided driver. Control transfers have no guaranteed bandwidth except for the bandwidth reserved for all control transfers on the bus.

A HID may be just one of multiple interfaces in a device. For example, a USB speaker might use isochronous transfers for audio and a HID interface for controlling volume, balance, treble, and bass.

Hardware requirements

To comply with the HID specification, the interface's endpoints and descriptors must meet several requirements.

Endpoints

All HID transfers use either the control endpoint or an interrupt endpoint. Every HID must have an interrupt IN endpoint for sending data to the host. An interrupt OUT endpoint is optional. Table 11-1 shows the transfer types and their typical use in HIDs.

Reports

The requirement for an interrupt IN endpoint suggests that every HID must have at least one Input report defined in the HID's report descriptor. Output and Feature reports are optional.

Control transfers

The HID specification defines six class-specific requests. Two requests, Set Report and Get Report, provide a way for the host and device to transfer reports to and from the device using control transfers. Set Idle and Get Idle set and read the Idle rate, which determines whether or not a device resends data that hasn't changed since the last report. Set Protocol and Get Protocol set and read a protocol value, which can enable a device to function with a simplified protocol when the full HID drivers aren't loaded on the host, such as during boot up.

Interrupt transfers

Interrupt endpoints provide a way to exchange data when the receiver must get the data periodically and with minimum delay. Control transfers can be delayed if the bus is very busy, while the bandwidth for interrupt transfers is guaranteed to be available after successful enumeration.

The ability to do Interrupt OUT transfers was added in USB 1.1, and the option to use an interrupt OUT pipe was added to version 1.1 of the HID specification.

Firmware requirements

The device's descriptors must include an interface descriptor for the HID class, a class-specific HID descriptor, and an interrupt IN endpoint descriptor. An interrupt OUT endpoint descriptor is optional. The firmware must also contain a class-specific report descriptor with information about the format and use of the report data.

A HID can support one or more reports. The report descriptor specifies the size and contents of the data in a device's report(s) and may also include information about how the receiver of the data should use the data. Values in the descriptor define each report as an Input, Output, or Feature report. The host receives data in Input reports and sends data in Output reports. A Feature report can travel in either direction.

Every device should support at least one Input report that the host can retrieve using interrupt transfers or control-transfer requests. Output reports are optional and can

Table 11-1: The transfer type used in a HID transfer depends on the chip's abilities and the requirements of the data being sent.

Transfer Type	Source of Data	Typical Data	Required Pipe?
Control	Device (IN transfer)	Data that doesn't have critical timing requirements.	yes
	Host (OUT transfer)	Data that doesn't have critical timing requirements, or any data if there is no OUT interrupt pipe.	
Interrupt	Device (IN transfer)	Periodic or low-latency data.	yes
	Host (OUT transfer)	Periodic or low-latency data.	no

use control or interrupt transfers. Feature reports are optional and always use control transfers.

Descriptors

As with any USB device, a HID's descriptors tell the host what it needs to know to communicate with the device. Listing 11-1 shows example device, configuration, interface, class, and endpoint descriptors for a HID with a vendor-specific function.

The host learns about the HID interface during enumeration by sending a Get Descriptor request for the configuration containing the HID interface. An interface descriptor specifies the HID interface. A HID class descriptor specifies the combined number of report and physical descriptors supported by the interface. During enumeration, the HID driver requests the report descriptor and any physical descriptors.

The HID interface

In the interface descriptor, bInterfaceclass = 0x03 to identify the interface as a HID. Other fields that contain HID-specific information in the interface descriptor are the bInterfaceSubclass and bInterfaceProtocol fields, which can specify a boot interface.

If bInterfaceSubclass = 0x01, the device supports a boot interface. A HID with a boot interface can communicate with the host even when the host hasn't loaded its HID drivers. This situation might occur when viewing the system setup screens that you can access on bootup or when using Windows Safe mode for system troubleshooting.

A keyboard or mouse with a boot interface can use a simplified protocol typically supported by the host's UEFI or BIOS. The UEFI or BIOS loads from non-volatile memory on bootup and is available in any OS mode. The HID specification defines

```
UCHAR device_descriptor[0x12] =
{
0x12,               // bLength           Descriptor size (18 bytes)
0x01,               // bDescriptorType   Descriptor type (device)
0x00, 0xx02,        // bcdUSB            USB spec. release 2.00
0x00,               // bDeviceClass      Class declared in interface desc.
0x00,               // bDeviceSubClass   Subclass code
0x00,               // bDeviceProtocol   Protocol code
0x08,               // bMaxPacketSize0   Endpoint zero maximum packet size
0x25, 0x09,         // idVendor          Vendor ID (0x0925)
0x34, 0x12,         // idProduct         Product ID (0x1234)
0x00, 0x01,         // bcdDevice         Device release number (0x0100)
0x01,               // iManufacturer     Manufacturer string index
0x02,               // iProduct          Product string index
0x00,               // iSerialNumber     Device serial number string index
0x01                // bNumConfigurations Number of configurations (1)
}

UCHAR configuration_descriptor[0x29] =
{
// Configuration descriptor

0x09,               // bLength           Descriptor size (9 bytes)
0x02,               // bDescriptorType   Descriptor type (configuration)
0x29, 0x00,         // wTotalLength      Length of this + subordinate
                    //                       descriptors (41)
0x01,               // bNumInterfaces    Number of interfaces
0x01,               // bConfigurationValueIndex of this configuration
0x00,               // iConfiguration    Configuration string index
0xA0,               // bmAttributes      bus powered, remote wakeup support
0x32,               // bMaxPower         Maximum power consumption (100 mA)

// Interface Descriptor

0x09,               // bLength           Descriptor size (9 bytes)
0x04,               // bDescriptorType   Descriptor type (interface)
0x00,               // bInterfaceNumber  Interface Number
0x00,               // bAlternateSetting Alternate Setting Number
0x02,               // bNumEndpoints     Number of endpoints
0x03,               // bInterfaceClass   Interface class (HID)
0x00,               // bInterfaceSubclass Interface subclass
0x00,               // bInterfaceProtocol Interface protocol
0x00,               // iInterface        Interface string index
```

Listing 11-1: Example descriptors for a vendor-specific HID. (Part 1 of 2)

```
// HID descriptor

0x09,                  // bLength             Descriptor size (9 bytes)
0x21,                  // bDescriptorType     Descriptor type (HID)
0x10, 0x01,            // bcdHID              HID release number (1.1)
0x00,                  // bCountryCode        Country code
0x01,                  // bNumDescriptors     Number class descriptors
0x22,                  // bDescriptorType     Class descriptor type (report)
0x2F, 0x00,            // wDescriptorLength   Report descriptor size (47 bytes)

// Interrupt IN endpoint descriptor

0x07,                  // bLength             Descriptor size (7 bytes)
0x05,                  // bDescriptorType     Descriptor type (endpoint)
0x81,                  // bEndpointAddress    Endpoint 1 IN
0x03,                  // bmAttributes        Transfer type (interrupt)
0x40, 0x00,            // wMaxPacketSize      Maximum packet size
0x0A,                  // bInterval           Polling interval (ms)

// Interrupt OUT endpoint descriptor

0x07,                  // bLength             Descriptor size (7 bytes)
0x05,                  // bDescriptorType     Descriptor type (endpoint)
0x01,                  // bEndpointAddress    Endpoint 1 OUT
0x03,                  // bmAttributes        Transfer type (interrupt)
0x40, 0x00,            // wMaxPacketSize      Maximum packet size
0x0A                   // bInterval           Polling interval (ms)
}
```

Listing 11-1: Example descriptors for a vendor-specific HID. (Part 2 of 2)

boot-interface protocols for keyboards and mice. If a device has a boot interface, bInterfaceProtocol indicates if the HID supports the keyboard (0x01) or mouse (0x02) function.

The HID Usage Tables document defines the report format for keyboards and mice that use the boot protocol. The system understands the boot protocol and assumes that a boot device will support the protocol, so there is no need to read a report descriptor from the device. Before sending or requesting reports, the system sends the HID-specific Set Protocol request to request to use the boot protocol. When the full HID drivers have been loaded, the driver can use the Set Protocol request to cause the device to switch from the boot protocol to the report protocol, which uses the report formats defined in the report descriptor. If the HID doesn't support a boot protocol, bInterfaceSubclass = 0x00.

HID class descriptor

The HID class descriptor (Table 11-2) identifies additional descriptors for HID communications. The class descriptor has seven or more fields depending on the number of additional descriptors.

Report descriptors

A report descriptor defines the format and use of the data in the HID's reports. If the device is a mouse, the data reports mouse movements and button clicks. If the device is a relay controller, the data specifies which relays to open and close. The descriptor format is flexible enough for use with devices with varied functions.

A report descriptor is a class-specific descriptor. The host retrieves the descriptor by sending a Get Descriptor request to the interface with the high byte of the wValue field set to 0x22.

Listing 11-2 is a report descriptor that defines an Input report, an Output report, and a Feature report. The device sends two bytes of vendor-defined data in the Input report. The host sends two bytes of vendor-defined data in the Output report. The Feature report is two bytes of vendor-defined data that the host can send to the device or request from the device.

Report descriptors similar to this example can serve many HIDs with vendor-specific functions. For a loop-back test, device firmware can copy received data from an Input report into an Output report to send back to the host. For a "lights and switches" application, firmware can use received Input report data to control LEDs and use Output reports to send logic states read at switches.

Each item in the report descriptor consists of a byte that identifies the item and one or more bytes containing the item's data. The HID specification defines item types that a report can contain. Chapter 12 has more about report formats. Here is the function of each item in the example report descriptor:

The **Usage Page** item (0x06) specifies the general function of the device, such as generic desktop control, game control, or alphanumeric display. The HID Usage Tables document provides values for different Usage Pages. Vendor-defined Usage Pages use the range 0xFF00–0xFFFF. In the example descriptor, the Usage Page is the vendor-defined value 0xFFA0.

The **Usage** item (0x09) specifies the function of an individual report in a Usage Page. For example, Usages available for generic desktop controls include mouse, joystick,

Table 11-2: The HID class descriptor specifies the length of the report descriptor. Information source: *Device Class Definition for Human Interface Devices (HID) Version 1.11*.

Offset (decimal)	Field	Size (bytes)	Description
0	bLength	1	Descriptor size in bytes.
1	bDescriptorType	1	This descriptor's type: 0x21 to indicate the HID class.
2	bcdHID	2	HID specification release number (BCD).
4	bCountryCode	1	Numeric expression identifying the country for localized hardware (BCD) or 0x00.
5	bNumDescriptors	1	Number of subordinate report and physical descriptors.
6	bDescriptorType	1	The type of a class-specific descriptor that follows. A report descriptor (required) is type 0x22.
7	wDescriptorLength	2	Total length of the descriptor identified above.
9	bDescriptorType	1	Optional. The type of a class-specific descriptor that follows. A physical descriptor is type 0x23.
10	wDescriptorLength	2	Total length of the descriptor identified above. Present only if bDescriptorType is present immediately above. May be followed by additional wDescriptorType and wDescriptorLength fields to identify additional physical descriptors.

and keyboard. Because the example's Usage Page is vendor-defined, all of the Usages in the Usage Page are vendor-defined also. In the example, the Usage is 0x01.

The **Collection (Application)** item (0xA1) begins a group of items that together perform a single function, such as keyboard or mouse. Each report descriptor must have an application collection.

The Collection contains three reports. Each report has these items:

A vendor-defined **Usage** applies to the data in the report.

A **Logical Minimum** and **Logical Maximum** specify the range of values that the report can contain. In the example, the values can range from zero to 255.

The **Report Size** item indicates how many bits are in each reported data item. In the example, each data item is eight bits.

The **Report Count** item indicates how many data items the report contains. In the example, each report contains two data items.

In the final item, the first byte specifies whether the report is an Input report (0x81), Output report (0x91), or Feature report (0xB1). The second byte contains

```
UCHAR report_descriptor[0x2F] =
{
0x06, 0xA0, 0xFF,        // Usage Page (vendor-defined)
0x09, 0x01,              // Usage (vendor-defined)

0xA1, 0x01,              // Collection (Application)

0x09, 0x03,              // Usage (vendor-defined)
0x15, 0x00,              // Logical Minimum (0)
0x26, 0xFF, 0x00,        // Logical Maximum (255)
0x75, 0x08,              // Report Size (8 bits)
0x95, 0x02,              // Report Count (2)
0x81, 0x02,              // Input report (Data, Variable, Absolute)

0x09, 0x04,              // Usage (vendor-defined)
0x15, 0x00,              // Logical Minimum (0)
0x26, 0xFF, 0x00,        // Logical Maximum (255)
0x75, 0x08,              // Report Size (8 bits)
0x95, 0x02,              // Report Count (2)
0x91, 0x02,              // Output report (Data, Variable, Absolute)

0x09, 0x05,              // Usage (vendor-defined)
0x15, 0x00,              // Logical Minimum (0)
0x26, 0xFF, 0x00,        // Logical Maximum (255)
0x75, 0x08,              // Report Size (8 bits)
0x95, 0x02,              // Report Count (2)
0xB1, 0x02,              // Feature report (Data, Variable, Absolute)

0xC0                     // End Collection
}
```

Listing 11-2: This report descriptor defines an Input report, an Output report, and a Feature report. Each report transfers two vendor-defined bytes.

additional information about the report data, such as whether the values are relative or absolute.

An **End Collection** item (0xC0) closes the Application Collection.

HID-specific requests

The HID specification defines six requests (Table 11-3) that transfer HID-specific data in control transfers.

Table 11-3: The HID class defines six control requests. Information source: *Device Class Definition for Human Interface Devices (HID) Version 1.11*

Request Number	Request	Data Source (Data stage)	wValue (high byte, low byte)	wIndex	Data Length (bytes) (wLength)	Data Stage Contents	Required?
0x01	Get Report	device	report type, Report ID	interface	report length	report	yes
0x02	Get Idle	device	00h, Report ID	interface	0x0001	idle duration	no
0x03	Get Protocol	device	0x0000	interface	0x0001	protocol	yes for HIDs that support a boot protocol
0x09	Set Report	host	report type, Report ID	interface	report length	report	no
0x0A	Set Idle	no Data stage	idle duration, Report ID	interface	–	–	no except for keyboards using the boot protocol
0x0B	Set Protocol	no Data stage	00h, protocol	interface	–	–	yes for HIDs that support a boot protocol

Get Report

Purpose: The host requests an Input or Feature report from a HID using a control transfer.

Request Number (bRequest): 0x01

Source of Data: device

Data Length (wLength): length of the report

Contents of wValue field: The high byte contains the report type (0x01 = Input, 0x03 = Feature), and the low byte contains the Report ID. The default Report ID is 0x00.

Contents of wIndex field: the number of the interface the request is directed to.

Contents of data packet in the Data stage: the report

Comments: The HID specification says that all HIDs must support this request. A host may enumerate and communicate with a HID that doesn't support the request, but future editions of the OS might enforce the requirement. See also Set Report.

Get Idle

Purpose: The host reads the current Idle rate from a HID.

Request Number (bRequest): 0x02

Source of Data: device

Data Length (wLength): 0x0001

Contents of wValue field: The high byte is 0x00. The low byte indicates the Report ID the request applies to. If the low byte is 0x00, the request applies to all of the HID's Input reports.

Contents of wIndex field: the number of the interface that supports this request.

Contents of data packet in the Data stage: the Idle rate expressed in units of 4 ms.

Comments: HIDs aren't required to support this request. See Set Idle for more details.

Get Protocol

Purpose: The host learns whether the boot or report protocol is currently active in the HID.

Request Number (bRequest): 0x03

Source of Data: device

Data Length (wLength): 0x0001

Contents of wValue field: 0x0000

Contents of wIndex field: the number of the interface that supports this request.

Contents of data packet in the Data stage: the protocol (0x00 = boot protocol, 0x01 = report protocol).

Comments: Boot devices must support this request. See also Set Protocol.

Set Report

Purpose: The host sends an Output or Feature report to a HID using a control transfer.

Request Number (bRequest): 0x09

Source of Data: host

Data Length (wLength): length of the report

Contents of wValue field: The high byte contains the report type (0x02 = Output, 0x03 = Feature), and the low byte contains the Report ID. The default Report ID is 0x00.

Contents of wIndex field: the number of the interface the request is directed to.

Contents of data packet in the Data stage: the report.

Comments: If a HID interface doesn't have an Interrupt OUT endpoint or if the host complies only with version 1.0 of the HID specification, this request is the only way the host can send data to the HID. HIDs aren't required to support this request. See also Get Report.

Set Idle

Purpose: conserves bandwidth by limiting the reporting frequency of an interrupt IN endpoint when the data hasn't changed since the last report.

Request Number (bRequest): 0x0A

Data Length (wLength): 0x0000

Contents of wValue field: The high byte sets the duration, or the maximum amount of time between reports. A value of 0x00 means that the HID will send a report only when the report data has changed or the duration time has elapsed. The low byte indicates the Report ID that the request applies to. If the low byte is 0x00, the request applies to all of the HID's Input reports.

Contents of wIndex field: the number of the interface that supports this request.

Comments: The duration is in units of 4 ms, which gives a range of 4–1,020 ms. No matter what the duration value, if the report data has changed since the last Input report sent, on receiving an interrupt IN token packet, the HID sends the data. If the data hasn't changed and the duration time hasn't elapsed since the last report, the HID returns NAK. If the data hasn't changed and the duration time has elapsed since the last report, the HID sends report data.

A duration value of 0x00 indicates an infinite duration: the HID sends a report only if the report data has changed and otherwise returns NAK. On enumerating a HID, the Windows HID driver attempts to set the idle rate to 0x00.

HIDs aren't required to support this request except for keyboards using the boot protocol. Not all device controllers have hardware support for the Idle rate. Device firmware can support the feature with help from a hardware timer. A HID can ignore the request by returning STALL. See also Get Idle.

Set Protocol

Purpose: The host specifies whether the HID should use the boot or report protocol.

Request Number (bRequest): 0x0B

Data Length (wLength): 0x0000

Contents of wValue field: the protocol (0x0000 = boot protocol, 0x0001 = report protocol).

Contents of wIndex field: the number of the interface that supports this request.

Comments: Boot devices must support this request. See also Get Protocol.

Transferring data

When enumeration is complete, the host has identified the device interface as a HID, established pipes with the interface's endpoints, and learned the report formats for sending and receiving data.

The host can then request reports using interrupt IN transfers and control transfers with Get Report requests. The device also has the option to support receiving reports using interrupt OUT transfers and control transfers with Set Report requests.

Writing firmware

Many device vendors provide HID examples.

Microchip provides HID example code for PIC microcontrollers for Microchip's compilers. The Microchip Libraries for Applications include generic HID, mouse, and other HID examples. See *janaxelson.com* for a generic HID example that supports exchanging reports via both interrupt and control transfers. Texas Instruments also provides HID example code for its MSP430 series.

Tools

Another option for users of Microchip device controllers is HIDmaker 32 from Trace Systems, Inc. A software wizard asks questions about your device and generates firmware to implement the Input, Output, and Feature reports you specify. The tool supports 8-, 16-, and 32-bit controllers with a less expensive version available for 8-bit controllers only. The tool also generates PC application code in several programming languages.

The HIDmaker Test Suite includes two other tools. The AnyHID application displays report descriptors and enables exchanging data with attached and enumerated HIDs except system mice and keyboards. USBwatch is a low-budget USB analyzer for HIDs. To use the analyzer, you add the provided code to your device firmware and connect the device's asynchronous serial port to a PC's serial port via RS-232 or a USB/serial-port adapter. The firmware writes debugging data to the serial port for display by the USBwatch application. USBwatch can display enumeration and application data. You can also define your own messages for firmware to send at locations you select in your code.

12

Human Interface Devices: Reports

Chapter 11 introduced the reports that HIDs use to exchange data. A report can be a basic buffer of bytes or a complex assortment of items with assigned functions and units. This chapter shows how to create reports to fit specific applications.

Report structure

The report descriptor provides information about the data the HID sends and receives. The descriptor identifies the device's function and can specify uses and units for the report data. Controls and data items describe values to be transferred in one or more reports. A control is a button, switch, or other physical entity that operates or regulates an aspect of a device. Everything else is a data item.

For vendor-specific devices intended for use with a vendor-provided application, the application often knows in advance the type, size, and order of the data in a report so there's no need to obtain this information from the device. For example, when the vendor of a data-acquisition unit creates an application for use with the unit, the vendor already knows the data format the device uses in its reports. At most, the application might check the Product ID and release number from the device descriptor to learn whether the application can request a particular setting or action. For applications like these, the host and device can exchange data in vendor-defined buffers without relying on the report descriptor to define what the buffers contain.

A tool that can help in creating and debugging report descriptors is the free RDD! HID Report Descriptor Decoder (*sourceforge.net*). From a command line, you can input data as hexadecimal strings or specify a file that contains hexadecimal strings or binary data, and the tool decodes the data and highlights any errors. The tool can also generate a C header file from provided data. The tool requires a Rexx interpreter, available free from multiple sources.

The USB-IF provides a free HID Descriptor Tool for creating HID report descriptors, but the tool hasn't been updated for many years and thus is of limited use.

Control and data item values

Several documents define values that reports may contain. The first place to look is the USB-IF's *HID Usage Tables*, which defines values for generic desktop controls, simulation controls, game controls, LEDs, buttons, telephone devices, and more. Other documents that define values are the main HID specification and the HID specifications for monitor, power, and point-of-sale devices.

Item format

The HID specification defines two report item types: short items and long items. As of HID 1.11, there are no defined Long items.

A Short item's 1-byte prefix specifies the item type, item tag, and item size. These are the elements that make up the prefix byte:

Bits	Contents	Description
1..0	Item size	Number of bytes in the item
3..2	Item type	Item scope: Main, Global, or Local
7..4	Item tag	Item function

The item size specifies how many data bytes the item contains. Note that an item size of 11_b corresponds to 4 data bytes (not 3):

Item Size (binary)	Number of Data Bytes
00	0
01	1
10	2
11	4

The item type specifies the scope of the item: Main (00_b), Global (01_b), or Local (10_b). This chapter has more information about these item types.

The item tag specifies the item's function.

The Main item type

A Main item defines or groups data items within a report descriptor. There are five Main item types. Input, Output, and Feature items each define fields in a type of report. Collection and End Collection items group related items within a report. The default value for all Main items is zero.

Input, Output, and Feature items

Table 12-1 shows supported values for Input, Output, and Feature items. Each item has a 1-byte prefix followed by one or two bytes that describe the report data.

An Input item applies to data a device sends to the host. An Input report contains one or more Input items. The host uses interrupt IN transfers or Get Report requests to request Input reports.

An Output item applies to data the host sends to the device. An Output report contains one or more Output items. Hosts can send Output reports using interrupt OUT transfers and Set Report requests.

A Feature report contains one or more Feature items. A Feature report's data can travel in either direction. Feature reports typically contain configuration settings that affect the overall behavior of the device or one of its components. For example, the host may have a virtual (on-screen) control panel to enable users to select and control a device's settings. The host uses control transfers with Set Report and Get Report requests to send and receive Feature reports.

Following each Input, Output, or Feature item prefix are up to 9 bits that describe the item's data. (An additional 23 bits are reserved.) An Input item prefix followed by 8 bits of item data has the value 0x81. The high four bits are set to 0x8 to indicate an

Table 12-1: The bits that follow Input, Output, and Feature Item prefixes describe the data in a report. Information source: *Device Class Definition for Human Interface Devices (HID) Version 1.11*.

Prefix	Item Data		
	Bit Number	**Meaning if bit = 0**	**Meaning if bit = 1**
Input (100000nn, where nn=the number of bytes in the data following the prefix) For example, use 0x81 for 1 byte of item data. Use 0x82 for 2 bytes of item data.	0	Data	Constant
	1	Array	Variable
	2	Absolute	Relative
	3	No wrap	Wrap
	4	Linear	Non-linear
	5	Preferred state	No preferred state
	6	No null position	Null state
	7	Reserved	
	8	Bit field	Buffered bytes
	9-31	Reserved	
Output (100100nn, where nn=the number of bytes in the data following the prefix) For example, use 0x91 for 1 byte of item data. Use 0x92 for 2 bytes of item data.	0	Data	Constant
	1	Array	Variable
	2	Absolute	Relative
	3	No wrap	Wrap
	4	Linear	Non-linear
	5	Preferred state	No preferred state
	6	No null position	Null state
	7	Non-volatile	Volatile
	8	Bit field	Buffered bytes
	9-31	Reserved	
Feature (101100nn, where nn=the number of bytes in the data following the prefix) For example, use 0xB1 for 1 byte of item data. Use 0xB2 for 2 bytes of item data.	0	Data	Constant
	1	Array	Variable
	2	Absolute	Relative
	3	No wrap	Wrap
	4	Linear	Non-linear
	5	Preferred state	No preferred state
	6	No null position	Null state
	7	Non-volatile	Volatile
	8	Bit field	Buffered bytes
	9-31	Reserved	

Input item, and the low four bits are set to 0x1 to indicate that the item data uses 1 byte. An Input item prefix followed by 9 bits of data has the value 0x82, with the low four bits set to 0x2 to indicate that the item data uses 2 bytes.

The bit functions are the same for Input, Output, and Feature items, except that Input items don't support the volatile/non-volatile bit. These are the uses for each bit:

Data | Constant. Data means that the contents of the item are modifiable (read/write). Constant means the contents are not modifiable (read-only).

Array | Variable. This bit specifies whether the data reports the state of every control (Variable) or just reports the states of controls that are asserted, or active (Array). Reporting only the asserted controls results in a more compact report for devices such as keyboards that have many controls (keys) but where only one or a few controls are asserted at the same time.

For example, if a keypad has eight keys, setting this bit to Variable would mean that the keypad's report would contain a bit for each key. In the report descriptor, the report size would be one bit, the report count would be eight, and the total amount of data sent would be eight bits. Setting the bit to Array would mean that each key has an assigned index, and the keypad's report would contain only the indexes of keys that are pressed. With eight keys, the report size would be three bits, which can report a key number in the range 0–7. The report count would equal the maximum number of simultaneous keypresses that could be reported. If the user can press only one key at a time, the report count would be 1 and the total amount of data sent would be just 3 bits. If the user can press all of the keys at once, the report count would be 8 and the total amount of data sent would be 24 bits.

An out-of-range value reported for an Array item indicates that no controls are asserted.

Absolute | Relative. Absolute means the value is based on a fixed origin. Relative means the data indicates the change from the previous reading. A joystick normally reports absolute data (the joystick's current position), while a mouse reports relative data (how far the mouse has moved since the last report).

No Wrap | Wrap. Wrap indicates that the value rolls over to the minimum if the value continues to increment after reaching its maximum and rolls over to the maximum if the value continues to decrement after reaching its minimum. An item specified as No Wrap that exceeds the specified limits may report a value outside the limits. This bit doesn't apply to Array data.

Linear | Non-linear. Linear indicates that the measured data and the reported value have a linear relationship. In other words, a graph of the reported data and the property being measured forms a straight line. In non-linear data, a graph of the reported data and the property being measured forms a curve. This bit doesn't apply to Array data.

Preferred State | No Preferred State. Preferred state indicates that the control will return to a particular state when the user isn't interacting with it. A momentary push-button has a preferred state (not pushed, or out) when no one is pressing the button. A toggle switch has no preferred state and remains in the last state selected by a user. This bit doesn't apply to Array data.

No Null Position | Null State. Null state indicates that the control supports a state where the control isn't sending meaningful data. A control indicates that it's in the null state by sending a value outside the range defined by its Logical Minimum and Logical Maximum. No Null Position indicates that any data sent by the control is meaningful data. A hat switch on a joystick is in a null position when it isn't being pressed. This bit doesn't apply to Array data.

Non-volatile | Volatile. The Volatile bit applies only to Output and Feature report data. Volatile means the device may change the value on its own, without host inter-action, and also when the host sends a report requesting to change the value. For example, users might request to change the value of a control by pressing a button on the device or by clicking a button on a virtual control panel to cause the host to send a report to the device. Non-volatile means that the device changes the value only when the host requests a new value in a report.

When the host is sending a report and doesn't want to change a volatile item, the value to assign to the item depends on whether the data is defined as relative or absolute. If a volatile item is defined as relative, a report that assigns a value of zero should result in no change. If a volatile item is defined as absolute, a report that assigns an out-of-range value should result in no change. This bit doesn't apply to Array data.

Bit Field | Buffered Bytes. Bit Field means that each bit or a group of bits in a byte can represent a separate piece of data. Buffered Bytes means that the data consists of one or more byte-wide values. The report size for Buffered Byte items must be eight. This bit doesn't apply to Array data. Note that this bit is bit 8 in the item's data so setting this bit requires two bytes of item data.

Collections

All report types use Collection and End Collection items to group related items. Following each Collection item (0xA1) in the report descriptor is a value indicating the collection type (Table 12-2). The End Collection item is a single byte (0xC0).

All report items must be in an application collection. Use of the other collection types is optional. All Main items between a Collection item and its End Collection item are

Table 12-2: Data values for the Collection and End Collection Main Item Tags. Information source: *Device Class Definition for Human Interface Devices (HID) Version 1.11.*

Value	Type	Description
0x00	Physical	Data at a single geometric point.
0x01	Application	Items that have a common purpose or carry out a function.
0x02	Logical	Items that describe a data structure.
0x03	Report	Wraps the fields in a report.
0x04	Named array	Array of selector usages.
0x05	Usage switch	Modifies the purpose or function of Usages in a collection.
0x06	Usage modifier	Modifies the purpose or function of a Usage.
0x07–0x7F	Reserved	–
0x80–0xFF	Vendor defined	–

part of the collection. Each collection must have a Usage tag (described below). Collections can be nested.

A top-level collection is a collection that isn't nested within another collection. A HID interface can have multiple top-level application collections with each representing a different HID function. For example, a keyboard with an embedded pointing device can have a single HID interface with two top-level collections, one for the pointing device's reports and one for the keyboard's reports. Unlike HIDs in separate interfaces in a composite device, these HID functions share interrupt endpoints.

The Global item type

Global items identify reports and describe the data in them, including characteristics such as the data's function, maximum and minimum allowed values, and the size and number of report items. A Global item tag applies to every item that follows until the next Global item tag. Thus a report descriptor doesn't have to repeat values that don't change from one item to the next. Table 12-3 shows the defined Global items.

Identifying the report

Report ID. A HID can support multiple reports of the same type with each report having its own Report ID and contents. This way, each report doesn't have to include every piece of data. Multiple reports are especially useful if the receiver of the data doesn't need frequent updates for all of the data.

In the report descriptor, a Report ID item applies to all items that follow until the next Report ID. If there is no Report ID item, the report uses the default ID of 0x00. A descriptor should not declare a Report ID of 0x00. Report IDs are specific to each report type, so a HID can have one report of each type with the default Report ID.

Table 12-3: There are twelve defined Global items. Information source: *Device Class Definition for Human Interface Devices (HID) Version 1.11*.

Item Type	Value (nn = the number of bytes that follow) (binary)	Description
Usage Page	000001nn	Specifies the data's usage or function.
Logical Minimum	000101nn	Smallest value that an item will report.
Logical Maximum	001001nn	Largest value that an item will report.
Physical Minimum	001101nn	The logical minimum expressed in physical units.
Physical Maximum	010001nn	The logical maximum expressed in physical units.
Unit exponent	010101nn	Base 10 exponent of units.
Unit	011001nn	Unit values.
Report Size	011101nn	Size of an item's fields in bits.
Report ID	100001nn	Prefix that identifies a report.
Report Count	100101nn	The number of data fields for an item.
Push	101001nn	Places a copy of the global item state table on the stack.
Pop	101101nn	Replaces the item state table with the last structure pushed onto the stack.
Reserved	110001nn– 111101nn	For future use.

However, if one report type uses multiple Report IDs, every report in the HID must have a declared Report ID. For example, if a descriptor declares Report IDs 0x01 and 0x02 for Feature reports, any Input or Output reports must also have a Report ID greater than 0x00.

In a transfer that uses a Set Report or Get Report request, the host specifies a Report ID in the Setup transaction in the low byte of the wValue field. In an interrupt transfer, if the interface supports more than one Report ID, the Report ID precedes the report data on the bus. If the interface supports only the default Report ID of 0x00, in interrupt transfers, the Report ID doesn't travel on the bus with the report data.

For Windows applications, the report buffer provided to an API function must be large enough to hold the report plus one byte for the Report ID even if using only Report ID 0x00. When a HID supports multiple Report IDs for Input reports of different sizes, the Windows HID driver requires applications to pass a buffer large enough to hold the longest report.

When a HID supports multiple reports of the same type and different sizes and the HID is sending a report whose data is a multiple of the endpoint's maximum packet size, for all but the HID's longest report, the HID indicates the end of the report by sending a ZLP.

For interrupt transfers that retrieve Input reports from HIDs with multiple Input Report IDs, the host's driver has no way to request a specific report from the device. The device firmware decides which report to place in the endpoint buffer to send to the host. At the host, the HID driver stores the received Report ID and report data.

Describing the data's use

The Global items that describe the data and how to use it are the Usage Page, Logical Minimum and Maximum, Physical Minimum and Maximum, Unit, and Unit Exponent. Each of these items helps the receiver of the report interpret the report's data. All but the Usage Page are involved with converting raw report data to values with units attached. The items make it possible for a report to contain data in a more compact form with the receiver of the data responsible for converting the data to meaningful values.

Usage Page. An item's Usage is a 32-bit value that identifies a function that a device performs. A Usage contains two values: the upper 16 bits are a Global Usage Page item and the lower 16 bits are a Local Usage item. The value in the Local Usage item is a Usage ID. The term *Usage* can refer to either the 32-bit value or the 16-bit Local value. To prevent confusion, some sources use the term Extended Usage to refer to the 32-bit value. Microsoft defines a USAGE type that is a 16-bit value that can contain a Usage Page or a Usage ID.

Multiple items can share a Usage Page while having different Usage IDs. After a Usage Page appears in a report, all Usage IDs that follow are in that Usage Page until the descriptor declares a new Usage Page.

The HID Usage Tables document defines many Usage Pages. There are Usage Pages for common device types including generic desktop controls (mouse, keyboard, joystick), digitizer, barcode scanner, camera control, and various game controls. A vendor can define Usage Pages using values from 0xFF00 to 0xFFFF.

Logical Minimum and Logical Maximum. The Logical Minimum and Logical Maximum define limits for reported values. The limits are expressed in logical units, which means that they use the same units as the values they apply to. For example, if a device reports values of up to 500 mA in units of 2 mA, the Logical Maximum is 250.

If the most significant bit of the highest byte is 1, the value is negative and is expressed as a two's complement. (To express a negative value as a two's complement, complement each bit and add 1 to the result. Perform the same operations to obtain the negative value represented by a two's complement.) Using 1-byte values,

0x00 to 0x7F represent the decimal values zero through +127, and 0xFF to 0x80 represent the decimal values -1 through -128.

The HID specification says that if both the Logical Minimum and Logical Maximum are considered positive, there's no need for a sign bit. To be safe, if the desired result is a minimum of zero and a maximum of 255, you can use a 2-byte value for the maximum:

```
0x15, 0x00,        // Logical Minimum
0x26, 0xFF, 0x00,  // Logical Maximum
```

Note that the Logical Maximum item tag is 0x26 (not 0x25) to indicate that the data that follows the tag is two bytes. Because the most-significant bit of the Logical Maximum is zero, the value is positive.

Converting units

The Physical Minimum, Physical Maximum, Unit Exponent, and Unit items define how to convert reported values into more meaningful units.

Physical Minimum and Physical Maximum. The Physical Minimum and Physical Maximum define the limits for a value when expressed in the units defined by the Units tag. In the earlier example of values of zero through 250 in units of 2 mA, the Physical Minimum is zero and the Physical Maximum is 500. The receiving device uses the logical and physical limit values to obtain the value in the desired units. In the example, reporting the data in units of 2 mA means that the value can transfer in a single byte, with the receiver of the data using the Physical Minimum and Maximum values to translate to mA. The price is a loss in resolution, compared to reporting 1 bit per mA. If the report descriptor doesn't specify these items, they default to the Logical Minimum and Logical Maximum.

Unit Exponent. The Unit Exponent specifies what power of 10 to apply to the value obtained after using the logical and physical limits to convert the value into the desired units. The USB 2.0 specification is unclear as to whether the exponent is limited to four bits, but common usage assumes this limit. A value of zero causes the value to be multiplied by 10^0, which is the same as applying no exponent. These are the codes:

Exponent	0	1	2	3	4	5	6	7	-8	-7	-6	-5	-4	-3	-2	-1
Code (hex)	00	01	02	03	04	05	06	07	08	09	0A	0B	0C	0D	0E	0F

For example, if the value obtained is 1234 and the Unit Exponent is 0x0E, the final value is 12.34.

Unit. The Unit tag specifies what units to apply to the report data after the value is converted using the Physical and Unit Exponent items. The HID specification defines codes for the basic units of length, mass, time, temperature, current, and luminous intensity. Most other units can be derived from these.

Specifying a Unit value can be more complicated than you might expect. Table 12-4 shows values to work from. A value can be as long as four bytes, with each nibble having a defined function. Nibble 0 (the least significant nibble) specifies the measurement system, either English or SI (International System of Units) and whether the measurement is in linear or angular units. Each of the nibbles that follow represents a quality to be measured with the value of the nibble representing the exponent to apply to the value. For example, a nibble with a value of 0x2 means that the corresponding value is in units squared. A nibble with a value of 0xD, which represents -3, means that the units are expressed as 1/units^3. These exponents are distinct from the Unit Exponent value, which is a power of ten applied to the data, rather than an exponent applied to the units.

Note that the basic SI units for length and temperature are meters and kilograms, but the HID specification uses centimeters and grams as basic units for the Unit tag.

Converting raw data

To convert raw data to values with units attached, three things must occur. The firmware's report descriptor must contain the information needed for the conversion. The sender must provide data that matches the report descriptor's specifications. And the receiver of the data must apply the conversions specified in the report descriptor.

Below are examples of descriptors and raw and converted data. Just because a tag exists in the HID specification doesn't mean you have to use it. If the application knows what format and units to use for the values it's going to send or receive, the firmware doesn't have to specify these items.

To specify time in seconds, up to a minute, the report descriptor might include this information:

Logical Minimum: 0x00

Logical Maximum: 0x3C (60)

Physical Minimum: 0x00

Physical Maximum: 0x3C (60)

Unit: 0x1003. Nibble 0 = 3 to select the English Linear measuring system (though in this case, any value from 1 to 4 would work). Nibble 3 = 1 to select time in seconds.

Unit Exponent: 0x00

Table 12-4: The units to apply to a reported value are a function of the measuring system and exponent values specified in the Unit item. Information source: *Device Class Definition for Human Interface Devices (HID) Version 1.11.*

Nibble Number	Quality Measured	Measuring System (Nibble 0 value)				
		None (0x0)	SI Linear (0x01)	SI Rotation (0x2)	English Linear (0x3)	English Rotation (0x4)
1	Length	None	Centimeter	Radian	Inch	Degree
2	Mass	None	Gram		Slug	
3	Time	None	Second			
4	Temperature	None	Kelvin		Fahrenheit	
5	Current	None	Ampere			
6	Luminous Intensity	None	Candela			
7	Reserved	None				

With this information, the receiver knows that the value sent equals a number of seconds.

To specify time in tenths of seconds up to a minute, increase the Logical Maximum and Physical Maximum and change the Unit Exponent:

Logical Minimum: 0x00

Logical Maximum: 0x0258 (600)

Physical Minimum: 0x00

Physical Maximum: 0x0258 (600)

Unit: 0x1003. Nibble 0 = 3 to select the English Linear measuring system. Nibble 3 = 1 to select time in seconds.

Unit Exponent: 0x0F. This represents an exponent of -1 to indicate that the value is expressed in tenths of seconds rather than seconds.

Sending values as large as 600 requires 2 bytes, which the firmware specifies in the Report Size tag.

To send a temperature value using one byte to represent temperatures from -20 to 110°F, the report descriptor might contain the following:

Logical Minimum: 0x80 (-128 decimal expressed as a hexadecimal two's complement)

Logical Maximum: 0x7F (127 decimal)

Physical Minimum: 0xEC (-20 expressed as a hexadecimal two's complement)

Physical Maximum: 0x6E (110 decimal)

Unit: 0x10003. Nibble 0 = 3 to select the English Linear measuring system. Nibble 4 = 1 to select degrees Fahrenheit.

Unit Exponent: 0x00

These values ensure the highest possible resolution for a single-byte report item, because the transmitted values can span the full range from 0 to 255.

In this case the logical and physical limits differ, so converting is required. This function accepts decimal values and returns the number of bits per logical unit:

```
private Single BitsPerLogicalUnit
    (Int32 logical_maximum,
    Int32 logical_minimum,
    Int32 physical_maximum,
    Int32 physical_minimum,
    Int32 unit_exponent)
{
    Single calculatedBitsPerLogicalUnit = Convert.ToSingle
        ((logical_maximum - logical_minimum) /
        ((physical_maximum - physical_minimum) *
        (Math.Pow(10, unit_exponent)))));

    return calculatedBitsPerLogicalUnit;
}
```

With the example values, the resolution is 1.96 bits per degree, or 0.51 degree per bit.

This function converts a logical value to the specified physical units:

```
private Single ValueInPhysicalUnits
    (Int32 value,
    Int32 logical_maximum,
    Int32 logical_minimum,
    Int32 physical_maximum,
    Int32 physical_minimum,
    Int32 unit_exponent)
{
    Single calculatedValueInPhysicalUnits = Convert.ToSingle
        (value *
        ((physical_maximum - physical_minimum) *
        (Math.Pow(10, unit_exponent))) /
        (logical_maximum - logical_minimum));

    return calculatedValueInPhysicalUnits;
}
```

If the value in logical units (the raw data) is 63, the converted value in the specified units is 32° F.

Describing the data's size and format

Two Global items describe the size and format of the report data.

Report Size specifies the size in bits of a field in an Input, Output, or Feature item. Each field contains one piece of data.

Report Count specifies how many fields an Input, Output, or Feature item contains.

For example, if a report has two 8-bit fields, Report Size is 0x08 and Report Count is 0x02. If a report has one 16-bit field, Report Size is 0x10 and Report Count is 0x01.

A single Input, Output, or Feature report can contain multiple items, each with its own Report Size and Report Count.

Saving and restoring Global items

The final two Global items enable saving and restoring sets of Global items. These items allow flexible report formats while using minimum storage space in the device.

Push places a copy of the Global-item state table on the CPU's stack. The Global-item state table contains the current settings for all previously defined Global items.

Pop is the complement to Push and restores the saved states of the previously pushed Global item states.

The Local item type

Local items specify qualities of the controls and data items in a report. A Local item's value applies to all items that follow within a Main item until the descriptor assigns a new value. Local items don't carry over to the next Main item; each Main item begins fresh with no Local items defined.

Local items relate to general usages, body-part designators, and strings. A Delimiter item enables grouping sets of Local items. Table 12-5 shows the values and meaning of each of the items.

Usage. The Local Usage item is the Usage ID that works together with the Global Usage Page to describe the function of a control, data, or collection.

The HID Usage Tables document lists many Usage IDs. For example, the Buttons Usage Page uses Local Usage IDs from 0x0001 to 0xFFFF to identify which button in a set is pressed, with a value of zero meaning no button pressed.

If a single Usage precedes a series of controls or data items, that Usage applies to all of the controls or data items. If multiple Usages precede controls or data items and the number of controls or data items equals the number of Usages, each Usage

Table 12-5: Local items can provide information about Usages, body parts, and strings. Information source: *Device Class Definition for Human Interface Devices (HID) Version 1.11.*

Local Item Type	Value (nn = the number of item bytes that follow) (binary)	Description
Usage	000010nn	The use for an item or collection.
Usage Minimum	000110nn	The starting Usage associated with the elements in an array or bitmap.
Usage Maximum	001010nn	The ending Usage associated with the elements in an array or bitmap.
Designator Index	001110nn	A Designator value in a physical descriptor. Indicates what body part applies to a control.
Designator Minimum	010010nn	The starting Designator associated with the elements in an array or bitmap.
Designator Maximum	010110nn	The ending Designator associated with the elements in an array or bitmap.
String Index	011110nn	Associates a string with an item or control.
String Minimum	100010nn	The first string index when assigning a group of sequential strings to controls in an array or bitmap.
String Maximum	100110nn	The last string index when assigning a group of sequential strings to controls in an array or bitmap.
Delimiter	101010nn	The beginning (1) or end (0) of a set of Local items.
Reserved	101011nn to 111110nn	For future use.

applies to one control or data item, with the Usages and the controls or data items pairing up in sequence.

In this example, the report contains two bytes. The first byte's Usage is X, and the second byte's Usage is Y.

```
Usage (X),
Usage (Y),
Report Count (0x02),
Report Size (0x08),
Input (Data, Variable, Absolute),
```

If multiple Usages preceded a series of controls or data items and the number of controls or data items is greater than the number of Usages, each Usage pairs up with one control or data item in sequence, and the final Usage applies to all of the remaining controls or data items.

In this example, the report is 16 bytes, Usage X applies to the first byte, Usage Y applies to the second byte, and a vendor-defined Usage applies to the third through 16th bytes.

```
Usage (X)
Usage (Y)
Usage (vendor defined)
Report Count (0x10),
Report Size (0x08),
Input (Data, Variable, Absolute)
```

Usage Minimum and Maximum. The Usage Minimum and Usage Maximum can assign a series of Usage IDs to the elements in an array or bitmap. The following example describes a report that contains the state (0 or 1) of each of three buttons. The Usage Minimum and Usage Maximum specify that the first button has a Usage ID of 0x01, the second button has a Usage ID of 0x02, and the third button has a Usage ID of 0x03:

```
Usage Page (Button Page)
Logical Minimum (0x00)
Logical Maximum (0x01)
Usage Minimum (0x01)
Usage Maximum (0x03)
Report Count (0x03)
Report Size (0x01)
Input (Data, Variable, Absolute)
```

Designator Index. For items with a physical descriptor, the Designator Index specifies a Designator value in a physical descriptor. The Designator specifies what body part the control uses.

Designator Minimum and Designator Maximum. When a report contains multiple Designator Indexes that apply to the elements in a bitmap or array, a Designator Minimum and Designator Maximum can assign a sequential Designator Index to each bit or array item.

String Index. An item or control can include a String Index to associate a string with the item or control. The strings are stored in the same format described in Chapter 4 for product, manufacturer, and serial-number strings.

String Minimum and Maximum. When a report contains multiple string indexes that apply to the elements in a bitmap or array, a String Minimum and String Maximum can assign a sequential String Index to each bit or array item.

Delimiter. A Delimiter defines the beginning (0x01) or end (0x00) of a local item. A delimited local item may contain alternate usages for a control. Different applications can thus define a device's controls in different ways. For example, a button may have a generic use (Button 1) and a specific use (for example, Send or Quit.).

Physical descriptors

A physical descriptor specifies the part or parts of the body intended to activate a control. For example, each finger might have its own assigned control. Similar physical descriptors are grouped into a physical descriptor set. A set consists of a header, followed by the physical descriptors. A physical descriptor is a HID-specific descriptor. The host can retrieve a physical descriptor set by sending a Get Descriptor request to the HID interface with 0x23 in the high byte of the wValue field and the number of the descriptor set in the low byte of the wValue field.

Physical descriptors are optional and rarely used. For most devices, these descriptors either don't apply or the information they provide has no practical use. The HID specification has more information on how to use physical descriptors.

Padding

To pad a descriptor so it contains a multiple of eight bits, a descriptor can include a Main item with no assigned Usage. This excerpt from a keyboard's report descriptor specifies an Output report that transfers five bits of data and three bits of padding:

```
Usage Page (LEDs)
Usage Minimum (0x01)
Usage Maximum (0x05)
Output (Data, Variable, Absolute) (five 1-bit LEDs)
Report Count (0x01)
Report Size (0x03)
Output (Constant) (3 bits of padding)
```

13

Human Interface Devices: Host Application

Chapter 10 showed how to obtain a handle to communicate with a device. This chapter shows how host applications can use handles to access HID-class devices.

HIDClass support routines

Windows provides HIDClass support routines with functions that applications can use to learn about a HID's reports and to send and receive report data.

The routines consider each report item to be either a button or value. A button is a control or data item that has a discrete, binary value, such as *on* (1) or *off* (0). Buttons include items represented by unique Usage IDs in the Buttons, Keyboard, and LED Usage pages. Any report item that isn't a button is a value usage. The report descriptor defines the range for each value usage.

Chapter 13

Table 13-1: Applications can use these functions to obtain information about a HID and its reports.

Function	Purpose
HidD_FreePreparsedData	Free resources used by HidD_GetPreparsedData.
HidD_GetAttributes	Retrieve a pointer to a structure containing the HID's Vendor ID, Product ID, and device release number.
HidD_GetPhysicalDescriptor	Retrieve a physical descriptor.
HidD_GetPreparsedData	Return a handle to a buffer with information about the HID's reports.
HidP_GetButtonCaps	Retrieve an array with information about the buttons in a top-level collection for a specified report type.
HidP_GetCaps	Retrieve a structure describing a HID's reports.
HidP_GetExtendedAttributes	Retrieve a structure with information about Global items the HID parser didn't recognize.
HidP_GetLinkCollectionNodes	Retrieve a structure with information about collections within a top-level collection.
HidP_GetSpecificButtonCaps	Like HidP_GetButtonCaps but can specify a Usage Page, Usage ID, and link collection.
HidP_GetSpecificValueCaps	Like HidP_GetValueCaps but can specify a Usage Page, Usage ID, and link collection.
HidP_GetValueCaps	Retrieve an array with information about the values in a top-level collection for a specified report type.
HidP_IsSameUsageAndPage	Determine if two Usages (each consisting of a Usage Page and Usage ID) are equal.
HidP_MaxDataListLength	Retrieve the maximum number of HIDP_DATA structures that HidP_GetData can return for a HID report type and top-level collection.
HidP_MaxUsageListLength	Retrieve the maximum number of Usage IDs that HidP_GetUsages can return for a report type and top-level collection.
HidP_TranslateUsagesToI8042ScanCodes	Map Usages on the HID_USAGE_PAGE_KEYBOARD Usage Page to PS/2 scan codes.
HidP_UsageAndPageListDifference	Retrieve the differences between two arrays of Usages (Usage Page and Usage ID).
HidP_UsageListDifference	Retrieve the differences between two arrays of Usage IDs.

Table 13-2: Applications can use these functions to retrieve strings from a HID.

Function	Purpose
HidD_GetIndexedString	Retrieve a specified string.
HidD_GetManufacturerString	Retrieve a manufacturer string.
HidD_GetProductString	Retrieve a product string.
HidD_GetSerialNumberString	Retrieve a serial-number string.

Requesting information about the HID

Table 13-1 lists routines that request information about a HID and its reports. Many applications use only a few of these routines. HidD_GetPreparsedData retrieves a pointer to a buffer that contains information about the HID's reports. HidP_GetCaps uses the pointer to retrieve a HIDP_CAPS structure that specifies what report types a device supports and provides information about the information in the reports. For example, the structure specifies the number of HIDP_BUTTON_CAPS structures that have information about a button or set of buttons. The application can call HidP_Get-ButtonCaps to retrieve these structures.

For values, the structure specifies the number of HIDP_VALUE_CAPS structures, and the application can call HidP_GetValueCaps to retrieve these structures.

The support routines also enable retrieving strings, including serial numbers. Table 13-2 lists these routines.

Sending and receiving reports

Table 13-3 lists routines that applications can use to send and receive reports using control transfers.

HidD_GetInputReport requests an Input report using a control transfer with a Get Report request. This function bypasses the HID driver's Input report buffer. HidD_SetOutputReport sends an Output report using a control transfer with a Set Report request.

For Feature reports, HidD_GetFeature retrieves a report using a control transfer and Get Report request and HidD_SetFeature sends a report using a control transfer and Set Report request. Note that HidD_SetFeature is not the same thing as the standard USB request Set Feature.

On failure or a timeout, these functions return with an error code.

For reading Input reports and writing Output reports using interrupt transfers, applications can use .NET's Filestream class. The FileStream class's Read and Write methods are synchronous—they block the program thread until the device responds or the Filestream closes. A better option is ReadAsync and WriteAsync, which don't

Table 13-3: Applications can use these routines to send and receive reports.

routine	Purpose
HidD_GetFeature	Read a Feature report.
HidD_GetInputReport	Read an Input report using a control transfer.
HidD_SetFeature	Send a Feature report.
HidD_SetOutputReport	Send an Output report using a control transfer.

block the application thread if the device doesn't have data to send or delays in accepting received data. These methods also support timeouts if the device doesn't respond within a specified time. The asynchronous methods were added in the .NET Framework 4.5, which doesn't install on Windows XP or earlier and thus aren't available on these earlier OSes.

An alternative to Filestreams is the ReadFile and WriteFile Windows API functions.

Providing and using report data

After retrieving a report, an application can use the raw data directly from the buffer or use HIDClass support routines to extract button or value data. In a similar way, an application can write data to be sent directly into a report's buffer or use HIDClass support routines to place the data in a buffer for sending.

Table 13-4 lists routines that extract information in received reports and store information in reports to be sent. For example, an application can find out what buttons have been pressed by calling HidP_GetButtons, which returns a buffer containing the Usage IDs of all buttons that belong to a specified Usage Page and are set to ON. An application can set and clear buttons in a report to be sent by calling HidP_SetButtons and HidP_UnsetButtons. Applications can retrieve and set values in a report using HidP_GetUsageValue and Hid_Set_UsageValue.

Managing HID communications

Table 13-5 lists routines that applications can use in managing HID communications.

Chapter 10 showed how to use HidD_GetHidGuid to obtain the device interface GUID for the HID class. HidD_SetNumInputBuffers requests to change the size of the HID driver's buffer for Input reports. A larger buffer can be helpful if the application might be too busy at times to read reports before the buffer overflows. The value set is the number of reports the buffer will hold, not the number of bytes. HidD_FlushQueue deletes any Input reports in the buffer.

Table 13-4: Applications can use these routines to extract information in retrieved reports and store information in reports to be sent.

routine	Purpose
HidP_GetButtons	Same as HidP_GetUsages.
HidP_GetButtonsEx	Same as HidP_GetUsagesEx.
HidP_GetData	Retrieve an array of structures with each structure identifying either the data index and state of a button control that is set to ON (1) or the data index and data for a value control.
HidP_GetScaledUsageValue	Retrieve a signed and scaled value from a report.
HidP_GetUsages	Retrieve a list of all of the buttons that are on a specified Usage Page and are set to ON (1).
HidP_GetUsagesEx	Retrieve a list of all of the buttons that are set to ON (1).
HidP_GetUsageValue	Retrieve the data for a specified value.
HidP_GetUsageValueArray	Retrieve data for an array of values with the same Usage ID.
HidP_InitializeReportForID	Set all buttons to OFF (0) and set all values to their null values if defined and otherwise to zero.
HidP_SetButtons	Same as HidP_SetUsages.
HidP_SetData	Sets the states of buttons and data in values in a report.
HidP_SetScaledUsageValue	Convert a signed and scaled physical number to a Usage's logical value and set the value in a report.
HidP_SetUsages	Set one or more buttons in a report to ON (1).
HidP_SetUsageValue	Set the data for a specified value.
HidP_SetUsageValueArray	Set the data for an array of values with the same Usage ID.
HidP_UnsetButtons	Same as HidP_UnsetUsages.
HidP_UnsetUsages	Set one or more buttons in a report to OFF (0).

Identifying a device

After obtaining a handle to a HID as described in Chapter 10, an application can use HIDClass support routines to find out whether the HID is the device the application wants to communicate with. The application can identify a device by its Vendor ID and Product ID or by searching for a device with a specific Usage, such as game controller.

Table 13-5: Applications can use these routines in managing HID communications.

Routine	Purpose
HidD_FlushQueue	Delete all Input reports in the buffer.
HidD_GetHidGuid	Retrieve the device interface GUID for HID-class devices.
HidD_GetNumInputBuffers	Retrieve the number of reports the Input report buffer can hold.
HidD_SetNumInputBuffers	Set the number of reports the Input report buffer can hold.
HidRegisterMinidriver	HID mini-drivers call this routine during initialization to register with the HID class driver.

The code examples in this chapter assume the following Imports and using statements:

```
using Microsoft.Win32.SafeHandles;
using System;
using System.Diagnostics;
using System.IO;
using System.Runtime.InteropServices;
using System.Threading;
using System.Threading.Tasks;
```

Reading the Vendor ID and Product ID

For vendor-specific HIDs that don't have standard Usages, searching for a device with a specific Vendor ID and Product ID can be useful. HidD_GetAttributes retrieves a pointer to a structure containing the Vendor ID, Product ID, and device release number.

Definitions

```
internal struct HIDD_ATTRIBUTES
{
    internal Int32 Size;
    internal UInt16 VendorID;
    internal UInt16 ProductID;
    internal UInt16 VersionNumber;

[DllImport("hid.dll", SetLastError = true)]
internal static extern Boolean HidD_GetAttributes
    (SafeFileHandle HidDeviceObject,
    ref HIDD_ATTRIBUTES Attributes);
```

Use

```
internal NativeMethods.HIDD_ATTRIBUTES DeviceAttributes;

// Example Product ID and Vendor ID values:

Int16 myProductID = 0x1234;
Int16 myVendorID = 0x0925;

DeviceAttributes.Size = Marshal.SizeOf(DeviceAttributes);

Boolean success = NativeMethods.HidD_GetAttributes
    (hidHandle, ref DeviceAttributes);

if (success)
{
    if ((DeviceAttributes.VendorID == myVendorId) &&
        (DeviceAttributes.ProductID == myProductId))
    {
        Debug.WriteLine("My device detected");
    }
    else
    {
        Debug.WriteLine("Not my device.");

        hidHandle.Close();
    }
}
```

How it works

The hidHandle parameter is a SafeFileHandle returned by CreateFile as shown in Chapter 10. A call to HidD_GetAttributes passes a HIDD_ATTRIBUTES structure with the Size member set to the structure's length. If the function returns true, the structure filled without error. The application can then compare the retrieved values with the desired Vendor ID and Product ID and device release number.

If the attributes don't indicate the desired device, the application should close the handle to the interface as shown in Chapter 10. The application can then move on to test the next HID in the device information set retrieved with SetupDiGetClassDevs, also shown in Chapter 10.

Getting a pointer to device capabilities

Another way to find out more about a device is to examine its capabilities. The first task is to call HidD_GetPreparsedData to get a pointer to a buffer with information about the device's capabilities.

Definitions

```
[DllImport("hid.dll", SetLastError = true)]
internal static extern Boolean HidD_GetPreparsedData
    (SafeFileHandle HidDeviceObject, ref IntPtr PreparsedData);
```

Use

```
var preparsedData = new IntPtr();

NativeMethods.HidD_GetPreparsedData(hidHandle, ref preparsedData);
```

How it works

The hidHandle parameter is the handle returned by CreateFile. The preparsedData variable points to the buffer containing the data. The application doesn't need to access the buffer's data directly. The code just needs to pass the returned pointer to another routine.

When finished using the PreparsedData buffer, the application should free system resources by calling HidD_FreePreparsedData as shown later in this chapter.

Getting the device's capabilities

HidP_GetCaps returns a pointer to a structure that contains information about the device's capabilities. The structure contains the HID's Usage Pages, Usages, report lengths, and the number of button-capabilities structures, value-capabilities structures, and data indexes that identify specific controls and data items in Input, Output, and Feature reports. An application can use the capabilities information to identify a specific HID and learn about its reports and report data. Not every item in the structure applies to all devices.

Definitions

```
internal struct HIDP_CAPS
{
    internal Int16 Usage;
    internal Int16 UsagePage;
    internal Int16 InputReportByteLength;
    internal Int16 OutputReportByteLength;
    internal Int16 FeatureReportByteLength;
    [MarshalAs(UnmanagedType.ByValArray, SizeConst = 17)]
        internal Int16[] Reserved;
    internal Int16 NumberLinkCollectionNodes;
    internal Int16 NumberInputButtonCaps;
    internal Int16 NumberInputValueCaps;
    internal Int16 NumberInputDataIndices;
    internal Int16 NumberOutputButtonCaps;
    internal Int16 NumberOutputValueCaps;
    internal Int16 NumberOutputDataIndices;
    internal Int16 NumberFeatureButtonCaps;
    internal Int16 NumberFeatureValueCaps;
    internal Int16 NumberFeatureDataIndices;
}

[DllImport("hid.dll", SetLastError = true)]
internal static extern Int32 HidP_GetCaps
    (IntPtr PreparsedData, ref HIDP_CAPS Capabilities);
```

Use

```
internal NativeMethods.HIDP_CAPS Capabilities;

Int32 result = NativeMethods.HidP_GetCaps
    (preparsedData, ref Capabilities);
```

How it works

The preparsedData parameter is the pointer returned by HidD_GetPreparsedData. When the function returns, the application can examine and use whatever values are of interest in the Capabilities structure. For example, to look for a joystick, look for Usage = 0x0004 and UsagePage = 0x0001.

InputReportByteLength, OutputReportByteLength, and FeatureReportByteLength are useful when setting buffer sizes for sending and receiving reports.

Getting capabilities of buttons and values

An application can also retrieve the capabilities of each button and value in a report. HidP_GetValueCaps returns a pointer to an array of structures containing information about the values in a report. The NumberInputValueCaps property of the HIDP_CAPS structure is the number of structures returned by HidP_GetValueCaps.

The items in the structures include many values obtained from the HID's report descriptor as described in Chapter 12. The items include the Report ID, whether a value is absolute or relative, whether a value has a null state, and logical and physical minimums and maximums. A LinkCollection identifier distinguishes between controls with the same Usage and Usage Page in the same collection. In a similar way, the HidP_GetButtonCaps function can retrieve information about a report's buttons. The information is stored in a HidP_ButtonCaps structure. Not every application needs this information.

Sending and receiving reports

The previous routines help in finding and learning about a device that matches what the application is looking for. On finding a device of interest, the application and device are ready to exchange data in reports.

Table 13-3 showed routines for exchanging reports using control transfers. Table 13-6 summarizes the transfer types the host uses with different report types. The application doesn't have to know or care which transfer type or endpoint the driver uses.

Sending Output reports with interrupt transfers

On obtaining a handle and learning the number of bytes in an Output report, an application can send a report to the HID. The example below places data to send in a buffer and uses a FileStream object to send the data asynchronously with a timeout if the device doesn't respond.

Use

```
private FileStream deviceData;

private async void SendOutputReport()
{
   const Int32 writeTimeout = 5000;
   var outputReportBuffer =
      new Byte[Capabilities.OutputReportByteLength];

   outputReportBuffer[0] = 0;
   outputReportBuffer[1] = 85;
   outputReportBuffer[2] = 83;
   outputReportBuffer[3] = 66;

   Action onWriteTimeoutAction = OnWriteTimeout;
```

Table 13-6: The transfer type used to send or receive a report can vary with the API function, operating system edition, and available endpoints.

Report Type	API Function or .NET Method	Transfer Type
Input	Filestream: Read, ReadAsync	Interrupt IN
	HidD_GetInputReport	Control, Get Report request
Output	Filestream: Write, WriteAsync	Interrupt OUT if available; otherwise control, Set Report request
	HidD_SetOutputReport	Control, Set Report request
Feature IN	HidD_GetFeature	Control, Get Report request
Feature OUT	HidD_SetFeature	Control, Set Report request

```
var cts = new CancellationTokenSource();
cts.CancelAfter(writeTimeout);
cts.Token.Register(onWriteTimeoutAction);

Task t = deviceData.WriteAsync
   (outputReportBuffer, 0, outputReportBuffer.Length,
   cts.Token);

await t;

switch (t.Status)
{
   case TaskStatus.RanToCompletion:
      success = true;
      Debug.Print("Output report written to device");
      break;
   case TaskStatus.Canceled:
      Debug.Print("Task canceled");
      break;
   case TaskStatus.Faulted:
      Debug.Print("Unhandled exception");
      break;
}
cts.Dispose();
}
```

```
private void OnWriteTimeout()
{
    if (deviceData != null)
    {
        deviceData.Dispose();
        Debug.Print("The attempt to send a report timed out.");
    }
}
```

How it works

The FileStream object deviceData provides methods for writing data to the device.

The SendOutputReport routine attempts to send a report to the device. The async modifier defines the routine as an async method, which doesn't block the calling routine's thread. In other words, while waiting for the data to transmit and be accepted by the device, the code that calls SendOutputReport can continue to respond to user input and other events. If the device doesn't accept the data within the specified time, the attempt to send data times out.

outputReportBuffer is the buffer that will store the data to be written to the device. The buffer's Length property is the OutputReportByteLength member in the HIDP_CAPS structure retrieved with HidP_GetCaps.

The first element in the buffer is the Report ID. If the interface supports only the default Report ID of zero, the Report ID doesn't transmit on the bus but still must be present in the buffer. The remaining elements hold the report data. In this example, the Report ID is zero and the report data is ASCII codes that spell "USB".

The writeTimeout constant sets the number of milliseconds to wait for the device to accept the data.

cts is a CancellationTokenSource object that sets up the timeout action. The CancelAfter method specifies the timeout value.

The cts object requires an Action delegate (onWriteTimeoutAction) for a routine that executes on a timeout (OnWriteTimeout).

To implement the timeout action, the Token property of cts registers the onWriteTimeoutAction delegate. The task t (an asynchronous operation) attempts to send the data and times out if the operation isn't complete when the timeout period elapsed.

deviceData's WriteAsync method names the buffer with data to send (outputReportBuffer), the offset to begin copying bytes from the buffer to the stream (0), the maximum number of bytes to write (outputReportBuffer.Length), and the token to monitor for cancellation requests (cts.Token).

The await operator waits for the task to complete or a timeout. While waiting for the write operation to complete, the routine that called SendOutputReport can perform other operations.

If the operation completes, t.Status has one of these states: RanToCompletion (success), Canceled (a cancellation was requested), or Faulted (unhandled exception).

The Dispose method stops the timeout timer and disposes of the resource. As an alternative to calling Dispose, you can wrap the code that uses cts in a using statement, which disposes of the resource on exiting the block of code:

```
using (var cts = new CancellationTokenSource())
{
    // Code that uses cts goes here.
}
```

If the write operation times out, the OnWriteTimeout routine executes. The timeout routine can dispose of the FileStream and perform any other needed actions.

If the HID has an interrupt OUT endpoint, the write operation initiates an interrupt transfer to send the report. Otherwise, the host uses a control transfer with a HID-class Set_Report request. The application doesn't have to know or care which transfer type the host uses.

Reading Input reports with interrupt transfers

In a similar way, an application can retrieve Input reports from a device. The example below requests report data asynchronously with a timeout if the device doesn't respond. The FileStream reads data that the HID driver has requested from the HID's interrupt IN endpoint.

Use

```
private FileStream deviceData;

private async void GetInputReport()
{
    const Int32 writeTimeout = 5000;
    var inputReportBuffer =
        new Byte[Capabilities.InputReportByteLength];

    Action onReadTimeoutAction = OnReadTimeout;

    var cts = new CancellationTokenSource();
    cts.CancelAfter(readTimeout);
    cts.Token.Register(onReadTimeoutAction);
```

```
Task<Int32> t = deviceData.ReadAsync
    (inputReportBuffer, 0, inputReportBuffer.Length,
    cts.Token);

Int32 bytesRead = await t;
switch (t.Status)
{
    case TaskStatus.RanToCompletion:
        success1 = 1;
        Debug.Print("Input report received from device");
            break;
    case TaskStatus.Canceled:
        Debug.Print("Task canceled");
            break;
    case TaskStatus.Faulted:
            Debug.Print("Unhandled exception");
            break;
    }
    cts.Dispose();
}

private void OnReadTimeout()
{
    deviceData.Dispose();
    Debug.Print("The attempt to send a report timed out.");}
}
```

How it works

The FileStream object deviceData reads data from the device.

The GetInputReport routine attempts to read a received report from the HID driver's buffer. As with the SendOutputReport routine, the async modifier defines the routine as an async method. While waiting for the device to send a report, the code that calls GetInputReport can continue to respond to user input and other events. If the device doesn't send a report within the specified time, the attempt to get data times out.

inputReportBuffer is the buffer that will store the received data. In the HIDP_CAPS structure retrieved with HidP_GetCaps, the value of the InputReportByteLength member is the minimum value to use for the buffer's Length property.

The readTimeout constant sets the number of milliseconds to wait for data from the device.

cts is a CancellationTokenSource object that sets up the timeout action. The CancelAfter method specifies the timeout value.

The cts object requires an Action delegate (onReadTimeoutAction) for a routine that will execute on a timeout (OnReadTimeout).

To implement the timeout action, the Token property of cts registers the onReadTimeoutAction delegate. The task t attempts to receive data and times out if the operation isn't complete when the timeout period elapsed.

deviceData's ReadAsync method passes the buffer that will hold received data (inputReportBuffer), the offset in the buffer to begin writing received data (0), the maximum number of bytes to read (inputReportBuffer.Length), and the token to monitor for cancellation requests (cts.Token).

The await operator waits for the task to complete or a timeout. While waiting for the read operation to complete, the routine that called GetInputReport can perform other operations.

If the operation completes, bytesRead holds the number of bytes received, and t.Status has one of these states: RanToCompletion (success), Canceled (a cancellation was requested), or Faulted (unhandled exception).

The Dispose method of cts stops the timeout timer and disposes of the resource.

The task completes successfully if one or more reports are available before the task times out. On success, the first element in inputReportBuffer is the Report ID. If the interface supports only the default Report ID of zero, the Report ID doesn't transmit on the bus but is present in the buffer. The report data follows the Report ID.

If the read operation times out, the OnReadTimeout routine executes, disposing of the Filestream and performing any other needed actions.

The read operation doesn't initiate traffic on the bus. The host begins requesting reports from the device after completing enumeration of the device. The host's HID driver stores received reports in a ring buffer. A request to get a report returns the oldest report in the buffer. If the driver's buffer is empty, the read operation waits for a report to arrive until a timeout occurs. If the buffer is full when a new report arrives, the buffer drops the oldest report.

Each handle with read access to the HID has its own Input buffer, so multiple applications and multiple devices can read the same reports.

If the application doesn't request reports as frequently as the device sends them, some reports will be lost. One way to keep from losing reports is to increase the size of the FileStream object's report buffer. If multiple reports are immediately available in the HID driver's buffer, and if inputReportBuffer's size and the maximum number of bytes parameter enable storing multiple reports, the read operation returns as many reports as will fit in inputReportBuffer. If you need to be absolutely sure not to lose a report, use Feature reports. Also see the tips in Chapter 3 about performing time-critical transfers.

The Idle rate introduced in Chapter 11 determines whether or not a device sends a report if the data hasn't changed since the last transfer.

If a read operation is timing out, these are possible reasons:

- The HID's interrupt IN endpoint is NAKing the IN token packets because the endpoint hasn't been armed to send report data. An endpoint's interrupt typically triggers only after endpoint sends data, so device firmware must arm the endpoint to send the first report before the first interrupt.

- The number of bytes the endpoint is sending doesn't equal the number of bytes in a report (for HIDs that use the default Report ID) or the number of bytes in a report + 1 (for HIDs that use other Report IDs).

- For HIDs with multiple Report IDs, the first byte doesn't match a valid Report ID.

Writing Feature reports

HidD_SetFeature attempts to send a Feature report to the device using a control transfer with a HID-class Set_Report request.

Definitions

```
[DllImport("hid.dll", SetLastError=true)]
internal static extern Boolean HidD_SetFeature
  (SafeFileHandle HidDeviceObject,
  Byte lpReportBuffer[],
  Int32 ReportBufferLength);
```

Use

```
var outFeatureReportBuffer =
  new Byte[Capabilities.FeatureReportByteLength];

outFeatureReportBuffer[0] = 0;
outFeatureReportBuffer[1] = 79;
outFeatureReportBuffer[2] = 75;

Boolean success = NativeMethods.HidD_SetFeature
  (hidHandle,
  outFeatureReportBuffer,
  outFeatureReportBuffer.Length);
```

How it works

HidD_SetFeature requires a handle to the HID, an array of bytes to write, and the array's length. The first byte in the outFeatureReportBuffer array is the Report ID. The array's length is the FeatureReportByteLength value in the HIDP_CAPS structure retrieved by HidP_GetCaps.

The function returns true on success. If the device continues to NAK the report data, the function times out and returns.

Writing Output reports with control transfers

In much the same way as HidD_SetFeature, HidD_SetOutputReport writes an Output report to the device using a control transfer and a Set_Report request. The function accepts a handle to the HID, a pointer to a byte array containing an Output report, and the number of bytes in the report plus one byte for the Report ID. The buffer's first byte is the Report ID.

Reading Feature reports

HidD_GetFeature requests a Feature report from a device using a control transfer with a HID-class Get_Feature request. The endpoint returns report data in the transfer's Data stage.

Definitions

```
[DllImport("hid.dll", SetLastError=true)]
internal static extern Boolean HidD_GetFeature
   (SafeFileHandle HidDeviceObject,
   Byte[] lpReportBuffer,
   Int32 ReportBufferLength);
```

Use

```
Byte[] inFeatureReportBuffer = null;
inFeatureReportBuffer =
   new Byte[Capabilities.FeatureReportByteLength];

inFeatureReportBuffer[0] = 0;

Boolean success = NativeMethods.HidD_GetFeature
   (deviceHandle,
   inFeatureReportBuffer,
   inFeatureReportBuffer.Length);
```

How it works

HidD_GetFeature requires a handle to the HID, an array to hold the retrieved report(s), and the array's length. The inFeatureReportBuffer array holds the retrieved report. The first byte in the array is the Report ID. The array's length is the FeatureReportByteLength value in the HIDP_CAPS structure retrieved by HidP_GetCaps.

The function returns true on success. If the device continues to return NAK in the Data stage of the transfer, the function times out and returns.

Reading Input reports with control transfers

In much the same way as HidD_GetFeature, HidD_GetInputReport requests an Input report to the device using a control transfer and a Get_Report request. The function accepts a handle to the HID, a pointer to a byte array that will hold the Input report, and the number of bytes in the report plus one byte for the Report ID. The buffer's first byte is the Report ID.

The function requests a report directly from the device, bypassing the HID driver's buffer

Closing communications

When finished communicating, the application should close any resources no longer needed.

Definitions

```
[DllImport("hid.dll", SetLastError=true)]
internal static extern Boolean HidD_FreePreparsedData
    (IntPtr PreparsedData);
```

Use

```
Boolean success = HidD_FreePreparsedData(preparsedData);
if (deviceData != null)
{
    deviceData.Dispose();
}
```

How it works

When finished using the PreparsedData buffer that HidD_GetPreparsedData returned, the application should call HidD_FreePreparsedData.

The FileStream class's Dispose method closes the Filestream, including closing its handle.

14

Using WinUSB for Vendor-defined Functions

For devices that perform vendor-defined functions that don't fit a standard class, Microsoft's WinUSB driver is an option. This chapter shows how to develop a device that uses the WinUSB driver and how to use the WinUSB API to access the device from applications.

Capabilities and limits

A device is a candidate for using the WinUSB driver if the device and its host computer(s) meet the requirements below.

Device requirements

The device:

- Exchanges application data using any combination of control, interrupt, bulk, or isochronous transfers.
- Has descriptors that specify a vendor-defined function.

Host requirements

The host:

- Is Windows XP SP2 or later (Windows 8.1 and later for isochronous transfers).

- Needs no more than one open handle to the device at once.

- Has a vendor-provided application to communicate with the device. Programming languages for the application can include Visual C# and other languages that can call Windows API functions. Windows 8.1 and later can run Windows Store apps created using the Windows.Devices.Usb namespace

Driver requirements

If the device has Microsoft OS descriptors that contain the CompatibleID "WINUSB" and a vendor-defined, device-specific value, the host can use the system-provided WinUSB INF file. Otherwise, the device must provide an INF file that matches the device's Vendor ID and Product ID to a vendor-defined GUID. Chapter 15 shows how to create descriptors to enable using the system INF file.

Device firmware

A WinUSB device has an interface descriptor with bInterfaceClass = 0xFF to specify a vendor-defined function. Listing 14-1 shows descriptors for an example WinUSB device with interrupt, bulk, and isochronous endpoints. The example also includes string descriptors.

The system-provided INF file places WinUSB devices in the USBDevice class. For devices in this class, under Windows 8 and later, Device Manager displays the contents of the iProduct string from the device's descriptors, if available, instead of using the generic description in the INF file.

For all transfer types, the host application and device firmware can define the meaning of transferred data in any way. For example, for a data-acquisition device, firmware might define a vendor-specific control request with bRequest = 0x01 to identify the request, wIndex indicating which sensor reading to return, and wLength equal to the number of bytes the device should return with the requested data. Or device firmware might send sensor data in a defined format on an interrupt or bulk endpoint. In a similar way, a host application can send data to a device using control, bulk, or interrupt transfers.

Microchip's USB Framework provides WinUSB firmware for Microchip microcontrollers. Texas Instruments also provides firmware for use with the WinUSB driver on the host.

```
UCHAR device_descriptor[0x12] =
{
// Device descriptor

0x12,              // bLength              Descriptor size in bytes
0x01,              // bDescriptorType      Descriptor type (Device)
0x00, 0x02,        // bcdUSB               USB release number (BCD) (2.00)
0x00,              // bDeviceClass         Class code
0x00,              // bDeviceSubClass      Subclass code
0x00,              // bDeviceProtocol      Protocol code
0x08,              // bMaxPacketSize0      Endpoint 0 maximum packet size
0x25, 0x09,        // idVendor             Vendor ID (Lakeview Research)
0x56, 0x14,        // idProduct            Product ID
0x00, 0x01,        // bcdDevice            Device release number (BCD)
0x01,              // iManufacturer        Manufacturer string index
0x02,              // iProduct             Product string index
0x00,              // iSerialNumber        Device serial number string index
0x01,              // bNumConfigurations   Number of configurations
}

UCHAR configuration_descriptor[0x3C] =
{
// Configuration descriptor

0x09,              // bLength              Descriptor size in bytes
0x02,              // bDescriptorType      Descriptor type (Configuration)
0x3C, 0x00,        // wTotalLength         Total length of this and
                   //                          subordinate descriptors (60)
0x01,              // bNumInterfaces       Number of interfaces
0x01,              // bConfigurationValue  Index of this configuration
0x00,              // iConfiguration       Configuration string index
0xE0,              // bmAttributes         Self powered, remote wakeup support
0x32,              // bMaxPower            Maximum power consumption (100 mA)
```

Listing 14-1: A device that uses the WinUSB driver can use these descriptors. (Part 1 of 4)

```
// Interface descriptor

0x09,            // bLength              Descriptor size in bytes
0x04,            // bDescriptorType      Descriptor type (Interface)
0x00,            // bInterfaceNumber     Interface number
0x00,            // bAlternateSetting    Alternate setting number
0x06,            // bNumEndpoints        Number of endpoints
0xFF,            // bInterfaceClass      Interface class (vendor specific)
0x00,            // bInterfaceSubclass   Interface subclass
0x00,            // bInterfaceProtocol   Interface protocol
0x00,            // iInterface           Interface string index

// Interrupt IN endpoint descriptor

0x07,            // bLength              Descriptor size in bytes
0x05,            // bDescriptorType      Descriptor type (Endpoint)
0x81,            // bEndpointAddress     Endpoint 1 IN
0x03,            // bmAttributes         Transfer type (interrupt)
0x08, 0x00,      // wMaxPacketSize       Maximum packet size
0x0A,            // bInterval            Polling interval (ms)

// Interrupt OUT endpoint descriptor

0x07,            // bLength              Descriptor size in bytes
0x05,            // bDescriptorType      Descriptor type (Endpoint)
0x01,            // bEndpointAddress     Endpoint 1 OUT
0x03,            // bmAttributes         Transfer type (interrupt)
0x08, 0x00,      // wMaxPacketSize       Maximum packet size
0x0A,            // bInterval            Polling interval (ms)

// Bulk IN endpoint descriptor

0x07,            // bLength              Descriptor size in bytes
0x05,            // bDescriptorType      Descriptor type (Endpoint)
0x82,            // bEndpointAddress     Endpoint 2 IN
0x02,            // bmAttributes         Transfer type (bulk)
0x40, 0x00,      // wMaxPacketSize       Maximum packet size
0x00,            // bInterval            Polling interval (ignored)
```

Listing 14-1: A device that uses the WinUSB driver can use these descriptors. (Part 2 of 4)

```
// Bulk OUT endpoint descriptor

0x07,              // bLength            Descriptor size in bytes
0x05,              // bDescriptorType    Descriptor type (Endpoint)
0x02,              // bEndpointAddress   Endpoint 2 OUT
0x02,              // bmAttributes       Transfer type (bulk)
0x40, 0x00,        // wMaxPacketSize     Maximum packet size
0x00,              // bInterval          Polling interval (ignored)

// Isochronous IN endpoint descriptor

0x07,              // bLength            Descriptor size in bytes
0x05,              // bDescriptorType    Descriptor type (Endpoint)
0x83,              // bEndpointAddress   Endpoint 3 IN
0x01,              // bmAttributes       Transfer type (isochronous)
0x08, 0x00,        // wMaxPacketSize     Maximum packet size
0x01,              // bInterval          Polling interval

// Isochronous OUT endpoint descriptor

0x07,              // bLength            Descriptor size in bytes
0x05,              // bDescriptorType    Descriptor type (Endpoint)
0x03,              // bEndpointAddress   Endpoint 3 OUT
0x01,              // bmAttributes       Transfer type (isochronous)
0x08, 0x00,        // wMaxPacketSize     Maximum packet size
0x01               // bInterval          Polling interval
}

UCHAR string_descriptor_0[0x04] =
{
// String descriptor 0

0x04,              // bLength            Descriptor size in bytes
0x03,              // bSTRING            Descriptor type (String)
0x09, 0x04         // wLANGID            Language ID (U.S. English)
}
```

Listing 14-1: A device that uses the WinUSB driver can use these descriptors. (Part 3 of 4)

```
UCHAR string_descriptor_1[0x24] =
{
// String descriptor 1

0x22,             // bLength           Descriptor size in bytes
0x03,             // bSTRING           Descriptor type (String)

// Manufacturer string, UTF-16LE Unicode: "Lakeview Research"

0x4C, 0x00, 0x61, 0x00, 0x6B, 0x00, 0x65, 0x00, 0x76, 0x00, 0x69, 0x00,
0x65, 0x00, 0x77, 0x00, 0x20, 0x00, 0x52, 0x00, 0x65, 0x00, 0x73, 0x00,
0x65, 0x00, 0x61, 0x00, 0x72, 0x00, 0x63, 0x00, 0x68, 0x00
}

UCHAR string_descriptor_2[0x2C] =
{
// String descriptor 2

0x2A,             // bLength           Descriptor size in bytes
0x03,             // bSTRING           Descriptor type (String)

// Product string, UTF-16LE Unicode: "WinUSB Example Device"

0x57, 0x00, 0x69, 0x00, 0x6E, 0x00, 0x55, 0x00, 0x53, 0x00, 0x42, 0x00,
0x20, 0x00, 0x45, 0x00, 0x78, 0x00, 0x61, 0x00, 0x6D, 0x00, 0x70, 0x00,
0x6C, 0x00, 0x65, 0x00, 0x20, 0x00, 0x44, 0x00, 0x65, 0x00, 0x76, 0x00,
0x69, 0x00, 0x63, 0x00, 0x65, 0x00
}
```

Listing 14-1: A device that uses the WinUSB driver can use these descriptors. (Part 4 of 4)

Accessing the device

Accessing a WinUSB device requires finding the device, initializing communications, and exchanging data using bulk, interrupt, isochronous, and control transfers as needed. The WinUSB driver's *winusb.dll* exposes functions that applications can call to obtain access to devices and to configure, and exchange data with them.

The code examples in this chapter assume the following using statements:

```
using Microsoft.Win32.SafeHandles;
using System;
using System.Runtime.InteropServices;
```

Creating a SafeWinUsbHandle

The WinUSB API provides a WinUsb_Initialize routine that returns a pointer to a handle for accessing a WinUSB device. As Chapter 10 explained, a SafeHandle is preferable to an IntPtr. WinUSB devices can't use any of the provided classes derived from SafeHandle, but you can derive a new SafeHandle class from one of the defined classes. The example here, adapted from Microsoft's example in the SafeHandle documentation, derives the SafeWinUsbHandle class from the provided class SafeHandleZeroOrMinusOneIsInvalid, which implements a handle where either zero or -1 is an invalid handle.

Definitions

```
[DllImport("winusb.dll", SetLastError = true)]
internal static extern Boolean WinUsb_Free
   (IntPtr InterfaceHandle);
```

Use

```
[SecurityPermission
   (SecurityAction.InheritanceDemand, UnmanagedCode = true)]
[SecurityPermission(SecurityAction.Demand, UnmanagedCode = true)]
internal class SafeWinUsbHandle : SafeHandleZeroOrMinusOneIsInvalid
{
   internal SafeWinUsbHandle()
      : base(true)
   {
      base.SetHandle(handle);
      this.handle = IntPtr.Zero;
   }

   [ReliabilityContract
      (Consistency.WillNotCorruptState, Cer.MayFail)]
   protected override bool ReleaseHandle()
   {
      if (!this.IsInvalid)
      {
         this.handle = IntPtr.Zero;
      }
      return NativeMethods.WinUsb_Free(handle);
   }
```

```csharp
public override bool IsInvalid
{
    get
    {
        if (handle == IntPtr.Zero)
        {
            return true;
        }
        if (handle == (IntPtr)(-1))
        {
            return true;
        }
        return false;
    }
}

public IntPtr GetHandle()
{
    if (IsInvalid)
    {
        throw new Exception("The handle is invalid.");
    }
    return handle;
}
}
```

Two security actions in the SecurityPermisson enumeration enable the derived class to use unmanaged code. The SecurityAction.InheritanceDemand action requires inherited classes to have permission to use unmanaged code. The SecurityAction.Demand action requires callers that access the class to have permission to use unmanaged code.

The constructor creates the SafeWinUsbHandle class and initializes the handle to IntPtr.Zero.

The ReleaseHandle method overrides the class's ReleaseHandle method to enable calling the WinUsb_Free API function to release the handle. The method's Reliability-Contract attribute indicates that the method may fail but on failure, data will be in a valid state.

Microsoft requires overriding the IsInvalid property in derived classes. The property returns true if the handle equals zero or -1.

The GetHandle method returns the handle or if the handle is invalid, throws an exception.

Obtaining a WinUSB handle

Before exchanging data with a WinUSB device, an application obtains a device path-name using SetupDi_ functions. The application can then use CreateFile to obtain a handle. The application must know the device interface GUID stored either in the device firmware or in the device's INF file. In the call to CreateFile, the dwFlagsandAttributes parameter must be set to FILE_FLAG_OVERLAPPED.

Chapter 8 discussed how to generate a GUID. Chapter 10 showed how to obtain a handle with CreateFile and use the handle to detect when a device is attached and removed.

After calling CreateFile to obtain a handle, the application calls WinUsb_Initialize to obtain a WinUSB interface handle. The application uses this handle for all communications with the interface.

Definitions

```
internal class DeviceInfo
{
    internal Byte BulkInPipe;
    internal Byte BulkOutPipe;
    internal Byte InterruptInPipe;
    internal Byte InterruptOutPipe;
    internal Byte IsochronousInPipe;
    internal Byte IsochronousOutPipe;
    internal UInt32 DeviceSpeed;
}

[DllImport("winusb.dll", SetLastError = true)]
internal static extern Boolean WinUsb_Initialize
    (SafeFileHandle DeviceHandle,
    ref SafeWinUsbHandle InterfaceHandle);
```

Use

```
private SafeWinUsbHandle winUsbHandle;
private DeviceInfo myDeviceInfo = new DeviceInfo();

var success = NativeMethods.WinUsb_Initialize
    (deviceHandle, ref winUsbHandle);
```

How it works

The DeviceInfo class holds information about a device and its endpoints. The device-Handle parameter is a handle to a WinUSB device returned by CreateFile. On success, WinUsb_Initialize returns true and winUsbHandle is a pointer to a WinUSB handle that the application can use to access the device.

Requesting an interface descriptor

The WinUsb_QueryInterfaceSettings function returns a structure with information about a WinUSB interface.

Definitions

```
internal struct USB_INTERFACE_DESCRIPTOR
{
    internal Byte bLength;
    internal Byte bDescriptorType;
    internal Byte bInterfaceNumber;
    internal Byte bAlternateSetting;
    internal Byte bNumEndpoints;
    internal Byte bInterfaceClass;
    internal Byte bInterfaceSubClass;
    internal Byte bInterfaceProtocol;
    internal Byte iInterface;
}

[DllImport("winusb.dll", SetLastError = true)]
internal static extern Boolean WinUsb_QueryInterfaceSettings
    (SafeWinUsbHandle InterfaceHandle,
    Byte AlternateInterfaceNumber,
    ref USB_INTERFACE_DESCRIPTOR UsbAltInterfaceDescriptor);
```

Use

```
var ifaceDescriptor = new NativeMethods.USB_INTERFACE_DESCRIPTOR();

var success = NativeMethods.WinUsb_QueryInterfaceSettings
    (winUsbHandle, 0, ref ifaceDescriptor);
```

How it works

The function accepts a pointer to a WinUsb handle and a bAlternateSetting number from the interface descriptor to indicate which interface setting to query. On success, the function returns true and a pointer to a USB_INTERFACE_DESCRIPTOR structure containing information from the requested interface descriptor.

For interfaces with alternate settings, you can create an array of USB_INTERFACE_DE-SCRIPTOR structures:

```
var ifaceDescriptors =
    new NativeMethods.USB_INTERFACE_DESCRIPTOR[2];
```

and query the interface settings by specifying the ifaceDescriptor array index for when querying the interface, for example, ifaceDescriptor[0] and ifaceDescriptor[1].

Identifying the endpoints

For each endpoint in the interface descriptor, an application can call WinUsb_QueryPipe to learn the endpoint's transfer type and direction. The myDeviceInfo structure can store the information.

Definitions

```
internal enum USBD_PIPE_TYPE
{
    UsbdPipeTypeControl,
    UsbdPipeTypeIsochronous,
    UsbdPipeTypeBulk,
    UsbdPipeTypeInterrupt,
}
internal struct WINUSB_PIPE_INFORMATION
{
    internal USBD_PIPE_TYPE PipeType;
    internal Byte PipeId;
    internal UInt16 MaximumPacketSize;
    internal Byte Interval;
}

[DllImport("winusb.dll", SetLastError = true)]
internal static extern Boolean WinUsb_QueryPipe
    (SafeWinUsbHandle InterfaceHandle,
    Byte AlternateInterfaceNumber,
    Byte PipeIndex,
    ref WINUSB_PIPE_INFORMATION PipeInformation);
```

Use

```
var pipeInfo = new NativeMethods.WINUSB_PIPE_INFORMATION();

private Boolean UsbEndpointDirectionIn(Int32 addr)
{
    var directionIn = false;

    if (((endpointAddress & 0X80) == 0X80))
    {
        directionIn = true;
    }
    return directionIn;
}
```

```csharp
private Boolean UsbEndpointDirectionOut(Int32 addr)
{
   var directionOut = false;
   if (((addr & 0X80) == 0))
   {
      directionOut = true;
   }
   return directionOut;

for (var i = 0; i <= ifaceDescriptor.bNumEndpoints - 1; i++)
{
   NativeMethods.WinUsb_QueryPipe
      (winUsbHandle,
       0,
       Convert.ToByte(i),
       ref pipeInfo);

   if (((pipeInfo.PipeType ==
      NativeMethods.USBD_PIPE_TYPE.UsbdPipeTypeBulk) &
      UsbEndpointDirectionIn(pipeInfo.PipeId)))
   {
      myDeviceInfo.BulkInPipe = pipeInfo.PipeId;


   }
   else if (((pipeInfo.PipeType ==
      NativeMethods.USBD_PIPE_TYPE.UsbdPipeTypeBulk) &
      UsbEndpointDirectionOut(pipeInfo.PipeId)))
   {
      myDeviceInfo.BulkOutPipe = pipeInfo.PipeId;


   }
   else if ((pipeInfo.PipeType ==
      NativeMethods.USBD_PIPE_TYPE.UsbdPipeTypeInterrupt) &
      UsbEndpointDirectionIn(pipeInfo.PipeId))
   {
      myDeviceInfo.InterruptInPipe = pipeInfo.PipeId;


   }
   else if ((pipeInfo.PipeType ==
            NativeMethods.USBD_PIPE_TYPE.UsbdPipeTypeInterrupt)
                & UsbEndpointDirectionOut(pipeInfo.PipeId))
   {
      myDeviceInfo.InterruptOutPipe = pipeInfo.PipeId;
   }
```

```
else if ((pipeInfo.PipeType ==
    NativeMethods.USBD_PIPE_TYPE.UsbdPipeTypeIsochronous) &
    UsbEndpointDirectionIn(pipeInfo.PipeId))
{
    myDeviceInfo.IsochronousInPipe = pipeInfo.PipeId;

}
else if ((pipeInfo.PipeType ==
        NativeMethods.USBD_PIPE_TYPE.UsbdPipeTypeIsochronous)
            & UsbEndpointDirectionOut(pipeInfo.PipeId))
{
    myDeviceInfo.IsochronousOutPipe = pipeInfo.PipeId;
}
}
```

How it works

The UsbEndpointDirectionIn and UsbEndpointDirectionOut functions enable query-ing the direction of an endpoint. The application can request and store information about each of the interface's endpoints in turn. The PipeId value equals bEnd-pointAddress in the endpoint descriptor. A valid endpoint has a PipeId greater than zero.

For interfaces with multiple alternate settings, you can create an array of pipeInfo structures:

```
var pipeInfo = new NativeMethods.WINUSB_PIPE_INFORMATION[2];
```

and specify the ifaceDescriptor and pipeInfo array index for each alternate interface when retrieving and setting pipe values.

Setting pipe policies

After identifying an endpoint, an application can set vendor-specific policies for transfers at the endpoint. Table 14-1 shows the policies.

Definitions

```
internal enum POLICY_TYPE
{
    SHORT_PACKET_TERMINATE = 1,
    AUTO_CLEAR_STALL,
    PIPE_TRANSFER_TIMEOUT,
    IGNORE_SHORT_PACKETS,
    ALLOW_PARTIAL_READS,
    AUTO_FLUSH,
    RAW_IO,
}
```

Table 14-1: The WinUsb_SetPipePolicy function can specify how the driver responds to various conditions when performing a transfer and whether data bypasses WinUSB's queuing and error handling.

Parameter	Value	Default	Description
SHORT_PACKET_TERMINATE	0x01	False	If True, terminate a write transfer that is a multiple of wMaxPacketSize with a ZLP.
AUTO_CLEAR_STALL	0x02	False	If True, clear a stall condition automatically.
PIPE_TRANSFER_TIMEOUT	0x03	Zero	Set a transfer timeout interval in milliseconds. Zero = never time out.
IGNORE_SHORT_PACKETS	0x04	False	If True, complete a read operation only on receiving the specified number of bytes. If False, complete a read operation on receiving the specified number of bytes or a short packet.
ALLOW_PARTIAL_READS	0x05	True	Sets the policy if the endpoint returns more data than requested. If True, complete the read operation and save or discard the extra data as specified by AUTO_FLUSH. If False, fail the read request.
AUTO_FLUSH	0x06	False	If True and ALLOW_PARTIAL_READS is also True, discard extra data. If False and ALLOW_PARTIAL_READS is True, save extra data and return it in the next read operation. If ALLOW_PARTIAL_READS is False, ignore.
RAW_IO	0x07	False	Determines whether calls to WinUsb_ReadPipe bypasses WinUSB's queuing and error handling, If True, calls pass directly to the USB stack, and the read buffer must be a multiple of wMaxPacketSize and less than the host controller's maximum per transfer. If False, calls don't pass directly to the USB stack, and the buffers don't have the size restrictions.

```
[DllImport("winusb.dll", SetLastError = true)]
internal static extern Boolean WinUsb_SetPipePolicy
   (SafeWinUsbHandle InterfaceHandle,
   Byte PipeID,
   UInt32 PolicyType,
   UInt32 ValueLength,
   ref Byte Value);

[DllImport("winusb.dll", SetLastError = true,
   EntryPoint = "WinUsb_SetPipePolicy")]
internal static extern Boolean WinUsb_SetPipePolicy1
   (SafeWinUsbHandle InterfaceHandle,
   Byte PipeID,
   UInt32 PolicyType,
   UInt32 ValueLength,
   ref UInt32 Value);
```

Use

```
private Boolean SetPipePolicy(SafeWinUsbHandle winUsbHandle, Byte
pipeId, UInt32 policyType, Byte value)
{
   var success = NativeMethods.WinUsb_SetPipePolicy
      (winUsbHandle, pipeId, policyType, 1, ref value);
   return success;
}

private Boolean SetPipePolicy(SafeWinUsbHandle winUsbHandle, Byte
pipeId, UInt32 policyType, UInt32 value)
{
   var success NativeMethods.WinUsb_SetPipePolicy1
      (winUsbHandle, pipeId, policyType, 4, ref value);

   return success;
}

var success = SetPipePolicy
        (winUsbHandle,
         myDeviceInfo.BulkOutPipe,
         Convert.ToUInt32
           (NativeMethods.POLICY_TYPE.IGNORE_SHORT_PACKETS),
         Convert.ToByte(false));

UInt32 pipeTimeout = 2000;
```

```
var success = NativeMethods.SetPipePolicy
        (winUsbHandle,
         myDeviceInfo.BulkOutPipe,
         Convert.ToUInt32
           (NativeMethods.POLICY_TYPE.PIPE_TRANSFER_TIMEOUT),
         pipeTimeout);
```

How it works

The WinUsb_SetPipePolicy function accepts a Byte for the value parameter for all policies except PIPE_TRANSFER_TIMEOUT, which requires a UInt32. To handle both types, the definition for WinUsb_SetPipePolicy accepts a Byte value, and the definition for the alias WinUsb_SetPipePolicy1 accepts a UInt32. Two overloaded SetPipePolicy functions accept different types for the value parameter and pass the parameter to WinUsb_SetPipePolicy or WinUsb_SetPipePolicy1.

The Byte parameters of WinUsb_SetPipePolicy have true/false meanings, so for readability, the SetPipePolicy function accepts a Boolean value, and the Convert.ToByte method converts the value to a Byte for passing to WinUsb_SetPipePolicy.

The example sets two policies for the bulk IN endpoint. In a similar way, you can set policies for all of an interface's endpoints. A companion function for reading pipe policies is WinUsb_GetPipePolicy.

Writing bulk and interrupt data

The WinUsb_WritePipe function can write data to bulk and interrupt endpoints.

Definitions

```
[DllImport("winusb.dll", SetLastError = true)]
internal static extern Boolean WinUsb_WritePipe
   (SafeWinUsbHandle InterfaceHandle,
    Byte PipeID,
    Byte[] Buffer,
    UInt32 BufferLength,
    ref UInt32 LengthTransferred,
    IntPtr Overlapped);
```

Use

```
Byte[] buffer = new Byte[2];
UInt32 bytesToWrite = 2;
UInt32 bytesWritten = 0;

buffer[0] = 72;
buffer[1] = 105;
bytesToWrite = Convert.ToUInt32(buffer.Length);
```

```
var success = NativeMethods.WinUsb_WritePipe
   (winUsbHandle,
   myDeviceInfo.bulkOutPipe,
   buffer,
   bytesToWrite,
   ref bytesWritten,
   IntPtr.Zero);
```

How it works

The WinUsb_WritePipe function accepts a pointer to a WinUSB handle obtained with WinUsb_Initialize, an endpoint address retrieved with WinUsb_QueryPipe, a buffer with data to send, the number of bytes to write, a variable that will hold the number of bytes written when the function returns, and a zero pointer to specify synchronous operation. The example creates a 2-byte buffer and stores 2 bytes in it.

The example is synchronous: the calling thread blocks until WinUsb_WritePipe returns. On success, the function returns True with the number of bytes written in bytesWritten. To send data using an interrupt transfer, change myDeviceInfo.bulkOutPipe to myDeviceInfo.interruptOutPipe.

The function returns on success or a timeout or other failure.

To cause the driver to terminate transfers that are exact multiples of wMaxPacketSize with ZLPs, call WinUsb_SetPipePolicy with SHORT_PACKET_TERMINATE = True. This option can be useful if the device firmware needs a way to identify the end of a transfer of unknown length.

Writing data without blocking

To write data asynchronously, or without blocking, you can use a delegate that initiates the operation and notifies the calling thread when the operation is complete.

To enable calling the code to write data, place the code from the example above in a routine:

```
internal void SendDataViaBulkTransfer
   (SafeWinUsbHandle winUsbHandle,
   DeviceInfo myDeviceInfo,
   UInt32 bytesToWrite,
   Byte[] dataBuffer,
   ref UInt32 bytesWritten,
   ref Boolean success)
{
   success = NativeMethods.WinUsb_WritePipe
      (winUsbHandle,
       myDeviceInfo.BulkOutPipe,
       dataBuffer,
       bytesToWrite,
       ref bytesWritten,
       IntPtr.Zero);
}
```

Then create a delegate for the routine to enable calling the routine asynchronously. The first step is to create a class of delegates with the same parameters as SendData-ViaBulk Transfer:

```
private delegate void SendToDeviceDelegate
   (SafeWinUsbHandle winUsbHandle,
   DeviceInfo myDevInfo,
   UInt32 bufferLength,
   Byte[] buffer,
   ref UInt32 lengthTransferred,
   ref Boolean success);
```

Then create a delegate of the SendToDeviceDelegate class:

```
SendToDeviceDelegate mySendToDeviceDelegate =
   SendDataViaBulkTransfer;
```

The delegate's BeginInvoke method has the same parameters as SendDataViaBulk-Transfer plus two additional parameters. GetBulkDataSent names the routine to call when the write operation completes, and the mySendToDeviceDelegate object passes information to the GetBulkDataSent routine:

```
mySendToDeviceDelegate.BeginInvoke
   (winUsbHandle,
    myDeviceInfo,
    bytesToWrite,
    dataBuffer,
    ref bytesWritten
    ref success,
    GetBulkDataSent,
    mySendToDeviceDelegate);
```

When SendDataViaBulkTransfer completes, the GetBulkDataSent routine executes:

```
private void GetBulkDataSent(IAsyncResult ar)
{
   UInt32 bytesWritten = 0;
   var deleg = ((SendToDeviceDelegate)(ar.AsyncState));
   deleg.EndInvoke(ref bytesWritten, ref success, ar);

   if (ar.IsCompleted)
   {
      Debug.WriteLine(bytesWritten);
      Debug.WriteLine(success);
   }
}
```

The EndInvoke method returns the parameters that BeginInvoke passed by reference. The IAsycnResult parameter's IsCompleted property returns true if the method completed.

Reading bulk and interrupt data

The WinUsb_ReadPipe function can read data from bulk and interrupt endpoints.

Definitions

```
[DllImport("winusb.dll", SetLastError = true)]
internal static extern Boolean WinUsb_ReadPipe
   (SafeWinUsbHandle InterfaceHandle,
   Byte PipeID,
   Byte[] Buffer,
   UInt32 BufferLength,
   ref UInt32 LengthTransferred,
   IntPtr Overlapped);
```

Use

```
Byte[] buffer = new Byte[64];
UInt32 bytesRead = 0;
UInt32 bytesToRead = 64;

var success = NativeMethods.WinUsb_ReadPipe
    (winUsbHandle,
    myDeviceInfo.bulkInPipe,
    buffer,
    bytesToRead,
    ref bytesRead,
    IntPtr.Zero);
```

How it works

The WinUsb_ReadPipe function accepts a pointer to a WinUSB handle obtained with WinUsb_Initialize, an endpoint address retrieved with WinUsb_QueryPipe, a buffer that will store the received data, the maximum number of bytes to read, a pointer to a buffer that will contain the number of bytes read when the function returns, and a zero pointer to specify synchronous operation. On success, the function returns true with the received data in the passed buffer and the number of bytes read in bytes-Read. To send data using interrupt transfers, change myDeviceInfo.bulkInPipe to myDeviceInfo.interruptInPipe.

The number of bytes read can depend on the policies set by WinUsb_SetPipePolicy.

Reading data without blocking

In the example above, the calling thread blocks until WinUsb_ReadPipe returns. As when writing data, you can read data without blocking by using a delegate to initiate the read operation and notify the calling thread when the operation is complete.

To enable calling the code to read data, place the code from the example above in a routine as shown in the example below.

```
internal void ReceiveDataViaBulkTransfer
   (SafeWinUsbHandle winUsbHandle,
   DeviceInfo myDeviceInfo,
   UInt32 bytesToRead,
   ref Byte[] dataBuffer,
   ref UInt32 bytesRead,
   ref Boolean success)
{
   var success = NativeMethods.WinUsb_ReadPipe
      (winUsbHandle,
       myDeviceInfo.BulkInPipe,
       dataBuffer,
       bytesToRead,
       ref bytesRead,
       IntPtr.Zero);
}
```

Then create a delegate for the routine to enable calling the routine asynchronously.

The first step is to create a class of delegates with the same parameters as Receive-DataViaBulk Transfer:

```
private delegate void ReceiveFromDeviceDelegate(
   SafeWinUsbHandle winUsbHandle,
   DeviceInfo myDeviceInfo,
   UInt32 bytesToRead,
   ref Byte[] dataBuffer,
   ref UInt32 bytesRead,
   ref Boolean success);
```

Then create a delegate of the ReceiveFromDeviceDelegate class:

```
ReceiveFromDeviceDelegate myReceiveFromDeviceDelegate =
   ReceiveDataViaBulkTransfer;
```

The delegate's BeginInvoke method has the same parameters as ReceiveDataViaBulk-Transfer plus two additional parameters. GetBulkDataReceived is the routine to call when the read operation completes, and the myReceiveFromDeviceDelegate object passes information to the GetBulkDataReceived routine:

```
myReceiveFromDeviceDelegate.BeginInvoke
   (winUsbHandle,
   myDeviceInfo,
   bytesToRead,
   ref dataBuffer,
   ref bytesRead,
   ref success,
   GetBulkDataReceived,
   myReceiveFromDeviceDelegate);
```

When ReceiveDataViaBulkTransfer completes, the GetBulkDataReceived routine executes:

```
private void GetBulkDataReceived(IAsyncResult ar)
{
   UInt32 bytesRead = 0;
   var success = false;
   Byte[] receivedDataBuffer = null;
   var deleg = ((ReceiveFromDeviceDelegate)(ar.AsyncState));

   deleg.EndInvoke
      (ref receivedDataBuffer,
       ref bytesRead,
       ref success, ar);

   if (ar.IsCompleted)
   {
      Debug.WriteLine(bytesRead);
      Debug.WriteLine(success);
      for (Int32 i = 0; i <= bytesRead - 1; i++)
      {
         Debug.WriteLine(receivedDataBuffer[i]);
      }
   }
}
```

The EndInvoke method returns the parameters that BeginInvoke passed by reference, including the received data. The IAsycnResult parameter's IsCompleted property returns true if the method completed.

Using vendor-defined control transfers

Another option for transferring data is to use vendor-defined requests sent using control transfers directed to the WinUSB interface.

Requests can use any value from 0x0000 to 0xFFFF for wValue and wLength in the Setup packet. If the request is directed to the device (bmRequestType bits 4..0 = 00000_b), the entire wIndex field is also available for any use. If the request is directed to an interface (bmRequestType bits 4..0 = 00001_b), the WinUSB driver passes the interface number in the low byte of wIndex so only the high byte is available for vendor use.

In the bmRequestType field, bits 6..5 equal 10_b to indicate a vendor-defined request. The bRequest field is a vendor-defined request number.

Definitions

```
internal struct WINUSB_SETUP_PACKET
{
    internal Byte RequestType;
    internal Byte Request;
    internal UInt16 Value;
    internal UInt16 Index;
    internal UInt16 Length;
}

[DllImport("winusb.dll", SetLastError = true)]
internal static extern Boolean WinUsb_ControlTransfer
    (SafeWinUsbHandle InterfaceHandle,
    WINUSB_SETUP_PACKET SetupPacket,
    Byte[] Buffer,
    UInt32 BufferLength,
    ref UInt32 LengthTransferred,
    IntPtr Overlapped);
```

Use

```
UInt32 bytesReturned = 0;
Byte[] dataStage = new Byte[2];
NativeMethods.WINUSB_SETUP_PACKET setupPacket;

// Use this for a vendor-specific request to an interface with a
// device-to-host Data stage.

// setupPacket.RequestType = 0XC1;

// Use this for a vendor-specific request to an interface with a
// host-to-device Data stage.

setupPacket.RequestType = 0X41;

setupPacket.Request = 1;
setupPacket.Value = 3;
setupPacket.Length = Convert.ToUInt16(dataStage.Length);

// For control write transfers (host-to-device Data stage),
// provide data for the Data stage. Example:

dataStage[0] = 65;
dataStage[1] = 66;
```

```
var success = NativeMethods.WinUsb_ControlTransfer
  (winUsbHandle,
  setupPacket,
  dataStage,
  Convert.ToUInt16(dataStage.Length),
  ref bytesReturned,
  IntPtr.Zero);
```

How it works

The WINUSB_SETUP_PACKET structure holds the contents of the fields in the Setup stage's data packet as described in Chapter 2. The application sets RequestType to the bmRequestType value for a vendor-specific request directed to an interface with bit 7 indicating the direction of the Data stage. The Request and Value fields are the desired values for bRequest (the request number) and wValue (vendor-defined data) in the request.

For requests directed to an interface, the WinUSB driver sets wIndex to the interface number of the WinUSB interface. For requests directed to the device (setupPacket.RequestType = 0x40 or 0xC0), the application can send a value in setupPacket.Index.

For a control write request, the application places the data to send to the device in an array. For a control read request, the application passes an array to hold data received from the device.

The setupPacket.Length field is the number of bytes in the request's Data stage.

The WinUsb_ControlTransfer function initiates a control transfer. The function passes a pointer to a WinUSB handle to the interface, a WINUSB_SETUP_PACKET structure, a pointer to a byte array that contains data to send or space for received data, the number of bytes to read or write, a pointer to variable that will contain the number of bytes read (for read operations), and a zero pointer to specify synchronous operation. For control write transfers, bytesReturned can be a null pointer. On success, the function returns True with the number of bytes read or written in the LengthTransferred parameter. For control read transfers, the passed array contains the received data.

Selecting an alternate interface

A device's default interface should request no isochronous bandwidth. To use isochronous transfers, the host should select an alternate interface that has one or more isochronous endpoints whose wPacketSize is greater than zero. WinUSB provides a function to select an alternate interface for this or other uses.

Definitions

```
[DllImport("winusb.dll", SetLastError = true)]
internal static extern Boolean WinUsb_SetCurrentAlternateSetting
   (SafeWinUsbHandle InterfaceHandle,
   Byte AlternateSetting);
```

Use

```
var success = NativeMethods.WinUsb_SetCurrentAlternateSetting
   (winUsbHandle,
   1);
```

How it works

The WinUsb_SetCurrentAlternateSetting function selects a bAlternateSetting value to use for the current interface. InterfaceHandle is a pointer to a WinUSB handle to the desired interface. AlternateSetting is the bAlternateSetting value in the interface descriptor with the desired endpoints. If using an array of interface descriptors, you can specify a descriptor from the array, for example:

```
ifaceDescriptors[1].bAlternateSetting
```

The function returns true on success.

Writing data: isochronous transfers

Isochronous OUT transfers require Windows 8.1 or later and a device that has an isochronous OUT endpoint and support for isochronous transfers.

Definitions

```
[DllImport("winusb.dll", SetLastError = true)]
internal static extern Boolean
WinUsb_RegisterIsochBuffer
   (SafeWinUsbHandle InterfaceHandle,
   Byte PipeID,
   Byte[] Buffer,
   UInt32 BufferLength,
   out IntPtr BufferHandle);

[DllImport("winusb.dll", SetLastError = true)]
internal static extern Boolean WinUsb_WriteIsochPipeAsap
   (IntPtr BufferHandle,
   UInt32 Offset,
   UInt32 Length,
   Boolean ContinueStream,
   IntPtr Overlapped);
```

```
[DllImport("winusb.dll", SetLastError = true)]
internal static extern Boolean WinUsb_UnregisterIsochBuffer
   (IntPtr BufferHandle);
```

Use

```
IntPtr bufferHandle = IntPtr.Zero;
var dataOutBuffer = new Byte[24];
var success = false;

// Store data to send in a buffer, for example:

for (var i = 0; i <= 23; i++)
{
   dataOutBuffer[i] = (Byte) (97 + i);
}

success = NativeMethods.WinUsb_RegisterIsochBuffer
   (winUsbHandle,
   myDeviceInfo.IsochronousOutPipe,
   dataOutBuffer,
   (UInt32) dataOutBuffer.Length,
   out bufferHandle);

success = NativeMethods.WinUsb_WriteIsochPipeAsap
   (bufferHandle,
   0,
   (UInt32) dataBuffer.Length,
   false,
   IntPtr.Zero);

success = NativeMethods.WinUsb_UnregisterIsochBuffer
   (bufferHandle);
```

How it works

WinUsb_RegisterIsochBuffer registers a buffer to use in isochronous transfers. The function accepts a handle to a WinUSB interface, a PipeID value obtained by WinUsb_QueryPipe, a buffer that will hold the isochronous data to send, the buffer's length in bytes, and a pointer that will hold a returned handle to the buffer. The function returns true on success.

WinUsb_WriteIsochPipeAsap writes data to an isochronous OUT endpoint using the next available frame number. The function accepts a buffer handle returned by WinUsb_RegisterIsochBuffer, an offset that specifies where in the buffer to start sending data, the buffer's size, a ContinueStream value, and either a pointer to an overlapped structure or IntPtr.Zero for a synchronous operation. If ContinueStream is true, the host will cancel the transfer if unable to schedule it in the first frame after the previous transfer. The function returns true on success.

When transfers are complete, WinUsb_UnregisterIsochBuffer releases the resources allocated by WinUsb_RegisterIsochBuffer.

An alternative to WinUsb_WriteIsochPipeAsap is WinUsb_WriteIsochPipe, which enables specifying a starting frame number for the transfer.

Reading data: isochronous transfers

Isochronous IN transfers require Windows 8.1 or later and a device that has an isochronous IN endpoint and support for isochronous transfers.

Definitions

```
internal struct USBD_ISO_PACKET_DESCRIPTOR
{
    internal UInt32 Offset;
    internal UInt32 Length;
    internal UInt32 Status;
}

[DllImport("winusb.dll", SetLastError = true)]
internal static extern Boolean WinUsb_ReadIsochPipeAsap
    (IntPtr BufferHandle,
    UInt32 Offset,
    UInt32 Length,
    Boolean ContinueStream,
    UInt32 NumberOfPackets,
    ref USBD_ISO_PACKET_DESCRIPTOR IsoPacketDescriptors,
    IntPtr Overlapped);
```

Use

```
IntPtr bufferHandle;
var dataInBuffer = new Byte[24];
UInt32 numberOfPackets = 3;
var isoPacketDescriptors =
    new NativeMethods.USBD_ISO_PACKET_DESCRIPTOR[numberOfPackets];

success = NativeMethods.WinUsb_RegisterIsochBuffer
    (winUsbHandle,
    myDeviceInfo.IsochronousInPipe,
    dataInBuffer,
    (UInt32) dataInBuffer.Length,
    out bufferHandle
```

```
success = NativeMethods.WinUsb_ReadIsochPipeAsap
    (bufferHandle,
    0,
    dataInBuffer.Length,
    false,
    numberOfPackets,
    ref isoPacketDescriptors[0],
    IntPtr.Zero);

for (var i = 0; i <= numberOfPackets - 1; i++) {
    Debug.WriteLine("packet offset = " +
        isoPacketDescriptors[i].Offset);
    Debug.WriteLine("packet length = " +
        isoPacketDescriptors[i].Length);
    Debug.WriteLine("packet status = " +
        isoPacketDescriptors[i].Status);
    for (var j = 0; j < isoPacketDescriptors [i].Length; j++)
    {
        Debug.WriteLine(dataInBuffer[j]);
    }
}
success = NativeMethods.WinUsb_UnregisterIsochBuffer
    (bufferHandle);
```

How it works

Reading isochronous data requires an array of USBD_ISO_PACKET_DESCRIPTOR structures. The array must have a structure for each packet to be received in a read operation. In each structure, on completing a read operation, Offset is the offset in bytes of the packet within the transfer buffer, Length is the number of bytes received in a packet, and Status is the USBD_STATUS code (defined in *usbdi.h* in the WDK) for the packet.

As with isochronous OUT transfers, the application must call WinUsb_RegisterIsoch-Buffer to register a buffer. For IN transfers, when the function returns, the buffer holds the received data.

WinUsb_ReadIsochPipeAsap requests data from an isochronous IN endpoint using the next frame number after any pending transfers on the endpoint. The function accepts a buffer handle returned by WinUsb_RegisterIsochBuffer, an offset that specifies where in the buffer to begin storing received data, the buffer's size, a ContinueStream value, the number of isochronous packets needed to hold the received data, a pointer to an array of USBD_ISO_PACKET_DESCRIPTOR structures, and either a pointer to an overlapped structure or IntPtr.Zero for a synchronous transfer. The function returns true on success.

The example requests to read three 8-byte packets. The USBD_ISO_PACKET_DE-SCRIPTOR structures contain information about the received data, and the data buffer registered by WinUsb_RegisterIsochBuffer contains the data.

When transfers are complete, WinUsb_UnregisterIsochBuffer releases the resources allocated by WinUsb_RegisterIsochBuffer.

An alternative to WinUsb_ReadIsochPipeAsap is WinUsb_ReadIsochPipe, which enables specifying a starting frame number for the transfer.

Closing communications

When finished communicating with a device, the application should free reserved resources.

Use

```
winUsbHandle.Close();
deviceHandle.Close();
```

How it works

The Close method marks each handle for releasing and freeing resources.

15

Using WinUSB's System INF File

For Windows 8 and later, the system-provided *winusb.inf* eliminates the need for a digitally signed, device-specific INF file. With supporting device firmware, the host system can detect a device that uses the WinUSB driver, and applications can find the device they want to communicate with.

To obtain a system INF tile to use with Windows versions previous to Windows 8, from the Microsoft Update Catalog, search on **windows phone winusb**, and download the associated *.cab* file, which contains *winusbcompat.cat* and *winusbcompat.inf*.

To use the system INF file, a device must support Microsoft OS 1.0 descriptors or Microsoft OS 2.0 descriptors. Microsoft OS 1.0 descriptors require Windows XP SP2 or later while Microsoft OS 2.0 Descriptors, which have greater capabilities, require Windows 8.1 or later.

Microsoft OS 1.0 descriptors

A WinUSB device that uses Microsoft OS 1.0 descriptors must provide these descriptors:

> Microsoft OS string descriptor
>
> Extended compat ID OS feature descriptor
>
> Extended properties OS feature descriptor.

Listing 15-1 shows example Microsoft OS 1.0 descriptors for a WinUSB device.

The descriptors are defined in a series of documents collectively titled *Microsoft OS 1.0 Descriptors Specification*.

The string descriptor must have an index of 0xEE and contain the signature "MSFT100". Windows XP SP1 and later request this string descriptor from vendor-defined devices on first attachment. A device that doesn't support the descriptor should return STALL.

After successfully retrieving a Microsoft OS string descriptor, the host requests Microsoft OS feature descriptors. The extended compat ID OS feature descriptor contains a Microsoft-defined ID that can help Windows locate a driver for device functions that don't have Windows-provided drivers. The extended properties OS feature descriptor can provide a GUID value that identifies a specific vendor-defined device function.

A WinUSB device that supports Microsoft OS 1.0 descriptors must have a device descriptor with bcdUSB = 0x0200 or higher.

Microsoft OS string descriptor

The Microsoft OS String Descriptor (Table 15-1) contains a qwSignature value that indicates that the device supports Microsoft OS descriptors.

The value for Microsoft OS String Descriptor version 1.00 is the UTF-16LE Unicode string "MSFT100". The string doesn't have a null termination. The string's seven 16-bit characters transmit LSB first on the bus:

```
0x4Ds, 0x00, 0x53, 0x00, 0x46, 0x00, 0x54, 0x00, 0x31, 0x00, 0x30,
0x00, 0x30, 0x00,
```

The bMS_VendorCode value enables the host to request additional Microsoft OS descriptors. The host passes the value in the bRequest field of the Setup packet for a Get Descriptor request. The value can be any vendor-defined byte except 0x00.

The host requests a Microsoft OS string descriptor by sending a Get Descriptor request with bmRequestType = 0x80, bRequest = 0x06 (Get Descriptor), wValue's high byte = 0x03 to request a string descriptor, wValue's low byte = 0xEE (the Microsoft-defined index for the descriptor), and wIndex = 0x0000. (Note that the USB 2.0

```
// Microsoft OS 1.0 String Descriptor

UCHAR ms_os_10_string_descriptor[0x12] =
{

0x12,                  // Descriptor size (18 bytes)
0x03,                  // Descriptor type (string)

// MSFT100 signature
0x4D, 0x00, 0x53, 0x00, 0x46, 0x00, 0x54, 0x00, 0x31, 0x00, 0x30, 0x00,
0x30, 0x00,

0x05,                  // Vendor-defined bMS_VendorCode
0x00                   // Pad byte
}

// Microsoft Extended Compat ID OS feature descriptor

UCHAR ms_extended_compat_id_os_feature_descriptor[0x28] =
{

0x28, 0x00,            // Descriptor size (40 bytes)
0x01, 0x00,            // Descriptor version number (1.00)
0x04, 0x00,            // Extended Compat ID OS descriptor identifier
0x01, 0x00,            // Number of custom property sections that follow
0x00, 0x00, 0x00, 0x00, 0x00, 0x00, 0x00,    // Reserved

0x00,                  //    bInterfaceNumber of the WinUSB interface
0x01,                  //    Reserved, set to 0x01
0x57, 0x49, 0x4E, 0x55, 0x53, 0x42, 0x00, 0x00,        // WINUSB ID
0x00, 0x00, 0x00, 0x00, 0x00, 0x00, 0x00, 0x00, 0x00,  // Secondary ID
0x00, 0x00, 0x00, 0x00, 0x00, 0x00                     // Reserved
}
```

Listing 15-1: These Microsoft OS 1.0 descriptors inform the host that the device uses the WinUSB driver. (Part 1 of 2)

```
// Microsoft extended properties OS feature descriptor

UCHAR ms_extended_properties_os_feature_descriptor[0x8E] =
{
0x8E, 0x00, 0x00, 0x00,     // Descriptor size in bytes (142 bytes)
0x00, 0x01,                 // Descriptor version number (1.00)
0x05, 0x00,                 // Extended Compat ID OS descriptor identifier
0x01, 0x00,                 // Number of custom property sections that
                            //   follow

0x84, 0x00, 0x00, 0x00,     // Length of custom property section
                            //   (132 bytes)
0x01, 0x00, 0x00, 0x00,     // String format (UTF-16LE Unicode)
0x28, 0x00,                 // Length of property name (40 bytes)

// Property Name (DeviceInterfaceGUID)

0x44, 0x00, 0x65, 0x00, 0x76, 0x00, 0x69, 0x00, 0x63, 0x00, 0x65, 0x00,
0x49, 0x00, 0x6E, 0x00, 0x74, 0x00, 0x65, 0x00, 0x72, 0x00, 0x66, 0x00,
0x61, 0x00, 0x63, 0x00, 0x65, 0x00, 0x47, 0x00, 0x55, 0x00, 0x49, 0x00,
0x44, 0x00, 0x00, 0x00,

0x4e, 0x00, 0x00, 0x00,     // Length of property data (78 bytes)

// Vendor-defined property data: {ecceff35-146c-4ff3-acd9-8f992d09acdd}

0x7B, 0x00, 0x65, 0x00, 0x63, 0x00, 0x63, 0x00, 0x65, 0x00, 0x66, 0x00,
0x66, 0x00, 0x33, 0x00, 0x35, 0x00, 0x2D, 0x00, 0x31, 0x00, 0x34, 0x00,
0x36, 0x00, 0x33, 0x00, 0x2D, 0x00, 0x34, 0x00, 0x66, 0x00, 0x66, 0x00,
0x33, 0x00, 0x2D, 0x00, 0x61, 0x00, 0x63, 0x00, 0x64, 0x00, 0x39, 0x00,
0x2D, 0x00, 0x38, 0x00, 0x66, 0x00, 0x39, 0x00, 0x39, 0x00, 0x32, 0x00,
0x64, 0x00, 0x30, 0x00, 0x39, 0x00, 0x61, 0x00, 0x63, 0x00, 0x64, 0x00,
0x64, 0x00, 0x7D, 0x00, 0x00, 0x00
}
```

Listing 15-1: These Microsoft OS 1.0 descriptors inform the host that the device uses the WinUSB driver. (Part 2 of 2)

specification says wIndex should contain a language ID, but Windows incorrectly uses 0x0000.)

If a device returns a string descriptor with the correct qwSignature, the host may request an extended compat ID OS feature descriptor and an extended properties OS feature descriptor.

Table 15-1: The Microsoft OS string descriptor contains a qwSignature value that indicates that the device supports Microsoft OS descriptors.

Offset (decimal)	Field	Size (bytes)	Description
0	bLength	1	Descriptor size in bytes (0x12)
1	bDescriptorType	1	The constant String (0x03)
2	qwSignature	14	UTF-16LE Unicode string "MSFT100" (for version 1.00)
16	bMS_VendorCode	1	Vendor-defined code (anything except 0x00)
17	bPad	1	0x00

Extended compat ID OS feature descriptor

The Microsoft-defined extended compat ID OS feature descriptor can identify a device that uses the WinUSB driver. The descriptor consists of a header followed by one or more function sections. A device can have only one extended compat ID OS feature descriptor.

Listing 15-2 shows the fields in an extended compat ID OS feature descriptor for a device that uses the WinUSB driver. The first five fields are the header, followed by a function section.

In the header:

wIndex = 0x0004 identifies the descriptor as an extended compat ID OS feature descriptor.

bCount contains the number of function sections that follow. A descriptor for a WinUSB device has one function section for each WinUSB interface in the device.

In the function section:

bFirstInterfaceNumber contains the bInterfaceNumber value of an interface descriptor for an interface that uses the WinUSB driver.

compatibleID contains ASCII codes for the string "WINUSB" followed by two zero bytes:

```
0x57, 0x49, 0x4e, 0x55, 0x53, 0x42, 0x00, 0x00
```

Devices with interfaces that use other drivers return other Microsoft-defined compatibleID values in a function section. Other functions with defined compatibleID values include RNDIS, Picture Transfer Protocol (PTP), Media Transfer Protocol (MTP), and Bluetooth radio.

For functions other than Bluetooth, the subCompatibleID field contains 0x0000000000000000.

Table 15-2: In a Microsoft extended compat ID OS feature descriptor, the first five fields are the header, followed by a function section.

Offset (decimal)	Field	Size (bytes)	Description
0	dwLength	4	Descriptor size in bytes (0x00000028)
4	bcdVersion	2	Version number in BCD format (Use 0x0100 for version 1.00)
6	wIndex	2	Extended compat ID descriptor identifier (0x0004)
8	bCount	1	The number of function sections that follow (1 function section per WinUSB interface)
9	RESERVED	7	Zeroes
16	bFirstInterfaceNumber	1	bInterfaceNumber of the first WinUSB interface
17	RESERVED	1	0x01
18	compatibleID	8	ASCII codes for "WINUSB" followed by 2 zero bytes
26	subCompatibleID	8	0x0000000000000000
34	RESERVED	6	0x000000000000

The host requests a Microsoft extended compat ID OS feature descriptor by sending a Get Descriptor request with bmRequestType = 0xC0 (to specify an IN data stage for a vendor request directed to the device), bRequest = the bMS_VendorCode from the OS string descriptor, wValue's high byte = 0x00, wValue's low byte = the bInterfaceNumber associated with the interface specified by the descriptor or 0x00 if the descriptor request is directed to the device, and wIndex = 0x0004 to specify the Extended Compat ID OS descriptor.

Because a device can have only one Microsoft Extended Compat ID OS feature descriptor, Microsoft advises that devices can ignore the low byte of wValue.

Because the host doesn't know the length of the descriptor in advance, the host typically begins by requesting the header's 16 bytes to learn the dwLength value, then resending the request with a request for dwLength bytes.

For descriptors with dwLength greater than 64 KB, the high byte of wValue contains a zero-based page number to enable the host to retrieve the entire descriptor using multiple requests.

Extended properties OS feature descriptor

Because devices with many different purposes may use the WinUSB driver, applications need a way to identify the specific device they want to communicate with. The Microsoft-defined extended properties OS feature descriptor can contain a vendor-defined GUID value that identifies a vendor-defined device function to application software. A device that provides an extended properties OS feature descriptor must also provide an extended compat ID OS feature descriptor.

The descriptor consists of a header followed by one or more custom property sections.

Listing 15-3 shows the fields in an extended properties OS feature descriptor that contains a GUID for a WinUSB device. The first four fields are the header, followed by one or more custom property sections.

In the header:

wIndex = 0x0005 to indicate that the descriptor is an extended properties OS feature descriptor.

wCount specifies the number of custom property sections that follow.

In the custom property section:

dwPropertyDataType = 0x00000001 to indicate UTF-16LE Unicode string.

wPropertyNameLength is the length in bytes of the bPropertyName field that follows.

bPropertyName contains the UTF-16LE Unicode string "DeviceInterfaceGUID" followed by two zero bytes.

dwPropertyDataLength is the length in bytes of the bPropertyData field that follows.

bPropertyData contains a vendor-defined, 76-byte UTF-16LE Unicode GUID value followed by 2 zero bytes. Here is an example:

`{ecceff35-146c-4ff3-acd9-8f992d09acdd}`

Each character is 2 bytes, and the GUID string includes the opening and closing curly brackets.

The GUID should be unique to a device capability that a host application can use to identify devices to communicate with. Multiple devices that have the same function and use the same communications protocols can use the same GUID.

The host requests a Microsoft extended properties OS feature descriptor by sending a Get Descriptor request with bmRequestType = 0xC0 (to specify an IN data stage and a vendor request directed to the device) or 0xC1 (for a request directed to an interface), bRequest = the bMS_VendorCode from the OS string descriptor, wValue's high byte = 0x00, wValue's low byte = the bInterfaceNumber associated with the descriptor, and wIndex = 0x0005 to specify the extended properties OS feature descriptor.

The *Microsoft OS 1.0 Descriptors Specification* shows how an extended properties OS feature descriptor can also configure power options such as enabling selective Suspend.

Table 15-3: A Microsoft extended properties OS feature descriptor can provide a vendor-defined GUID value that identifies a specific device.

Offset (decimal)	Field	Size (bytes)	Description
0	dwLength	4	Descriptor size in bytes (0x008e)
4	bcdVersion	2	Version number in BCD format (0x0100)
6	wIndex	2	Extended compat ID descriptor identifier (0x0005)
8	wCount	2	The number of custom property sections that follow
9	dwSize	4	Length of the custom property section in bytes (0x00000084)
13	dwPropertyDataType	4	0x00000001 = UTF-16LE Unicode string
17	wPropertyNameLength	2	Length of bPropertyName in bytes (0x0028)
19	bPropertyName	40	Null-terminated UTF-16LE Unicode string "DeviceInterfaceGUID" followed by 2 zero bytes
59	dwPropertyDataLength	4	Length of bPropertyData (0x0000004e)
63	bPropertyData	78	GUID value expressed as a UTF-16LE Unicode string followed by 2 zero bytes

Enumeration

If a device returns the compatID "WINUSB" in an extended compat ID OS feature descriptor, the OS assigns the WinUSB driver to the device. Applications can use the DeviceInterfaceGUID returned in an extended properties OS feature descriptor to open a handle to the device.

A device that doesn't support the Microsoft OS string descriptor or another requested Microsoft OS descriptor should return STALL. However, some devices don't handle the request for a Microsoft OS string descriptor correctly and may even fail to complete enumeration after receiving the request. For this reason, a Windows host requests the Microsoft OS string descriptor only on the first enumeration attempt, whether or not the request was successful on previous attachments.

During debugging of the descriptors, you may want to force the host to request the Microsoft OS descriptors again. To do so, delete the device's entry in the system registry here:

```
HKEY_LOCAL_MACHINE\SYSTEM\CurrentControlSet\Control\usbflags\
    <VVVVPPPPRRRR>
```

using these values from the device descriptor:

VVVV is the device's idVendor

PPPP is the device's idProduct

RRRR is the devices bcdDevice

Then remove and reattach the device to re-enumerate.

Microsoft OS 2.0 descriptors

Microsoft OS 2.0 descriptors remove the need to request a Microsoft string descriptor and the problems that can result and also add capabilities to the descriptors.

A WinUSB device that supports Microsoft OS 2.0 descriptors provides these descriptors:

BOS descriptor

Microsoft OS 2.0 platform capability descriptor

Microsoft OS 2.0 compatible ID descriptor

Microsoft OS 2.0 registry property descriptor

Listing 15-2 shows example Microsoft OS 2.0 descriptors for a WinUSB device.

Microsoft OS 2.0 descriptors add the ability to assign the WinUSB driver to an entire composite device and to return descriptors that apply to specific Windows versions.

In the device descriptor, bcdUSB must equal 0x0210 or higher to enable supporting the BOS descriptor.

The document that defines the descriptors is *Microsoft OS 2.0 Descriptors Specification*.

Microsoft OS 2.0 platform capability descriptor

A BOS descriptor (see Chapter 4) tells the host that the device supports one or more device capability descriptors. As Table 15-4 shows, for WinUSB devices, the BOS descriptor has one subordinate descriptor, the Microsoft OS 2.0 platform capability descriptor. A host can request the BOS descriptor's five bytes to learn the length of the full BOS descriptor set, then request wTotalLength bytes to retrieve the BOS descriptor and its subordinate descriptor.

The Microsoft OS 2.0 platform capability descriptor tells the host that the device supports Microsoft OS 2.0 descriptors.

The first 20 bytes are the header:

bDevCapabilityType field = 0x05 to indicate that the descriptor defines a device capability specific to a particular platform or operating system (Windows).

PlatformCapabilityUUID holds a 128-bit value that is unique to the device capability. To indicate Microsoft OS 2.0 platform capability, the field contains this UUID:

D8DD60DF-4589-4CC7-9CD2-659D9E648A9F

```
// BOS descriptor with platform capability descriptor

UCHAR platform_capability_descriptor[0x21] = {
// BOS descriptor

0x05,                          // Descriptor size (5 bytes)
0x0F,                          // Descriptor type (BOS)
0x21, 0x00,                    // Length of this + subordinate descriptors
                               // (33 bytes)
0x01,                          // Number of subordinate descriptors

// Microsoft OS 2.0 Platform Capability Descriptor

0x1C,                          // Descriptor size (28 bytes)
0x10,                          // Descriptor type (Device Capability)
0x05,                          // Capability type (Platform)
0x00,                          // Reserved

// MS OS 2.0 Platform Capability ID (D8DD60DF-4589-4CC7-9CD2-659D9E648A9F)

0xDF, 0x60, 0xDD, 0xD8,
0x89, 0x45,
0xC7, 0x4C,
0x9C, 0xD2,
0x65, 0x9D, 0x9E, 0x64, 0x8A, 0x9F,

0x00, 0x00, 0x03, 0x06,        // Windows version (8.1) (0x06030000)
0x9E, 0x00,                    // Size, MS OS 2.0 descriptor set (158 bytes)
0x01,                          // Vendor-assigned bMS_VendorCode
0x00                           // Doesn't support alternate enumeration
}
```

Listing 15-2: These Microsoft OS 2.0 descriptors inform the host that the device uses the WinUSB driver. (Part 1 of 2)

```
// Microsoft OS 2.0 Descriptor Set

UCHAR ms_os_20_descriptor_set[0x9E] = {

0x0A, 0x00,                       // Descriptor size (10 bytes)
0x00, 0x00,                       // MS OS 2.0 descriptor set header
0x00, 0x00, 0x03, 0x06,           // Windows version (8.1) (0x06030000)
0x9E, 0x00,                       // Size, MS OS 2.0 descriptor set (158 bytes)

// Microsoft OS 2.0 compatible ID descriptor

0x14, 0x00,                             // Descriptor size (20 bytes)
0x03, 0x00,                             // MS OS 2.0 compatible ID descriptor
0x57, 0x49, 0x4E, 0x55, 0x53, 0x42, 0x00, 0x00,   // WINUSB string
0x00, 0x00, 0x00, 0x00, 0x00, 0x00, 0x00, 0x00,   // Sub-compatible ID

// Registry property descriptor

0x80, 0x00,               // Descriptor size (130 bytes)
0x04, 0x00,               // Registry Property descriptor
0x01, 0x00,               // Strings are null-terminated Unicode
0x28, 0x00,               // Size of Property Name (40 bytes)

//Property Name ("DeviceInterfaceGUID")

0x44, 0x00, 0x65, 0x00, 0x76, 0x00, 0x69, 0x00, 0x63, 0x00, 0x65, 0x00,
0x49, 0x00, 0x6E, 0x00, 0x74, 0x00, 0x65, 0x00, 0x72, 0x00, 0x66, 0x00,
0x61, 0x00, 0x63, 0x00, 0x65, 0x00, 0x47, 0x00, 0x55, 0x00, 0x49, 0x00,
0x44, 0x00, 0x00, 0x00,

0x4E, 0x00,               // Size of Property Data (78 bytes)

// Vendor-defined Property Data: {ecceff35-146c-4ff3-acd9-8f992d09acdd}

0x7B, 0x00, 0x65, 0x00, 0x63, 0x00, 0x63, 0x00, 0x65, 0x00, 0x66, 0x00,
0x66, 0x00, 0x33, 0x00, 0x35, 0x00, 0x2D, 0x00, 0x31, 0x00, 0x34, 0x00,
0x36, 0x00, 0x33, 0x00, 0x2D, 0x00, 0x34, 0x00, 0x66, 0x00, 0x66, 0x00,
0x33, 0x00, 0x2D, 0x00, 0x61, 0x00, 0x63, 0x00, 0x64, 0x00, 0x39, 0x00,
0x2D, 0x00, 0x38, 0x00, 0x66, 0x00, 0x39, 0x00, 0x39, 0x00, 0x32, 0x00,
0x64, 0x00, 0x30, 0x00, 0x39, 0x00, 0x61, 0x00, 0x63, 0x00, 0x64, 0x00,
0x64, 0x00, 0x7D, 0x00, 0x00, 0x00
}
```

Listing 15-2: These Microsoft OS 2.0 descriptors inform the host that the device uses the WinUSB driver. (Part 2 of 2)

Table 15-4: The 5-byte BOS descriptor serves as a header that informs the host about the subordinate Microsoft OS 2.0 platform device capability descriptor.

Offset (decimal)	Field	Size (bytes)	Description
0	bLength	1	Descriptor size in bytes (0x05).
1	bDescriptorType	1	BOS (0x0F)
2	wTotalLength	2	The number of bytes in this descriptor and all of its subordinate descriptors (0x0021)
4	bNumDeviceCaps	1	The number of device capability descriptors subordinate to this BOS descriptor (0x01)
5	bLength	1	Descriptor size in bytes (0x1C)
6	bDescriptorType	1	DEVICE CAPABILITY (0x10)
7	bDevCapabilityType	1	PLATFORM (0x05)
8	bReserved	1	Reserved, (0x00)
9	MS_OS_20_Platform_Capability_ID	16	128-bit value that identifies a platform-specific device capability: D8DD60DF-4589-4CC7-9CD2-659D9E648A9F
25	dwWindowsVersion	4	Windows version (Windows 8.1 = 0x00000603)
29	wMSOSDescriptorSet-TotalLength	2	Length in bytes of the MS OS 2.0 descriptor set (0x9E)
31	bMS_VendorCode	1	Vendor-defined code, can be anything except 0x00
32	bAltEnumCode	1	0x00 or a non-zero bAltInterface value for use by the Microsoft OS 2.0 Set Alternate Enumeration request

When expressed as text, a UUID consists of five groups of 2-character hexadecimal values separated by hyphens. Confusingly, each of the first three groups is considered to be a single hexadecimal value, while the final two groups are considered to be sequences of bytes. For the groups that represent single values, the LSB transmits first. For the other groups, the bytes transmit in sequence as expressed. So the UUID transmits in this order:

```
0xDF, 0x60, 0xDD, 0xD8,
0x89, 0x45,
0xC7, 0x4C,
0x9C, 0xD2,
0x65, 0x9D, 0x9E, 0x64, 0x8A, 0x9F
```

Following the header are additional fields.

dwWindowsVersion is the lowest Windows version the descriptor requires. The value is an NTDDI version constant from *sdkddkver.h* in the WDK and must be set to Windows 8.1 or later.

wMSOSDescriptorSetTotalLength is the length in bytes of the Microsoft OS 2.0 descriptor set supported by the device (0x9E for a WinUSB device that provides a compatible ID descriptor and a registry property descriptor with a GUID).

bMS_VendorCode is a vendor-defined value that performs the same function as this value does in a Microsoft OS 1.0 string descriptor.

bAltEnumCode may contain a non-zero value to indicate support for the Microsoft OS 2.0 Set Alternate Enumeration request. This request informs the device that it may return non-default descriptors during enumeration. Regardless of the value in this field, for WinUSB devices that support an alternate interface setting, a host can use the WinUsb_SetCurrentAlternateSetting function to select an alternate interface setting.

Microsoft OS 2.0 descriptor set

For a WinUSB device that uses the system INF file, the Microsoft OS 2.0 descriptor set consists of a 10-byte Microsoft OS 2.0 descriptor set header followed by a Microsoft OS 2.0 compatible ID descriptor and a Microsoft OS 2.0 registry property descriptor (Table 15-5). The descriptor set may also contain additional descriptors as described later in this chapter.

The Microsoft OS 2.0 compatible ID descriptor provides the "WINUSB" string that specifies that the device uses the WinUSB driver. The Microsoft OS 2.0 registry property descriptor provides a Device Interface GUID that applications can use to find a WinUSB device with a specific function.

The host requests the Microsoft OS 2.0 descriptor set by sending a Get Descriptor request with these values:

bmRequestType = 0xC0 to specify a vendor request with an IN data stage directed to the device.

bRequest = the bMS_VendorCode from the platform capability descriptor.

wValue = 0x00.

wIndex = 0x0007 to specify a Microsoft OS 2.0 descriptor.

In the header:

wLength = the length in bytes of the header (0x0A).

wDescriptorType = 0x0000 to indicate a Microsoft OS 2.0 descriptor set header.

dwWindowsVersion has the same meaning as in the Microsoft OS 2.0 platform capability descriptor.

wTotalLength must match wMSOSDescriptorSetTotalLength in the Microsoft OS 2.0 platform capability descriptor.

Table 15-5: For a WinUSB device, the Microsoft OS 2.0 descriptor set consists of a Microsoft OS 2.0 descriptor set header followed by a Microsoft OS 2.0 compatible ID feature descriptor and a Microsoft OS 2.0 registry property feature descriptor.

Offset (decimal)	Field	Size (bytes)	Description
0	wLength	2	Header length (0x0A)
2	wDescriptorType	2	MSOS20_SET_HEADER_DESCRIPTOR (0x0000)
4	dwWindowsVersion	4	Windows version (Windows 8.1 = 0x00000603)
8	wTotalLength	2	Length in bytes of the header and the descriptor that follows (0x009E)
10	wLength	2	Descriptor length in bytes (0x0014)
12	wDescriptorType	2	MS_OS_FEATURE_COMPATIBLE_ID (0x0003)
14	CompatibleID	8	ASCII codes for "WINUSB" followed by two zero bytes
22	SubCompatibleID	8	0x0000000000000000
30	wLength	2	Descriptor length in bytes (0x0080)
32	wDescriptorType	2	MS_OS_20_FEATURE_REG_PROPERTY (0x0004)
34	wPropertyDataType	2	0x0001 = null-terminated Unicode string
36	wPropertyNameLength	2	Length of bPropertyName in bytes (0x0028)
38	PropertyName	40	UTF-16LE Unicode string "DeviceInterfaceGUID" followed by 2 zero bytes
78	wPropertyDataLength	2	Length of bPropertyData (0x004E)
80	PropertyData	78	GUID value expressed as a UTF-16LE Unicode string followed by 2 zero bytes

In the compatible ID feature descriptor:

wLength is the length in bytes of the descriptor (0x0014).

wDescriptorType = 0x0003 to indicate Microsoft OS 2.0 compatible ID feature descriptor.

CompatibleID = the ACSII codes for "WINUSB" followed by two zero bytes:

0x57, 0x49, 0x4E, 0x55, 0x53, 0x42, 0x00, 0x00

SubCompatibleID = 0x0000000000000000.

In the registry property feature descriptor:

wLength is the length in bytes of the descriptor (0x0080).

wDescriptorType = 0x0004 to indicate a Microsoft OS 2.0 registry property feature descriptor.

The final five fields have the same values as contained in the Microsoft OS 1.0 extended properties descriptor:

wPropertyDataType = 0x00000001 to indicate text values are UTF-16LE Unicode strings.

wPropertyNameLength is the length in bytes of the PropertyName field that follows.

PropertyName contains the UTF-16LE Unicode string "DeviceInterfaceGUID" followed by two zero bytes.

wPropertyDataLength is the length in bytes of the PropertyData field that follows.

PropertyData contains a vendor-defined, 76-byte UTF-16LE Unicode GUID value followed by 2 zero bytes, for example:

`{ecceff35-146c-4ff3-acd9-8f992d09acdd}`

Each character is 2 bytes, and the GUID string includes the opening and closing curly brackets.

For the registry property descriptor, Microsoft warns that Windows uses only the values retrieved in the device's first enumeration. During debugging, if you want to edit the descriptor, change the device's Product ID or delete the device's original registry entry, then remove and reattach the device.

A registry property descriptor can add other registry entries such as the SelectiveSuspendEnabled property.

The *Microsoft OS 2.0 Descriptors Specification* document defines additional descriptors:

> For descriptors that apply to a single configuration or function, the descriptor set can include a configuration subset or function subset header with subordinate descriptors.

> The Microsoft OS 2.0 minimum resume time descriptor can specify shorter required times for detecting and resuming from the Suspend state. The descriptor applies only to USB 2.0 speeds.

> The Microsoft OS 2.0 model ID descriptor provides a 128-bit value that uniquely identifies a physical device.

> The Microsoft OS 2.0 CCGP device descriptor requests the host to treat the device as a composite device.

Enumeration

If a device returns a Microsoft OS 2.0 platform capability descriptor and a Microsoft OS 2.0 descriptor set with the compatID "WINUSB", Windows assigns the WinUSB driver to the device. Applications can use the DeviceInterfaceGUID in the descriptor set's registry property descriptor to open a handle to the device.

16

Using Hubs to Extend and Expand the Bus

A hub is an intelligent device that provides attachment points for devices and manages the devices' connections on the bus. Devices that plug directly into the host computer connect to the bus's root hub. Other devices can connect to external hubs downstream from the root hub.

A hub manages power, helps initiate communications with newly attached devices, and passes traffic up and down the bus. To manage power, a hub provides current to attached devices and limits current on detecting an over-current condition. To help initiate communications with devices, the hub detects and informs the host of newly attached devices and responds to requests that relate to status and control of the hub's ports. The hub's role in passing traffic up and down the bus varies with the speeds of the host, device, and hubs between them.

This chapter presents essentials about hub communications. You don't need to know every detail about hubs in order to design a USB peripheral, but understanding what a hub does can help in understanding how devices are detected and communicate

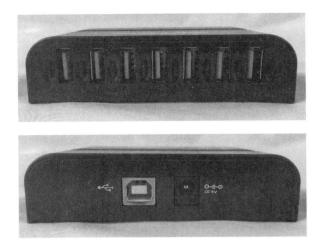

Figure 16-1. The front of this hub (top) has seven downstream-facing ports with Standard-A receptacles on the front, and the back (bottom) has an upstream-facing port with a Standard-B receptacle and a power connection.

on the bus, how to help ensure devices get the bandwidth they need, and the limits to extending a bus with hubs.

USB 2.0

Each external USB 2.0 hub has one port, or attachment point, that connects in the upstream direction (toward the host) (Figure 16-1). The upstream-facing port may connect directly to the host's root hub or to a downstream-facing port on another external hub. Every hub has one or more downstream-facing ports. Most downstream ports have a receptacle for attaching a cable. An exception is a hub in a compound device, whose downstream-facing ports connect to functions embedded in the device. Hubs with one, two, four, and seven downstream ports are common. A hub may be self powered or bus powered. As Chapter 17 explains, bus-powered hubs are limited because you can't attach high-power devices to them.

A USB 2.0 hub acts as a remote processor with store-and-forward capabilities. As needed, the hub converts between high-speed upstream communications and low- and full-speed downstream communications. The hub also performs other functions that help make efficient use of bus time.

USB 1.1 hubs, which support only low and full speeds, are no longer in common use, but understanding the operation of a USB 1.1 hub can help in understanding USB 2.0 hubs. A USB 1.1 hub doesn't convert between speeds; it just passes received traffic up

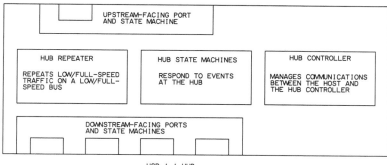

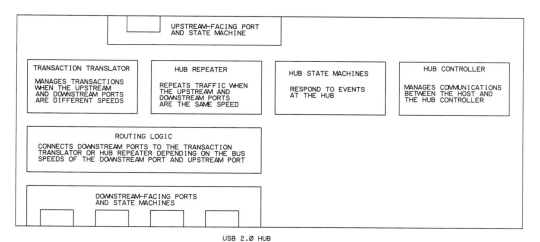

Figure 16-2. A USB 2.0 hub contains one or more transaction translators and routing logic that enables a hub on a high-speed bus to communicate with low- and full-speed devices. A USB 1.1 hub doesn't convert between bus speeds. (Content from: *Universal Serial Bus Specification Revision 2.0.*)

or down the bus. For traffic to and from low-speed devices, a USB 1.1 hub changes the edge rate and signal polarity but not the bit rate.

Controller chips for hubs contain dedicated silicon to perform hub functions. Due to timing requirements, implementing a hub function with a general-purpose device controller chip isn't feasible. Compound devices can use chips that contain an embedded hub and a generic device controller.

An external USB 2.0 hub contains a hub repeater and a hub controller (Figure 16-2). The hub repeater passes USB traffic between the upstream hub (which may be on the host) and attached and enabled downstream devices. The hub controller manages communications between the host and the hub repeater. State machines control the hub's response to events at the hub repeater and upstream and downstream ports. A USB 2.0 hub also has one or more transaction translators and routing logic that enable low- and full-speed devices to communicate on a high-speed bus.

The host's root hub is a special case. The host controller performs many of the functions that the hub repeater and hub controller perform in an external hub, so a root hub may contain little more than routing logic and downstream ports.

The hub repeater

The hub repeater re-transmits the packets it receives, sending them on their way up or down stream with minimal changes. The hub repeater also detects when a device is attached and removed, establishes the connection of a device to the bus, detects bus faults such as over-current conditions, and manages power to the device.

A USB 2.0 hub repeater has two modes of operation depending on the upstream bus speed. When the hub connects upstream to a full-speed bus segment, the repeater functions as a low- and full-speed repeater. When the hub connects upstream to a high-speed bus segment, the repeater functions as a high-speed repeater. The repeaters in USB 1.1 hubs always function as low- and full-speed repeaters.

The low- and full-speed repeater

When a USB 2.0 hub's upstream port connects to a full- or low-speed port, the hub doesn't send or receive high-speed traffic but instead functions identically to a USB 1.1 hub.

A low- and full-speed repeater re-transmits all low- and full-speed packets received from the host, including data that has passed through one or more additional hubs, to all enabled, full-speed, downstream ports. Enabled ports include all ports with attached devices that are ready to receive communications from the hub. Devices with ports that aren't enabled include devices that the host controller has stopped communicating with due to errors or other problems, devices in the Suspend state, and devices that aren't yet ready to communicate because they have just attached or are in the process of exiting the Suspend state.

The hub repeater doesn't translate, examine the contents of, or process the traffic to or from full-speed ports. The repeater just regenerates the edges of the signal transitions and passes the traffic on.

Low-speed devices never see full-speed traffic. The hub identifies a low-speed packet by the PRE packet identifier that precedes the packet. The hub repeats the low-speed packets, and only these packets, to any enabled low-speed ports. The hub also repeats low-speed packets to its full-speed downstream ports because a full-speed port could connect to a hub that in turn connects to a low-speed device. To give hubs time to make their low-speed ports ready to receive data, the host adds a delay of at least four full-speed bit widths between the PRE packet and the low-speed packet.

Compared to full speed, traffic in a low-speed cable segment varies not only in speed, but also in edge rate and polarity. A hub whose downstream port connects directly to a low-speed device uses low speed's edge rate and polarity when communicating with the device. When communicating upstream, the hub uses full-speed's faster edge rate and an inverted polarity compared to low speed. The hub repeater converts between the edge rates and polarities as needed. Chapter 19 has more on the signal polarities, and Chapter 20 has more about edge rates.

The high-speed repeater

A USB 2.0 hub uses a high-speed repeater when the hub's upstream port connects to a high-speed bus segment. In this case, the hub sends and receives all upstream traffic at high speed even if the traffic is to or from a low- or full-speed device. Routing logic in the hub determines whether traffic to or from a downstream port passes through a transaction translator.

Unlike a low- and full-speed repeater, a high-speed repeater re-clocks received data to minimize accumulated jitter. In other words, instead of just repeating received transitions, a high-speed repeater uses its own local clock to time transitions when retransmitting. The edge rate and polarity don't change. An elasticity buffer allows for small differences between the hub's clock frequency and the timing of the received data. When the buffer is half full, the received data begins clocking out.

The transaction translator

Every USB 2.0 hub must have one or more transaction translators to manage communications with low- and full-speed devices. When the hub's upstream port connects at high speed, the hub's transaction translator communicates upstream at high speed while enabling low- and full-speed devices to continue to communicate at low and full speeds. The transaction translator stores received data and forwards, or transmits, the data toward its destination at the appropriate speed.

The transaction translator frees bus time by enabling other communications to use the bus while a hub completes a low- or full-speed transaction with a device. Transaction translators can also enable low- and full-speed devices to use more bandwidth than the host could allocate on a shared low/full-speed bus.

For traffic to and from low- and full-speed devices, the high-speed repeater communicates with the transaction translator, which manages transactions with the devices.

A hub can use a single transaction translator for all ports, or the hub can have as many as one transaction translator per port. To find out if a hub has one or multiple transaction translators, open Device Manager, locate the hub under **Universal Serial**

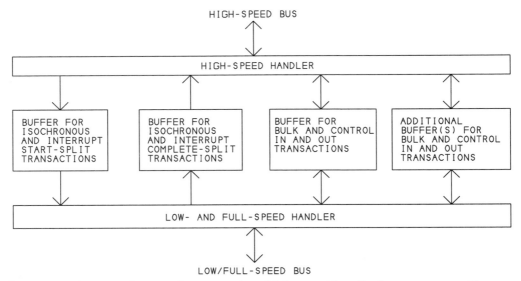

Figure 16-3. A transaction translator contains a high-speed handler for upstream traffic, buffers for storing information in split transactions, and a low- and full-speed handler for downstream traffic to low- and full-speed devices. Content from: *Universal Serial Bus Specification Revision 2.0.*

Bus controllers, right-click the hub's entry, select **Properties**, and view the **Advanced** tab.

Sections

The transaction translator contains three sections (Figure 16-3). The high-speed handler communicates with the host at high speed. The low/full-speed handler communicates with devices at low and full speeds. Buffers store data used in transactions with low- and full-speed devices. Each transaction translator has to have at least four buffers: one for interrupt and isochronous start-split transactions, one for interrupt and isochronous complete-split transactions, and two or more for control and bulk transfers.

Managing split transactions

When a USB 2.0 host wants to communicate with a low- or full-speed device that connects to a hub on a high-speed bus, the host initiates a split transaction with the USB 2.0 hub that is nearest the device and communicating upstream at high speed. Figure 16-4 shows the transactions that make up a split transaction.

1. THE HOST INITIATES AND COMPLETES THE START-SPLIT TRANSACTION WITH THE HUB.

2. THE HUB INITIATES AND COMPLETES THE TRANSACTION WITH THE DEVICE.

3. THE HOST INITIATES AND COMPLETES THE COMPLETE-SPLIT TRANSACTION WITH THE HUB.

Figure 16-4. In a transfer that uses split transactions, the host communicates at high speed with a USB 2.0 hub, and the hub communicates at low or full speed with the device. Information source: *Universal Serial Bus Specification Revision 2.0.*

One or more start-split transactions contain the information the hub needs to complete the transaction with the device. The transaction translator stores information received from the host and completes the start-split transaction with the host.

On completing a start-split transaction, the hub performs the function of a host controller in carrying out the transaction with the device. The transaction translator initiates the transaction in the token phase, sends data or stores received data or status information as needed in the data phase, and sends or receives a status code as needed in the handshake phase. The hub uses low or full speed as required in its communications with the device.

After the hub has had time to exchange data with the device, in all transactions except isochronous OUTs, the host initiates one or more complete-split transactions to retrieve the information returned by the device and stored in the transaction translator's buffer. The hub performs these transactions at high speed.

Table 16-1 compares the structure and contents of transactions with low- and full-speed devices at different bus speeds.

Table 16-1: When a low- or full-speed device has a transaction on a high-speed bus, the host uses start-split (SSPLIT) and complete-split (CSPLIT) transactions with the USB 2.0 hub that is nearest the device and communicating upstream at high speed.

Bus Speed	Transaction Type	Transaction Phase		
		Token	Data	Handshake
Low/full-speed communications with the device	Setup, OUT	PRE if low speed, LS/FS token	PRE if low speed, data	status (except for isochronous)
	IN	PRE if low speed, LS/FS token	data or status	PRE if low speed, status (except for isochronous)
High-speed communications between a USB 2.0 hub and host in transactions with a low- or full-speed device	Setup, OUT (isochronous OUT has no CSPLIT transaction)	SSPLIT, LS/FS token	data	status (bulk and control only)
		CSPLIT, LS/FS token	–	status
	IN	SSPLIT, LS/FS token	–	status (bulk and control only)
		CSPLIT, LS/FS token)	data or status	–

Bulk and control transfers

For bulk and control transfers, in the start-split transaction, the USB 2.0 host sends the start-split token packet (SSPLIT), followed by the usual low- or full-speed token packet and any data packet destined for the device. The USB 2.0 hub that is nearest the device and communicating upstream at high speed returns ACK or NAK. The host is then free to use the bus for other transactions. The device knows nothing about the transaction yet.

After returning ACK in a start-split transaction, the hub has two responsibilities. The hub must complete the transaction with the device and also must continue to handle any other bus traffic received from the host or other attached devices.

To complete the transaction, the hub converts the packet or packets received from the host to the appropriate speed, sends them to the device and stores the data or handshake returned by the device. Depending on the transaction, the device may send data, a handshake, or nothing. For IN transactions, the hub sends a handshake packet to the device. To the device, the transaction has proceeded at the expected low or full speed and is now complete. The device has no knowledge that the transaction is a split transaction. The host hasn't yet received the device's response.

While the hub is completing the transaction with the device, the host may initiate other bus traffic that the device's hub must handle as well. Separate hardware modules within the hub handle the two functions. When the hub has had enough time to complete the transaction with the device, the host begins a complete-split transaction with the hub.

In a complete-split transaction, the host sends a complete-split token packet (CSPLIT), followed by a low- or full-speed token packet to request the data or status information the hub has received from the device. The hub sends the information. The transfer is now complete at the host. The host doesn't send an ACK to the hub. If the hub doesn't have the packet ready to send, the hub sends NYET, and the host retries later. The device is unaware of the complete-split transaction.

Interrupt and isochronous transfers

In split transactions in interrupt and isochronous transfers, the process is similar but with stricter timing. The goals are to transfer data to the host as soon as possible after the device has data available to send and to transfer data to the device just as the device is ready to receive new data. To achieve this timing, isochronous transactions with large packets use multiple start splits or complete splits and transfer a portion of the data in each.

Unlike with bulk and control transfers, start-split transactions in interrupt and isochronous transfers have no handshake phase, just the start-split token followed by an IN or OUT token and for OUT transactions, data.

In an interrupt transaction, the hub schedules the start split in the microframe just before the earliest time that the hub is expected to begin the transaction with the device. For example, assume that the microframes in a frame are numbered in sequence, 0–7. If the start split is in microframe 0, the transaction with the device can occur as early as microframe 1. The device may have data or a handshake response to send to the host as early as microframe 2, and the host schedules time for three complete-split transactions in microframes 2, 3, and 4. If the hub doesn't yet have the information to return in a complete split, the hub sends NYET and the host retries.

Full-speed isochronous transactions can transfer up to 1023 bytes. To ensure that the data transfers as soon as the device has data to send or is ready to receive data, transactions with large packets use multiple start splits or complete splits with up to 188 data bytes in each. This amount is the maximum quantity of full-speed data that fits in a microframe. A single transaction's data can require up to eight start-split or complete-split transactions.

In an isochronous IN transaction, the host schedules complete-split transactions in every microframe where the host expects the device to have at least a portion of the data to send. Requesting the data in smaller chunks ensures that the host receives the data as quickly as possible. The host doesn't have to wait for all of the data to transfer from the device at full speed before beginning to retrieve the data.

In an isochronous OUT transaction, the host sends the data in one or more start-split transactions. The host schedules the transactions so the hub's buffer will never be empty but will contain as few bytes as possible. Each SPLIT packet contains bits that indicate the data's position in the low- or full-speed data packet (beginning, middle, end, or all). There is no complete-split transaction.

Bandwidth use of low- and full-speed devices

Because a USB 2.0 hub acts as a host controller in managing transactions, low- and full-speed devices share low- and full-speed bandwidth only with devices that use the same transaction translator. A hub may provide one transaction translator for all ports, but a single hub can also provide a transaction translator for each port that connects to a low- or full-speed device.

If two full-speed devices each have a dedicated transaction translator on a high-speed bus, each device can use all of the transaction translator's downstream, full-speed bandwidth. When the hub(s) convert to high speed, the full-speed traffic uses little of the high-speed bandwidth.

However, for bulk transactions, the extra transaction with the host in each split transaction can result in lower throughput for a full-speed device that connects to a hub on a busy bus that is also carrying high-speed bulk traffic.

The hub controller

A USB 2.0 hub controller manages communications between the host and the hub. As it does for all devices, the host enumerates a newly detected hub to learn about it. The hub descriptor retrieved during enumeration tells the host the number of ports on the hub. After enumerating the hub, the host requests to know if the hub has any attached devices. If so, the host enumerates these as well.

The host finds out if a device is attached to a port by sending the hub-class request Get Port Status. This is similar to the standard Get Status request but is directed to a hub and provides a port number in the wIndex field. The hub returns two 16-bit values that indicate whether a device is attached and other information such as whether the device is in the Suspend state.

The hub controller is also responsible for disabling any port that caused loss of bus activity or babble. Loss of bus activity occurs when a packet doesn't end with the expected EOP. Babble occurs when a device continues to transmit beyond the EOP.

Each hub has a Status Change endpoint configured for interrupt IN transfers. A USB 2.0 host polls the endpoint to find out if the hub has any changes to report. On each poll, the hub controller returns NAK if there have been no changes or data that indicates a specific port or the hub itself as the source of the change. After a reported change, the host sends requests to find out more about the change and take whatever action is needed. For example, if the hub reports attachment of a new device, the host attempts to enumerate the device.

Speed

An external USB 2.0 hub's downstream ports must support low, full, and high speeds. In the upstream direction, if a USB 2.0 hub's upstream segment is high speed, the hub communicates at high speed. Otherwise, the hub communicates upstream at low and full speeds.

Filtering traffic according to speed

Low-speed devices aren't capable of receiving full-speed data so hubs don't repeat full-speed traffic to low-speed devices. Otherwise, a low-speed device would try to interpret full-speed traffic as low-speed data and might even mistakenly see what looks like valid data. Full- or high-speed data on a low-speed cable could also cause problems due to radiated electromagnetic interference (EMI). In the other direction, hubs repeat received low-speed data upstream.

Low- and full-speed devices aren't capable of receiving high-speed data, so USB 2.0 hubs don't repeat high-speed traffic to these devices, including USB 1.1 hubs.

Detecting device speed

On attachment, every USB 2.0 device must support either low or full speed. A hub detects whether an attached device is low or full speed by detecting which signal line is more positive on an idle line. Figure 16-5 illustrates. As Chapter 4 explained, the hub has pull-down resistors of 14.25k–24.8kΩ on D+ and D-. A newly attached device has a pull-up of 900–1575Ω on either D+ for a full-speed device or D- for a low-speed device. When a device attaches to a port, the line with the pull-up is more positive than the hub's logic-high input threshold. The hub detects the voltage, assumes a device is attached, and determines the speed by detecting which line is pulled up.

After detecting a full-speed device, a USB 2.0 hub determines whether the device supports high speed by using the high-speed detection handshake. The handshake occurs during the Reset state that the hub initiates during enumeration. If the handshake succeeds, the device removes its pull-up and communications are at high speed. A USB 1.1 hub ignores the attempt to handshake, and the failure of the handshake informs the device that it must use full speed. Chapter 19 has more about the handshake.

Maintaining active links

SOF packets keep full- and high-speed devices from entering the Suspend state on an otherwise idle bus. On an idle, full-speed bus, the host continues to send an SOF

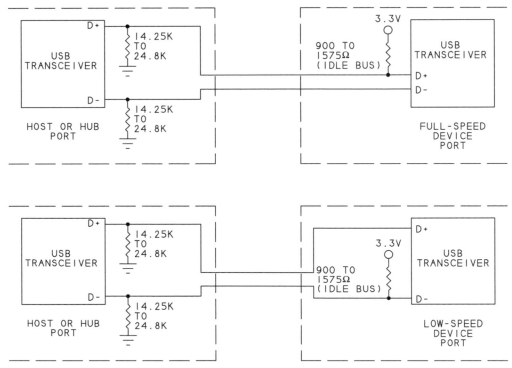

Figure 16-5. The device's port has a stronger pull-up than the hub's port. The location of the pull-up tells the hub whether the device is low or full speed. High-speed devices are full speed at attachment. Information source: *Universal Serial Bus Specification Revision 2.0*.

once per frame, and hubs pass these packets on to their full-speed devices. On an otherwise idle, high-speed bus, the host continues to send an SOF once per microframe, and hubs pass these packets on to their high-speed devices. A full-speed device that connects to a USB 2.0 hub that communicates upstream at high speed will also receive an SOF once per frame from the hub.

Low-speed devices don't see the SOFs. Instead, at least once per frame, hubs must send their low-speed devices a low-speed End-of-Packet (EOP) signal (defined in Chapter 19). This signal functions as a keep-alive signal that keeps a device from entering the Suspend state on a bus with no low-speed activity. A host can also request a hub to suspend the bus at a single port. Chapter 17 has more on how hubs manage the Suspend state.

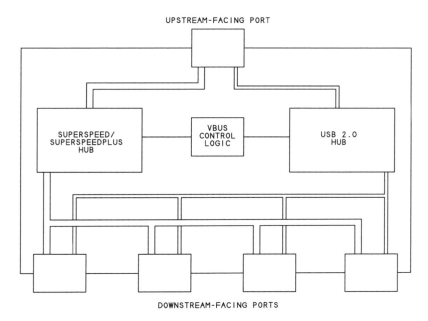

Figure 16-6. A USB 3.1 hub contains a USB 2.0 hub and a hub for SuperSpeed and SuperSpeedPlus. Information source: *Universal Serial Bus 3.1 Specification Revision 1.0.*

USB 3.1

A USB 3.1 hub contains both a USB 2.0 hub that supports low, full, and high speeds and an Enhanced SuperSpeed hub that contains a SuperSpeed hub and a Super-SpeedPlus hub (Figure 16-6). The USB 2.0 and Enhanced SuperSpeed hubs operate independently except for sharing logic to control VBUS. The host enumerates a USB 3.1 hub as two hubs. Hubs are the only devices with ports that can communicate upstream at the same time at both Enhanced SuperSpeed and high speed.

Bus speeds

The speed of a hub's upstream port determines what bus speeds are available to downstream ports. If the upstream port connects at SuperSpeedPlus, the hub can communicate with downstream devices at any speed. If the upstream port connects at SuperSpeed, the hub can communicate with downstream devices at SuperSpeed and all USB 2.0 speeds. If the upstream port connects at high speed, the hub can communicate downstream at low, full, and high speeds. If the upstream port connects at full speed, the hub can communicate downstream at low and full speeds. A

371

downstream-facing hub port that connects internally to an embedded device can support a single speed.

At the hub's upstream port, traffic to and from downstream devices operating at SuperSpeed or SuperSpeedPlus use the Enhanced SuperSpeed data wires, and traffic to and from downstream low-, full-, and high-speed devices uses the USB 2.0 data wires. As with USB 2.0 hubs, all upstream traffic on the USB 2.0 wires uses high speed (unless a USB 1.1 hub is upstream from the hub).

SuperSpeed

The SuperSpeed components in a USB 3.1 hub include a repeater/forwarder for data and a hub controller. The hub repeats DPs and stores and forwards header packets. A hub may partially store a DP before beginning to repeat it. The hub must be able to store eight header packets directed to the same downstream port and eight header packets received at a downstream port.

Like the hub repeater in a USB 2.0 hub, the repeater/forwarder re-transmits received packets, detects device attachment and removal, establishes the connection of a device to the bus, detects bus faults such as over-current conditions, and manages power to the device.

Buffers help manage traffic that passes through the hub. Buffers enable storing packet headers for later delivery to a downstream device that must exit a low-power mode before receiving traffic. Buffers also enable receiving asynchronous messages from multiple downstream devices at once and holding received payload data to repeat. To enable retrying, after transmitting a DP, the buffer retains the packet until receiving a link-level acknowledgment.

As in a USB 2.0 hub, a SuperSpeed hub controller manages communications between the host and the hub. The hub sends status information using an interrupt IN Status Change endpoint. A hub with information to report sends an ERDY TP to the host.

SuperSpeedPlus

The SuperSpeedPlus components in a USB 3.1 hub include a SuperSpeedPlus hub controller, a SuperSpeedPlus upstream controller, and a SuperSpeedPlus downstream controller for each port. (USB 3.0 hubs don't have these components.) The hub uses a store-and-forward architecture, where the hub can store one or more received data packets before sending them up or down stream. The result is more efficient scheduling compared to the repeater/forwarder architecture used by hubs operating at SuperSpeed.

The upstream controller buffers packets received from upstream, buffers and arbitrates to determine priority for packets waiting to transmit upstream, and routes received packets to a downstream controller or the hub controller. The downstream controllers buffer packets received from downstream, buffer and arbitrate to determine priority for packets waiting to transmit downstream, and route received packets to the upstream controller.

A SuperSpeedPlus hub has these abilities that are not available on a SuperSpeed hub:

- Schedule simultaneous transactions for SuperSpeed endpoints and SuperSpeedPlus IN endpoints.

- Intermingle and reorder packets on the SuperSpeedPlus bus.

Managing traffic

During hub enumeration, the host sends a Set Hub Depth request to assign a hub-depth value to the hub. The value equals the number of additional upstream hubs that lie in the path between the hub and the root hub. Hubs that connect directly to the root hub have a hub depth of zero. Any hubs that connect to downstream ports on those hubs have a hub depth of one. Any hubs that connect to those hubs have a hub depth of two, and so on up to a maximum hub depth of four. The USB 2.0 specification defines the root hub as tier 1 in the bus topology, so hub depth equals the hub's tier - 2.

Unlike USB 2.0 hubs, USB 3.1 hubs don't broadcast downstream traffic but instead direct traffic only toward the target device. Using routing instead of broadcasting enables ports to enter a low-power state when not communicating with the host even if the bus is carrying traffic to other devices. In the upstream direction, hubs route all traffic to the host as with USB 2.0.

On receiving a packet from the host, a hub uses its hub-depth value and a Route String in the packet header to determine whether the hub should process the packet or route the packet to a downstream port. The Route String has five 4-bit fields. Each field contains information that applies to one of up to five external hubs in the path that the packet travels. The hub-depth value identifies which 4-bit field in a received Route String applies to the hub. The field contains either a port number to route the packet to or zero if the packet's destination is the hub itself. Because the Route String's fields are four bits, a USB 3.1 hub can have at most 15 downstream ports. A hub that isn't configured assumes all packets are directed to itself.

The hub class

Hubs are members of the hub class, which is the only device class defined in the USB 2.0 and USB 3.1 specifications.

Hub descriptors

The hub descriptor informs the host of hub-specific capabilities such as supported modes for power switching and overcurrent protection. For USB 3.1 hubs, the hub descriptor has additional fields to support USB 3.1 capabilities. A host can request the descriptor with a Get Hub Descriptor control request.

A hub that connects at SuperSpeed must return a SUPERSPEED_USB device capability descriptor that describes supported speeds and features and latency values for SuperSpeed communications. A hub that connects at SuperSpeedPlus must return a SUPERSPEED_PLUS device capability descriptor that describes supported features and capabilities for SuperSpeedPlus communications. Enhanced SuperSpeed hubs also support the CONTAINER_ID device capability descriptor, which identifies the device instance. The Container ID is the same value for the USB 2.0 and USB 3.1 hub functions in a device.

Hub class requests

A host can use hub-class requests to obtain status information, set and clear hub and port features, and monitor and control transaction translators.

17

Managing Power

The USB interface can provide power to devices when they need it, conserve power when devices are idle, and charge batteries. Hosts and devices that support the *USB Power Delivery Rev. 2.0, v1.0* specification can use higher bus voltages and currents, fine-tune power delivery, and even reverse the flow so a device provides power to the host.

This chapter shows how USB manages power, including how to decide if a device can be bus-powered or requires its own power supply.

Power options

The USB cable includes power and ground lines that can provide power to devices. A device can provide its own power supply, rely entirely on bus power, or use both bus power and self power. Devices that use their own power must at minimum be able to detect the presence of the VBUS voltage on the cable.

The capabilities described below don't include the expanded capabilities of *USB Power Delivery Rev. 2.0, v1.0*, detailed later in this chapter.

Using bus current

USB 2.0 defines a low-power device as a device that draws up to 100 mA from the bus and a high-power device as a device that draws up to 500 mA from the bus. A self-powered device can draw up to 100 mA from the bus and as much power as is available from the device's supply.

A self-powered USB 2.0 device may draw up to 100 mA from the bus any time the device isn't in the Suspend state. This capability enables the device's USB interface to function if a device's power supply is off and the host detects and enumerates the device. Otherwise, if a device's pull-up is bus powered and the rest of the interface is self powered, the host will detect the device but won't be able to communicate with it.

A high-power device must be able to enumerate at low power. On connecting to the bus, a USB 2.0 device can draw up to 100 mA of bus current until the host has configured the device unless the device is required to enter the Suspend state as explained below. After retrieving a configuration descriptor, the host examines the amount of current requested in bMaxPower, and if the current is available, the host sends a Set Configuration request to select the configuration. The device can then draw up to the value specified in bMaxPower from the bus. In practice, hosts and hubs are likely to allocate either 100 mA or 500 mA to a device rather than the amount requested in bMaxPower. Hosts and hubs that support *USB Power Delivery Rev. 2.0, v1.0* can manage bus current more precisely.

The current limits are absolute maximums, not averages. Also, VBUS can be as high as 5.5V, and a higher voltage can result in greater current consumption.

Except as defined in *USB Power Delivery Rev. 2.0, v1.0*, a device must never provide upstream power. Even the pull-up on D+ or D- must remain unpowered until VBUS is present. A device that provides upstream power can cause problems that include a host PC that doesn't boot or doesn't resume from the Suspend state, a hub that doesn't enumerate its downstream devices, and failure of an upstream device. The USB-IF's compliance testing includes a back-voltage test to verify that a device doesn't provide upstream power. A self-powered device must connect to VBUS to detect its presence even if the device never uses bus power. If VBUS is removed, the device must remove power from the pull-up within 10 s.

Devices that connect at SuperSpeed and SuperSpeedPlus follow the same rules for using power but with higher limits of 150 mA for low-power and self-powered devices and 900 mA for high-power devices.

Current limits on attachment

Originally, the USB specification required devices to support entering the Suspend state from any powered state. Meeting this requirement proved difficult, and the *USB 2.0 Connect Timing Update* ECN loosened the rules for just-connected devices.

The ECN specifies that devices aren't required to enter the Suspend state and reduce their use of bus current until 1 s after connecting even if the condition of the upstream bus segment would otherwise mandate entering Suspend. A USB 2.0 device is considered to be connected when the device has pulled up D+ or D-.

Detecting device attachment

USB hosts in embedded systems may turn off VBUS to save power but may still need the ability to detect device attachment even when VBUS is off. Chapter 21 describes the Attach Detection Protocol (ADP), which enables device detection when VBUS is off.

The *Device Capacitance* ECN to the USB 2.0 specification requires a device's VBUS line to have sufficient capacitance to enable using the Attach Detection Protocol (ADP). The ECN mandates a capacitance of 1–10 µF between VBUS and GND on a device's upstream-facing port.

Bus voltage

The nominal voltage between VBUS and GND in a USB cable is 5 V, but VBUS at a host or hub's downstream port can be anywhere in the range 4.45–5.5 V. Cable and connector losses further reduce the voltage available at a device's port. ECNs to the USB 2.0 and USB 3.1 specifications raised the maximum VBUS voltage from 5.25 V to 5.5 V. On links that use USB Type-C connectors, which can carry up to 5 A, a higher voltage can help ensure that the downstream voltage is valid despite electrical losses.

These are the minimum and maximum valid voltages for connectors on downstream-facing ports:

Hub Type	USB Version	Available Current per Port (mA)	VBUS at Hub Port (V)	
			Minimum	Maximum
High power	2.0	500	4.75	5.5
	3.1	900	4.45	5.5
Low power	2.0	100	4.4	5.5
	3.1	150	4.45	5.5

When VBUS is at least 4.4 V at the upstream hub's port, low-power USB 2.0 devices must fully function, and high-power USB 2.0 devices attached to low-power ports must at minimum respond to enumeration requests. All USB 3.1 devices must at minimum respond to enumeration requests when VBUS is at least 4.0 V at the device's upstream-facing port. Transient conditions can cause the voltage to drop briefly by a few additional tenths of a volt.

USB controller chips typically use a power supply of 5 V, 3.3 V, or even 1.2 V. Devices powered at 3.3 V or 1.2 V can use a low-dropout linear regulator to obtain the needed supply voltage from VBUS. For devices that need +5 V, a step-up switching regulator can produce the needed voltage from VBUS.

Bus-powered devices

A bus-powered device doesn't need to provide a battery or a power supply that connects to a wall socket. Without an internal power supply, the device can be physically smaller, lighter in weight, and cheaper to manufacture. Figure 17-1 will help you decide whether a device can use bus power.

A device that requires up to 100 mA can be bus powered from any host or hub. A device that requires up to 500 mA can use bus power when attached to a self-powered hub or any host except some battery-powered hosts.

An Enhanced SuperSpeed device on a USB 3.1 bus can draw up to 150 mA from any USB 3.1 hub and up to 900 mA when attached to any host or self-powered hub except some battery-powered hosts.

Except when connected to a USB charger, no device should draw more than 100 mA (USB 2.0) or 150 mA (USB 3.1) until the host has issued a Set Configuration request for a configuration that allows more current. Devices must limit their power consumption further when in the Suspend state.

Of course, devices such as cameras that need to function when not attached to a host need self power. Self power can use batteries or power from a wall socket. Because a device in the Suspend state should draw very little current from the bus, some devices need their own power supplies to enable operating when the device's bus segment is suspended.

During enumeration, the host learns whether the device is self powered or bus powered and the maximum current the device will draw from the bus. All hubs must have over-current protection that blocks excessive current to a device.

Hub power

Power use on hubs has special considerations. A hub must control power to its downstream devices and must monitor power consumption and take action when devices try to draw an amount of current that would present a safety hazard.

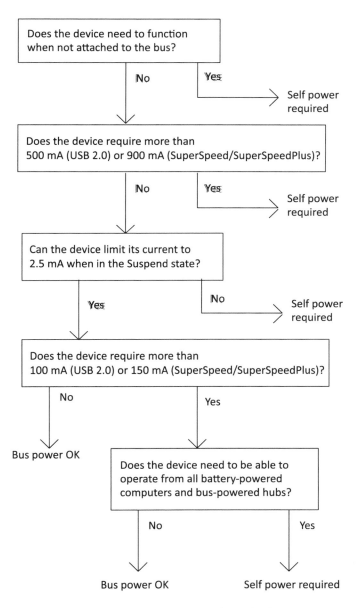

Figure 17-1. Some devices can draw all of their power from the bus.

Power sources

The root hub gets its power from the host. External hubs may be self-powered or bus-powered.

If the host uses power from a wall socket or another external source, a USB 2.0 root hub must be capable of supplying 500 mA to each port on the hub. If the host is battery-powered, the root hub may supply either 500 mA or 100 mA to each port. A high-power hub supplies 500 mA per port. A low-power hub supplies 100 mA per port.

All of a bus-powered, USB 2.0 hub's downstream devices must be low power because the hub can draw no more than 500 mA and the hub itself will use some current, leaving less than 500 mA for all attached devices combined. Thus two bus-powered hubs shouldn't connect in series. The upstream hub can guarantee no more than 100 mA to each downstream port, and that amount doesn't leave enough current to power a second hub that also has one or more downstream ports that each require 100 mA.

An exception is a bus-powered compound device, which consists of a hub and one or more downstream, non-removable devices. In this case, the hub's configuration descriptor can report the maximum power required by the hub's electronics plus its non-removable device(s). The configuration descriptors for the non-removable device(s) report that the devices are self-powered with bMaxPower = 0x00. The hub descriptor indicates whether a hub's ports have removable devices.

Like other high-power, bus-powered devices, a USB 2.0 bus-powered hub can draw up to 100 mA until configured and up to 500 mA after being configured. During configuration, the hub must manage the available current so its devices and the hub combined don't exceed the allowed current.

Like other self-powered devices, a self-powered USB 2.0 hub may also draw up to 100 mA from the bus so the hub interface can continue to function when the hub's power supply is off. If the hub's power is from an external source such as AC power from a wall socket, the hub is high power and must be capable of supplying 500 mA to each port on the hub. If the hub uses battery power, the hub may supply 100 mA or 500 mA to each port on the hub.

When a self-powered hub's power supply is removed or turned off, the hub must remain in the Configured state, transition its downstream ports to the Powered Off state, and inform the host of the change via the hub's Status Change endpoint.

USB 3.1 hubs can provide up to 900 mA per port if high power and 150 mA per port if low power. If a USB 3.1 hub's upstream-facing port isn't connected, the hub doesn't provide power to the downstream-facing ports unless the hub supports the USB battery charging specification.

Over-current protection

As a safety precaution, hubs must be able to detect an over-current condition, which occurs when the current used by the total of all devices attached to the hub exceeds a set value. On detecting an over-current condition, a hub's port circuits limit the current at the port, and the hub informs the host of the problem.

The current that triggers the over-current actions must be less than 5 A. To allow for transient currents, the over-current value should be greater than the total of the maximum allowed currents for the devices. In the worst case, seven high-power, bus-powered, USB 2.0 downstream devices can legally draw up to 3.5 A. So a supply for a self-powered hub with up to seven downstream ports would provide much less than 5 A at all times unless something goes very wrong. A single hub can implement multiple over-current gangs.

A device can briefly draw a larger inrush current on attachment to the bus. The over-current protection circuits typically don't see the inrush current because a capacitor downstream from the protection provides the stored energy. But a too-large inrush current can cause the VBUS voltage on adjacent ports to drop, causing attached devices to disconnect. For this reason, compliance tests measure inrush current.

Power switching

A bus-powered hub must support power switching that can provide and cut off power to downstream ports in response to control requests. A single switch may control all ports, or the ports may switch individually. A self-powered hub must support switching its ports to the Powered Off state and may also support power switching using control transfers.

Conserving power

With a couple of exceptions described below, all USB devices must support the low-power Suspend state. Additional low-power states enable conserving power with faster transitions from a low-power state and less stringent requirements compared to Suspend.

USB 2.0 Link Power Management

The *USB 2.0 Link Power Management (LPM) Addendum* to the USB 2.0 specification defines four USB link power management states. USB 3.1 devices must support link power management when operating at high speed. USB 2.0 devices may also support link power management. A link consists of a cable segment and the two ports, or link partners, that the cable connects.

The document assigns new names to states defined in the USB 2.0 specification and adds the new L1 (Sleep) state:

L0 (On). The link is carrying data or is able to do so. When not carrying data, the link carries SOF (full and high speed) or keep-alive (low speed) signals.

L1 (Sleep). The link doesn't carry data or SOF/keep-alive signals. The device may reduce power consumption.

L2 (Suspend). The link doesn't carry data or SOF/keep-alive signals. The device must reduce power consumption.

L3 (Off). The link is powered off, disconnected, or disabled and isn't capable of performing data signaling.

The *USB 2.0 Phase-locked SOFs* ECN to the USB 2.0 specification can help isochronous devices save power. To comply with the ECN, SOFs issued on exiting the Sleep or selective Suspend states must be in phase lock with the SOFs that preceded the low-power state. Isochronous devices can thus enter a low-power state and maintain synchronization to SOFs on returning to full power.

Suspend

The L2 Suspend state reduces a device's use of bus power when the host doesn't need to communicate. Beginning 1 s after connecting, a USB 2.0 device must enter the Suspend state when the bus has had no activity for 3 ms.

While in the Suspend state, a device must draw no more than 2.5 mA from the bus. A device that needs to function when the host has ceased communicating may need to be self-powered. However, many device controllers can consume very little power while remaining able to detect activity requiring attention on an I/O pin and wake the host as needed.

There are two exceptions to the requirement to support the Suspend state. The *USB Power Delivery Rev. 2.0, v1.0* specification defines a USB Suspend Supported flag that enables a host to inform a device that the device may ignore the requirement to reduce current in the Suspend state. And devices that use USB Type-C connectors and have a negotiated maximum current of 1.5 A or 3.0 A can ignore the requirement to reduce current in the Suspend state.

On ports that use USB Type-C connectors, the VCONN pin should provide no more than 7.5 mA in the Suspend state.

Global and selective suspends

In a global suspend, a USB 2.0 host stops communicating with the entire bus, which carries no traffic or SOFs. When a full- or high-speed device detects that no SOF has arrived for 3 ms, the device enters the Suspend state. Low-speed devices enter the

Suspend state when they haven't received a low-speed keep-alive signal for 3 ms. A device must be in the Suspend state within 10 ms of no bus activity.

A host may also request a selective suspend of an individual port. The host issues the class-specific Set Port Feature request to a hub with wIndex set to a port number and wValue set to PORT_SUSPEND. The request instructs the hub to stop sending any traffic, including SOFs or low-speed keep-alives, to the specified port.

Windows implements global suspend by selectively suspending each device in turn, beginning with the farthest downstream devices.

Current limits for suspended devices

A device in the Suspend state should consume maximum of 2.5 mA of bus current averaged over 1 s. The limit includes current through the pull-up on D+ or D-.

The USB 2.0 specification originally defined a limit of just 500 µA for devices that don't support remote wakeup. However, the limit was difficult for many devices to meet, and the *Suspend Current Limit Changes* ECN raised the limit, which also applies to USB 3.1 devices.

Configured bus-powered hubs and configured bus-powered compound devices can draw up to 12.5 mA in the Suspend state. So a bus-powered hub can consume 2.5 mA while providing 2.5 mA for each of up to four downstream ports.

Resuming communications

To resume communications on a suspended bus, a USB 2.0 host places the bus in the Resume state (the K state, defined in Chapter 19) for at least 20 ms. The host follows the Resume with a low-speed EOP. The host then resumes sending SOFs and any other communications. (For low-speed devices, the upstream hub issues low-speed keep-alive signals instead of SOFs.) For selectively suspended devices, a host can request a hub to resume communications with a downstream-facing port by issuing a Clear Port Feature(PORT_SUSPEND) request.

A device that wants to be able to request to resume communications indicates support for remote wakeup in the configuration descriptor's bmAttributes field. The host enables remote wakeup by sending a Set Port Feature(DEVICE_REMOTE_WAKEUP) request to the hub port that is the device's link partner.

A suspended device with remote wakeup enabled can request to resume communications by driving the upstream bus segment in the Resume state for 1–15 ms. The device then places its drivers in a high-impedance state to enable receiving traffic from the upstream hub. The resume signaling propagates upstream to the first non-suspended hub, which may be the root hub.

After the resume signaling completes, the device again receives SOFs or low-speed keep-alives and other traffic. A device may initiate a Resume any time after the bus has been idle for at least 5 ms. The host must allow a device at least 10 ms to recover from a Resume.

Some device controllers require firmware support to monitor the bus to determine when to enter the Suspend state, while other controllers handle the task entirely in hardware. A device's serial interface engine typically handles the resume signaling without firmware support.

When a device uses bus power, firmware may need to control power to external circuits, removing power on entering the Suspend state and restoring power on resuming. A power switch with soft-start capability can reduce current surges when switching. Micrel Inc. is one source for power-distribution switches suitable for use with USB devices. Each switch contains one or more high-side MOSFET switches with soft-start capability that minimizes inrush current.

Sleep

The L1 Sleep state provides a way for devices to reduce power consumption without having to meet the Suspend state's stringent requirements. The Sleep state also enables faster transitions to and from the powered state. A major purpose in defining the Sleep state was to provide a more effective mechanism for power conservation on mobile, battery-powered systems.

In the Sleep state, a device receives no USB traffic including SOFs or keep-alive signaling. The device can reduce power consumption but isn't required to do so.

To place a device in the Sleep state, a host issues a Set_and_Test(PORT_L1) request to the hub that is the device's link partner. A hub that supports the Sleep state then initiates an LPM transaction to the device by issuing a token packet with an EXT Packet ID, followed by an extended token packet with an LPM Packet ID (0011_b). (Chapter 2 covered Packet IDs.) In the LPM token packet, the bmAttributes field requests the Sleep state and provides information used in resume signaling (Table 17-1).

A device that receives an EXT token packet followed by an LPM token packet can return ACK (ready to transition to the Sleep state), NYET (not ready to transition to the Sleep state), STALL (requested link state not supported), or no response (the device doesn't support the transaction type or detected an error).

The hub NAKs the Data stage of the Set_and_Test request as needed until the downstream device returns ACK or STALL or fails to respond after three attempts. The hub then returns a completion code in the Data stage of the request.

To resume communications with a device in the Sleep state, a host issues a Clear Port Feature(PORT_L1) request to the device's link partner. The hub then initiates resume signaling with the device. The signaling is identical to a resume from Suspend except for timing. The HIRD value in the LPM token packet indicates how long the hub will

Table 17-1: In an LPM extended token packet, the bmAttributes field provides information about the requested Sleep state.

Bits	Field	Description
3..0	bLinkState	0001_b = L1 (Sleep).
		Other values reserved.
7..4	HIRD	Host initiated resume duration (encoded value)
8	bRemoteWake	1 = the device can wake the host.
		0 = the device cannot wake the host.
10..9	Reserved	For future use.

hold the line in the Resume state when exiting Sleep. The encoded value can specify a range from 50 µs to 1.2 ms.

If in the LPM token packet, bRemoteWake = 1, the device can request to wake the host by driving the line in the Resume state for 50 µs.

A host that doesn't support the Sleep state will never request it. Devices that don't support the Sleep state can return STALL or no response to token packets that contain the LPM Packet ID.

Enhanced SuperSpeed power management

Enhanced SuperSpeed offers more ways to conserve power, including new low-power states and latency tolerance messages that help the host manage power on the bus and for the system.

If you're developing a device that must use as little power as possible, you might choose a USB 3.1 controller even if the device doesn't require Enhanced Super-Speed's bus rate. With Enhanced SuperSpeed's fast data transfers and new low-power states, some devices can save significant power by entering a low-power state between transactions.

Link states

Enhanced SuperSpeed defines four operational link states:

- U0 is normal operation and is the highest link state. This is the only state where the link can carry packets.

- U1 is a low-power state with fast transitions to U0. The state has no mandated reduction in bus current, but the link carries no signaling and the device can implement power-saving measures.

- U2 is a more aggressive low-power state with slower transitions to U0. The state has no mandated reduction in bus current, but the link carries no signaling, and the device can turn off clock circuits and implement other power-saving measures that require more time to transition to U0.

- U3 is the Suspend state and is the lowest link state. The link carries no signaling, and a device whose port is in U3 can draw up to 2.5 mA of bus current. A device in the Suspend state must detect Warm Reset (defined in Chapter 19) and wakeup signaling. A device that supports remote wakeup must be capable of sending wakeup signaling.

Managing the transitions between states in a device may require firmware support.

In addition to the above states, which apply to links, an Enhanced SuperSpeed device can have one or more functions that are in the function suspend state (defined below) while the link and other function(s) in the device remain in a higher-power state.

For each device, the host calculates U1 and U2 System Exit Latency values that are a measure of the time required to transition from U1 or U2 to U0. For devices with interrupt or isochronous endpoints, the host uses these values in determining whether the device can initiate U1 or U2. If the corresponding Latency value plus one bus interval is greater than the shortest service interval on the device, the host doesn't allow the device to initiate the low-power state.

A link that is in U0 and is not transmitting data or other packets is in the logical idle state. A SuperSpeed port in logical idle transmits encoded bytes of 0x00. A SuperSpeedPlus port in logical idle transmits encoded bytes of 0x5A. A link in U1, U2, or U3 is in the electrical idle state and carries no signaling.

Changing states

Link-level communications control the state of a link. The host doesn't need to know the state of every link on the bus. To conserve power, if a link has no pending upstream traffic, a hub transitions its upstream-facing port to the lowest link state possible. In other words, if a hub's downstream-facing ports are in U1 and U2, the hub can place its upstream-facing port in U1. If all of the ports are in U2, the hub can reduce power further by placing its upstream-facing port in U2. Only a host can request a transition to U3. When a host or hub wants to communicate with a device, any links in the communication path that aren't in U0 must transition to U0.

The mechanism for changing a power state varies with the state, who initiated the change, and whether the change applies to an entire link or a function in a device. Hubs implement host-programmable inactivity timers for each downstream-facing port for use in determining when to enter U1 and U2. Isochronous Timestamp packets don't prevent a device from entering a low-power state. To exit a low-power state, a link uses a hardware handshake implemented using low-frequency periodic signaling (LFPS), defined in Chapter 19.

U1

A host, hub, or device can request a transition to U1. The host can send a hub-specific Set Port Feature(PORT_LINK_STATE) request for a downstream-facing port on a hub. The hub then uses hardware-generated link commands to implement the state change on the link. When a hub's downstream-facing port is in U0 and an inactivity timer detects no bus activity on the port for the timer's specified period, the hub uses link commands to request to transition the link to U1. A device can use a device-specific policy in deciding when to request U1 entry via link commands. In all cases, the link partner can refuse to change to the requested state for example, if the port will soon have traffic to send or doesn't support U1.

When a host or device has a packet ready to transmit, a hardware handshake initiates exit from U1 to U0.

U2

When a link is in U1, if the downstream port supports U2 and the link partners' U2 inactivity timers time out, the link silently transitions to U2. When a host or device has a packet ready to transmit, a hardware handshake initiates exit from U2 to U0.

U3

Unlike USB 2.0, Enhanced SuperSpeed buses don't support global suspend, where the host places the entire bus in the Suspend state by ceasing to send timing markers. Enhanced SuperSpeed supports only selective suspend and function suspend.

In selective suspend, a device enters the Suspend state on detecting that the device's link is in U3. Set Port Feature (PORT_LINK_STATE, U3) requests a hub to place a downstream-facing port and its link in U3. The hub uses hardware-generated link commands to implement the state change on the link. The downstream device enters the Suspend state on detecting that the link is in U3.

To suspend the entire bus, the host must request each downstream port on the bus to enter U3. When all of a hub's downstream ports are in U3, a host places the hub's upstream link in U3. Only a host can request to place a link in U3, and hubs must accept requests to place an enabled downstream port in U3.

To wake a device, the host sends a Set Port Feature(PORT_LINK_STATE, U0) request to the downstream-facing hub port that is the device's link partner. The hub uses hardware-generated link commands to transition the link to U0. On detecting that the link is in U0, the downstream device exits the Suspend state. A device can initiate exit from U3 via LFPS as described below under Function Suspend.

Function suspend

For finer power control, an Enhanced SuperSpeed host can place an individual function in the function suspend state while allowing other functions in a device to continue to communicate on the bus. To suspend a function, the host issues a Set Port Feature(FUNCTION_SUSPEND) request to an interface. In the high byte of wIndex, bit 0 requests the suspend state or normal operation, and bit 1 enables or disables function remote wakeup.

To resume communications with a suspended function, a host issues a Set Port Feature(FUNCTION_SUSPEND) request for normal operation. Note that exiting function suspend uses Set Port Feature rather than Clear Port Feature. If the device's link isn't in U0, the downstream-facing hub port that is the device's link partner uses LFPS to initiate the transition to U0. The hub then resumes communicating with the function.

A function with remote wakeup enabled can request to wake by sending a DEV_NOTIFICATION TP with a Function Wake notification. If the device's link isn't in U0, before sending the notification, the device uses LFPS to transition the link to U0. The signaling propagates upstream from the device until reaching a hub that isn't in U3 and then propagates back downstream to the device requesting the wakeup.

If the host places a device in the Suspend state when one or more functions are suspended, the functions remain suspended when the device wakes. The host or device must then initiate exiting function suspend for the individual function(s). Both composite and non-composite devices can use function suspend.

Informing the host of delays

Hubs help manage bus traffic by informing the host of delays caused by a device's being in a low-power state. On receiving a header packet addressed to a port in a low-power state, the hub sends a deferred header packet to the host, which halts communication attempts with the device. When the target port has transitioned to U0, the hub sends the header packet to the device with the Deferred bit set in the Link Control Word. To inform the host that the device is ready to communicate, the device sends an ERDY TP.

Latency tolerance messages

Enhanced SuperSpeed hosts can save additional power by obtaining information about the maximum delay each device can tolerate between sending an ERDY TP and receiving a response from the host. The host can use more aggressive power management with devices that can tolerate long delays. The protocols for obtaining this information include the Set Feature(LTM_ENABLE) and Set SEL requests and DEV_NOTIFICATION TPs with Latency Tolerance Message Device notifications. The

SuperSpeed USB device capability descriptor indicates whether a device supports Latency Tolerance Message notifications.

Using PING

If a host initiates an isochronous transaction with a device in a low-power state, the device might be unable to transition to U0 in time to send or receive data in the scheduled service interval. To prevent this problem, the host uses PING and PING_RESPONSE TPs. Before beginning the isochronous transfer, the host sends a PING TP, which causes all links between the device and host to transition to U0. The device returns a PING_RESPONSE TP when the device is ready to transfer data. The host must send the PING far enough in advance of a scheduled transfer to enable the transfer to take place on time.

This use of PING is unrelated to the high-speed PING protocol described in Chapter 2.

Advanced power delivery capabilities

The *USB Power Delivery Rev. 2.0, v1.0* specification defines hardware and protocols for bus currents as high as 5 A, VBUS voltages up to 20 V, more precise power management, and even the ability to reverse the flow of current so a device can provide power to a host. Revision 2.0 of the specification expanded the capabilities and added support for USB Type-C connectors.

Requirements

A device that supports *USB Power Delivery Rev. 2.0, v1.0* can be a Provider that sources current, a Consumer that sinks current, or both. To use Power Delivery (PD) capabilities, both the upstream-facing port (UFP) and downstream-facing port (DFP) in a link must have PD-capable connectors and system support for PD protocols.

A host learns about a PD-capable device in the PD Capability descriptors returned in the device's BOS descriptor set.

A USB Power Delivery Capability descriptor informs the host if the device supports USB Power Delivery and battery charging and also indicates if the device's upstream and downstream ports are Providers, Consumers, or both.

A Battery Info Capability descriptor contains information relating to charging such as a threshold value that defines when the battery is considered fully charged.

Each Consumer port has a PD Consumer Port Capability descriptor that specifies operating voltages and power consumption. When a device is using PD protocols, the values in this descriptor override the bMaxPower value in the configuration descriptor.

Each Provider port has a Provider Port descriptor that indicates if the port supports PD, battery charging, or both and provides information about the capabilities of power sources.

A series of PD-specific requests get and set PD-specific features, status, and data.

The device descriptor for a PD-capable device attached to a PD-capable port reports that the device is self-powered even if the device is drawing all of its power from the bus. The device instead reports its power needs in the PD Consumer Port Capability descriptor.

USB Power Delivery ports can use USB Type-C connectors or PD versions of USB 2.0 and USB 3.1 Series-A and Series-B connectors. Chapter 20 has more about these connectors.

Negotiating power

On power up, a PD-capable port uses the voltage and current limits defined in the USB 2.0 or USB 3.1 specification. To negotiate a PD Contract for a different VBUS voltage, maximum current, or direction of current flow, two PD-capable ports in a cable segment communicate using either a Binary Frequency Shift Keying (BFSK) modulated carrier on the VBUS line or the Communications Channel (CC) line available on USB Type-C cables.

The communications use Start of Packet (SOP) communications that each begin with an encoded symbol called a K-code.

An SOP communication can contain a Control Message or Data Message. Control Messages help manage data flow and are always 16 bits. Data Messages provide information in a Data Object and vary in length. A Power Data Object details the capabilities of a power source or the needs of a power sink. A Request Data Object is used in negotiating a contract. A BIST Data Object requests a test mode. A Vendor Defined Data Object contains a Vendor Defined Message.

A device can have a Device Policy Manager that monitors and controls power delivery in the device. A USB host can provide a System Policy Manager that coordinates power resources on attached devices that have Device Policy Managers. On systems that don't have a System Policy Manager, two attached PD-capable ports can still negotiate power on their local link. A Policy Engine implements power policies on a local port.

In links that use USB Type-C connectors, even if the host or hub and the device don't support *USB Power Delivery Rev. 2.0, v1.0,* a host or hub can make up to 3 A available to a device

Role swapping

PD links that use USB Type-C connectors can support three types of role swapping: Power Role (PR) Swap, Data Role (DR) Swap, and VCONN Swap. As the name suggests, in a Power Role Swap, the power consumer becomes the provider and the power provider becomes the consumer. In a Data Role Swap, the UFP becomes the DFP, and the DFP becomes the UFP. In a VCONN swap, the provider of the VCONN supply in the connector (see Chapter 20) switches to the opposite port.

To request a role swap, a port sends a PR, DR, or VCONN swap message.The DR swap protocol performs a similar function to OTG's Host Negotiation Protocol but the devices don't need to meet OTG requirements such as using a Micro-AB connector.

When a USB host doesn't have power due to a dead battery or other reason, the *USB Power Delivery Rev. 2.0, v1.0* and USB Type-C specifications define protocols that enable an attached device to power VBUS if the device can function as a Provider.

For links with Series-A and Series-B connectors, a device that wants to provide power begins by powering VBUS at a reduced current level. On detecting VBUS, a host port that wants to receive power sends a bitstream of alternating zeros and ones. On detecting the bitstream, after a delay to allow the host to stop the bitstream and get ready to receive power, the device port can provide full power. A device that doesn't detect the bitstream within a specified time removes VBUS but may delay, reapply the voltage and try again for a response.

Vendor-defined messages

USB Power Delivery Rev. 2.0, v1.0 defines a Vendor Defined Message (VDM) format that supports messages with vendor-defined content. A VDM resides in a Vendor Defined Data Object sent in a Data Message.

A VDM must contain a Standard or Vendor ID (SVID), which is either a USB Vendor ID or a Standard ID (SID). A SID is a 16-bit value the USB-IF assigns to an industry standard. For example, the SID for USB Power Delivery is 0xFF00.

A Structured VDM contains a command. Structured VDMs enable Modal Operation, where a host can request a device to enter one or more Alternate Modes defined by a vendor or standard. Alternate Modes are valid only between a host and a directly connected device.

An Unstructured VDM uses a vendor-defined message format.

Power management under Windows

Windows PCs manage power according to the *Advanced Configuration and Power Interface Specification* (ACPI) maintained by the UEFI Forum (*uefi.org*). A system that implements ACPI power management enables the OS to conserve power, including suspending the USB bus, when the computer is idle.

Computer power states

Various power states specify power usage by the computer and its devices. Except for S0 Low Power Idle, which is defined by Microsoft, the ACPI Specification defines the states below.

Working

S0. The system is on. USB devices that aren't in use may be suspended.

S0 Low Power Idle (InstantGo). In Microsoft's InstantGo state, the computer uses little power yet keeps needed applications and devices available. A computer enters the InstantGo state whenever the display is off. Tasks such as printing and playing music can continue. To support InstantGo, a computer must have solid-state drives and other low-power components, and the OS must support aggressive power saving. Computers that support InstantGo don't use the S3 state.

Sleep

S1. The display is off and drives are powered down. USB buses are suspended, but VBUS remains powered. This state is no longer in use.

S2. The processor loses power and the processor context and contents of the cache are lost. This state is not implemented.

S3. The PCI bus's main power supply is off and memory isn't accessed, but system memory continues to be refreshed. USB buses are suspended. The PCI bus's auxiliary supply (V_{AUX}) is powered. USB devices may wake the system.

Hibernate

S4. The system context is saved to disk. USB buses are powered off.

Soft Off

S5. The system context is not saved. The system consumes minimal power and requires a restart to return to the working state.

Mechanical Off

G3. The computer is switched off by mechanical means, consumes no power except for the real-time clock, and requires a restart to return to the working state.

You can view and change a system's power-management options in **Control Panel > Power Options.** Click **Change when a computer sleeps > Change advanced power settings** for options such as enabling USB selective suspend and configuring low-power settings.

Utilities

Windows and the WDK provide utilities for viewing and managing power states.

Displaying and initiating power changes

The Windows command-line utility *Powercfg* can display power-management information and initiate transitions to low-power states.

This command lists all available sleep states on the system:

```
powercfg /a
```

This command lists the devicename of each device that can wake the computer:

```
powercfg /devicequery wake_armed
```

To enable or disable a device's ability to wake the system, use these commands with a devicename returned from devicequery wake_armed:

```
powercfg /deviceenablewake <devicename>
powercfg /devicedisablewake <devicename>
```

To view all commands, enter:

```
powercfg /?
```

Testing and debugging power management

The command-line *PwrTest* utility can list all available power states and initiate transitions to sleep, hibernate, InstantGo, and shutdown for USB devices. PwrTest is in the free Microsoft USB Test Tool (MUTT) software package.

To run PwrTest, open a command prompt with administrator privileges. One way to do so is to search the computer for **command**, then right-click **Command Prompt** and select **Run as Administrator.** Or create a shortcut to *%SystemRoot%\System32\cmd.exe*, right-click the shortcut, and select **Run as Administrator.**

PwrTest supports a variety of scenarios for monitoring and testing power management including sleep states, battery usage, and power usage by drives, monitors, and other devices.

This command places the system in the S4 power state for 60 seconds and resumes:

```
pwrtest /scenario /sleep /p:60 /s:4
```

To view all scenarios, enter:

```
pwrtest
```

To view the options for a scenario, enter:

```
pwrtest /<scenario> /?
```

Some scenarios require provisioning a test computer using Visual Studio. Microsoft provides instructions for doing so.

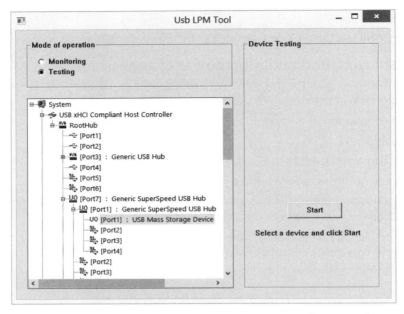

Figure 17-2. The USBLPM tool can test and monitor power states of USB 3.0 devices under Windows 8 and higher.

Monitoring and testing power states

Under Windows 8 and higher, the USBLPM tool can monitor the power states of USB 3.0 ports, verify correct transitions between states, and enable and disable U1 and U2 states on devices (Figure 17-2). USBLPM is included in the MUTT software package.

Battery charging

The USB-IF's *Battery Charging Specification* defines interfaces and protocols for USB host and hub ports and dedicated devices that operate as USB chargers. With host and device support for the specification, devices can draw charging currents of up to 1.5 A and can charge batteries that are too weak to enable the device to enumerate. The ability to use a USB connector for charging is convenient for users and lowers manufacturing cost because devices doesn't need vendor-specific connectors or cables for charging.

Any device can receive charging current from a standard USB port on a host or hub, but a USB charging port contains charger-detection circuits to enable a device to detect a connection to a USB charger that doesn't enumerate the device.

The information below is current as of Revision 1.2 of the specification. The specification was released before the USB 3.1 specification so there are no references to SuperSpeedPlus.

The *USB Power Delivery Rev. 2.0, v1.0* specification also supports battery charging using the Battery Info Capability descriptor and other protocols.

Charger types

The Battery Charging specification defines five types of chargers:

Term	Meaning	Comment
SDP	Standard Downstream Port	Standard host or hub port
CDP	Charging Downstream Port	Host or hub port with expanded charging capabilities
DCP	Dedicated charging port	Doesn't enumerate the device
ACA	Accessory charging adapter	Can charge an OTG device that is also communicating with a device
ACA-Dock	ACA-Dock	ACA that uses a vendor-specific connection

Figure 17-3 illustrates.

- A standard downstream port (SDP) is a downstream-facing port that doesn't have expanded abilities to support charging. An attached downstream device in the Suspend state should draw no more than the allowed Suspend current.

- A charging downstream port (CDP) is a downstream-facing port on a host or hub that supports charger detection and can provide 1.5 A at any time. A device that connects to a host charger by pulling up D+ or D- can draw charging current even if the host has placed the device in the Suspend state. A CDP must have a Standard-A receptacle.

- A dedicated charging port (DCP) resides on a charging device that provides power but doesn't enumerate the attached device. The charging port connects its D+ and D- lines together via a resistor of 200 Ω maximum and must limit the charging current to less than 1.5 A. The charging port has a Standard-A receptacle or a captive cable with a Micro-B plug. Any device with a DCP is a USB charger.

- An Accessory Charging Adapter (ACA) enables an OTG device to charge from a CDP, DCP, or other charger while also communicating with a USB device. The ACA attaches to an OTG device using a captive cable that terminates in a Micro-A plug. The ACA's charger port connects to a CDP or DCP using a Micro-B receptacle or a

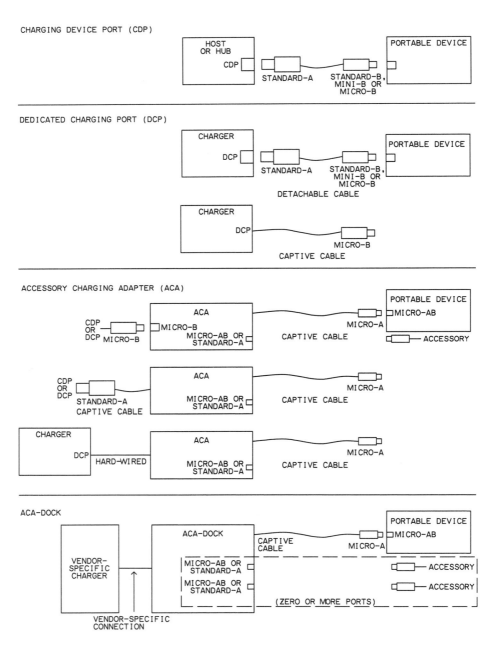

Figure 17-3. A charging port can be on a charging downstream port on a host or hub, a dedicated charging port on a charger, an accessory charging adapter, or an ACA-Dock.

captive cable with a Standard-A plug, or the ACA may be hard-wired to a charger. The accessory port has a Micro-AB or Standard-A receptacle that can connect to a device supported by the OTG device.

- An ACA-Dock has a similar function to an ACA but must use a vendor-specific charger connection and may have zero or more accessory ports. The ACA-Dock attaches to an OTG device using a captive cable that terminates in a Micro-A plug. The ACA's charger port connects to a vendor-defined charger using a vendor-specific connection. If present, one or more accessory ports each have a Micro-AB or Standard-A receptacle that can connect to a device supported by the OTG device. Because the OTG device being charged has a single Micro-AB port, an ACA-Dock that contains more than one accessory port must incorporate a hub.

A device uses the ID pin on the device's Micro-AB receptacle in detecting attachment of an ACA or ACA-Dock. Chapter 20 has more about connector types.

A charger that wants to provide more than 1.5 A can use cables with USB Type-C connectors with currents up to 3 A or use *USB Power Delivery Rev. 2.0, v1.0* protocols with USB Type-C cables that support currents up to 5 A.

Battery Charging Specification Revision 1.2 precedes the *On-The-Go and Embedded Host Supplement to the USB Revision 2.0* specification, which first permitted embedded hosts to use Micro-AB receptacles. Thus the charging specification doesn't mention embedded hosts using ACAs and ACA-Docks to charge.

Charger detection

After detecting the presence of VBUS, a device can detect attachment to a USB charger by driving D+ to the VDAT_SRC voltage (0.5 V–0.7 V) and detecting the voltage on D-. If D- is greater than VDAT_REF (0.4 V maximum), the device is attached to a USB charger.

A CDP that detects a voltage between 0.4 V and 0.8 V on D+ drives D- to VDAT_SRC, which exceeds VDAT_REF. On a DCP, D+ and D- are connected together and thus both exceed VDAT_REF. Hosts and hubs that don't function as USB chargers pull D- to ground via a 15K resistor, which brings D- below VDAT_REF.

A device attached to a USB charger can determine the charger type after pulling up D+ (full speed) or D- (low speed) and detecting the voltage on the line not pulled up:

Device Speed	Action	Detected Voltage	Charger Type
Full	Pull D+ high	D- is low	Host or hub
		D- is high	Dedicated
Low	Pull D- high	D+ is low	Host or hub
		D+ is high	Dedicated

High-speed-capable devices attach at full speed. SuperSpeed devices use these charger-detect protocols on the D+ and D- lines in the USB 3.0 cable.

To ensure valid voltages when connecting, a low-speed device must draw less than 100 mA (USB 2.0) or 150 mA (SuperSpeed) when pulling up D-. The specification provides timing requirements and other restrictions for implementing charger detection.

Charging dead or weak batteries

A dead-battery provision (DBP) in the Battery Charging Specification allows some devices with dead or weak batteries to draw up to 100 mA of bus current for 45 minutes or until the batteries are charged to a weak-battery threshold, whichever occurs sooner. A device whose battery has charged to the weak battery threshold is capable of powering up and enumerating. The device vendor defines the weak-battery threshold voltage.

Only devices that are capable of operating stand-alone from battery power may use DBP current, and the only allowed use of DBP current is to bring a device to its weak-battery threshold.

18

Testing and Debugging

Along with the chip-specific development boards and debugging software described in Chapter 6, a variety of other hardware and software tools can help in testing and debugging USB devices and their host software. This chapter introduces tools available from the USB-IF and other sources and explain what's involved in passing tests for the Certified USB logo and Windows logos.

Tools

Without a doubt the most useful tool for USB device developers is a protocol analyzer for monitoring USB traffic and other bus events. The analyzer captures, decodes, and displays data and events on the bus. You can see what happened during enumeration, detect and examine protocol and signaling errors, view data transferred during control, interrupt, bulk, and isochronous transfers, and focus on specific details of any transfer.

A hardware analyzer uses a combination of hardware and software, while a software analyzer consists only of software that runs on the device's host computer. The capabilities of the two types overlap, but each can also record and display information that isn't available to the other type.

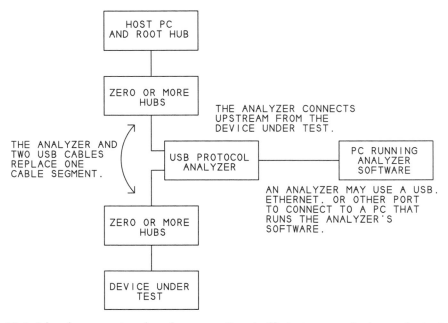

Figure 18-1. A hardware protocol analyzer monitors traffic between a device under test and the device's host. An interface to a PC (or logic analyzer) enables viewing the captured data.

Another useful tool is a traffic generator, which emulates a host or device and offers precise control over what goes out on the bus.

Hardware protocol analyzers

A hardware protocol analyzer captures the signals in a cable segment without affecting the traffic in the segment. The analyzer connects in a cable segment upstream from the device under test (Figure 18-1). To enable viewing the captured traffic, the analyzer also connects to a PC or logic analyzer. A connection to a PC may use USB or another interface such as Ethernet. Instead of a PC interface, some protocol analyzers connect to logic analyzers from Agilent or Tektronix.

With a hardware analyzer, you can see the data in the cable down to the individual bytes that make up each packet. There's no question about what the host or device did or didn't send. For example, if the host sends an IN token packet, you can see whether the device returned data or NAK. You can view the packets in every stage of a control request. Time stamps enable you to see how often the host accesses an endpoint.

Analyzers are available from multiple vendors and in a range of prices. As a rule, support for higher speeds increases the price, with low/full-speed analyzers having the lowest cost.

In this chapter, I use an Ellisys analyzer and Ellisys Visual USB Analysis software to illustrate what a hardware analyzer can do.

The hardware

The Ellisys Explorer 260 USB 2.0 analyzer requires two USB host controllers, one that communicates with the analyzer and one that controls the bus segment being monitored. Both host controllers can be in the same PC, but for high-bandwidth traffic, two PCs can prevent overflow errors.

One USB cable connects the analyzer to the PC running Ellisys Visual USB Analysis software. The PC detects the analyzer as a USB device that uses a driver provided by Ellisys.

Two additional USB cables and the analyzer replace a cable segment upstream from the device being monitored. The combined length of the two cables should total 3 m or less because the cables and the analyzer's electronics together must emulate an ordinary cable segment of 5 m or less.

The software

The Ellisys Visual USB Analysis Software enables you to start and stop data logging and to save, view, and print the results. Figure 18-2 shows data captured by an analyzer. You can specify the amount, type, and format of data the displayed. For less detail, you can elect to hide individual packets, repeated NAKs, and other information. You can specify criteria to display such as specific devices, endpoints, speeds, status codes, and control requests.

A Details pane provides more information about a request, transaction, packet, or other item in a row in the application's main window (Figure 18-3). A Data pane displays the individual bytes in hexadecimal and ASCII. You can also search for specific items, including events, token-packet types, traffic to and from a specific device or endpoint, and data.

Additional software modules add support for triggering on events, decoding class-specific information, and exporting captured data in text, XML, and other formats.

Item	Device	Endpoint	Interface	Status	Speed	Payload	Time
Enter text here	Ent...	Ente...	Ente...	E...	E...	Enter text here	Enter text here
⚡ Reset (4.1 s)							0.000 000 000
⚡ Suspended (104.9 ms)							4.060 097 517
⚡ Reset (11.1 ms)							4.162 029 783
⚡ High speed Detection Handshake				TIME...			4.172 038 633
⊟ GetDescriptor (Device)	0 (14)	0		OK	FS	8 bytes (12 01 00 02 00 00 00 08)	4.192 482 633
⊟ → SETUP transaction	0 (14)	0		ACK	FS	8 bytes (80 06 00 01 00 00 40 00)	4.192 482 633
→ SETUP packet	0	0			FS		4.192 482 633
→ DATA0 packet					FS	8 bytes (80 06 00 01 00 00 40 00)	4.192 485 867
← ACK packet				ACK	FS		4.192 494 500
⊞ ← IN transaction (9)	0 (14)	0		NAK	FS	No data	4.192 580 150
⊟ ← IN transaction	0 (14)	0		ACK	FS	8 bytes (12 01 00 02 00 00 00 08)	4.192 591 033
→ IN packet	0	0			FS		4.192 591 033
← DATA1 packet					FS	8 bytes (12 01 00 02 00 00 00 08)	4.192 594 350
→ ACK packet				ACK	FS		4.192 602 917
⊟ → OUT transaction	0 (14)	0		ACK	FS	No data	4.192 611 650
→ OUT packet	0	0			FS		4.192 611 650
→ DATA1 packet					FS	No data	4.192 614 883
← ACK packet				ACK	FS		4.192 618 183
⚡ Reset (10.6 ms)							4.193 537 450
⚡ High speed Detection Handshake				TIME...			4.203 546 317
⊟ SetAddress (14)	0 (14)	0		OK	FS	No data	4.223 732 933
⊟ → SETUP transaction	0 (14)	0		ACK	FS	8 bytes (00 05 0E 00 00 00 00 00)	4.223 732 933
→ SETUP packet	0	0			FS		4.223 732 933
→ DATA0 packet					FS	8 bytes (00 05 0E 00 00 00 00 00)	4.223 736 167
← ACK packet				ACK	FS		4.223 744 800
⊞ ← IN transaction (7)	0 (14)	0		NAK	FS	No data	4.223 804 517
⊟ ← IN transaction	0 (14)	0		ACK	FS	No data	4.223 813 067
→ IN packet	0	0			FS		4.223 813 067
← DATA1 packet					FS	No data	4.223 816 383
→ ACK packet				ACK	FS		4.223 819 617

Figure 18-2. Ellisys provides the Visual USB application for use with the company's analyzers. This example shows transactions and other events that occurred when a device was attached downstream from the analyzer

Software protocol analyzers

A software-only protocol analyzer runs on the host computer of the device being tested. You can view traffic to and from any device that connects to any of the computer's host controllers.

A software analyzer can display driver information that a hardware analyzer can't see. As Chapter 8 explained, Windows drivers communicate with USB devices using I/O Request Packets (IRPs) that contain USB Request Blocks (URBs). A software analyzer can show the IRPs and URBs that a driver has submitted and the responses received from a device.

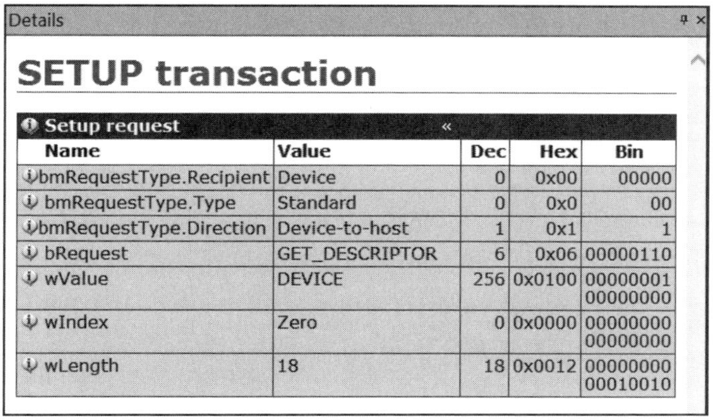
Details

SETUP transaction

Setup request

Name	Value	Dec	Hex	Bin
bmRequestType.Recipient	Device	0	0x00	00000
bmRequestType.Type	Standard	0	0x0	00
bmRequestType.Direction	Device-to-host	1	0x1	1
bRequest	GET_DESCRIPTOR	6	0x06	00000110
wValue	DEVICE	256	0x0100	00000001 00000000
wIndex	Zero	0	0x0000	00000000 00000000
wLength	18	18	0x0012	00000000 00010010

Figure 18-3. The Details pane in Ellisys' Visual USB software has more information about a request, transaction, packet, or other event.

However, software analyzers can't show anything the host-controller or hub hardware handles without software intervention. For example, the analyzer won't show how many times an endpoint NAKed a transaction before returning an ACK or the precise time a transaction occurred on the bus.

Some software analyzers use a filter driver that loads when the operating system loads the driver for the device being monitored. Because the filter driver doesn't load until the host has enumerated the device, the analyzer can't show the enumeration requests and other events that occur at device attachment.

Open-source tools

One option for a software analyzer uses two open-source tools: USBPcap (*desowin.org*) to capture the data and WireShark (*wireshark.org*) to decode and display the captured data.

The first step in using these tools is to find the device's root hub. To keep the capture free of clutter, attach the device to a host controller that has a minimum of downstream devices that are generating traffic. With the device attached, run USBPcap from a command prompt to view a numbered list of root hubs and their downstream devices (Figure 18-4).

To start the capture, find your target device in the list and enter its root-hub number and a filename for the captured data.

To view the data, run WireShark and open the file created by USBPcap (Figure 18-5). Wireshark decodes the captured URBs including the contents of standard control

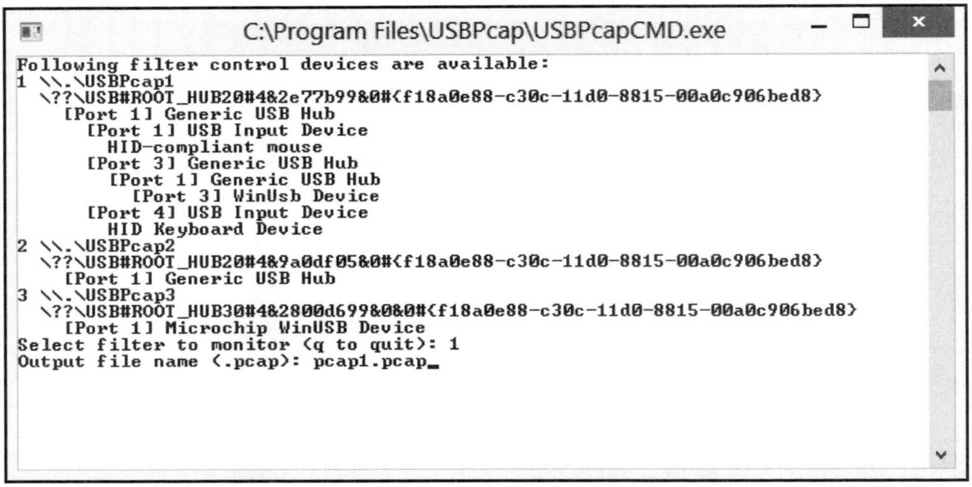

Figure 18-4. USBPcap can capture data at a root hub.

transfers and class-specific data for the audio, smart card, HID, hub, mass storage, and video classes. You can also view raw data for any transaction.

If you attach a device while USBPcap is running, the capture includes enumeration data beginning with the first Get Descriptor request.

Event tracing for Windows

Another option for viewing USB data uses the Event Tracing for Windows (ETW) capabilities supported by Windows 7 and later. Viewing USB data requires two tools: Logman to capture the data and Netmon to display the data.

Capturing data with Logman

The Windows command-line utility Logman captures USB ETW event traces. To start a trace, you enter commands to create a trace, specify what to include, and start logging. Another series of commands stops the trace and copies it to a file for viewing. *Logman.exe* is in *%SystemRoot%\system32*.

An alternative to typing or pasting the commands each time is to place them in a batch file. Listing 18-1 shows a batch file that captures all USB 2.0 and USB 3.0 traffic until the user presses a key, then stops and saves the capture. These are the commands In the batch file:

logman create defines a trace with the collection name **usbtrace** and the destination of the path and filename specified by the **-o** parameter. The **-nb** option specifies the

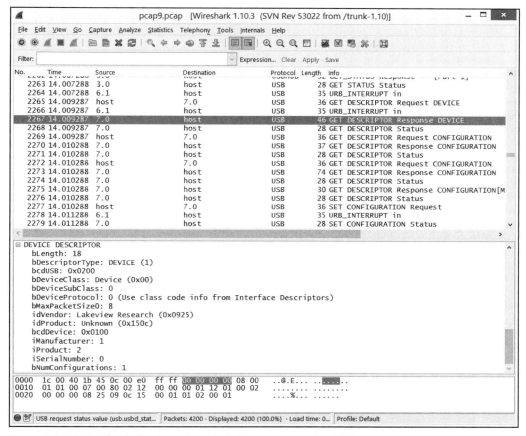

Figure 18-5. WireShark displays decoded data captured by USBPcap.

minimum and maximum number of buffers to use for trace data. The **-bs** option specifies the buffer size in KB.

logman update names a provider to log. The example uses multiple commands to capture all data downstream from USB 2.0 and USB 3.0 host controllers. To capture only data downstream from USB 2.0 controllers, delete or comment out (with **rem**) the lines that contain USBXHCI, UCX, and USBHUB3. To capture only data downstream from USB 3.0 controllers, delete or comment out the lines that contain USB-PORT and USBHUB.

You can find all named providers in the system with this command:

logman query providers

logman start initiates logging.

```
rem @ECHO OFF
logman create trace usbtrace -o %SystemRoot%\Tracing\usbtrace.etl
 -nb 128 640 -bs 128
logman update trace usbtrace -p Microsoft-Windows-USB-USBXHCI
 (Default,PartialDataBusTrace)
logman update trace usbtrace -p Microsoft-Windows-USB-UCX
 Default,PartialDataBusTrace)
logman update trace -n usbtrace -p Microsoft-Windows-USB-USBHUB3
 (Default,PartialDataBusTrace)
logman update trace usbtrace -p Microsoft-Windows-USB-USBPORT
logman update trace usbtrace -p Microsoft-Windows-USB-USBHUB
logman update trace usbtrace -p Microsoft-Windows-Kernel-IoTrace 0
 2
logman start usbtrace

ECHO "Logging data. To stop logging, press any key."

PAUSE

logman stop usbtrace
logman delete usbtrace
move %SystemRoot%\Tracing\usbtrace.etl
 %SystemRoot%\Tracing\usbtrace_000001.etl
```

Listing 18-1: This batch file logs all USB 2.0 and USB 3.0 data until the user presses a key, then saves the result in a file.

The **pause** command stops execution of the batch file until you press a key. When you have logged the events you want to view, press a key to continue.

logman stop stops the logging.

logman delete deletes the data collection query.

The **move** command copies the log file (the first file specified) to the named location (the second file specified).

To run the batch file or execute other logman commands, open a command prompt with administrator privileges as described in Chapter 17.

Viewing data with Netmon

The Netmon utility and USB parsers enable viewing data captured with logman. Both are free from the Microsoft Download Center. You will also need the WDK.

A Netmon parser is a text file that contains the information needed to display events for a specific protocol. Netmon parsers have the extension *.npl*. The WDK provides USB parsers.

Before using Netmon to view USB events, you need to make the USB parsers available to Netmon. To do so requires using the Windows PowerShell application and allowing execution of PowerShell scripts.

PowerShell provides a command-line interface and scripting language for performing system administration tasks. To allow execution of PowerShell scripts, search the computer for **powershell**, right-click **Windows PowerShell**, and select **Run as administrator**. In the PowerShell window that appears, enter this command:

Set-ExecutionPolicy RemoteSigned -Force

Close PowerShell and reopen it. This time it's not necessary to run as administrator.

A user-defined Parser Profile can make USB parsers available to Netmon. The provided PowerShell script *NplAutoProfile.ps1* adds Netmon parsers from the current directory to a Parser Profile named AutoProfile. To add the USB parsers to AutoProfile, enter these commands in PowerShell, editing the path to the *Network Monitor Parsers\usb* directory to match your system as needed:

cd "C:\Program Files (x86)\Windows Kits\8.0\Tools\x86\Network Monitor Parsers\usb"
..\NplAutoProfile.ps1

The commands switch to the USB parsers directory and execute the NplAutoProfile script.

Close PowerShell. Now you can run NetMon, select AutoProfile, and open traces captured by logman.

To run Netmon, search the computer for **netmon** and click **netmon.exe**.

In Netmon, to select the AutoProfile you created, click **Tools** > **Options** > **Parser Profiles**, select **AutoProfile**, and click **Set as Active**.

To load the captured data, click **Open Capture** and select the *.etl* file created by logman. Figure 18-6 shows an example.

You will likely see a long list of events. With filters, you can narrow the display to items of interest.

For example, to view Get Descriptor requests, in the Frame Summary window, in the Description column, find an item containing:

USBPort:Dispatch URB_FUNCTION_GET_DESCRIPTOR_FROM_DEVICE

Right-click the item and select **Add 'Description' to Display Filter**

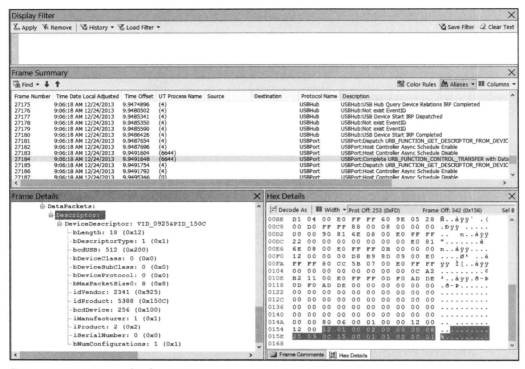

Figure 18-6. Netmon displays USB events captured by logman.

Or enter this text in the Display Filter window:

Description=="USBPort:Dispatch URB_FUNCTION_GET_DESCRIPTOR_FROM_DEVICE"

In the Display Filter window, click **Apply**.

The Frame Summary window now displays only URBs for Get Descriptor requests (Figure 18-7).

The Frame Details windows shows information about the item currently selected in the Frame Summary window.

To view the Get Descriptor request, in the Frame Details window, expand:

UsbPort: Dispatch URB_FUNCTION_GET_DESCRIPTOR_FROM_DEVICE

and scroll down. Expand:

SetupPacket: GET_DESCRIPTOR

to view the requested descriptor.

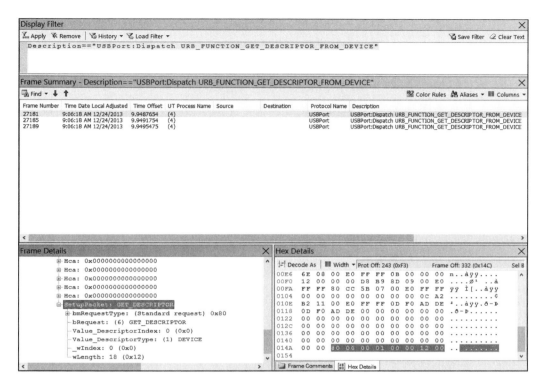

Figure 18-7. With Netmon's filtering, you can home in on a specific USB request such as Get Descriptor.

Here is an example:

```
- SetupPacket: GET_DESCRIPTOR
+ bmRequestType: (Standard request) 0x80
  bRequest: (6) GET_DESCRIPTOR
  Value_DescriptorIndex: 0 (0x0)
  Value_DescriptorType: (1) DEVICE
  _wIndex: 0 (0x0)
  wLength: 18 (0x12)
```

If you see:

Value_DescriptorType: (1) DEVICE

you have a request for the device descriptor. If not, select other events in the Frame Details window until you find the request for the device descriptor.

When you find the request, make a note of the event's Frame Number.

To view the returned descriptor, follow the steps below to clear the filters and look for the response in a frame that follows the request.

In the Display Filter window, click **Clear Text**, then **Apply**.

Scroll to the Frame Number you noted for the request. In a frame that follows, look for an event with this description:

USBPort:Complete URB_FUNCTION_CONTROL_TRANSFER with Data

If you prefer to narrow the possibilities before searching, you can create and apply a filter:

Description=="USBPort:Complete URB_FUNCTION_CONTROL_TRANSFER with Data"

To view the decoded contents of the device descriptor, expand the items in the Frame Details window.

Here is an example showing the fields in a device descriptor:

```
- DeviceDescriptor: VID_0925&PID_150C
    bLength: 18 (0x12)
    bDescriptorType: 1 (0x1)
    bcdUSB: 512 (0x200)
    bDeviceClass: 0 (0x0)
    bDeviceSubClass: 0 (0x0)
    bDeviceProtocol: 0 (0x0)
    bMaxPacketSize0: 8 (0x8)
    idVendor: 2341 (0x925)
    idProduct: 5388 (0x150C)
    bcdDevice: 256 (0x100)
    iManufacturer: 1 (0x1)
    iProduct: 2 (0x2)
    iSerialNumber: 0 (0x0)
    bNumConfigurations: 1 (0x1)
```

In a similar way, you can find and examine requests for other descriptors. You can also view URBs that request and send USB data for any purpose.

To add a filter from a value in the Frame Details window, right-click the item and select **Add Selected Value to Display Filter**. For example, to display only events for a specific device, you can filter on the idVendor and idProduct values.

The WDK's USB parsers don't decode class-specific data such as mass-storage commands, but you can view the hexadecimal data.

Traffic generators

Sometimes it's useful to be able to control bus traffic and signaling beyond what you can do from host software and device firmware. Some hardware protocol analyzers can also function as traffic generators that emulate a host or device and give you precise control over the traffic that the emulated host or device places on the bus. In addition to generating valid traffic, a traffic generator can introduce errors such as bit-stuff and CRC errors. Some vendors of protocol analyzers also offer stand-alone traffic generators or analyzers with traffic-generator capabilities

Compliance testing

The USB-IF offers testing opportunities for developers of USB products. Passing the tests is a requirement for a product's displaying a Certified USB logo. Compliance tools, checklists, and documentation are available at *usb.org*.

The USB-IF's compliance program provides tests for peripherals, hubs, host systems, OTG devices, silicon building blocks, cable assemblies, and connectors.

Compliance testing checks to see if a product meets requirements of relevant USB specifications. No test suite can check for every possible violation of a specification, but the goal of the USB-IF's tests are to make a good effort to verify that a device operates without problems at every supported speed, with every supported host controller type, under hubs, and on buses loaded with other devices. The tests check for valid values in descriptors, issue requests that a device might not be expecting, verify proper operation when entering and leaving low-power states, and look for other violations that are likely to cause problems in the field.

An important requirement of compliance testing is adhering to the *no silent failure* rule. A device may be unable to function in a situation such as needing more bandwidth or power than is available. When a device can't function, the host computer must not leave the user wondering what is wrong but instead should display a message that informs the user why the device isn't working.

When a product passes its required compliance tests, the USB-IF asserts that the product has "reasonable measures of acceptability" and adds the product to its Integrators List of compliant devices. On receiving a signed license agreement, the USB-IF authorizes the product to display a Certified USB logo. Even if you don't submit your device to formal compliance testing, you can use the tests to verify your device's performance.

You can submit a device for compliance testing at a USB-IF compliance workshop or an independent lab authorized by the USB-IF. The USB-IF's compliance workshops are open only to USB-IF members, are free of charge, and include demonstrated operation tests where the device performs its intended purpose when attached downstream from hubs and with other attached devices. Testing by independent labs doesn't require demonstrated operation testing because it's impractical for the labs to set up these tests. To save time and expense, before submitting a product for compliance testing, you should perform the tests as fully as possible on your own.

Checklists

The USB-IF's compliance checklists contain a series of questions about a product's specifications and behavior. There are checklists for peripherals, hubs, hub and peripheral silicon, and host systems. The USB 2.0 USB Compliance Checklist for peripherals covers mechanical design, device states and signals, operating voltages, and power consumption. Accompanying each question is a reference to a section in the USB specification with more information. You should be able to answer yes to each relevant question on a checklist that applies to your device. The USB 3.0 checklist for peripherals asks only if the silicon, connectors, and cables are on the USB Integrators List and whether any USB pins are used for anything other than USB.

USB Command Verifier software

The USB-IF's Command Verifier software performs tests of the device framework protocols, current measurement, and interoperability. The USB20CV version tests USB 2.0 protocols and requirements under EHCI, OHCI, and UHCI host controllers. The USB30CV version tests USB 2.0 and USB 3.0 protocols and requirements under xHCI host controllers.

Each version replaces the system's host-controller driver with a test-stack driver and on exiting, restores the original driver. Before installing and running the software, review the readme file and release notes. It doesn't hurt to create a Windows restore point before running the software in case something goes wrong and you need to recover your system's original state.

Running USB30CV

USB30CV requires a PC with a recent Windows version and an xHCI host controller.

When you run USB30CV, after the stack switch, Device Manager lists the xHCI host controller as *xhci compliance test host controller*.

If the PC has multiple xHCI host controllers, the software will ask you to select the host controller to use for the stack switch. To find which host controller is upstream from your device, start Device Manager and select **View** > **Devices by Connection**. (See Chapter 9.) Look for the host controllers under these or similar headings: **ACPI x64-based PC** > **Microsoft ACPI-Compliant System** > **PCI Express Root Complex**. Look for one or more items with USB 3.0 eXtensible Host Controller in the name. Expand these items and their subordinate hubs and search for your device. When you find the device, double-click its host controller's entry. In the **General** tab, note the displayed **Location**.

The USB-IF recommends running USB30CV only on hosts that are using Microsoft's USB drivers. The system mouse and keyboard must attach either directly to the root hub of the host controller whose driver is being switched or under a host controller that isn't having its driver switched.

To enable performing the stack switch, you must turn off User Account Control (UAC) and reboot. The setup instructions for the software detail the steps to do so on different Windows versions.

If you have non-functioning USB ports after exiting USB30CV, it's likely that the software didn't complete the stack switch for some reason. Running and exiting USB30CV again may fix the problem, or you can try rolling back the test driver in Device Manager or powering down the system and rebooting.

Running USB20CV

USB20CV functions much like USB30CV but tests devices attached under ECHI, OHCI, and UHCI host controllers.

To enable performing the stack switch, you must turn off User Account Control (UAC) and also disable driver signature enforcement. The setup instructions for the software detail the steps needed to perform these actions on different Windows versions.

Device Framework tests

USB20CV and USB30CV each include USB 2.0 Device Framework tests to verify that a USB 2.0 device or a USB 3.0 device operating at a USB 2.0 speed responds correctly to standard control requests. USB30CV also includes Device Framework tests for USB 3.0 devices operating at SuperSpeed (and presumably will be updated to include SuperSpeedPlus).

A USB 2.0 device must pass the Device Framework tests under EHCI, UHCI, and OHCI hosts using USB20CV and also under an xHCI host using USB30CV.

About the tests

In the USB 2.0 Device Framework tests, the host issues standard control requests defined in Chapter 9 of the USB 2.0 specification and performs additional checks on the information returned by a device (Figure 18-8). For example, on retrieving a device descriptor, the software checks to see that the bMaxPacketSize0 value is valid for the device's speed and that the bDeviceClass value is either a value for a defined class or 0xFF (vendor-defined). The software resets and enumerates the device when the device is in the default, address, and configured states and in every supported configuration.

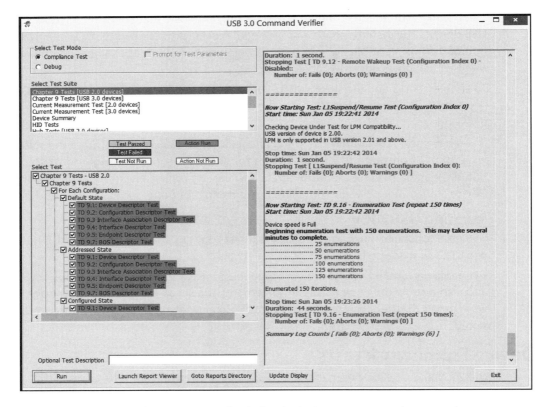

Figure 18-8. USBCV's Chapter 9 tests check the device's responses to the control requests defined in Chapter 9 of the USB specification.

The Chapter 9 tests also include these:

- Enumerate the device multiple times with different addresses.
- Verify that all bulk and interrupt endpoints can be halted and unhalted with Set Feature and Clear Feature requests.
- Ensure that the device returns STALL in response to receiving a request for an unsupported descriptor type.
- Ensure that the device returns STALL in response to receiving a Set Feature request for an unsupported feature.
- Suspend and resume the device.
- If the device supports remote wakeup, suspend the device and request the user to perform an action to wake the device.

The software has two modes. Compliance Test mode runs the entire test suite. Debug mode enables selecting and running a single test within the suite and offers more control, such as selecting a configuration to use when running a test.

Additional test suites in both USB20CV and USB30CV provide tests for devices in the HID, USB 2.0 hub, mass-storage, personal-healthcare, and video classes and devices that return OTG descriptors. USB30CV also has tests for USB 3.0 link-layer and UASP protocols. USB 3.0 hubs have their own testing tool, HUB30CV.

Interoperability tests

Interoperability (*interop* for short) tests emulate a user's experience by testing a device with different host controllers and with a variety of other USB devices in use at the same time. Using USB20CV, a A USB 2.0 device must pass the interop tests under EHCI, UHCI, and OHCI hosts, including testing under a tier of five external hubs using maximum-length cables and under hubs operating at full and high speeds. Using USB30CV, a USB 2.0 device must pass the interop tests when attached to the root port of an xHCI host.

The USB 2.0 interop tests are documented in the USB-IF's *Full and Low Speed Electrical and Interoperability Compliance Test Procedure*. (The document, though not its title, was updated to include high speed.) The USB 3.0 interop tests are documented in the USB-IF's *xHCI Interoperability Test Procedures For Peripherals, Hubs, Hosts*.

USB 2.0 Gold Tree

The USB 2.0 tests use a Gold Tree configuration that contains a variety of hubs and other devices on the bus with the device under test. Check the USB-IF Compliance Updates page for any updates to the configuration. All of the Gold Tree components are for use with USB20CV except the xHCI adapter, which USB30CV uses. These are the components of the USB 2.0 Gold Tree:

Host system

- USB host system with a multicore processor, EHCI with embedded UHCI and PCI Express slots with compliant downspread spread-spectrum clocking (SSC).

- PCI Host Adapter, EHCI with embedded OHCI.

- PCI Host Adapter, xHCI.

Hubs

- Six self-powered hubs, high speed, with at least four exposed downstream ports each.

- One bus-powered hub operating at full speed, with at least two exposed downstream ports. (May be a compound device.)

Other devices

- One mouse, low speed, using interrupt transfers.
- Two mass-storage devices, high speed, using bulk transfers.
- One camera, high speed, using isochronous transfers.

The devices attach to the host in the configuration shown in Figure 18-9. Test labs can provide Gold Tree hardware setups for testing.

On attachment, the host must enumerate and install the driver for the device. If needed, the user may specify the driver's location. The device must operate properly while the other devices in the Gold Tree are also operating. The device must also continue to operate properly after each of these actions under the EHCI host:

- Detach the device's cable at the downstream-facing port and reattach to the same port.
- Unless the device has a hard-wired cable, detach the device's cable at the upstream-facing port and reattach to the same port.
- Do a warm boot. (**Start** > **Shutdown** > **Restart**.)
- Enter the S3 system power state and resume.
- Enter the S4 system power state and turn on.
- For devices that support remote wakeup, enter the S3 system power state and have the device wake the system.
- Stop operation of the device and attach the device to a root port.

Additional device tests under UHCI and OHCI hosts include device operation, Suspend and resume, and warm boot.

A high-speed device must also be fully functional at full speed unless the USB-IF grants a waiver. The test specification has more details about the tests.

A device should demonstrate device operation and pass the appropriate Chapter 9 tests at each bus speed the device supports.

SuperSpeed Interop Tree

USB30CV uses a SuperSpeed Interop Tree defined in *USB Implementers Forum xHCI Interoperability Test Procedures For Peripherals, Hubs, Hosts*. The document specifies a tree similar to the USB 2.0 Gold Tree but using only an XHCI host, using USB 3.0 hubs, and adding SuperSpeed peripherals.

Current measurement

The Current Measurement tests measure the bus current a device draws when in the unconfigured, configured, and Suspend states. In the unconfigured state, the device

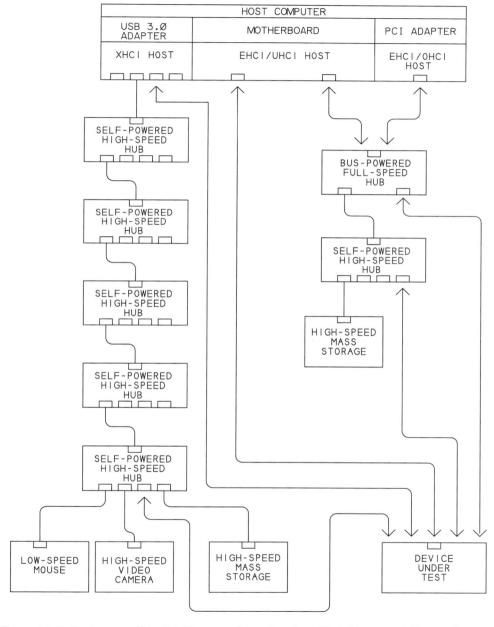

Figure 18-9. Devices use this Gold Tree configuration for USB 2.0 interopability testing.

should draw no more than 100 mA (USB 2.0) or 150 mA (SuperSpeed). When configured, the device should draw no more than the amount specified in the bMaxPower field of the configuration descriptor for the currently active configuration. In the Suspend state, the device should draw no more than 2.5 mA.

Electrical tests

Devices must also pass tests of signal quality, receiver sensitivity, timing, inrush current, and other aspects of electrical performance.

Documentation of the tests for full- and low-speed devices are in the *Full and Low Speed Electrical and Interoperability Compliance Test Procedure*. Documentation and tools for high speed and SuperSpeed tests are in additional documents and files on the USB-IF's website.

Certified USB Logo

A device that passes compliance testing is eligible to display the Certified USB logo. The logo indicates if a device supports SuperSpeed, SuperSpeedPlus, high speed, Certified Wireless USB, and USB OTG (Figure 18-10). To use the logo, you must sign the USB-IF Trademark License Agreement. If you're not a member of the USB-IF, you must pay a logo administration fee ($3500 at this writing). The logo is different from the USB icon described in Chapter 19.

A device can earn a USB logo without passing every test. At its discretion, the USB-IF may grant a waiver of a requirement. For example, before the specification increased the limit for all devices, the USB-IF granted waivers to devices that drew up to 2.5 mA in the Suspend state. In considering whether to grant a waiver, the USB-IF considers the effect of the violation on the user's experience and other USB products, the product's market size, and the vendor's cost to correct the violation.

Windows hardware certification

The Windows Hardware Certification Program licenses Windows logos for display by products that meet Microsoft's standards for compatibility, reliability, and security. To earn the right to display a logo on a product and its marketing materials, the vendor must submit test logs that demonstrate that the product meets Microsoft's requirements.

Benefits of a Windows logo include increased customer confidence in the product, the ability to distribute drivers via Windows Update, and inclusion in the Windows Certified Products List.

Figure 18-10. Devices that pass compliance testing can display a Certified USB logo. The logo indicates if the device supports high speed, SuperSpeed, SuperSpeedPlus, OTG, or Wireless USB as appropriate. (Images courtesy of the USB Implementers Forum.)

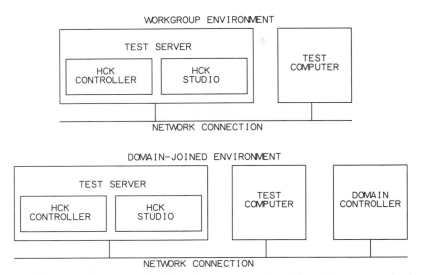

Figure 18-11. Windows Hardware Certification tests require at least two networked computers.

Participating in the Hardware Certification program requires establishing a Windows Certification account and signing a Logo License Agreement and Windows Certification Program Testing Agreement.

Microsoft charges no fee for hardware certification, but each vendor must pay a fee to obtain a Microsoft Authenticode certificate that identifies the company and provides a code-signing ID for submitting files. Multiple vendors offer certificates. At this writing, the per-year fees are in the $200–$500 range.

The description that follows is an overview of the Hardware Certification process. Check the Windows hardware certification web page and the WDK for full details and updates.

Windows hardware certification

The Windows Hardware Certification Kit (HCK) is a free test framework for certifying hardware devices and their drivers. Certification is limited to devices whose function matches one of the Microsoft-defined product types (for example, keyboard, storage, camera, USB hub). A device that doesn't fit a defined function can't display a Windows logo but can use a signed driver, and Windows Update can distribute the driver.

An HCK test environment requires a minimum of two computers with a network connection. The environment has these components (Figure 18-11):

The HCK test server, or controller, runs the Windows HCK Controller and Windows HCK Studio software. Windows HCK Controller manages the tests, and Windows HCK Studio selects and schedules tests. The HCK test server must be running a recent version of Windows Server. The HCK Controller and HCK Studio software can run on the same computer or on different computers. Beginning with Windows 8.1, the HCK test server can also run HCK test suites from a command-prompt window or from Visual Studio.

The HCK test computer, or client computer, is the host computer for the target device under test. The HCK test computer must be running the Windows version under test for certification. For testing USB devices, the test computer must have an xHCI controller and either an EHCI controller or a high-speed hub. A single HCK test server can have multiple HCK test computers.

The HCK test server and test computer may be two computers in the same workgroup, or you can join the computers using a third computer that functions as a domain controller. The domain controller must be running Windows Server with Active Directory Domain Services installed.

To test a device, from HCK Studio, you add the test computer to a machine pool, create a project, and select the target device. The software detects the device features that interact with Windows and generates a set of tests. When a device has passed all required tests, HCK Studio can create a submission package to complete the certification process.

The HCK test categories include device fundamentals, connectivity, and function.

Device fundamentals includes PnP, driver, and power tests.

For USB devices, the connectivity tests relate to USB communications. The vendor must submit the test ID that the USB-IF provides on passing compliance tests. Additional tests verify that the device:

- Responds only to its assigned bus address.
- Responds properly to standard descriptor requests.
- Is available within 500 ms after the system exits the S3 or S4 power state.
- Is configured within 100 ms after host software enables the device.
- Responds properly to repeated enumeration requests.
- Responds properly to suspend and resume requests.
- Resumes properly after the system exits the S3 power state (repeated tests).
- Enumerates under ECHI and xHCI host controllers and under full-speed, high-speed, and SuperSpeed hubs.
- Handles simulated failures initiated by the Windows USB client driver feature of

the USB 3.0 driver stack.

- For devices with serial numbers, returns a unique serial number (tests two devices with the same Vendor ID and Product ID).
- Has no default interface that consumes isochronous bandwidth.
- Responds properly to a request for a Microsoft ContainerID descriptor.

A USB 3.0 device must:

- Always connect at SuperSpeed when SuperSpeed is available.
- Respond properly to Function Suspend and Selective Suspend.

Hubs have additional tests.

The function category tests device functions such as audio, storage, input, imaging, and streaming.

Windows 7 and Windows 8 each have their own logo. A single logo indicates compatibility with Windows 8 and Windows RT.

For developers of device drivers, the USB client driver verifier included in Windows 8 and higher can help in creating robust drivers by simulating various failures. The HCK includes a USB Verifier Test that runs simulated test cases.

Driver signatures

A Windows software driver for a USB device must have a digital signature provided by a catalog (*.cat*) file associated with the driver or embedded in the driver itself. Windows uses digital signatures to identify the source, or publisher, of a driver and to verify that driver files haven't been modified since the driver was signed.

When a driver package passes HCK testing, the vendor can submit the test logs to obtain a Windows Hardware Quality Labs (WHQL) release signature for the driver package. Microsoft distributes drivers with WHQL signatures through the Windows Update program.

During testing and debugging, a developer can test-sign a driver using tools provided with Visual Studio and the WDK.

An INF file can name a catalog file that contains cryptographic hash values that identify the driver's files. A digitally signed catalog file serves as a digital signature that the OS uses to determine whether the driver files have been altered since the signature was created. Each INF file has a single catalog file, but one INF file can support multiple devices. Any change in an INF file, including adding or editing a Product ID, device release number, or string, requires a new digital signature.

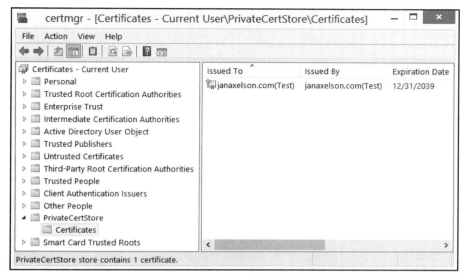

Figure 18-12. The Certificate Manager shows a system's certificate stores and their contents.

Windows keeps information relating to digital signatures in databases called *certificate stores*. To view the certificate stores, open the Certificate Manager snap-in, *certmgr.msc* (Figure 18-12), typically in *\%SystemRoot%\system32*. The default view displays certificates organized by logical stores.

The Trusted Publishers store lists Certificates from certification authorities that are trusted by the system's Software Restriction policies. Users with administrator privileges can add publishers to this store. The Trusted Root Certification Authorities certificate store contains information about CAs that have met Microsoft's requirements. Users with administrator privileges can add private CAs to this store.

PrivateCertStore can contain certificates used to test-sign drivers.

Whether Windows allows a driver to be installed varies depending on the Windows edition, the security settings, whether the user installing the driver has administrator privileges, and whether the driver is signed. If the driver is signed, successful installation can depend on the source of the signature, whether the driver publisher's certificate is in the system's Trusted Publishers certificate store, and whether the CA that issued the publisher's certificate is in the Trusted Root Certification Authorities certificate store.

The 64-bit Windows editions require signed drivers. The 32-bit Windows editions will install unsigned drivers but may display warnings depending on system settings.

A driver signed by the Windows hardware certification program installs without triggering security warnings. For other signed drivers, a dialog box with a security warning may appear if the driver publisher's certificate isn't in the computer's Trusted Publishers certificate store. In the dialog box, selecting the option to always trust software from the publisher adds that publisher to the system's Trusted Publishers certificate store.

Test-signing a driver

As mentioned in Chapter 9, you can test-sign a driver for use on a single machine at no charge. To enable test-signing of drivers, you first create a test certificate on the system. Then to test-sign a driver, you add an entry for a catalog file in the INF file and create and test-sign the catalog file.

Create a test certificate

To test-sign drivers, the development PC must have a digital certificate that verifies the system's identity. A PC needs only one certificate to support test-signing of multiple drivers.

Visual Studio includes the MakeCert tool, which can create a digital certificate for use in test-signing drivers. You can run MakeCert from the Visual Studio Command Prompt. From the Programs menu, select **Microsoft Visual Studio <version> > Visual Studio Tools**. Right-click **Developer Command Prompt for <version>** and select **Run as Administrator.**

Here is an example command to enter in the Visual Studio Command Prompt window (as one line):

MakeCert -r -pe -ss PrivateCertStore -n CN=janaxelson.com(Test) janaxelsonTest.cer

where

-r specifies that the certificate is self-signed (not signed by a CA).

-pe specifies that the private key associated with the certificate can be exported, for example to removable media or another computer.

-ss PrivateCertStore supplies the name of the certificate store that contains the test certificate. Microsoft's documentation recommends using PrivateCertStore as the certificate store for a test certificate to keep it separate from other certificates in the computer.

CN=janaxelson.com(Test) identifies the certificate.

janaxelsonTest.cer is the file that will contain the test certificate.

After executing the command, the CertMgr snap-in should show the certificate janaxelson.com(Test) in the example) in **PrivateCertStore > Certificates**.

Install the test certificate

To enable verifying a test signature, the test certificate must be installed in both the Trusted Root Certification Authorities certificate store and the Trusted Publishers certificate store in the PC that will verify the test signature.

Visual Studio's CrtMgr tool (*certmgr.exe*), typically in the WDK's *\bin\x86* or *\bin\x64* directory, can install a certificate. Note that CrtMgr (*certmgr.exe*) is different from Certificate Manager (*certmgr.msc*).

Run *certmgr.exe* from the Visual Studio Command Prompt.

This command adds the certificate *janaxelsonTest.cer* to the Trusted Root Certification Authorities certificate store on the test computer:

CertMgr.exe /add janaxelsonTest.cer /s /r localMachine root

where

/add janaxelsonTest.cer specifies the certificate to add to the store. Be sure to include the *.cer* extension.

/s specifies that the certificate store is a system store.

/r localMachine specifies that the certificate store is under the HKEY_LOCAL_MACHINE registry key.

root is the certificate store name for trusted root CAs. Supported store names are members of .NET's StoreName enumeration.

In a similar way, this command adds janaxelsonTest.cer to the Trusted Publishers certificate store on the test computer:

CertMgr.exe /add janaxelsonTest.cer /s /r localMachine trustedpublisher

Enable test-signing

By default, Windows disables the ability to load test-signed kernel-mode code. To enable loading test-signed code, open a command prompt as administrator and enter:

Bcdedit.exe -set TESTSIGNING ON

and reboot.

To turn test-signing off, enter:

Bcdedit.exe -set TESTSIGNING OFF

To enable turning test-signing on, you may need to disable Secure Boot in the PC's UEFI Firmware Settings.

Reference a catalog file in the INF file

Chapter 9 introduced the syntax of INF files. To reference a catalog file in an INF file, add an entry in the Version section of the INF file:

CatalogFile=Filename.Cat

where

Filename.Cat is the name of the catalog file to be created. For example:

CatalogFile=Cdclvr.Cat

If needed, the entry can specify a platform:

CatalogFile.ntamd64=Cdclvramd64.Cat
CatalogFile.ntx86=Cdclvrx86.Cat

Each catalog file referenced in the INF file must have a unique name.

Create the catalog file

To create a catalog file for an INF file, use Visual Studio's Inf2Cat tool. At the Visual Studio command prompt, enter:

Inf2Cat /driver:DriverPath /os:WindowsVersionList

where

/driver:DriverPath is the directory that contains the INF file. Inf2Cat will attempt to create a catalog file for every INF file in the directory so if you want to create a catalog file for a single INF file, be sure it's the only one in the directory.

/os:WindowsVersionList specifies the Windows versions that Inf2Cat will verify signing requirements for.

For example, this command:

Inf2Cat /driver:c:\Users\jan\Documents\lvrcdc /os:7_X86,7_X64,8_X86,8_X64

creates a catalog file for the INF file in *c:\Users\jan\Documents\lvrcdc* and verifies the signing requirements for Windows 7 and Windows 8, 32-bit and 64-bit versions.

Do include a space before each parameter list. (A parameter list begins with "/".)

Do not add spaces within the parameter lists. For example, don't use a space between **/os:** and the first OS specifier or between the comma-separated OS specifiers. If the filename or path contains spaces, enclose the filename and path in quotes.

To copy a path, in Windows Explorer, click to the right of the displayed path in the address bar. The path will change to a full path, highlighted for copying. For example, this:

Libraries > Documents > lvrcdc

changes to:

c:\Users\jan\Documents\lvrcdc

To paste a copied path and filename in the command line, right-click and select **Paste**. If pasting quotes, be sure to paste straight, not curly, quotes.

To view the supported Windows version identifiers and other help for the tool, at the command prompt, enter **Inf2Cat** with no options.

Test-sign the catalog file

To test-sign a catalog file, use Visual Studio's SignTool utility. At the Visual Studio Command prompt, enter (as one line):

SignTool sign /v /s TestCertStoreName /n TestCertName /t http://timestamp.verisign.com/scripts/timstamp.dll CatalogFileName.cat

where

sign configures SignTool to sign a catalog file.

/v configures SignTool to display messages.

/s TestCertStoreName supplies the name of a test certificate store

/n TestCertName supplies the name of the test certificate installed in TestCertStore-Name.

/t http://timestamp.verisign.com/scripts/timstamp.dll supplies the URL to a publicly-available time-stamp server.

CatalogFileName.cat is the name of the catalog file to be signed. If the command says the catalog file can't be found, include the file's path in the command.

For example (as one line):

SignTool sign /v /s PrivateCertStore /n janaxelson.com(Test) /t http://timestamp.verisign.com/scripts/timstamp.dll c:\Users\jan\Documents\lvrcdc\lvrcdc.cat

Note there is no "e" in **timstamp.dll**.

Assign the driver to a device

On attaching a device with a test-signed driver, Windows should assign the driver without complaint. If necessary, on first attachment, point to the location of the device's INF file.

Another option for installing unsigned drivers is to disable driver signature enforcement in the startup setting on boot up. Select the Advanced Boot Option **Disable Driver Signature Enforcement**. On the next reboot, driver signature enforcement will be re-enabled.

Microsoft USB Test Tool (MUTT)

The Microsoft USB Test Tool (MUTT) software package and MUTT devices can help in testing host controllers, drivers, and devices.

MUTT devices

A MUTT device is a circuit board that emulates a USB 2.0 or USB 3.0 device or a hub. MUTT devices are designed by Microsoft and available from hardware vendors listed on the Microsoft Hardware Dev Center website.

The MUTT Pack is a MUTT device that contains a USB 2.0 hub with two downstream ports. One port connects on-board to a Cypress FX2 device controller that can control hub operations. The second, exposed port is available for attaching a device under test. The SuperMUTT Pack is similar but contains a USB 3.0 hub.

For testing host-controller hardware and hubs, the MUTT and SuperMUTT devices contain an FX2 or FX3 device that simulates USB 2.0 or USB 3.0 traffic. These devices have no hub or downstream port.

MUTT Software Package

The MUTT Software Package contains a variety of tools for testing. The software is a free download from the Hardware Dev Center.

MUTTUtil tests host controllers, hubs, and other devices with the Microsoft USB driver stack. Tests for devices include turning VBUS on and off and setting and clearing an overcurrent condition. You can run USB-IF and HCK tests with a device connected to a MUTT Pack or SuperMUTT Pack.

The USB3HWVerifierAnalyzer command-line tool logs hardware events. The software flags errors including bad responses to standard requests and bad data returned in response to standard requests. The device being monitored must connect under a USB 3.0 host. You can log events for all hardware or specify a Vendor ID and/or Product ID. You can view the logged events in real time or after logging is completed, you can view the *.etl* log in Netmon or convert the log to a text file for viewing.

USBStress performs a variety of tests in random order on a MUTT device.

USBTCD initiates control, bulk, and isochronous data transfers for performance measurements.

Chapter 17 introduced these additional MUTT utilities:

USBLPM monitors USB 3.0 link states and can test transitions between the U0, U1, and U2 states.

PwrTest can list available power states and initiate transitions to different states.

19

Packets on the Bus

Understanding how data is encoded on the bus can help in understanding the capabilities and limits of devices. This chapter presents the essentials of the USB's encoding and data formats for USB 2.0 and USB 3.1.

USB 2.0

The USB 2.0 specification defines bus states that correspond to signal voltages on the bus or conditions that the voltages signify. Different cable segments may be in different bus states. For example, in response to a request from the host, a hub might place one of its downstream ports in the Reset state while its other ports are in the Idle state. Low/full speed and high speed each have different defined bus states.

Low speed and full speed bus states

Low and full speed use the same bus states though some are defined differently depending on the speed of the cable segment. A low-speed segment is a segment between a low-speed device and its nearest hub. A full-speed segment is any other segment that carries data at low- or full-speed bit rates.

Differential 0 and Differential 1

When transferring data, the two states on the bus are Differential 0 and Differential 1. A Differential 0 exists when D+ is a logic low and D- is a logic high. A Differential 1 exists when D+ is a logic high and D- is a logic low. Chapter 19 describes the voltage levels.

The Differential 0s and 1s don't translate directly into zero and one data states but instead indicate either a change in logic level, no change in logic level, or a bit stuff, as explained later in this chapter.

Single-ended 0

The Single-ended 0 (SE0) state occurs when both D+ and D- are logic low. The bus uses the SE0 state when entering the EOP, Disconnect, and Reset states.

Single-ended 1

The complement of SE0 is the Single-ended 1 (SE1). This state occurs when both D+ and D- are logic high. SE1 is an invalid bus state and should never occur.

Data J and Data K

In addition to the Differential 0 and Differential 1 states, which are defined by voltages, USB also defines two Data bus states, J and K. These are defined by whether the bus state is Differential 0 or Differential 1 and the speed of the cable segment:

Bus State	Data State	
	Low Speed	Full Speed
Differential 0	Data J	Data K
Differential 1	Data K	Data J

Defining the J and K states in this way makes it possible to use one terminology to describe an event or logic state even though the voltages on low- and full-speed lines differ. For example, a Start-of-Packet state exists when the bus changes from Idle to the K state. On a full-speed segment, the state occurs when D- becomes more positive than D+, while on a low-speed segment, the state occurs when D+ becomes more positive than D-.

Idle

In the Idle state, no drivers are active. On a full-speed segment, D+ is more positive than D-, while on a low-speed segment, D- is more positive than D+. Shortly after device attachment, a hub determines whether a device is low or full speed by checking the voltages on the Idle bus at the device's port.

Resume

When a device is in the Suspend state, a Data K state at the device's port signifies a resume from Suspend.

Start-of-Packet

The Start-of-Packet (SOP) bus state exists when the lines change from the Idle state to the K data state. Every transmitted low- or full-speed packet begins with an SOP.

End-of-Packet

The End-of-Packet (EOP) state exists when a receiver has been in the SE0 state for at least one bit time followed by a Data J state for at least one bit time. A receiver may optionally accept a shorter minimum time for the Data J state. Every transmitted low- or full-speed packet ends with an EOP.

Disconnect

A downstream port is in the Disconnect state when an SE0 has persisted for at least 2.5 µs.

Connect

A downstream port enters the Connect state when the bus has been in the Idle state for at least 2.5 µs and no more than 2.0 ms.

Reset

When an SE0 has lasted for 10 ms, the device must be in the Reset state. A device may enter the Reset state after an SE0 of at least 2.5 µs. A full-speed device that is capable of high-speed communications performs the high-speed handshake during the Reset state.

On exiting the Reset state, a device must be operating at its correct speed and must respond to communications directed to the default address (0x00).

High speed bus states

Many of the high-speed bus states correspond to states for low and full speed, but a few are unique to high speed, and some low/full-speed states have no equivalents at high speed.

High-speed Differential 0 and Differential 1

The two bus states that exist when transferring high-speed data are High-speed Differential 0 and High-speed Differential 1. As with low and full speeds, a High-speed Differential 0 exists when D+ is a logic low and D- is a logic high, and a High-speed Differential 1 exists when D+ is a logic high and D- is a logic low. The voltage requirements differ at high speed, however, and high speed has additional requirements for AC differential levels.

High-speed Data J and Data K

The definitions for High-speed Data J and Data K states correspond to the definitions for full-speed J and K.

Bus State	Data State (high speed)
Differential 0	High-speed Data K
Differential 1	High-speed Data J

Chirp J and Chirp K

The Chirp J and Chirp K bus states are present only during the high-speed detection handshake. The handshake occurs when a USB 2.0 hub has placed a downstream bus segment in the Reset state. In a Chirp J, D+ is more positive than D-, and in a Chirp K, D- is more positive than D+.

A high-speed device must use full speed on attaching to the bus. The high-speed detection handshake enables a high-speed device to tell a USB 2.0 hub that the device supports high speed and to transition to high-speed communications.

As Chapter 4 explained, shortly after detecting device attachment, a device's hub places a device's port and bus segment in the Reset state. When a high-speed-capable device detects the Reset, the device places its line in the Chirp K state for 1–7 ms. A hub that communicates upstream at high speed detects the Chirp K and in response, sends an alternating sequence of Chirp K and Chirp J. The sequence continues until shortly before the Reset state ends. On detecting the Chirp K and Chirp J sequence, the device disconnects its full-speed pull-up, enables its high-speed terminations, and enters the Default state. A hub that communicates upstream at low/full speed ignores the device's Chirp K. The device doesn't see the answering sequence and knows that communications must take place at full speed.

High-speed Squelch

The High-speed Squelch state indicates an invalid signal. High-speed receivers must include circuits that detect the Squelch state, indicated by a differential bus voltage of 100 mV or less.

High-speed Idle

In the High-speed Idle state, no high-speed drivers are active and the low/full-speed drivers assert SE0. Both D+ and D- are between -10 mV and +10 mV.

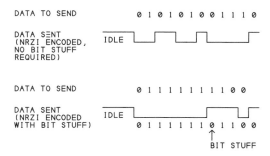

Figure 19-1. In NRZI encoding, a zero causes a change and a 1 causes no change. Bit stuffing adds a zero after six consecutive 1s.

Start of High-speed Packet

A Start-of-High-speed Packet (HSSOP) exists when a segment changes from the High-speed Idle state to the High-speed Data K state. Every high-speed packet begins with a Start of High-speed Packet.

End of High-speed Packet

An End of High-speed Packet (HSEOP) exists when the bus changes from the High-speed Data K or Data J state to the High-speed Idle state. Every high-speed packet ends with an End of High-speed Packet.

High-speed Disconnect

Removing a high-speed device from the bus also removes the high-speed line terminations at the device. Removing the terminations causes the differential voltage at the hub's port to double. A differential voltage of at least 625 mV on the data lines indicates the High-speed Disconnect state. USB 2.0 hubs contain circuits that detect this voltage.

Data encoding

All data on a USB 2.0 bus is encoded using a format called *non-return to zero inverted* (NRZI) with bit stuffing. The encoding ensures that the receiver remains synchronized with the transmitter without the overhead of sending a separate clock signal or Start and Stop bits with each byte.

If you use an oscilloscope or logic analyzer to view USB data on the bus, you'll find that reading the bits isn't as easy as matching voltage levels to logic levels. Instead of defining logic zeros and ones as voltages, NRZI encoding defines logic zero as a voltage change, and logic one as a voltage that remains the same. Figure 19-1 shows an example. Each logic zero results in a change from the previous state. Each logic one results in no change in the voltages. The bits transmit least-significant-bit first.

Fortunately, USB hardware performs the encoding and decoding automatically so device developers and programmers don't have to do it. As Chapter 18 showed, a protocol analyzer decodes the data for you.

Staying synchronized

Unlike other interfaces, USB requires no Start and Stop bits or clock line in the cable. Instead, USB 2.0 synchronizes the sender and receiver by using bit stuffing and SYNC fields. These extra bits add some overhead, but the amount is minimal, especially with large packets.

Bit stuffing

The encoding uses bit stuffing because the receiver synchronizes on transitions. Data that is all zeros has plenty of transitions. But for data that contains a long string of 1s, the lack of transitions could cause the receiver to get out of sync.

After six consecutive 1s, the transmitter stuffs, or inserts, a zero (represented by a transition). The bit stuffing ensures at least one transition for every seven bit widths. The receiver detects and discards any bit that follows six consecutive 1s. The overhead for bit-stuffing in random data is just 0.8%, or one stuff bit per 125 data bits.

SYNC field

Because devices and the host don't share a clock, the receiver has no way of knowing exactly when a transmitter will send a transition that marks the beginning of a new packet. Thus, each packet begins with a SYNC field to enable the receiving device to align, or synchronize, its clock to the transmitted data. For low and full speeds, the SYNC pattern is eight bits: KJKJKJKK. The transition from Idle to the first K serves as a sort of Start bit that indicates the arrival of a new packet.

For high speed, the SYNC pattern is 32 bits: fifteen KJ repetitions, followed by KK. A high-speed hub repeating a packet can drop up to four bits from the beginning of the sync field, so a SYNC field repeated by the fifth external hub in series can be as short as 12 bits.

The alternating Ks and Js provide transitions for synchronizing, and the final two Ks mark the end of the field. After receiving the SYNC pattern, the receiving device can accurately clock in the remaining bits in the packet. The price for synchronizing is adding between 8 and 32 bit times to each packet. Large packets are thus more efficient than smaller ones.

End of packet

An EOP returns the bus to the Idle state in preparation for the next SYNC field. The EOP signal is different for low/full and high speed.

The low- or full-speed EOP is an SE0 that lasts for two bit widths.

At high speed, the signal is more complicated. High-speed receivers treat any bit-stuff error as an end of packet, so an HSEOP must cause a bit-stuff error.

For all high-speed packets except SOFs, the HSEOP is an encoded byte of 01111111_b without bit stuffing. If the preceding bit was a J, the HSEOP is KKKKKKKK. The initial zero causes the first bit to be a change of state from J to K, and the following 1s mean that the rest of the bits don't change. If the preceding bit was a K, the HSEOP is JJJJJJJJ. The initial zero causes the first bit to be a change of state from K to J, and the following 1s mean that the rest of the bits don't change. In either case, the sequence of seven 1s causes a bit stuff error.

In high-speed SOFs, the HSEOP is 40 bits. This larger packet allows a hub time to detect the doubled differential voltage that indicates that a device has been removed from the bus. The encoded byte begins with a zero, followed by 39 ones, which results in an HSEOP consisting of 40 Js or 40 Ks. As with low and full speeds, this sequence results in a bit-stuff error that the receiver treats as an EOP.

Timing accuracy

One tradeoff of increased speed is stricter timing requirements. High speed has the strictest timing, while low speed is the most tolerant. These are the tolerances for the clock at each speed:

Speed	Tolerance (percent)
Low	1.5
Full	0.25
High	0.05

Devices typically derive their timing from a crystal. Many factors can affect a crystal's frequency, including initial accuracy, capacitive loading, aging of the crystal, supply voltage, and temperature. Because of its wider tolerance, low speed can use inexpensive ceramic resonators instead of quartz crystals

The signaling rate at a host or USB 2.0 hub must be within 0.05%, of the specified rate at all speeds. The frame intervals must be accurate as well, at 1 ms ±500 ns per frame or 125.0 ±62.5 µs per microframe. Each hub has its own timing source and synchronizes its transmissions to the host's SOF signals in each frame or microframe.

The USB specification also defines limits for data jitter, which is small variations in the timing of the individual bit transitions. Factors that affect data jitter are differences in the rise and fall times of the drivers, clock jitter, and random noise.

Packet format

As Chapter 2 explained, all USB 2.0 data travels in packets, which contain information in defined fields. Table 19-1 shows the fields that USB 2.0 packets contain.

SYNC

Each packet begins with an 8-bit SYNC field, defined earlier. The SYNC Field serves as the Start-of-Packet delimiter.

Packet identifier

The packet identifier field (PID) is 8 bits. Bits 3..0 identify the packet type and bits 7..4 are the complement of these bits for use in error checking.

Chapter 2 introduced the PID codes for token, data, handshake and special packets. The lower two bits identify the PID type, and the upper two bits identify the specific PID.

Address

The address field is seven bits that identify the device the host is communicating with.

Endpoint

The endpoint field is four bits that identify an endpoint number within a device.

Frame number

The frame-number field is eleven bits that identify the frame. The host sends this data in the SOF packet that begins each frame or microframe. Following 0x7FF, the number rolls over to zero. A full-speed host maintains an 11-bit counter that increments once per frame. A high-speed host maintains a 14-bit counter that increments once per microframe. Only bits 3–13 of the microframe counter transmit in the frame number field, so the frame number increments once per frame, with eight microframes in sequence having the same frame number.

Data

The Data field may range from 0–1024 bytes for USB 2.0 and from 0–1023 bytes for USB 1.1. The transfer type may limit the maximum size.

Table 19-1: USB 2.0 packets contain fields with defined contents.

Field Name	SIze (bits)	Packet Types	Purpose
SYNC	8	all	Start of packet and synchronization
PID	8	all	Identify the packet type
Address	7	IN, OUT, Setup	Identify the function address
Endpoint	4	IN, OUT, Setup	Identify the endpoint
Frame Number	11	SOF	Identify the frame
Data	USB 2.0: 0 to 8192 (1024 bytes) USB 1.1: 0 to 8184 (1023 bytes)	Data0, Data1	Data
Token CRC	5	IN, OUT, Setup	Detect errors
Data CRC	16	Data0, Data1	Detect errors

CRC

The CRC field is 5 bits for address and endpoint fields and 16 bits for data fields. The transmitting hardware normally inserts the CRC bits and the receiving hardware does the required error checking.

Inter-packet delay

USB 2.0 carries data from multiple sources, in both directions, on one pair of wires. Data can travel in just one direction at a time. To ensure that the previous transmitting device has had time to switch off its driver, the bus requires a brief delay between the end of one packet and the beginning of the next packet in a transaction. This delay is short, however, and devices must switch directions quickly.

The USB specification defines the delays differently for low/full and high speed. The delays are handled by hardware and require no support in code.

Test modes

For use in compliance testing, the USB 2.0 specification added five test modes that all host controllers, hubs, and high-speed-capable devices must support.

An upstream-facing port enters a test mode in response to a Set Feature request with TEST_MODE in the wValue field. A downstream-facing port enters a test mode in response to the hub-class request Set Port Feature with PORT_TEST in the wValue field. In both cases, the wIndex field contains the port number and the test number. All downstream ports on a hub with a port to be tested must be in the suspended, disabled, or disconnected state.

An upstream-facing port exits the test mode when the device powers down and back up. A downstream-facing port exits the test mode when the hub is reset.

The test modes enable testing characteristics such as output drive level on D+ and D-, output impedance, low-level output voltage, loading characteristics, device squelch-level circuits, rise and fall times, eye pattern, jitter, and the disconnect-detection threshold.

USB 3.1

The signaling rates, dual-simplex interface, and new power-management capabilities of Enhanced SuperSpeed require different encoding, packet formats, and low-level protocols. The transmitter scrambles and encodes data to be sent on the bus, and the receiver decodes and de-scrambles the received data.

Data scrambling

Data scrambling eliminates repetitive patterns in the data, spreading the radiated EMI over a wider frequency spectrum and helping meeting FCC requirements. To scramble data to be transmitted, a free-running linear feedback shift register implements a polynomial defined in the USB 3.1 specification. The transmitter XORs the output of the shift register with the data bits. Descrambling uses a complementary mechanism to recover the unscrambled data.

SuperSpeed scrambles all transmitted data. SuperSpeedPlus scrambles symbols in data blocks and may scramble symbols in control blocks depending on the symbol type. Scrambling can be disabled for debugging.

Encoding

SuperSpeed uses 8b/10b data encoding as specified in ANSI INCITS 230-1994. Other interfaces that use this encoding include PCI Express, Gigabit Ethernet and IEEE-1394b. The encoding converts each byte value to a 10-bit Data Symbol for transmitting. The encoded data has no more than five ones or zeros in series and contains equal numbers of ones and zeros over time.

As with USB 2.0 data, frequent transitions enable the receiver to synchronize with the transmitted data without requiring a separate clock line. The roughly equal numbers of transmitted ones and zeros provide DC balance, which prevents errors due to a DC component, or offset, in the signal. The encoding also enables error detecting by monitoring the number of received ones and zeros over time.

Because the encoded data has more bits than the data being encoded, extra symbols are available to perform special functions. Data Symbols represent values from 0x00 to 0xFF and Special Symbols perform functions used in framing data and managing link-level communications.

The SuperSpeed signaling rate, or speed of the bits on the wires in each direction, is 5 Gbps. The USB 3.1 specification refers to the rate as 5 GT/s (GigaTransfers / s). The 8b/10b encoding increases the number of bits to be transmitted by 25%, so 5 Gbps on the bus translates to 4 Gbps, or 500 MB/s, of unencoded data. Framing, error detecting, and other protocols reduce the theoretical maximum data throughput to around 460 MB/s in each direction.

SuperSpeedPlus has less overhead due to its use of 128b/132b encoding, where a 132-byte payload contains 128 bytes of data. The transmitter prepends a 4-bit Block Header to a 128-bit payload made up of sixteen 8-bit symbols. The header indicates whether the payload contains a data block or a control block.

The SuperSpeedPlus signaling rate is 10 Gbps. The USB 3.1 specification refers to the rate as 10 GT/s (GigaTransfers / s). The 128b/132b encoding increases the number of bits to be transmitted by about 3.1%, so 10 Gbps on the bus translates to 9.69 Gbps, or 1.21 GB/s, of unencoded data. Other overhead reduces the theoretical maximum data throughput to around 1.1 GB/s in each direction.

Link layer

An Enhanced SuperSpeed link is the physical and logical connection between two ports. The physical connection consists of a cable segment and the two ports, or link partners, that the cable connects. The link partners manage the link by communicating using link commands and other signaling when the wires aren't carrying other traffic.

Each port provides state machines and buffers to manage the connection and data transfers with the link partner. State machines generate link commands to acknowledge received header packets, recover from errors, implement flow control, and manage power on the link. An upstream-facing port must detect when its link has been idle for 10 μs and send a special link command to indicate that the port is present.

Link commands transmit when the link isn't carrying TPs. Downstream-facing ports detect device connection and removal and wakeup signaling. Link-layer protocols define how the link manages buffers, frames packets, and detects received packets. The link layer also handles training and synchronizing to establish connectivity between a device (which may be a hub) and its upstream link partner. To synchronize, a link partner transmits defined series of bytes called Ordered Sets, which the receiving link partner detects. SuperSpeed and SuperSpeedPlus use different Ordered Sets and have other differences in synchronizing protocols.

Reset

Enhanced SuperSpeed uses two categories of reset. A PowerOn Reset restores memory, registers, and other storage in the device to their default power-on states. An InBand Reset resets port settings and places the link in the U0 state while remaining powered. Two types of InBand Reset are the Warm Reset and Hot Reset. A Warm Reset uses low-frequency periodic signaling (defined below) and takes around 100 ms. A Hot Reset uses link-level training sequences of Ordered Sets, is much faster, and leaves more settings unchanged in the device.

The host requests an in InBand reset by issuing a hub-class Set Port Feature(Port_Reset) or SetPortFeature(BH_Port_Reset) request to the hub that is the target device's link partner. On receiving a request for a BH_Port_Reset, the hub issues a Warm Reset to the device. On receiving a request for a Port_Reset, if the link is in U3, the hub uses a Warm Reset, and if the link is in U0, the hub uses a Hot Reset. For other states, the USB 3.1 specification defines how a hub decides which reset to use.

Signaling

USB 3.1 links use low-frequency periodic signaling (LFPS) to implement functions such as exiting low-power states, performing Warm Resets, and link training. The signaling consists of bursts of a frequency in the range 10–50 MHz. This type of signaling is easy to generate and uses little power. Each defined LFPS signal has a specified burst length and, for some signals, a repeat rate. For example, the Polling.LFPS signal is a 1.0-µs burst that repeats every 6–14 µs.

Link partners operating at SuperSpeedPlus use a signaling method called LFPS Based PWM Signaling (LBPS) to find their highest shared capabilities.

Negotiating speed

The Polling state handles negotiating port capability and link training. On entering the Polling.LFPS substate, Enhanced SuperSpeed ports transmit the Polling.LFPS signal. A SuperSpeedPlus-capable port uses this signal to negotiate the highest data rate supported by both link partners.

To announce SuperSpeedPlus capability, a port transmits a SuperSpeedPlus Capability Declaration that consists of a Polling.LFPS signal using the SCD1 pattern. In this pattern, the port transmits the code 0010_b with the binary values encoded as different repeat rates.

A SuperSpeedPlus link partner continually transmits the SCD1 pattern. If a link partner doesn't receive an SCD1 pattern in 16 consecutive Polling.LFPS signals, the port switches to SuperSpeed operation and stops transmitting the SCD1 pattern in the Polling.LFPS signal.

On receiving two SCD1 patterns, a SuperSpeedPlus link partner enters the Polling.LFPSPlus substate and begins transmitting a second pattern called SCD2. On receiving two SCD2 patterns, the port transitions to the Polling.PortMatch substate where the link partners use LBPM to discover the highest capabilities shared by the SuperSpeedPlus link partners.

For a more in-depth discussion of low-level USB 3.0 protocols than presented here, see the book *USB 3.0 Technology* by Donovan Anderson and Jay Trodden.

20

Electrical and Mechanical Interface

All of the protocols and program code in the world are no use if the signals don't make it down the wires in good shape. The electrical and mechanical interface play an important part in making USB a reliable way to transfer information.

This chapter presents the essentials about drivers and receivers and options for cables and connectors for USB 2.0 and USB 3.1 plus a discussion of ways to connect other than with conventional cables, including wireless options.

USB 2.0

A USB 2.0 cable connects to transceivers that send and receive data on the bus. The device can use any of a number of different connectors.

Transceivers

The electrical signals on a USB 2.0 cable vary depending on the speed of the cable segment. Low-, full-, and high-speed signaling each use a different edge rate, which is a measure of the rise and fall times of the voltages on the lines and thus the amount of time required for an output to switch. The transceivers and supporting circuits that produce and detect the bus signals also vary depending on speed.

At any USB 2.0 speed, a transceiver must withstand the shorting of D+, D-, or both to GND, the other data line, or the cable shield at the connector. A requirement to withstand shorting to VBUS was reduced to a recommendation with the *5V Short Circuit Withstand Requirement Change* ECN to the USB 2.0 specification. Research showed that shorts to VBUS are extremely unlikely and that removing the requirement would allow reduced silicon area and power savings on chips.

Cable segments

A cable segment connects a device (which may be a hub) to an upstream hub (which may be a root hub at the host). A segment's speed depends on the speed of the final downstream device and the speeds supported by the host and any upstream hubs. Figure 20-1 illustrates.

A low-speed segment exists only between a low-speed device and its immediate upstream hub. A low-speed segment carries only low-speed data and uses low-speed's edge rate and an inverted polarity compared to full speed.

A full-speed segment exists between a full-speed device and its immediate upstream hub. Full-speed devices include USB 1.1 hubs, which may carry data to and from low-speed devices that connect to downstream ports on the hub. In this situation, the low-speed data on the full-speed segment uses low-speed's bit rate but full speed's polarity and edge rate. The hub that connects to the low-speed device converts between low and full speed's polarity and edge rates. Full-speed segments never carry data at high speed. A high-speed-capable device that connects to a USB 1.1 hub communicates at full speed.

When a device communicates at a USB 2.0 speed and all upstream hubs are USB 2.0 or USB 3.1, all segments are high speed with one exception. As noted above, if the device is low or full speed, the segment between the device and its nearest upstream hub is low or full speed. All data in a high-speed segment travels at high speed. The transaction translator in a downstream hub converts between low or full speed and high speed as needed. A USB 3.1 hub uses its USB 2.0 hub controller for USB 2.0 traffic.

On attachment, all USB 2.0 devices must communicate at low or full speed. When possible, a high-speed-capable device transitions from full to high speed during the high-speed detection handshake shortly after the host detects device attachment.

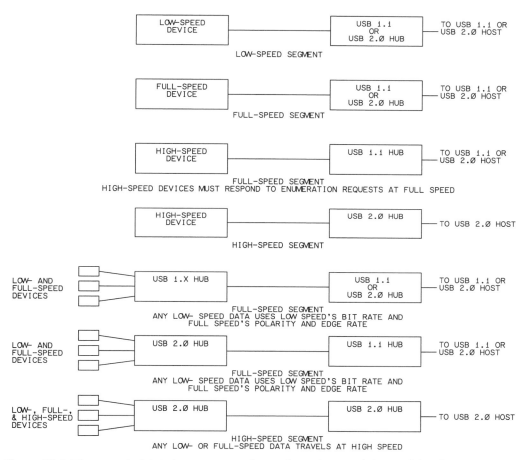

Figure 20-1. The speed of data in a segment depends on the capabilities of the device and its upstream hub.

Low-speed and full-speed transceivers

Transceivers for low and full speeds can have a simpler design compared to transceivers for high speed.

Differences

Low-speed data differs electrically from full-speed data in three ways. The bit rate is slower, at 1.5 Mbps compared to 12 Mbps for full speed. The polarity of low-speed traffic is inverted compared to full speed. And low speed has a slower edge rate compared to full speed. Figure 20-2 illustrates. The slower edge rate reduces the high-fre-

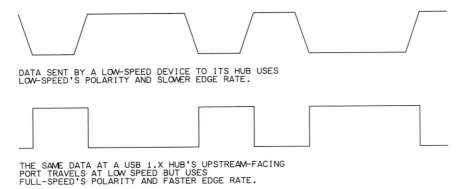

DATA SENT BY A LOW-SPEED DEVICE TO ITS HUB USES
LOW-SPEED'S POLARITY AND SLOWER EDGE RATE.

THE SAME DATA AT A USB 1.X HUB'S UPSTREAM-FACING
PORT TRAVELS AT LOW SPEED BUT USES
FULL-SPEED'S POLARITY AND FASTER EDGE RATE.

Figure 20-2. a USB 1.1 hub converts between low- and full-speed's polarities and edge rates. (Not drawn to scale.)

quency energy and reflected voltages on the line and makes it possible to use cables that have less shielding and are thus cheaper to make and physically more flexible.

The transceiver's hardware doesn't care about signal polarity. The transceiver just retransmits the logic levels at its inputs. A driver that supports both speeds, such as a driver for a hub's downstream port, must switch between the two edge rates as needed.

Circuits

Figure 20-3 shows port circuits for low- and full-speed devices. Each transceiver contains a differential driver and receiver for sending and receiving data on the bus's twisted pair.

When transmitting data, the driver has two outputs that are 180 degrees out of phase: when one output is high, the other is low. A single driver can support both low and full speeds with an input that selects the edge rate.

The differential receiver detects the voltage difference between the lines. A differential receiver has two inputs and defines logic levels in terms of the voltage difference between the inputs. The output of the differential receiver is also specified as a logic-high or logic-low voltage referenced to ground.

Each port has two single-ended receivers that detect the voltages on D+ and D- with reference to signal ground. The logic states of the receivers' outputs indicate whether the bus is low or full speed or if the bus is in the SE0 state.

The drivers' output impedances plus a series resistor at each driver's output act as source terminations that reduce reflected voltages when the outputs switch. The series resistors may be on-chip or external to the chip.

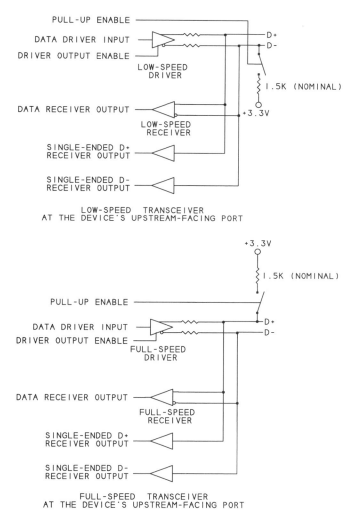

Figure 20-3. A low-speed device has a pull-up on D-, while a full-speed device has a pull-up on D+. Information source: *Universal Serial Bus Specification Revision 2.0.*

Pull-up and pull-down values

The pull-up resistor on D+ or D- at a device's upstream-facing port enables the hub to detect whether the device is low speed or full speed. The hub's downstream-facing port has pull-down resistors on D+ and D-.

On devices with detachable cables, the pull-up resistors must connect to a positive voltage of 3.0–3.6 V. Devices with captive cables can instead use an alternate means of termination, including connecting the resistor directly to VBUS. In selecting an alternate means of termination, the designer must ensure that all signal levels meet USB 2.0 requirements.

The USB 2.0 Engineering Change Notice *Pull-up/pull-down resistors* loosens the tolerances for pull-up and pull-down resistors that connect to a voltage source of 3.0–3.6 V. The original values were 1.5 kΩ ±5% for the pull-ups and 15 kΩ ±5% for the pull-downs. The new values for the pull-ups are 900–1575 Ω when the bus is idle and 1425–3090 Ω when the upstream device is transmitting. A 1.5 kΩ ±5% resistor meets both requirements. For the pull-downs, the resistance can be anywhere in the range 14.25 k–24.80 kΩ. The tolerances were loosened to make it easier to include the resistors on chip without requiring laser trimming of the values.

High-speed transceivers

A high-speed device must support control transfers at full speed, so the device must contain transceivers to support both full and high speeds and logic to switch between them. A high-speed-capable device's upstream-facing transceivers aren't allowed to support low speed. In an external USB 2.0 hub, the downstream transceivers at ports with user-accessible connectors must support all three speeds.

Why 480 Megabits?

The developers of the USB 2.0 specification chose high speed's rate of 480 Mbps for several reasons. The frequency is slow enough to allow using the same cables and connectors as full speed. Components can use CMOS processes and don't require the advanced compensation used in high-speed digital signal processors. Tests of high-speed drivers showed 20–30% jitter at 480 Mbps. Because receivers can be designed to tolerate 40% jitter, this bit rate allows a good margin of error. And 480 is an even multiple of 12, so a single crystal can support both full and high speeds.

The use of separate drivers for high speed makes it easy to add high speed to an existing full-speed design. Current-mode drivers were chosen because they can handle high speeds.

Circuits

Figure 20-4 shows upstream-facing transceiver circuits in a high-speed-capable device, and Figure 20-5 shows downstream-facing transceiver circuits in a USB 2.0 hub. The USB 2.0 specification requires downstream-facing transceivers, and thus all hosts and hubs (except hosts in embedded systems), to support all three speeds.

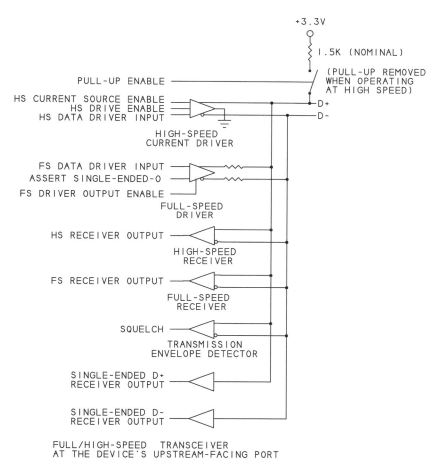

Figure 20-4. The upstream-facing port on a high-speed device must also support full-speed communications. Information source: *Universal Serial Bus Specification Revision 2.0.*

High speed requires its own drivers, so a high-speed device must contain two sets of drivers. For receiving, a transceiver may use a single receiver to handle all speeds or separate receivers for full speed and high speed.

When a high-speed driver transmits data, a current source drives one line with the other line at ground. The current source may be active all the time or active only when transmitting. A current source that is active all the time is easier to design but consumes more power. USB 2.0 requires devices to meet signal-amplitude and timing requirements beginning with the first symbol in a packet, and this requirement complicates the design of a current source that is active only when transmitting. If

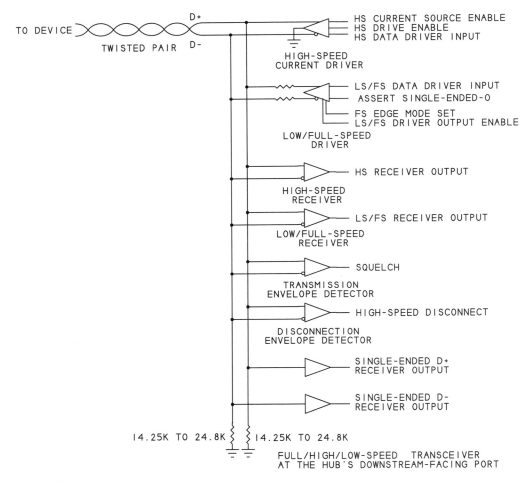

Figure 20-5. The downstream-facing ports on USB 2.0 hubs must support all three speeds (except ports with embedded or permanently attached devices). Information source: *Universal Serial Bus Specification Revision 2.0.*

the driver keeps its current source active all the time, the driver can direct the current to ground when not transmitting on the bus.

In a high-speed-capable transceiver, the output impedance of the full-speed drivers has a tighter tolerance compared to full-speed-only drivers (45Ω ±10%, compared to 36 Ω ±22%). The high-speed bus uses the full-speed drivers as electrical terminations and requires higher values for impedance matching. Full-speed drivers that aren't part of a high-speed transceiver don't require a change in output impedance.

When the high-speed drivers are active, the full-speed drivers bring both data lines low (SE0 state). Each driver and its series resistor then function as a 45-Ω termination to ground. Because each end of the cable segment has a driver, the line has a termination at both the source and the load. The double termination quiets the line more effectively than the source-only series terminations in full-speed segments. Using the full-speed drivers as terminations reduces the number of components.

The USB 2.0 specification provides eye-pattern templates that show required high-speed transmitter outputs and receiver sensitivity. High-speed receivers must also meet new specifications that require the use of a differential time-domain reflectometer (TDR) to measure impedance characteristics.

All high-speed receivers must include a differential envelope detector to detect the Squelch (invalid signal) state indicated by a differential bus voltage of 100 mV or less. The downstream-facing ports on USB 2.0 hubs must also include a high-speed-disconnect detector that detects when a device has been removed from the bus.

Other new responsibilities for high-speed-capable devices include managing the switch from full to high speed and handling new protocols for entering and exiting the Suspend and Reset states.

Switching to high speed

In a low- or full-speed device, a pull-up on one of the signal lines indicates device speed. When a low- or full-speed device attaches to or is removed from the bus, the voltage change due to the arrival or removal of the pull-up informs the hub of the change. High-speed-capable devices always attach at full speed, so hubs detect attachment of high-speed-capable devices in the same way as for full-speed devices.

As Chapter 19 explained, the switch to high speed occurs after the device has been detected during the Reset initiated by the hub's downstream port. A high-speed-capable device must support the high-speed handshake that informs the hub that the device is capable of high speed. When switching to high speed, the device removes its pull-up from the bus.

Detecting removal of a high-speed device

Because a device has no pull-up at high speed, the hub has to use a different method to detect removal of high-speed devices. Removing a device from the bus also removes the differential terminations, and the removal causes the differential voltage at the hub's port to double. On detecting the doubled voltage, the hub knows the device is no longer attached.

The hub detects the voltage by measuring the differential bus voltage during the extended End of High-speed Packet (HSEOP) in each high-speed Start-of-Frame Packet (HSSOP). A differential voltage of at least 625 mV indicates a disconnect.

Suspending and resuming at high speed

As Chapter 17 explained, USB 2.0 devices must enter the low-power Suspend state when the bus has been in the Idle state for at least 3 ms and no more than 10 ms. When the bus has been idle for 3 ms, a high-speed device switches to full speed. The device then checks the state of the full-speed bus to determine whether the host is requesting a Suspend or Reset. If the bus state is SE0, the host is requesting a Reset, and the device prepares for the high-speed-detect handshake. If the bus state is Idle, the device enters the Suspend state. On exiting the Suspend state, the device resumes at high speed.

Signal voltages

Chapter 19 introduced USB's bus states. The voltage that corresponds to a state varies depending on the speed of the cable segment. The difference in the specified voltages at the transmitter and receiver mean that a signal can have some noise or attenuation and the receiver will still see the correct logic level.

Low and full speeds

Table 20-1 shows the driver output voltages for low/full and high speeds. At low and full speeds, a Differential 1 exists at the driver when the D+ output is at least 2.8 V and the D- output is no greater than 0.3 V referenced to the driver's signal ground. A Differential 0 exists at the driver when D- is at least 2.8 V and D+ is no greater than 0.3 V referenced to the driver's signal ground.

At a low- or full-speed receiver, a Differential 1 exists when D+ is at least 2V referenced to the receiver's signal ground, and the difference between D+ and D- is greater than 200 mV. A Differential 0 exists when D- is at least 2 V referenced to the receiver's signal ground, and the difference between D- and D+ is greater than 200 mV. However, a receiver may optionally have less stringent definitions that require only a differential voltage greater than 200 mV, ignoring the requirement for one line to be at least 2 V.

High speed

At high speed, a Differential 1 exists at the driver when both the D+ output is at least 0.36 V and the D- output is no greater than 0.01 V referenced to the driver's signal ground. A Differential 0 exists at the driver when D- is at least 0.36 V and D+ is no greater than 0.01 V referenced to the driver's signal ground.

At a high-speed receiver, the input must meet the requirements shown in the eye-pattern templates in the USB 2.0 specification. The eye patterns specify maximum and minimum voltages, rise and fall times, maximum jitter in a transmitted signal, and the maximum jitter a receiver must tolerate. The USB 2.0 specification explains how to make the measurements.

Table 20-1: High speed has different driver and receiver voltage specifications compared to low and full speed.

Parameter	Low/Full Speed (V)	High Speed (V)
VOUT low minimum	0	-0.010
VOUT low maximum	0.3	0.010
VOUT high minimum	2.8	0.360
VOUT high maximum	3.6	0.440
VIN low maximum	0.8	Limits defined by the eye-pattern templates in the USB 2.0 specification
VIN high minimum	2.0	

Cables and connectors

The USB 2.0 specification includes cable and connector requirements that help ensure that signals will make it to their destinations without errors due to noise. The cable specifications also limit noise that radiates from the cable. To reduce problems, use cables and connectors that are certified, indicating that they have passed USB-IF compliance tests. This section describes cables with Standard-A and Series-B connectors. USB 2.0 devices and hosts can also use USB Type-C connectors and cables as described later in this chapter.

Conductors

USB 2.0 cables provide conductors for power, ground, and USB 2.0 communications. The cables contain wires for VBUS, ground, the D+ and D- signal wires, and a drain wire that connects to the cable shield (Table 20-2). Chapter 17 detailed the voltage and current limits for VBUS. The signal wires carry the data. Unlike the RS-232 interface, which has a TX line to carry data in one direction and an RX line for the other direction, USB 2.0's pair of wires carries a single differential signal, and data travels in one direction at a time.

In a full/high-speed USB cable, the signal wires must be a twisted pair of two insulated conductors that spiral around each other with a twist every few inches. Twisting is effective for reducing low-frequency, magnetically coupled signals such as 60-Hz power-line noise.

In a full/high-speed cable, the signal wires must have a differential characteristic impedance of 90 Ω. This value is a measure of the input impedance of an infinite, open line and determines the initial current on the lines when the outputs switch. The characteristic impedance for a low-speed cable isn't defined because the slower edge rates mean that the initial current doesn't affect the logic states at the receiver.

Table 20-2: A USB 2.0 cable has four wires plus a drain wire.

Wire	Name	Use	Color
1	VBUS	+5V	Red
2	D-	Signal pair negative	White
3	D+	Signal pair positive	Green
4	GND	Ground reference	Black
Shell	Shield	Drain wire	–

The USB 2.0 specification lists requirements for the cable's conductors, shielding, and insulation (Table 20-3). These are the major requirements for full/high-speed cables:

Signal wires: twisted pair, 28 AWG minimum diameter.

Power and ground: non-twisted, 28 AWG minimum diameter.

Inner shield: aluminum metalized polyester surrounding the two twisted pairs.

Outer shield: braided, tinned copper or equivalent braided material.

Drain wire: stranded, tinned copper wire, 28 AWG minimum diameter between the inner and outer shields.

The specification also lists requirements for a cable's durability and performance.

A low-speed cable must have the same inner shield and drain wire required for full speed. The USB 2.0 specification also recommends, but doesn't require, a braided outer shield and a twisted pair for data, as on full- and high-speed cables.

The USB 1.1 specification did not require shielding for low-speed cables on the premise that the slower rise and fall times made shielding unnecessary. The shielding requirement was added in USB 2.0 not because the USB interface is noisy in itself, but because the cables are likely to attach to computers that are noisy internally. Shielding helps keep the cable from radiating this noise and thus helps in passing FCC tests. The downside is that USB 2.0's low-speed cables are more expensive to make and physically less flexible.

A low-speed device can use a full-speed cable if the cable meets all of the low-speed cable requirements including the typical maximum length of 3 m and not using a standard USB connector type at the device end.

Connectors

The USB 2.0 specification allows these options for the USB receptacle on a device: Standard B (also called Std B or just "B"), Mini B, and Micro B. Collectively, these are the Series-B connectors. Figure 20-6 shows cable plugs that mate with the receptacles. Another option for devices is a captive cable, which uses a vendor-specific connector or is permanently attached to the device.

Table 20-3: The requirements for cables and related components differ for full/high-speed cables and cables that attach to low-speed devices.

Specification	Low Speed	Full/High Speed
Maximum length (typical) (m)	3	5
Inner shield and drain wire required?	yes	
Braided outer shield	recommended	required
Twisted pair	recommended	required
Common-mode impedance (Ω)	not specified	30 ±30%
Differential Characteristic impedance (Ω)	not specified	90
Cable skew (picoseconds)	< 100	
Wire gauge (AWG)	28 minimum diameter	
DC resistance, plug shell to plug shell (Ω)	0.6	
Cable delay	18 ns (one way)	5.2 ns/m
pull-up location at the device	D-	D+
Detachable cable OK?	no	yes
Captive cable OK?	yes	

Conventional USB 2.0 hosts use the Standard A (also called Std A or "A") receptacle. USB OTG devices use the Micro-AB receptacle, which can accept a Micro-A or Micro-B plug. Embedded Hosts as defined in the *On-The-Go and Embedded Host Supplement to the USB Revision 2.0 Specification* may also use the Micro-AB receptacle. (See Chapter 21.) "Series-A" refers to Standard-A and Micro-A connectors .

Figure 20-6. Approved cable plugs include (from left) Standard-A for hosts and Standard-B, Mini-B, and Micro-B for devices.

Figure 20-7. A USB icon identifies USB plugs (left) and receptacles (right). A "+" at a receptacle indicates support for high speed.

The USB 2.0 specification defines the Standard series connectors. ECNs to the USB 2.0 specification define the Mini and Micro series connectors.

Mini and Micro plugs have an additional ID pin. OTG devices use the ID pin to identify the type of plug inserted. Table 20-4 shows the pinout for the connectors.

All of the connectors are keyed so you can't insert a plug the wrong way. The connections for D+ and D- are recessed so the power lines connect first on attachment.

USB plugs and some receptacles have a USB icon (Figure 20-7). A USB 2.0 receptacle that supports high speed may have a "+" to indicate high-speed support. Receptacles should install so the USB icon on the top of the plug is visible to users inserting a plug. Only cable assemblies that have passed compliance tests may display the USB 3.1 icon (Figure 20-8).

As Chapter 17 explained, Standard-A and Series-B PD connectors support capabilities defined in the *USB Power Delivery Rev. 2.0, v1.0* specification. USB 2.0 devices can also use USB Type-C connectors, described later in this chapter.

Detachable and captive cables

USB 2.0 defines cables as being either *detachable* or *captive*. From the names, you might think that a detachable cable is one you can remove while a captive cable is permanently attached to its device. In reality, a captive cable can be removable as long as its downstream connector is *not* one of the standard USB connector types.

TM & © 2008 USB-IF. All rights reserved.

Figure 20-8. USB 3.1 cable assemblies must pass compliance tests to earn the right to display the SuperSpeedPlus icon. (Image courtesy of the USB Implementers Forum.)

Table 20-4: The Mini-B and Micro-B plugs have an additional ID pin to enable OTG devices to detect the plug type.

Pin	Standard A, Standard B	Mini-B, Micro-B
1	VBUS	VBUS
2	D-	D-
3	D+	D+
4	GND	ID: open or > 1MΩ
5	Not present	GND
Shell	Shield	Shield

A detachable USB 2.0 cable must be full/high speed, with a Standard-A plug for the upstream connection and a Series-B plug for the downstream connection. A captive cable may be low or full/high speed. The upstream end has a Standard-A plug. For the downstream connection, a captive cable can be permanently attached or use a removable, non-standard connector type. The non-standard connection doesn't have to be hot pluggable, but the Standard-A connection must be hot pluggable. Requiring low-speed cables to be captive eliminates the possibility of trying to use a low-speed cable in a full- or high-speed segment.

OTG products have other cable options described in Chapter 21.

Cable length

USB 1.0 specified maximum lengths for cable segments. A full-speed segment could be up to 5 m and a low-speed segment could be up to 3 m. USB 1.1 and later dropped the length limits in favor of a discussion of the characteristics that limit a cable's ability to meet timing and voltage specifications. On full- and high-speed cables, the limits are due to signal attenuation, cable propagation delay (the amount of time it takes for a signal to travel from driver to receiver), and voltage drops on the VBUS and GND wires. Except for cables with Micro-B plugs, the maximum cable delay is 26 ns. On low-speed cables, the length is limited by the rise and fall times of the signals, the capacitive load presented by the segment, and voltage drops on the VBUS and GND wires. The maximum cable delay is 18 ns.

USB 1.0's limits are still good general guidelines for all USB 2.0 cables except those with Micro-B plugs. Cables with Micro-B plugs have a shorter defined maximum cable delay (10 ns) and a specified maximum length of 2 m.

Bus length

A bus can have up to 5 external hubs in a tier so using 5-m cables, a device can be up to 30 m from its host. If the device is low speed, the limit is 28 m because the cable the connects to the low-speed device can be no more than 3 m. Using cables with

Micro-B connectors also reduce the maximum distance due to the 2-m limit for these cables. The limit on the number of hubs is due to the electrical properties of the hubs and cables and the resulting delays in propagating signals along the cable and through a hub.

USB 3.1

USB 3.1 cables have additional wires and other requirements to enable carrying Enhanced SuperSpeed data.

Transmitters and receivers

For Enhanced SuperSpeed data, each direction has a dedicated pair of wires with a differential transmitter at one end and a differential receiver at the opposite end. The hardware interface is based on the PCI Express (PCIe) Gen 2 interface used in expansion buses in PCs. In a PC, the bus uses multiple lanes to transfer multiple bits in the same direction at once. Enhanced SuperSpeed use a single lane with one signal pair for each direction. The SuperSpeedPlus interface doubles the interface's signaling rate.

An Enhanced SuperSpeed transmitter must contain a circuit that detects an attached receiver's load of 18–30 Ω. An RC charging circuit can perform this function. As Chapter 19 explained, a SuperSpeedPlus-capable port uses LFPS polling messages to determine whether to communicate at SuperSpeed or SuperSpeedPlus.

Cables and connectors

The USB 3.1 specification defines cables and Series-A and Series-B connectors that carry USB 2.0 signals, Enhanced SuperSpeed signals, and power. Compared to USB 3.0, USB 3.1 adds requirements to reduce EMI and RFI, especially at SuperSpeedPlus. All new cable designs intended for use with SuperSpeed or SuperSpeedPlus should meet USB 3.1's requirements.

This section describes USB 3.1 Series-A and Series-B connectors and cables. USB 3.1 devices and hosts can also use Type-C connectors and cables as described later in this chapter.

Compatibility

Figure 20-9 shows connectors on a USB 3.0 cable. USB 3.1 connectors have the same form factor but have additional requirements as detailed below.

USB 3.1 cables and connectors are backwards compatible with USB 2.0. Plugs on USB 2.0 cables fit USB 3.1 receptacles. A USB 2.0 cable attached to a USB 3.1 host or hub can carry low-, full-, and high-speed data.

Figure 20-9. A USB 3.0/3.1 Standard-A plug (left) fits a USB 2.0 receptacle, but a USB 3.0/3.1 Standard-B plug (right) requires a USB 3.0 or USB 3.1 receptacle. The plugs shown are USB 3.0 plugs.

A USB 3.1 Standard-A plug fits a USB 2.0 Standard-A receptacle so you can use a USB 3.1 cable to attach a USB 3.1 device to a USB 2.0 host or hub and communicate at a USB 2.0 speed. USB 3.1 Series-B plugs don't fit USB 2.0 Series-B receptacles so you need a USB 2.0 cable to attach a USB 2.0 device to a USB 3.1 host or hub.

To communicate at Enhanced SuperSpeed, all cables and receptacles in the links between the device and host must be USB 3.1. (USB 3.0 hosts can optionally use USB 3.0 cables and receptacles.).

Conductors

A USB 3.1 cable has ten wires (Table 20-5), which include USB 2.0's power, ground, and unshielded pair plus two shielded pairs, each with a drain wire, for Enhanced SuperSpeed. The Enhanced SuperSpeed interface is dual simplex: each direction has its own pair of wires, each pair has its own ground, or drain, wire, and data can travel in both directions at once. (Full duplex is also has dedicated wires for each direction but uses a single, common ground wire.)

The Enhanced SuperSpeed wires can be shielded twisted pairs, twinaxial cable (twinax), or coaxial cable (coax). Twinax is similar to coax but has two inner conductors instead of one. The characteristic impedance of shielded twisted pairs should be 90Ω.

USB 3.1 doesn't specify wire gauges but provides electrical data for typical values (26–34 AWG for signal pairs) and recommends using the smallest-diameter gauges that meet the electrical requirements of the cable assembly. Cable flexibility, which

Table 20-5: A USB 3.1 cable has additional wires to support Enhanced SuperSpeed. Information source: *Universal Serial Bus 3.1 Specification Revision 1.0.*

Wire	Signal Name	Description
1	PWR	VBUS power
2	D-	Unshielded differential pair, negative (USB 2.0)
3	D+	Unshielded twisted pair, positive (USB 2.0)
4	GND_PWRrt	Ground for power return
5	P1-	Shielded differential pair,1, negative (SuperSpeed/SuperSpeedPlus)
6	P1+	Shielded differential pair 1, positive (SuperSpeed/SuperSpeedPlus)
7	P1_Drain	Drain wire for SDP1.
8	P2-	Shielded differential pair 2, negative (SuperSpeed/SuperSpeedPlus)
9	P2+	Shielded differential pair 2, positive (SuperSpeed/SuperSpeedPlus)
10	P2_Drain	Drain wire for SDP2. Connects to pin 7 on the connectors.
Braid	Shield	External braid terminated onto metal shell of plug

generally decreases with the AWG number, may also be a consideration. The cable's outer diameter must be in the range 3–6 mm.

USB 3.1 cables must have metal braid surrounding all of the wires and terminating at the metal shell.

For the Enhanced SuperSpeed signal pairs, USB 3.1 tightens USB 3.0's specifications for differential characteristic impedance, insertion loss (attenuation), and crosstalk. USB 3.1 removed USB 3.0's specified color for each wire.

Cable length

The USB 3.1 specification doesn't provide maximum cable lengths and just says that cables must meet the requirements for voltage drop and cable assembly loss. The USB Type-C cable specification does provide practical maximum lengths for Enhanced SuperSpeed (presented later in this chapter).

Connectors

USB 3.1 Series-A and Series-B connectors have five additional pins for the two Enhanced SuperSpeed signal pairs and the two drain wires, which terminate at the same pin. Figure 20-10 shows the connectors.

Table 20-6 shows the pin assignments for USB 3.1 Standard-A, Standard-B, and Micro-B connectors. Table 20-7 shows which plugs can attach to different receptacle types. A USB 3.1 device can have a USB 3.1 Standard-B or USB 3.1 Micro-B receptacle or a captive cable with a USB 3.1 Standard-A plug. A USB 3.1 host has a USB 3.1 Standard-A receptacle.

Except for the Mini-B, all USB 2.0 plugs can mate with a USB 3.1 receptacle of the same series. A USB 2.0 Standard-A plug fits a USB 3.1 Standard-A receptacle, a USB 2.0 Standard-B plug fits a USB 3.1 Standard-B receptacle, and a USB 2.0 Micro-B plug fits a USB 3.1 Micro-B receptacle. There is no USB 3.1 Mini-B receptacle. Of course, cables with USB 2.0 plugs can't carry Enhanced SuperSpeed traffic.

The USB 3.1 Standard-A plug and receptacle have the same form factors as the USB 2.0 Standard-A plug and receptacle. Thus a USB 3.1 Standard-A plug will mate with a USB 2.0 Standard-A receptacle. To support Enhanced SuperSpeed, USB 3.1 Standard-A connectors use a 2-tier contact system with five additional pins behind the four USB 2.0 pins on the plug.

For the Enhanced SuperSpeed signal pairs, the cable connects each transmit pin to its corresponding receive pin. For example, StdA_SSTX+ connects to StdB_SSRX+ or MicB_SSRX+, and StdA_SSTX- connects to StdB_SSRX- or MicB_SSRX-. In other words, RX and TX in the signal names refer to the direction of data flow at the connector. Also note that becaues the Micro-B connector has an ID pin, the Standard-B and Micro-B connectors use different pins for some signals.

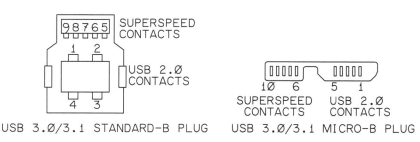

Figure 20-10. USB 3.1 connectors have additional pins for the SuperSpeed wires. (Not drawn to scale.)

Table 20-6: The signals on a USB 3.1 connector vary according to the connector type. Information source: *Universal Serial Bus 3.1 Specification Revision 1.0.*

Pin	Signal		
	Standard-A	**Standard-B**	**Micro-B**
1	VBUS	VBUS	VBUS
2	D-	D-	D-
3	D+	D+	D+
4	GND	GND	ID
5	StdA_SSRX+	StdB_SSTX+	GND
6	StdA_SSRX-	StdB_SSTX-	MicB_SSTX-
7	GND_DRAIN	GND_DRAIN	MicB_SSTX+
8	StdA_SSTX-	StdB_SSRX-	GND_DRAIN
9	StdA_SSTX+	StdB_SSRX+	MicB_SSRX-
10	—	—	MicB_SSRX+
12	INSERTION DETECT	—	—
13	(USB Power Delivery, receptacle only)	—	—

To ensure signal quality at SuperSpeedPlus, USB 3.1 adds requirements for connectors including a back-shield, ground tabs, and additional grounding spring tabs for receptacles.

 As Chapter 17 explained, USB 3.1 Standard-A PD and Series-B PD connectors support capabilities defined in *USB Power Delivery Rev. 2.0, v1.0.* USB 3.1 devices can also use USB Type-C connectors, described later in this chapter. The USB 3.1 specification deprecated the Powered-B connector defined in the USB 3.0 specification

Host-to-host cables

USB 2.0 forbids cables that connect two hosts except for bridge cables that contain device controllers with a shared buffer. USB 3.1 defines a USB 3.1 Standard-A to USB 3.1 Standard-A cable for debugging and other specialized host-to-host applications with driver support. In the cable, VBUS, D-, and D+ have no connection.

USB Type-C cables

Following many years of incremental additions to the Series-A and Series-B connectors, in 2014, the USB 3.0 Promoter Group started fresh with the USB Type-C connectors and cables defined in the *Universal Serial Bus Type-C Cable and Connector Specification.*

Table 20-7: USB 3.1 connectors are backwards compatible with USB 2.0 connectors. Information source: *Universal Serial Bus 3.1 Specification Revision 1.0*.

Unit	Connector	Mates with
USB 2.0 host	USB 2.0 Standard-A receptacle	USB 2.0 Standard-A plug
USB 3.1 host	USB 3.1 Standard-A receptacle	USB 3.1 Standard-A plug
USB 2.0 device	USB 2.0 Standard-B receptacle	USB 2.0 Standard-B plug
	USB 2.0 Mini-B receptacle	USB 2.0 Mini-B plug
	USB 2.0 Micro-B receptacle	USB 2.0 Micro-B plug
	Captive cable with USB 2.0 Standard-A plug	USB 2.0 Standard-A receptacle USB 3.1 Standard-A receptacle
USB 3.1 device	USB 3.1 Standard-B receptacle	USB 2.0 Standard-B plug USB 3.1 Standard-B plug
	USB 3.0 Micro-B receptacle	USB 2.0 Micro-B plug USB 3.1 Micro-B plug
	Captive cable with USB 3.1 Standard-A plug	USB 2.0 Standard-A receptacle USB 3.1 Standard-A receptacle

USB Type-C connectors are not backwards compatible with Standard-A and Series-B connectors. A USB Type-C receptacle requires a USB Type-C plug, and a USB Type-C plug doesn't fit a Standard-A or Series-B receptacle. However, hosts and devices with USB Type-C connectors can use the cables described below to attach to ports that have Standard-A or Series-B receptacles.

Benefits

USB Type-C connectors and cables have many benefits:

- No need to determine which side is up when attaching a plug. The plugs work either way.

- No need to determine which end of the cable goes where. The same plug fits both host and device receptacles.

- Small form factor, with receptacle height of just 3 mm.

- Enhanced support for *USB Power Delivery Rev. 2.0, v1.0*, including communication over a new Configuration Channel.

- New Sideband Use wires and the ability to re-assign pin functions to support protocols other than USB.

- Secure connectors with side latches that "click" on attachment and hold the plug in the receptacle.

- Lower EMI and RFI emissions.
- Support for USB 2.0 and USB 3.1 communications.

Due to their many benefits, the USB Type-C connectors will likely come to dominate the market as manufacturers release new products.

Cables and connectors

Compared to cables that use Series-A and Series-B connectors, USB Type-C cables have additional wires to support new abilities.

Conductors

The USB Type-C specification defines two cable types for links that have USB Type-C connectors at both ends.

A *USB Full-Featured Type-C cable* has a USB 2.0 signal pair, two complete sets of Enhanced SuperSpeed shielded pairs (8 wires), two Sideband Use (SBU) wires, a Configuration Channel (CC) wire, VBUS, ground, and optional duplicate VBUS and ground wires. All USB Full-Featured Type-C cables are electronically marked cables as defined below and support a VCONN connection that can power circuits in the plug.

A *USB 2.0 Type-C cable* lacks the Enhanced SuperSpeed shielded pairs and SBU wires. If the cable is an electronically marked cable, the plugs support a VCONN connection that can power circuits in the plug.

Cables that use shielded twisted pairs or twinax for the differential pairs also have a ground return wire for each pair. In coax, the shield is the ground return. A braided shield must enclose all of the wires in the cable. The shield terminates at the metal shells on the plugs.

Cable length

The USB Type-C specification provides practical maximum lengths for cables (Table 20-8). Note that the maximum length decreases as the signaling rate increases: 2 m for SuperSpeed and 1 m for SuperSpeedPlus. USB 2.0 Type-C cables also have shorter maximum lengths compared to cables with Standard-A and Series-B connectors.

Connectors

Table 20-9 shows the pin connections in USB Type-C connectors. The specification defines two types of plugs. A USB Full-Featured Type-C plug supports Enhanced SuperSpeed and USB 2.0. A USB 2.0 Type-C plug supports only USB 2.0 communications and has no connections to USB 3.1 signals or Sideband Use pins. A single USB Type-C receptacle is defined for use with both USB 2.0 and USB 3.1 ports.

To support attaching the plugs in either orientation, USB Type-C receptacles have duplicate sets of pins for both USB 2.0 data and USB 3.1 data.

Table 20-8: The USB Type-C cable specification gives these practical length limits for cables that have one or more USB Type-C connectors.

Speed	Connector Type, Second Plug	Maximum Length (m)
USB 3.1 Gen 2	USB Type-C, USB 3.1 Standard-A, USB 3.1 Standard-B, USB 3.1 Micro-B	1
USB 3.1 Gen 1	USB Type-C	2
USB 2.0	Micro-B	2
	USB Type-C, Standard-A, Standard-B, Mini-B	4

Table 20-10 shows the connections at the cable plugs. As in other USB 3.1 cables, in cables that have USB Full-Featured Type-C connectors, the pins for each Enhanced SuperSpeed transmit pair connect to corresponding receive pins at the opposite end. For example, each SSTXp1 pin connects to SSRXp1 at the opposite end, and each SSTXn1 pin connects to SSRXn1 at the opposite end. The two SBU wires also cross-connect, with SBU1 on each connector wired to SBU2 on the opposite connector.

Figure 20-11 shows the options for a mating receptacle and plug. Depending on the plug's orientation when it attaches, SSTXp2 (B2) on the receptacle might connect to SSTXp2 (B2) or SSTXp1 (A2) on the plug, SSTXn2 (B3) might connect to SSTXn2 (B3) or SSTXn1 (A3), and so on down the line.

All USB Type-C connectors can support currents of 5 A. All USB Type-C cables can support currents of 3 A, while electronically marked USB Type-C cables may support currents up to 5A.

In addition to new side latches to hold the plug securely in the receptacle, the rated number of insertion/extraction cycles is 10,000, much higher than the ratings for other USB plugs except USB 3.1 Micro-series connectors.

Because there is only one receptacle design, hubs must clearly mark their upstream-facing port and downstream-facing ports.

New cable connections

USB Type-C connectors provide several new pins to support detecting cable attachment and orientation, powering circuits in the plug, and a new data path to support communications that use other than USB protocols.

Table 20-9: USB Type-C connectors provide access to power, USB 2.0 and USB 3.1 data, and a Configuration Channel. Information source: *Universal Serial Bus Type-C Cable and Connector Specification Revision 1.0*

Pin	Signal	Description
A1	GND	Cable return current path
A2	SSTXp1	Transmit signal pair 1, positive (SuperSpeed/SuperSpeedPlus)[1]
A3	SSTXn1	Transmit signal pair 1, negative (SuperSpeed/SuperSpeedPlus)[1]
A4	VBUS	Bus power
A5	CC1 (receptacle)/ CC (plug)	Configuration Channel
A6	Dp1	USB 2.0 differential pair 1, positive (USB 2.0)
A7	Dn1	USB 2.0 differential pair 1, negative (USB 2.0)
A8	SBU1	Sideband Use[2]
A9	VBUS	Bus power
A10	SSRXn2	Receive signal pair 2, negative (SuperSpeed/SuperSpeedPlus)[1]
A11	SSRXp2	Receive signal pair 2, positive (SuperSpeed/SuperSpeedPlus)[1]
A12	GND	Cable return current path
B1	GND	Cable return current path
B2	SSTXp2	Transmit signal pair 2, positive (SuperSpeed/SuperSpeedPlus)[1]
B3	SSTXn2	Transmit signal pair 2, negative (SuperSpeed/SuperSpeedPlus)[1]
B4	VBUS	Bus power
B5	CC2/ VCONN	Configuration Channel 2 (receptacle) plug power (plug)
B6	Receptacle: Dp2 Plug: no contact present	USB 2.0 differential pair 2, positive (USB 2.0) (receptacle) no contact present (plug)
B7	Receptacle: Dn2 Plug: no contact present	USB 2.0 differential pair 2, negative (USB 2.0) (receptacle) no contact present (plug)
B8	SBU2	Sideband Use[2]
B9	VBUS	Bus power
B10	SSRXn1	Receive signal pair 1, negative (SuperSpeed/SuperSpeedPlus)[1]
B11	SSRXp1	Receive signal pair 1, positive (SuperSpeed/SuperSpeedPlus)[1]
B12	GND	Cable return current path

[1]No connection on USB 2.0 Type-C plug.

[2]Connected on USB 2.0 Type-C plug only if required for specified purpose.

Table 20-10: In a USB Full-Featured Type-C cable, the Enhanced SuperSpeed and SBU wires cross-connect TX/RX and SBU1/SBU2.

Plug 1		Cable connection	Plug 2	
Pin	Signal		Signal	Pin
A1, B1, A12, B12	GND	connects to	GND	A1, B1, A12, B12
A4, B4, A9, B9	VBUS	connects to	VBUS	A4, B4, A9, B9
A5	CC	connects to	CC	A5
B5	VCONN	connects to	VCONN	B5
A6	Dp1	connects to	Dp1	A6
A7	Dn1	connects to	Dn1	A7
A2	SSTXp1	connects to	SSRXp1	B11
A3	SSTXn1	connects to	SSRXn1	B10
B11	SSRXp1	connects to	SSTXp1	A2
B10	SSRXn1	connects to	SSTXn1	A3
B2	SSTXp2	connects to	SSRXp2	A11
B3	SSTXn2	connects to	SSRXn2	A10
A11	SSRXp2	connects to	SSTXp2	B2
A10	SSRXn2	connects to	SSTXn2	B3
A8	SBU1	connects to	SBU2	B8
B8	SBU2	connects to	SBU1	A8

Configuration channel

Host and device ports can use the Configuration Channel (CC) to detect attachment and plug orientation, establish downward facing port (DFP) and upward-facing port (UFP) roles, and configure VBUS, VCONN, Alternate Modes, and Accessory Modes.

The cable's CC wire can carry messages to negotiate a USB Power Delivery (PD) Contract as described in Chapter 17. The Configuration Channel uses Bi-phase Mark Coded (BMC) communications, a method of encoding similar to differential Manchester encoding where each bit has at least one level change and the average DC component is zero.

When two dual-role ports (DRPs) connect, a protocol on the CC pins establishes which port functions as the host. The ports can then use a PD DR Swap message to swap roles, or a device can swap roles by emulating detach and reattach.

VCONN

A USB Type-C cable has a single CC wire, but USB Type-C receptacles have two CC pins, CC1 and CC2. In USB Full-Featured Type-C cables, the CC pin that doesn't con-

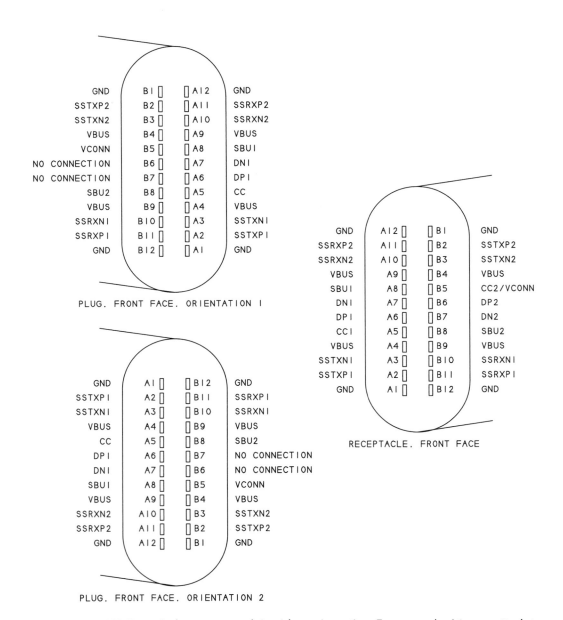

Figure 20-11. USB Type-C plugs can attach in either orientation. For example, A1 may attach to A1 or B1, A2 may attach to A2 or B2, and so on.

nect in the cable functions as the VCONN +5V source to power circuits in electronically marked cables. VCONN must be able to provide a minimum 1 W of power.

Electronically marked cables can report characteristics such as the cable's vendor and maximum current. The information travels in a Discover Identity command in a Vendor Defined Message as defined in *USB Power Delivery Rev. 2.0, v1.0*. All USB Full-Featured Type-C cables and any cable rated for more than 3 A must be electronically marked and must support *USB Power Delivery Rev. 2.0, v1.0* protocols.

The DFP provides VCONN initially, but PD protocols can swap the VCONN source. VCONN is always +5V and the voltage is isolated from the opposite end of the cable. Electronically marked cables can use VBUS instead of VCONN to power circuits in the plug.

A VCONN-powered accessory is a device with a UFP that supports an Alternate Mode and that can operate when powered by VCONN.

Sideband use

The Sideband Use (SBU) wires provide two new signal paths for specific applications. The signals are used in Alternate Modes as defined in *USB Power Delivery Rev. 2.0, v1.0*, an Audio Adapter Accessory Mode defined in the USB Type-C specification, and a Debug Accessory Mode to be defined in a later revision of the USB Type-C specification. The use of these pins is limited to uses defined in USB specifications.

Data routing

To configure the USB Type-C interface for Enhanced SuperSpeed data, the ports use the CC wire to identify which of the two sets of signal pairs to use for communications.

Connections

Depending on the orientation of the plugs, the CC wire in the cable may connect to CC1 on both receptacles, to CC2 on both receptacles, or to CC1 on one receptacle and CC2 on the other. In addition, the DFP may supply VCONN, and the UFP may be a conventional USB device or a device that supports one or more Alternate Modes or an Accessory Mode. Using the CC wire, the ports can detect each of these conditions.

Figure 20-12 shows example connections for a cable that connects to CC1 on both ports with the DFP supplying VCONN.

On CC1 and CC2, a DFP on a host or hub has a pull-up, a current source, or another means to detect a termination, or resistance to ground, at the opposite end of the cable. If using default USB power with a pull-up to +5V, the resistor's value is 56 kΩ. Ports with higher current capabilities use different, lower, values to enable the UFP

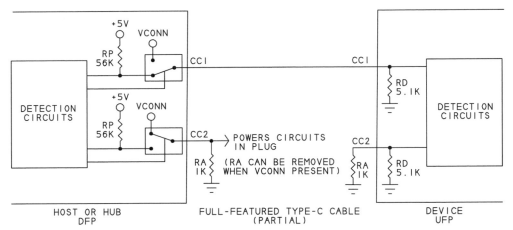

Figure 20-12. In this example, the CC wire in the cable connects to CC1 on both ports, and the DFP supplies VCONN to the plug's circuits. Information source: *Universal Serial Bus Type-C Cable and Connector Specification Revision 1.0.*

on the device to detect the amount of current the DFP can provide. The specified values also vary with the pull-up voltage. A UFP has a 5.1 kΩ pull-down on CC1 and CC2.

A powered cable is a cable that requires VCONN to power its circuits. In a powered cable, the CC pins that don't connect to the CC wire initially present a 1 kΩ load to ground. On detecting VCONN, the cable can remove this load.

Detecting attachment and orientation

On connecting a UFP to a DFP, the pull-down on the UFP causes the voltage to drop at the DFP's receptacle. The DFP detects an attached device by detecting this voltage drop.

On detecting the voltage drop, the DFP knows which signal pairs to use for Enhanced SuperSpeed data, and the port switches the pairs to the port's circuits in the host or hub. If CC1 connects, Enhanced SuperSpeed data uses transmit signal pair 1 and receive signal pair 1. If CC2 connects, Enhanced SuperSpeed data uses transmit signal pair 2 and receive signal pair 2. The USB Type-C specification leaves it to the vendor to decide how to implement the switch. The other set of Enhanced SuperSpeed signal pairs in the cable remains unused unless put to use in an Alternate Mode or Accessory Mode as described later in this chapter.

On detecting attachment, the DFP applies VBUS and applies VCONN on the CC pin that doesn't connect to the CC wire.

The UFP detects attachment by detecting the presence of VBUS. The CC pin with the higher voltage is connected to the CC wire. As on the DFP, the UFP switches the appropriate Enhanced SuperSpeed pins to the port's circuits.

The device is then ready for enumeration at Enhanced SuperSpeed. As Chapter 17 explained, USB Type-C ports that support role swapping can use PD protocols to swap power and data roles.

Both ports must continue to monitor the lines to detect detach. On the DFP, detach is indicated by a rise in voltage on the pin that connects to CC. On detecting detach, the DFP removes VBUS. On the UFP, detach is indicated by a loss of VBUS. On detach, the DFP resumes monitoring for a new attachment.

For USB 2.0 data, the USB Type-C receptacle has two sets of contacts with the two D+ pins shorted together and the two D- pins shorted together. The cable has a single pair of USB 2.0 data wires that may connect to either pair depending on orientation.

Legacy cables and adapters

To enable connecting a host or device with a USB Type-C connector to a device or host with a Series-B or Series-A receptacle, the USB Type-C specification defines legacy USB cables and two adapters.

A cable with a USB Full-Featured Type-C plug may have any of these plugs at the opposite end: USB Full-Featured Type-C, USB 3.1 Standard-A, USB 3.1 Standard-B, or USB 3.1 Micro-B. To minimize the number of defined cable types, there are no defined cables using USB 3.0 Standard-A or Series-B connectors. A cable with a USB 2.0 Type-C plug may have any of these plugs at the opposite end: USB 2.0 Type-C, USB 2.0 Standard-A, USB 2.0 Standard-B, USB 2.0 Mini-B, or USB 2.0 Micro-B.

Also allowed are an adapter with a USB Full-Featured Type-C plug and USB 3.1 Standard-A receptacle (for flash drives), an adapter with a USB 2.0 Type-C plug and USB 2.0 Micro-B receptacle, and captive cables. Adapters that convert a USB Type-C receptacle to a Standard-A or Series-B connector are not allowed.

Because the Standard-A and Series-B plugs don't have CC or SBU pins or a VCONN source, those capabilities aren't available on cables where one end has a Standard-A or Series-B plug.

To enable detecting attachment and plug orientation, a cable that connects a USB Type-C receptacle to a USB 3.1 or USB 2.0 Standard-A receptacle has a single CC pin with a pull-up to indicate a connection to a DFP. A cable that connects a USB Type-C receptacle to a USB 3.1 or USB 2.0 Series-B receptacle has a single CC pin with a pull-down to indicate a connection to a UFP.

A DRP initially alternates between UFP and DFP roles until the connected port detects attachment to a UFP or DFP.

A USB Type-C cable that connects two hosts or two devices isn't functional but causes no harm.

Alternate modes

Every device with a USB Type-C receptacle must support USB communications (except for dedicated charging ports as defined in the battery charging specification). Devices may optionally also support one or more Alternate Modes that support alternate functions. An alternate mode can reassign pins in the cable to new functions. The USB Type-C specification gives the example of a PCIe bridge that communicates using the otherwise unused shielded pairs and the SBU wires.

To enter and exit an Alternate Mode, a device uses PD Vendor Defined Messages. A device that has no other USB function must at minimum support the billboard class to identify the device. Alternate Modes require a direct connection to a host with no hubs between.

Accessory modes

The USB Type-C specification defines an Audio Adapter Accessory Mode that uses the USB 2.0 data pins and the SBU pins to provide four analog audio signals. Revision 1.0 of the specification also refers to a Debug Adapter Accessory Mode to be defined in a later revision of the document.

To enable detecting devices that use the Accessory Modes, the Audio Adapter has pull-ups on both CC pins, and the Debug Adapter has pull-downs on both CC pins.

Other ways to connect

Besides using conventional cables, USB devices can connect using inter-chip connections, electrically isolated interfaces, long-distance interfaces, and wireless technologies.

Inter-Chip

USB was developed as an interface to connect computers and peripherals via cables. But USB has also found uses in products that contain a host and an embedded or removable peripheral. In these products, communications between the host and peripheral don't require standard USB cables or connectors and can use lower supply voltages.

USB 2.0

Two USB-IF standards for this type of interface are the *Inter-Chip USB Supplement* for low and full speeds and the *High-Speed Inter-Chip USB Electrical Specification* for high speed.

For both interface types, all of the following are true:

- The distance between the host and peripheral is 10 cm or less.
- The host doesn't allow peripheral attachment or removal while the inter-chip supply voltage is present.
- The interface can use a vendor-specific cable or on-board connection (circuit-board traces).

An interface that complies with the Inter-Chip USB Supplement must meet these requirements:

- The host always supports full speed and supports low speed if the host communicates with a low-speed peripheral. The peripheral may support low or full speed.
- The interface supports one or more of six defined supply-voltage classes with nominal voltages in the range 1–3 V.

The low/full speed interface draws no bus current when idle. To save additional power, hardware can switch out the bus pull-up and pull-down resistors during traffic signaling.

The High-Speed Inter-Chip USB Electrical Specification defines an interface that uses a high-speed inter-chip (HSIC) synchronous serial interface. The interface uses 240-MHz double data rate (DDR) signaling, which transfers data on both the rising and falling clock edges. A 240-MHz clock thus supports a 480-Mbps bit rate.

An interface that complies with the High-Speed Inter-Chip USB Electrical Specification must meet these requirements:

- The host and peripheral support high speed.
- The interface uses 1.2 V LVCMOS voltages.

The HSIC interface consumes power only when a transfer is in progress.

USB 3.0

For USB 3.0 products that contain a host and an embedded or removable peripheral, the *Inter-Chip Supplement to the USB Revision 3.0 Specification* describes SuperSpeed Inter-Chip (SSIC) connections. Presumably, a USB 3.1 update to the standard is forthcoming.

Isolated interfaces

Galvanic isolation can be useful in preventing electrical noise and power surges from coupling into a circuit. Circuits that are galvanically isolated from each other have no ohmic connection. Typical methods of isolation include using a transformer to transfer power by magnetic coupling and optoisolators to transfer digital signals by optical coupling.

USB devices shouldn't require isolation in conventional environments such as offices and classrooms. For medical or industrial environments or other locations where devices might benefit from isolation, USB's timing requirements and USB 2.0's use of a single pair of wires for both directions make it difficult to isolate a device from its host. One solution is to isolate the non-USB components the device controller connects to. For example, in a motor controller with a USB interface, the motor and control circuits can be isolated from the USB controller and bus.

Maxim's MAX3420E interface chip can be suitable for electrically isolating a USB device from its host. The chip uses a 3- or 4-wire SPI bus to connect to a processor that sends and receives USB data. Electro-isolators on each line of the SPI bus can isolate the interface chip and USB data from the processor and its upstream hubs and host.

Another option is to use an isolated hub. Several sources offer hubs with isolated low/full-speed downstream ports. Wireless links, described later in this chapter, offer another way to cut the cable.

Long distance links

The USB specifications prohibit extension cables that extend a segment by connecting a second cable in series. An extension cable for the upstream side of a cable would have a Standard-A plug on one end and a Standard-A receptacle on the other, while an extension cable for the downstream side would have a Series-B plug and Series-B receptacle. A USB Type-C extension cable would have a plug and a receptacle. Prohibiting extension cables eliminates the temptation to stretch a segment beyond the interface's electrical limits. Extension cables are available, but just because you can buy one doesn't mean that it's a good idea or that the cable will work. Instead, to extend the distance between a host and device, use hubs.

An exception to the no-extension-cable rule is an active extension cable that contains a hub, a downstream port, and a cable. This type of cable works because it contains the required hub. Depending on the attached device, the hub may need its own power supply.

The USB Type-C specification defines an active cable that contains conditioning circuits that may support longer cable lengths. The specification doesn't detail how the conditioning circuits might work.

One option for long distances is to use an adapter as a bridge that converts between USB and Ethernet, RS-232, RS-485, or another interface suitable for longer distances. The remote device supports the long-distance interface rather than USB.

Another approach for long distances is to access USB devices using a local Ethernet network. A product that uses this method is the AnywhereUSB hub from Digi International. The hub contains one or more host controllers that communicate with the host PC over an Ethernet connection using the Internet Protocol (IP). The hub can attach to any Ethernet port in the PC's local network. The host drivers for the USB devices are on the PC. PC applications can access many USB devices that connect to the AnywhereUSB hub and use bulk and interrupt transfers. The interface has increased latency due to the added protocol layer.

Software-only products for accessing USB devices over a network include USB Network Gate from Eltima, USB over Network from Fabula Tech, and USB Redirector from Incentives Pro. To use these products to access a device attached to another computer in a network, you must install software on the PC the device attaches to and the PC(s) that will access the device.

Going wireless

Replacing a USB cable with a wireless connection isn't an easy task. USB transactions involve communicating in both directions with tight timing requirements. For example, when a USB 2.0 host sends a token and data packet in the Data stage of an interrupt OUT transaction, the device must respond quickly with ACK or another code in the handshake packet.

But the idea of a wireless connection for USB devices is so compelling that multiple technologies have become available to incorporate USB in wireless applications. In many implementations, the wireless links use wired devices that serve as wireless bridges, or adapters. The bridge uses USB to communicate with the host and a wireless interface to communicate with the peripheral. The peripheral contains a wireless bridge to convert between the wireless interface and the peripheral's circuits.

Wireless USB

The USB-IF's *Wireless Universal Serial Bus Specification* defines Wireless USB. Revision 1.1 was released in 2010.

Wireless USB supports speeds of up to 480 Mbps at 3 m and 100 Mbps at 10 m. The interface supports power-saving modes and uses encryption for security. The technology is ultrawideband (UWB) radio, which transmits in short bursts at very low power over a wide frequency spectrum. The UWB technology is defined in the ISO/IEC 26907/8 specifications, which evolved from specifications developed by the nonprofit WiMedia Alliance.

A USB host can have a built-in Wireless USB interface or a wired connection to a USB device that functions as a host wire adapter (HWA) that communicates via Wireless USB. In a similar way, a USB device can have a built-in Wireless USB interface or a wired connection or direct attachment to a device wire adapter (DWA) that communicates via Wireless USB.

A Wireless USB host can support up to 127 devices that each communicate directly with the host. A host and its devices form a Wireless USB Cluster. All communications are between the host and a device. Wireless USB doesn't use hubs though a DWA may have an embedded hub that enables wired USB devices to communicate wirelessly.

Hosts and devices use a protocol to establish a secure relationship where all communications sent wirelessly are encrypted.

Products with Wireless USB interfaces have been slow to reach the market in part because Wi-Fi hubs and other Wi-Fi devices have competed more successfully for the same market.

Media Agnostic USB

In 2014, the USB-IF released a Media Agnostic (MA) USB specification to enable using USB drivers to communicate over a variety of wireless and wired interfaces.

The first expected use for MA USB is 1-Gbps wireless communications based on the WiGig Serial Extension (WSE) 1.2 specification from the Wi-Fi Alliance. The Wi-Fi Alliance transferred the WSE specification to the USB-IF for use in MA USB. WiGig uses unlicensed 60-GHz frequencies for short-range communications.

Cypress WirelessUSB

For low-speed devices, including HID-class devices, Cypress Semiconductor offers the WirelessUSB technology. An obvious market is wireless keyboards, mice, and game controllers. With a wireless range of up to 50 m, the technology is also useful for building and home automation and industrial control. The wireless interface uses radio-frequency (RF) transmissions at 2.4 GHz in the unlicensed Industrial, Scientific, and Medical (ISM) band.

A WirelessUSB system consists of a WirelessUSB bridge and one or more WirelessUSB devices (Figure 20-13). The bridge translates between USB and the wireless protocol and medium. The WirelessUSB device carries out the device's function (mouse, keyboard, game controller) and communicates with the bridge.

The bridge contains a USB-capable microcontroller and a WirelessUSB transceiver chip and antenna. The WirelessUSB device contains a Cypress PsOC or another microcontroller and a WirelessUSB transmitter or transceiver chip and antenna. A device with a transceiver is 2-way: the device can communicate in both directions. A device with just a transmitter is 1-way: the device can send data to the host but can't receive data or status information. In both the bridge and device, the transmitter and transceiver chips use SPI to communicate with their microcontrollers.

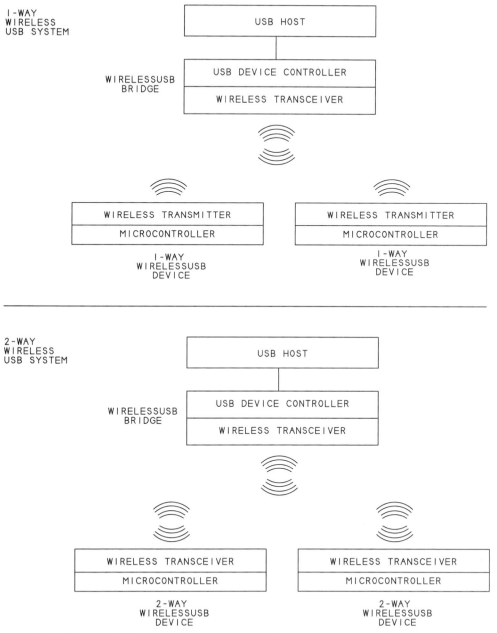

Figure 20-13. WirelessUSB provides a way to design low-speed devices that use a wireless interface.

In a 2-way system, when a device has data to send to the host, the device's microcontroller writes the data to the transceiver chip, which encodes the data and sends it through the air to the bridge's transceiver. On receiving the data, the bridge returns an acknowledgment to the device, decodes the data, and sends the data to the host in conventional USB interrupt or control transfers. On failing to receive an acknowledgment from the bridge, the device resends the data.

When the host has data to send to the device, the host writes the data to the bridge's USB controller, which returns ACK (if not busy and the data is accepted) and passes the data to the bridge's transceiver. The transceiver encodes the data and sends it through the air to the WirelessUSB device. The device returns an acknowledgment to the bridge. On receiving a NAK or no reply, the bridge resends the data.

In a 1-way system, a device sends data to the host in much the same way as in a 2-way system except the device receives no acknowledgment from the host. To help ensure that the bridge and host receive all transmitted data, the device sends its data multiple times. Sequence numbers enable the bridge to identify previously received data.

With both systems, the host thinks it's communicating with an ordinary HID and has no knowledge of the wireless link.

A WirelessUSB link can have data throughput of up to 62.5 kbps, but low-speed throughput is limited by the USB bandwidth available for low-speed control and interrupt transfers. A device and its bridge must use the same frequency/code pair. A single WirelessUSB bridge can use multiple frequency/code pairs to communicate with multiple devices. For faster performance, the microcontroller can use burst reads to read multiple registers in the WirelessUSB chip in sequence.

Other options

Other ways to use USB in wireless devices include various wireless bridges and a wireless networking option.

Chapter 7 introduced two USB classes for wireless data. A device in the IrDA bridge class can use bulk transfers to communicate over an infrared link. A device in the wireless controller class can use Bluetooth to communicate over an RF link.

ZigBee is an inexpensive, low-power, RF interface suitable for building and industrial automation and other applications that transmit at up to 250 kbps and over distances of up to 500 m. DLP Design's DLP-RF1-Z 2.4GHz Transceiver module provides a way to monitor and control a Zigbee interface from a USB port. The module's USB controller is FTDI's FT245BM. One or more DLP-RF2-Z 2.4GHz Transceiver modules can communicate with the DLP-RF1-Z.

Another option is a vendor-specific wireless bridge that uses infrared, RF, or other wireless modules designed for use in robotics and other low- to moderate-speed applications. The bridge functions as a wired USB device that also supports a wireless interface. A remote device that supports the wireless interface carries out the periph-eral's function. Firmware passes received wireless data to the host and passes received USB data to the device.

To use an existing USB device wirelessly, you may be able to use one of the USB/Ethernet products described earlier in this chapter along with a wireless net-work interface between the host PC and the hub/server.

21

Hosts for Embedded Systems

A conventional USB host has many responsibilities. The host must support multiple bus speeds, manage communications with many device types, and provide current to every device that connects to the root hub. Embedded systems might also need to access USB devices but might not have the resources to support all of the responsibilities of a conventional USB host.

Embedded systems that operate as USB hosts can take advantage of alternatives that relax some requirements and offer new capabilities tailored to the needs of small systems. This chapter presents options for small systems.

The Targeted Host

An embedded system is a device that contains a processor programmed to carry out a dedicated task or related set of tasks. Embedded systems typically access a limited number of device types. For example, a camera might print to a USB printer. A data-acquisition device might store data in a USB drive. Products like these can perform their functions without having to support all of the requirements of a conventional host.

Some embedded systems have the additional requirement of needing to support both USB host and device functions. For example, a camera might function as a device that connects to a host for uploading images and as a host that connects to a printer for printing photos.

Three specifications define requirements and capabilities for hosts in small systems. The *On-The-Go and Embedded Host Supplement to the USB Revision 2.0 Specification* applies to hosts of any speed, while the *On-The-Go and Embedded Host Supplement to the USB Revision 3.0 Specification* adds information specific to SuperSpeed-capable products and presumably will be updated for USB 3.1. The USB 3.1 specification defines connectors for use with Enhanced SuperSpeed Targeted Hosts.

The Targeted Peripheral List

The supplements define requirements for USB hosts that provide a Targeted Peripheral List (TPL). A host that provides a TPL is a *Targeted Host*.

The TPL names devices that the manufacturer has successfully tested with the host. For example, a camera might list manufacturers and model numbers of supported printers. Other printer models may also work, but the list enables users to find and use known good peripherals. The specifications don't say where the list must appear.

On attachment of an unsupported peripheral, including a hub on a system that doesn't support hubs, a Targeted Host shouldn't fail silently but should provide a message or other indicator to inform the user that the host doesn't support the device. The message should have enough information so the user doesn't have to refer to a manual or other documentation to understand the failure.

A Targeted Host can support external hubs or require all devices to attach directly to a host port. A host that supports hubs can support the hub class, including providing 500 mA (USB 2.0) or 900 mA (USB 3.0) to bus-powered hubs, or the host can support specific hub models. On attachment of a hub when the TPL doesn't support hubs, a user message should say specifically that the Targeted Host doesn't support hubs.

Targeted Host types

Two types of Targeted Hosts are the Embedded Host and the On-The-Go (OTG) device (Figure 21-1).

An Embedded Host has one or more host ports and may also have one or more device ports. An OTG device has a single port that can function as both a host port and a device port.

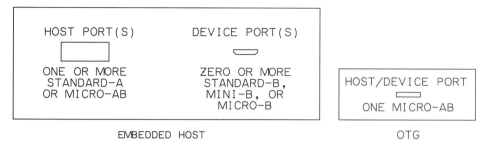

Figure 21-1. An Embedded Host system can have multiple USB ports, while an OTG device has a single dual-role port.

Bus current

Targeted Hosts have more flexible requirements for providing bus current. The ability for a device to draw up to 500 mA or 900 mA per port reduces cost because many devices can rely on bus power instead of external power supplies. Bus power is also convenient for users, who don't have to find a place to plug in a power supply for the device. But providing this much current, or even the 100 mA that USB 2.0 battery-powered hosts must provide, can be a burden for small systems, and many devices don't need this much current. Some self-powered devices might not need bus power at all.

An Embedded Host or an OTG device with a Micro-A plug inserted must provide the greater of 8 mA of bus current or the maximum amount the devices on the TPL require, up to 500 mA (USB 2.0) or 900 mA (USB 3.0).

Like conventional hosts, Targeted Hosts can suspend the bus to save power, and devices can use remote wakeup to request communications when the bus is suspended.

Turning off bus power

Targeted Hosts can leave VBUS unpowered until detecting plug insertion by a variety of methods, depending on the receptacle type:

- Micro-AB receptacle: detect insertion of a Micro-A plug by monitoring the voltage on the Micro-AB receptacle's ID pin.

- Series-A receptacle: detect insertion of a Series-A plug using Attach Detection Protocol (ADP) signaling, required if the host runs an application on attachment to a specific device.

- Standard-A or PD Standard-A receptacle: as defined in the *USB Power Delivery Rev. 2.0, v1.0* specification, use the Insertion Detect pin to detect plug insertion

- PD Standard-A receptacle: use the PD Detect pins to detect insertion of PD Standard-A plugs.

Targeted Hosts may also turn off VBUS when a plug is present and the bus is idle. The host restores power to VBUS on detecting plug removal followed by insertion using any of the methods described above and also on these events:

- If the host has an SRP-capable peripheral on the TPL, detect Session Request Protocol (SRP) signaling or any user input. (See below for a definition of SRP.)

- If the host communicates over USB only in response to a user action, detect the user action.

Attach Detection Protocol

Conventional USB 2.0 hosts detect device attachment by monitoring for a voltage change on the D+ or D- data line. But the USB 2.0 specification forbids devices from powering the pull-up resistor on D+ or D- when VBUS is absent except to do data-line pulsing for the Session Request Protocol as described below. The Attach Detection Protocol (ADP) provides a way for a host or device to detect attachment when VBUS is absent.

A host performs ADP probing by discharging the VBUS line, then measuring the time required for a known current to charge the line to a known voltage. If the line doesn't charge within the expected time, no device is present. The probing repeats about every 1.75 s. Host support for ADP is optional. Hubs don't support ADP probing so if a hub lies between the host and device, the host can't use ADP probing. Devices can also use ADP probing to detect attachment to a host.

Both USB 2.0 and SuperSpeed Targeted Hosts and devices can use ADP. Host and device controllers typically require additional hardware to support ADP.

Session Request Protocol

If the host has turned off VBUS, a device that supports the Session Request Protocol (SRP) can use SRP to request restoring VBUS and beginning a new session.

To request to restore VBUS, a device performs data-line pulsing, which consists of switching in the pull-up on D+ for 5–10 ms. Within 5 seconds of detecting data-line pulsing, the host must turn on VBUS and reset the bus.

A Targeted Host must respond to SRP if the host ever turns off VBUS while a Series-A plug is inserted. Hubs don't recognize SRP signaling, so if a hub lies between the host and device, the device can't use SRP.

In violation of the USB 2.0 specification, some self-powered devices keep D+ pulled up when VBUS isn't present. To prevent problems with these devices, on detecting that D+ is pulled up for a period longer than 10 ms, a host should disable responding to SRP until D+ goes low, indicating that the device has been removed.

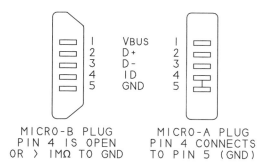

VBUS
D+
D-
ID
GND

MICRO-B PLUG
PIN 4 IS OPEN
OR > 1MΩ TO GND

MICRO-A PLUG
PIN 4 CONNECTS
TO PIN 5 (GND)

Figure 21-2. The ID pin tells the OTG device is the attached plug is a Micro-A or Micro-B.

USB 2.0 and SuperSpeed Targeted Hosts can use SRP. Host hardware can provide support for SRP. For example, chips in Microchip's PIC32MX family include register bits for monitoring the VBUS voltage and switching in the pull-up on D+.

The Micro-AB receptacle

Chapter 20 introduced the Micro-AB receptacle, which accepts both Micro-A and Micro-B plugs. OTG devices must use the Micro-AB receptacle. The *On-The-Go and Embedded Host Supplement to the USB Revision 2.0, version 1.1* specifies that Embedded Hosts may also use Micro-AB receptacles.

The *Micro-USB Cables and Connectors* specification defines the USB 2.0 Micro-AB receptacle and Micro-A and Micro-B plugs. The USB 3.1 specification defines a Micro-AB receptacle and Micro-A and Micro-B plugs for Enhanced SuperSpeed. The USB 3.1 Micro-AB receptacle adds contacts for Enhanced SuperSpeed and can accept a USB 3.1 Micro-B, USB 3.1 Micro-A, USB 2.0 Micro-B, or USB 2.0 Micro-A plug. USB 3.1 Micro-A and Micro-B plugs don't fit USB 2.0 Micro-AB receptacles.

There is no approved Micro-A receptacle so Micro-A plugs must attach to a Micro-AB receptacle. The USB-IF deprecated the Mini-AB receptacle defined in version 1.0 of the OTG specification.

Micro-A and Micro-B plugs include an ID pin that enables a device with a Micro-AB receptacle to detect whether a Micro-A or Micro-B plug is inserted. On a Micro-B plug, the ID pin is open or connected to the ground pin by a resistance greater than 1 MΩ. (The *MicroUSB Micro-B ID Pin Resistance* ECN raised the minimum value from its original 100 kΩ.) On a Micro-A plug, the ID pin connects to the GND pin (Figure 21-2).

At the Micro-AB receptacle, a pull-up resistor much lower than 1 MΩ on the ID pin enables identifying the type of an attached plug. If the pin is a logic low, the plug is a Micro-A, and if the pin is a logic high, the plug is a Micro-B.

Embedded Hosts

The host ports of an Embedded Host function much like the ports in conventional PCs but without the need to support the bus speeds and bus currents the targeted peripherals don't need.

Differences from conventional host ports

Table 21-1 compares the requirements for USB 2.0 Embedded Host ports and conventional host ports.

A USB 2.0 Embedded Host can support just about any combination of speeds needed for the targeted peripherals. If all of the targeted peripherals use low speed or all use full speed, the system needs to support only one speed. A system that supports high speed must also support full speed. All host ports should support the same speeds and devices.

A SuperSpeed-capable Embedded Host must also support operation as a USB 2.0 Embedded Host at full speed, with support for high speed recommended and support for low speed required only if needed by a device on the TPL.

Host connectors

An Embedded Host can have one or more host ports. The port(s) can use any combination of Standard-A and Micro-AB receptacles.

An Embedded Host with a Micro-AB receptacle requires a cable with a Micro-A plug and a plug that mates with the desired peripheral. Because the Micro-AB receptacle can also accept a Micro-B plug, a user could use a Series-A-to-Micro-B cable to mistakenly connect another host port to an Embedded Host's Micro-AB receptacle. To prevent two voltage sources from connecting on VBUS, an Embedded Host with a Micro-AB receptacle should enable VBUS only when the port's ID pin is logic low, indicating that a Micro-A plug is inserted.

Designers of products that have both Standard-A and Series-B receptacles should use product design, labeling, and product literature to inform users of the product's function. In particular, the product's design and labeling should make it clear that the product isn't a hub.

Functioning as a USB device

An embedded system with USB host support can also provide a device port and function as a USB device. For example, a data logger might have a host port that connects to a drive for saving data and a device port that connects to a PC for uploading data. Unlike OTG devices, which can perform only one function at a time, a system

Table 21-1: USB 2.0 Embedded Hosts have different requirements compared to conventional USB 2.0 hosts.

Capability or Feature	Conventional Host	USB 2.0 Embedded Host
Communicate at high speed	Yes	Must support all devices on the TPL. May support high, full, and low speeds; high and full speeds; full and low speeds; full speed only; or low speed only.
Communicate at full speed	Yes	
Communicate at low speed	Yes	
Support external hubs	Yes	Optional
Provide Targeted Peripheral List	No	Yes
Minimum available bus current per port	500 mA (100 mA if battery-powered)	8 mA or the amount needed by targeted peripherals, whichever is greater
OK to turn off VBUS when unneeded?	No except as defined in USB Power Delivery	Yes
Connector	1 or more Standard-A receptacles	1 or more Standard-A and/or Micro-AB receptacles

with conventional host and device ports can function as a host and device at the same time.

OTG devices

An OTG device can function as both a limited-capability host and a peripheral, switching roles as needed. When connected to a host, including an OTG device functioning as a host, the OTG port functions as a device port. When connected to a peripheral on the OTG device's TPL, including an OTG device functioning as a peripheral, the OTG port functions as a host port.

Compared to Embedded Host systems, OTG adds complexity by requiring the ability to function as a peripheral and requiring support for role-swapping protocols. But OTG reduces the hardware cost and product size by using a single connector for both functions.

An alternative to an OTG device is a Dual-Role Device (DRD) as defined in the USB Type-C connector specification. A DRD has a USB Type-C connector and can function as a host or device. Protocols defined in the Type-C specification enable the device to detect which role to use when connected to a host or device with a USB Type-C connector and to swap roles when connected to another DRD.

Requirements

To support OTG, the Targeted Host must have a hardware OTG port and support for protocols for role switching. Table 21-2 compares the requirements of a USB 2.0 conventional host and a USB 2.0 OTG device functioning as a host.

Table 21-2: USB 2.0 OTG hosts have different requirements compared to conventional USB hosts.

Capability or Feature	USB 2.0 Conventional Host	USB 2.0 OTG device Functioning as a Host
Communicate at high speed	Yes	As needed to support targeted peripherals
Communicate at full speed	Yes	Yes
Communicate at low speed	Yes	As needed to support targeted peripherals (not allowed when operating as a peripheral)
Support external hubs	Yes	Optional
Provide Targeted Peripheral List	No	Yes
Function as a peripheral	Requires a separate device port	Yes, when not functioning as a host
Support Attach Detection Protocol (ADP)	Optional	Optional
Support Session Request Protocol (SRP)	Optional	Yes if the device supports HNP as a B-device; otherwise optional
Support Host Negotiation Protocol (HNP)	No	Yes as an A-device; yes as a B-device if the TPL includes an OTG device
Minimum available bus current per port	500 mA (100 mA if battery-powered)	8 mA or the amount needed by targeted peripherals, whichever is greater
OK to turn off VBUS when unneeded?	No	Yes
Connectors	1 or more Standard-A	1 Micro-AB

An USB 2.0 OTG device must provide all of the following:

- A Targeted Peripheral List (TPL).
- The ability to function as a host that can communicate with one or more full-speed devices. Support for high speed and low speed is required only as needed by devices on the TPL.
- The ability to function as a full-speed peripheral. Functioning as a high-speed peripheral is optional. The peripheral function must not use low speed.
- When functioning as an A-device (Micro-A plug inserted), support for the Host Negotiation Protocol (HNP) for role swapping. When functioning as a B-device, support for HNP is required if the TPL includes OTG devices.
- If the device ever turns off VBUS with a Micro-A plug inserted, the ability to respond to the Session Request Protocol (SRP). If the device supports HNP when functioning as a B-device (Micro-B plug inserted), the ability to initiate SRP.

- Support for remote wakeup.
- One and only one Micro-AB receptacle.
- When functioning as the A-device, the ability to provide the bus current required by peripherals on the TPL.
- A display, indicators, or other way to communicate with users.

An OTG device that supports operating as a SuperSpeed host must also support operating as a USB 2.0 host. If the host function supports SuperSpeed, support for host operation at high speed is recommended.

An OTG device that supports operation as a USB 2.0 host but not as a SuperSpeed host may support operation as a SuperSpeed peripheral. If the peripheral function supports SuperSpeed, support for high speed operation as a peripheral is recommended.

When functioning as a host, the OTG device can communicate with the devices in its TPL. The targeted peripherals can be any combination of other OTG devices and peripheral-only devices.

OTG communications occur in sessions. A session begins when VBUS rises above the session-valid threshold voltage and ends when VBUS falls below that voltage. To conserve power, an OTG device that is providing power on VBUS can remove bus power when the bus is idle.

Cables and connectors

An OTG device has one and only one Micro-AB receptacle, which can accept a Micro-A plug or a Micro-B plug. Figure 21-3 shows cabling options. Two USB 2.0 OTG devices connect to each other via a cable with a Micro-A plug on one end and a Micro-B plug on the other end. It doesn't matter which device has which plug.

A host or upstream hub connects to an OTG device via a Standard-A-to-Micro-B cable. A peripheral with a Micro-B receptacle connects to an OTG device with a Micro-A-to-Micro-B cable. A peripheral with a permanently attached cable with a Micro-A plug attaches directly to the OTG device.

A peripheral with a Standard-B or Mini-B receptacle or a captive cable must use an adapter to connect to an OTG device (Figure 21-4). The adapter, defined in the *Micro-USB Cables and Connectors* specification, has a Micro-A plug and a Standard-A receptacle. The Micro-A plug attaches to the OTG device. The Standard-A receptacle accepts a Standard-A plug from a captive or detachable cable that connects to a peripheral. The adapter is the only approved adapter for use with Series-A and Series-B cables.

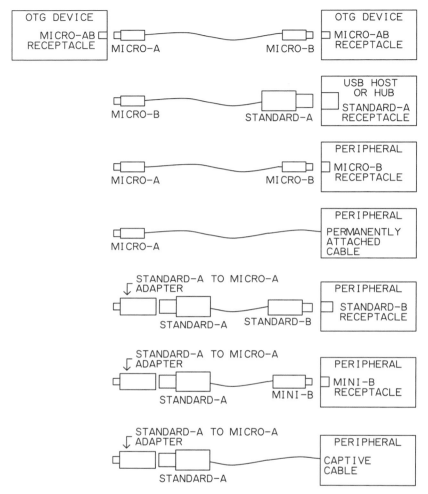

Figure 21-3. An USB 2.0 OTG device can communicate with a USB host or a device on the OTG device's target peripheral list.

The A-Device and B-Device

Every OTG connection is between an *A-device* and a *B-device*. An OTG port with a Micro-A plug inserted is an A-Device. The device at the other end of the cable, which can be another OTG device or a conventional peripheral, is the B-device. On attachment, the A-device functions as the host, and the B-device functions as the periph-

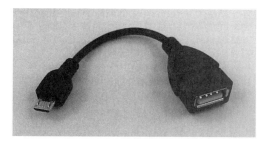

Figure 21-4. This adapter enables connecting an OTG device with a Micro-AB receptacle to a device that uses a captive cable or a detachable cable with a Standard-A plug.

eral. Two connected OTG devices can use the Host Negotiation Protocol (HNP) to swap roles.

The A-device is always the source of VBUS even when functioning as a peripheral. An OTG device must detect the resistance at the OTG connector's ID pin and implement the host or device function accordingly.

To connect an OTG device to a conventional host, use a cable with a Micro-B plug for the OTG port and a Standard-A plug for the host. When connected to a conventional host, the OTG device functions as a peripheral.

To connect an OTG port to a conventional peripheral, use the adapter described above along with a cable that has a Standard-A plug and a Series-B plug. Cables with a Micro-A plug and either a Standard-B plug or Mini-B plug are not allowed. When connected to a conventional peripheral, the OTG device functions as a host only.

The OTG descriptor

The OTG descriptor tells the host whether an attached B-device supports ADP, SRP, and HNP. Any B-device that supports ADP, SRP, or HNP must return an OTG descriptor in response to a Get Descriptor request for the configuration descriptor.

The OTG specification doesn't say where to insert the descriptor, but typically the OTG device returns the OTG descriptor immediately following the configuration descriptor. The OTG device must also return the descriptor in response to a Get Descriptor(OTG) request.

Table 21-3 shows the contents of the descriptor. The bmAttributes field tells whether the device supports various OTG protocols. An A-device doesn't need to know in advance if a device supports SRP, but the information is useful in compliance testing.

Table 21-3: The OTG descriptor informs the host about support for OTG protocols.

Offset	Field	Size	Description
0	bLength	1	Descriptor length (0x05)
1	bDescriptorType	1	OTG (0x09)
2	bmAttributes	1	Protocols supported as B-device (1 = supported): D0: SRP D1: HNP D2: ADP D3: RSP (USB 3.1) D4–D7: reserved, set to zero
3	bcdOTG	2	OTG and EH supplement revision number in BCD format (release 2.0 = 0x0200). This field is present only if the revision number >= 2.

Host Negotiation Protocol (HNP)

The Host Negotiation Protocol (HNP) enables a B-device to request to function as a host. HNP means that users who connect two USB 2.0 OTG devices don't have worry about which end of the cable goes where. As needed, the devices use HNP to swap roles.

When two OTG devices connect to each other, the A-device enumerates the B-device in the same way that a standard USB host enumerates its devices. During enumeration, the A-device retrieves the B-device's OTG descriptor, which indicates whether the B-device supports HNP.

If the B-device supports HNP, the A-device can send a Set Feature control request with a request code of b_hnp_enable (0x03). The request informs the B-device that it can use HNP to request to function as the host when the bus is suspended.

At any time after enumerating, an A-device that has no communications for the B-device can suspend the bus. The B-device then can use HNP to request to communicate. The B-device might use HNP in response to user input such as pressing a button, or firmware can initiate HNP without user intervention.

Support for HNP ensures that an OTG B-device can request to communicate with the peripheral function of an attached and supported OTG device. If the TPL includes no OTG devices, the OTG B-device isn't required to support HNP because the supported peripherals will never use it.

Standard hubs don't recognize HNP signaling. If a hub is between the A-device and the B-device, the A-device must not send the hnp_enable request and the B-device can't use HNP.

When idle or functioning as a host, an OTG device should switch in its pull-down resistors on D+ and D-. When functioning as a peripheral, an OTG device should disable its pull-down resistor only on D+.

Requesting to operate as a host

This is the protocol the B-device uses to request to operate as the host:

1. The A-device suspends the bus.

2. If the devices were communicating at full speed, the B-device removes itself from the bus by switching out its pull-up resistor on D+. If the devices were communicating at high speed, the B-device enters full-speed mode by switching in its pull-up on D+ briefly. The B-device then switches the pull-up out. The bus segment is in the SE0 state.

3. The A-device detects the SE0 state and connects to the bus as a device by switching in its pull-up resistor on D+, placing the bus segment in the J state.

4. The B-device detects the J state and resets the bus.

5. The B-device enumerates the A-device and can perform other communications with the device.

Returning to operation as a peripheral

When finished communicating, the B-device returns to its role as a peripheral using the following protocol:

1. The B-device stops all bus activity and may switch in its pull-up resistor.

2. The A-device detects a lack of activity for at least 3 ms, enters full-speed mode if communicating at high speed, and switches out its pull-up resistor or removes VBUS to end the session.

3. If VBUS is present and the B-device didn't switch in its pull-up in Step 1, the B-device switches in its pull-up to connect as a peripheral.

4. If VBUS is present, the A-device can reset the bus and enumerate and communicate with the B-device or end the session by removing VBUS.

Requesting device status

During an active OTG session, a host learns if a device wants to function as a host by initiating a control transfer with a Get_Status request with wIndex = 0xF000. In the Data stage of the request, the device returns 0x01 if the device wants to function as the host or 0x00 if not. During active sessions between two OTG devices, the host must issue the request every 1–2 s. On receiving a request to function as the host, the currently active host must suspend the bus within 2 s to enable the remote device to initiate HNP.

Hardware Support

OTG controllers may have hardware support for HNP. For example, chips in the Microchip PIC32MX family contain register bits to detect a connect condition on the port, control the pull-up on D+, and enable and disable host operations.

Role Swap Protocol

Instead of HNP, two directly connected OTG devices operating at SuperSpeed use the Role Swap Protocol (RSP) to swap roles. With RSP, an A-device or B-device functioning as a peripheral can request to function as a host, and a B-device functioning as a host can release its host function to an A-device.

These are the steps for a role swap using RSP:

1. The OTG device operating as a peripheral issues a DEV_NOTIFICATION TP with a HOST_ROLE_REQUEST notification and the notification's RSP Phase field set to INITIATE.

2. To release the host role, an OTG device operating as a host sends a Set_Feature(NTF_HOST_REL) request.

3. The OTG device operating as a peripheral confirms that the device is ready for the role swap by issuing a Device Notification TP(HOST_ROLE_REQUEST) notification with RSP Phase set to CONFIRM.

4. The OTG device operating as a host then initiates the role swap by issuing a Warm Reset. Following the Warm Reset, the device previously operating as the host starts up as a peripheral, and the device previously operating as the peripheral starts up as a host.

In one case, the ability to communicate at SuperSpeed depends on the cable's orientation. If the A-device supports SuperSpeed only as a peripheral and the B-device supports SuperSpeed as a host, the link uses a USB 2.0 speed because the A-device, which must be the initial host, doesn't support SuperSpeed as a host. To use SuperSpeed, the user must reverse the cable. When operating at SuperSpeed, this type of link can't use RSP because the B-device doesn't support SuperSpeed as a host. To swap roles, the B-device must disconnect and reconnect at a USB 2.0 speed to enable using HNP.

Choosing a development platform

Because of the host's many responsibilities, adding USB host capability to a small embedded system can seem like a daunting task. But a variety of hardware and programming platforms can help ease the way.

Comparing options

Host hardware and firmware are available for just about any need. Systems that need capabilities comparable to conventional PCs can use high-end processors targeted to embedded applications. Cost-sensitive systems that need good performance can use mid-range microcontrollers with USB host support either on-chip or in an external controller. Where high performance isn't essential, even 8-bit microcontrollers can access USB devices by interfacing to host modules that manage USB protocols. Many processors and USB interface chips with host ports also support OTG functions.

The amount and type of programming the developer needs to provide host communications varies depending on the host hardware and the amount and type of firmware support for host communications. On some platforms, the OS or a host module handles many or all of the low-level USB host functions. With other hardware, the developer must provide firmware for these tasks. When the hardware needs firmware support, chip vendors typically provide example code. Table 21-4 compares options for implementing an Targeted Host in an embedded system.

Embedded PC

USB was created as an interface for PCs, and OSes such as Linux and Windows have rich support for USB host communications. An embedded PC can take advantage of this built-in support by using a Linux distribution or Windows edition targeted to small systems.

In an embedded PC, applications can access devices in much the same way that applications access devices on conventional PCs. The OS manages enumeration and other low-level protocols and provides drivers for popular USB device classes.

Embedded PCs can use many of the same development tools used for developing mainstream PC applications. You can use boards with Linux or Windows installed or install an OS yourself on suitable hardware.

The ever-evolving Windows Embedded family includes editions suitable for smartphones, point-of-sale devices, automotive applications, and more. Windows Embedded editions include USB host drivers and support for USB classes.

Linux has a variety of distributions that are targeted to embedded systems and have USB host support. The Android OS, based on Linux, also supports the USB host function. Two books that focus on USB communications in Linux embedded systems are my *USB Embedded Hosts* and Rajaram Regupathy's *Bootstrap Yourself with Linux-USB Stack*. For USB under Android, see *Unboxing Android USB* by Rajaram Regupathy.

For sources of hardware for Windows Embedded, Microsoft maintains a web page of Windows Embedded Board Support Packages. For a similar list for Linux, see *elinux.org*.

Table 21-4: Many hardware options are available for implementing hosts in embedded systems.

System Type	Sources	Host Communications Support
Embedded PC with host controller	Products listed on the Windows Embedded Board Support Packages web page and elinux.org	Linux or Windows API, other protocols supported by the OS and programming environment
General-purpose microcontroller with on-chip host controller	Atmel, Cypress Semiconductor, Freescale Semiconductor Inc., Microchip Technology	Libraries from chip provider
External host interface chip used with general-purpose microcontroller	Maxim Integrated Products, Inc.	Libraries from chip provider
Processor with on-chip host module	FTDI (Vinculum VNC2)	Vendor-specific API

General-purpose microcontroller

A general-purpose microcontroller or other processor with an on-chip host controller allows full control of the firmware with low per-unit cost. The downside is the effort needed to program host communications. Firmware typically manages device detecting and enumeration, communications down to the transaction level, and bus power. Chip vendors often provide firmware libraries that implement basic host communications and provide a foundation for application programming.

Sources for microcontrollers and processors with on-chip host controllers include Atmel, Cypress, Freescale, and Microchip.

Interface chip

A microcontroller or other processor that doesn't have an on-chip USB host controller can use an external host interface chip. Maxim's MAX3421E is similar to the MAX-3420E introduced in Chapter 6 but adds the ability to function as a full- and low-speed host.

Host module

For projects that don't have the firmware resources to support USB protocols, a USB host module can be a solution. The module manages enumeration and low-level communications and supports commands or an API for accessing popular device types. FTDI's VNC2 (Vinculum II) is a host module with built-in support for accessing drives, keyboards, and other devices. A free ebook that focuses on the VNC2, *Embedded USB Design By Example* by John Hyde, is available from FTDI.

The VNC2 has an on-chip processor core that supports an API for accessing USB devices. FTDI provides a C compiler for the processor. Supported USB device classes includes mass storage, hub, HID, still image, and audio. The module can also communicate with FTDI's FT232x USB UART devices.

The VNC2 also supports an alternate mode that can use an asynchronous serial (UART), SPI, or parallel interface to an external processor. The processor uses defined commands to exchange data with USB devices. The VNC2 handles the USB protocols and communications. This mode emulates the first-generation Vinculum.

***

I hope you've found this book useful. For example code, updates, and more, please visit my website: *janaxelson.com*. I wish you success with your USB projects!

Index

Index